MEDIEVAL TEXTS
AND STUDIES

MEDIEVAL TEXTS
AND STUDIES

C. R. CHENEY

OXFORD
AT THE CLARENDON PRESS
1973

Oxford University Press, Ely House, London W. 1

GLASGOW NEW YORK TORONTO MELBOURNE WELLINGTON
CAPE TOWN IBADAN NAIROBI DAR ES SALAAM LUSAKA ADDIS ABABA
DELHI BOMBAY CALCUTTA MADRAS KARACHI LAHORE DACCA
KUALA LUMPUR SINGAPORE HONG KONG TOKYO

ISBN 0 19 8223994

© *Oxford University Press 1973*

*Printed in Great Britain
at the University Press, Oxford
by Vivian Ridler
Printer to the University*

Preface

FRIENDS have encouraged me to select and republish essays which I have written over the years, but I have not found selection easy. I must explain the plan of this book. While the lectures and papers I have chosen range over a fairly wide variety of topics, most of them concern church history and letters in the twelfth and thirteenth centuries, apart from the introductory chapter which was an inaugural lecture. They are here because they either turn on critical problems presented by well-known sources or print and discuss newly-found texts. I hope that they may be useful to students of history and diplomatic in general and, in particular, to those interested in the way in which medieval laws and letters were drafted and transmitted, chronicles composed, forgeries perpetrated. For it is only when historians cultivate in themselves an awareness of these matters that they can properly weigh the evidence of the written word—the written word on which we rely so much and which can so seldom be taken at face value.

In editing these papers, published over the space of thirty-four years, I retain their original form with little change. A few corrections have been made; pointers to more recent literature are added here and there; but I have abstained from attempting total revision. In the first preparation and later improvement of the papers I have had help from many: from my wife above all, but also from colleagues and pupils in such numbers that I cannot possibly name them. I ask them all to accept my thanks.

Publishers and editors of journals have kindly allowed me to reprint in this book as indicated: The Cambridge University Press (1), *The Bulletin of the John Rylands Library* (2, 13, 18), *The Bulletin of the Institute of Historical Research* (3, 4, 5), Professor Bruno Paradisi and the Società Italiana per l'Istoria del Diritto (6), Professor Stephan Kuttner and the Institute of Medieval Canon Law (7), *The Jurist* (8), Éditions Sirey (9), *Recherches de théologie ancienne et médiévale* (10), The Toronto University Press (11), *The English Historical Review* (12), *Cîteaux: Commentarii Cistercienses* (14), Miss Joan Godber and the Bedfordshire Historical Record Society (15), The Manchester University Press (16), and M. l'Abbé Jean Marilier on behalf of the Association des Amis de S. Bernard (17).

C. R. CHENEY

Contents

Abbreviations

Ann. Mon.	*Annales monastici*, ed. H. R. Luard (RS), 5 vols. 1864–9.
BIHR	*Bulletin of the Institute of Historical Research*, University of London.
BJRL	*Bulletin of the John Rylands Library*, Manchester.
B.M.	British Museum.
C. & S.	*Councils & Synods, with other documents relating to the English Church*, vol. ii: 1205–1313, ed. F. M. Powicke and C. R. Cheney (Oxford, 1964).
CPL	*Calendar of Entries in the Papal Registers relating to Great Britain and Ireland. Papal Letters*, vol. i: 1198–1304 (HMSO 1894).
CYS	Canterbury and York Society.
D. & C.	Dean and Chapter.
EHR	*English Historical Review.*
JEH	*Journal of Ecclesiastical History.*
JL	*Regesta pontificum Romanorum . . . ad annum 1198*, ed. P. Jaffe, 2nd ed. S. Loewenfeld, etc. 2 vols. Leipzig, 1885–8.
Migne	*Patrologiae latinae cursus completus*, ed. J. P. Migne. 221 vols. Paris, 1844–64.
Mon. Ang.	*Monasticon anglicanum*, by William Dugdale, ed. J. Caley, H. Ellis, and B. Bandinel. 6 vols. in 8. 1817–30.
Pott.	*Regesta pontificum Romanorum a.d. 1198–1304*, ed. A. Potthast. 2 vols. Berlin, 1874–5.
P.R.O.	Public Record Office, London.
PUE	*Papsturkunden in England*, ed. W. Holtzmann (Abhandlungen der Gesellsch. der Wissensch. zu Göttingen, phil.-hist. Kl., neue Folge xxv (1930–1), dritte Folge 14–15 (1935–6) and 33 (1952). 3 vols.
RS	Rolls Series.
Rymer	*Foedera, conventiones*, etc., ed. T. Rymer, re-ed. A. Clarke, etc. (Record Com.). 3 vols. in 6. 1816–30.
Wilkins	*Concilia Magnae Britanniae et Hiberniae*, ed. D. Wilkins. 4 vols. 1737.

1. The Records of Medieval England*

LESS than twenty years ago Cambridge first found it desirable to establish a chair of medieval history. Cambridge, some may say, had got on with its study of the Middle Ages very well without this post. There was plenty of activity both in the Faculty of History and outside: Lapsley continued the tradition of Maitland, and Chadwick, Whitney, and Coulton were at work, not to mention those of a younger generation. Why, then, create a new office? What debates preceded the decision, whether they were long or acrimonious, I have not inquired; but the post was set up in 1937 and three Cambridge scholars in turn have distinguished it and justified its existence: Previté-Orton, Brooke, Knowles. It has been my privilege to know them all as friends and to learn much from each. As regards the first two, many here knew them better than I and abler men have written assessments of their work; while, to our joy and advantage, the time is not ripe for a funeral oration upon the third. Convention forbids me to speak much about the present Regius Professor, and I will only say this: Cambridge is fortunate to have in him a fine teacher —by precept and by example—and the foremost historian of the medieval religious Orders in England. He examines critically the records of monastic economy and discipline; he explores the recesses of medieval mystical experience and scholastic thought; and he presents what he finds with rare objectivity and grace. In his work we see combined those virtues of historical writing which we associate with former spacious times and those which conform to new and austere standards of scholarship.

The last two occupants of this chair used the occasion of an inaugural lecture to survey the prospect of medieval historical studies in Cambridge. My subject is related to this, but not

* An inaugural lecture delivered in Cambridge, 25 Nov. 1955, and first published by the Cambridge University Press in 1956.

identical; for I have been with you too short a space of time to be qualified to comment on the work being done here, either in teaching undergraduates or in advanced historical studies. (So far as one can distinguish local traditions in these things, my own first teachers belong to the traditions of Oxford and Manchester, and it is in those universities that I have spent the greater part of my academic life.)

Today I shall look at just one aspect of the present activities of medieval historians in England as a whole: the zeal for investigating archives. I shall resolutely avoid some other topics which weigh on a medievalist's mind nowadays: questions of teaching, and questions of popularizing. They well deserve to be discussed. But a historian may sometimes be pardoned for thinking more about his job than about his audience, and for going on with the tasks of examining material, analysing and comparing, without bothering about the simplification of what is never simple and the making of bricks without straw.

I want to do a little stocktaking. That metaphor is not, perhaps, well chosen; for I do not mean the shopkeeper's task, which is to calculate what goods are most in demand, what are sold out, what can be bought from the manufacturer. Thomas Gray, it is true, wrote as Regius Professor to William Mason in 1768: 'I profess Modern History and languages in a little shop of mine at Cambridge.' But the historian does not—or should not—purvey ready-made goods. He tries to re-create and discover. In this process, however, he cannot, like Lord Foppington, replace books with the natural sprouts of his brain. His most subtle, most intangible inquiries are those which most need precise factual information. The poetic, imaginative element in the greatest history comes of intense familiarity with what we call 'the sources'. Even of the giants among historians it may be said that, as with Antaeus, their strength departs once their feet leave the ground. A remark made by one who was both philosopher and historian should often spring to a historian's mind: 'As accumulated learning stifles the mental powers, so original thinking has been known to bring about a puffy unsubstantial mental condition.'

To return to my task, and my metaphor of stocktaking,

I want to inspect not a shop but a workshop, to see how the historian of medieval England is provided nowadays with raw materials, and to see whether he has apt and sharp tools. With the finer and rarer elements of scholarship, the insight and integrity without which mere learning will not make a historian, I shall hardly be concerned.

Written historical materials are often classified under the two headings of literary sources and records or documents. The division is convenient rather than logical or precise, for the line of demarcation (like many medieval frontiers) is hard to find. It is convenient, too, for the bibliographers, archivists and librarians, rather than for historians. On the literary side we put biographies, romances, annals, chronicles, and, with some hesitancy, private letters. Records, on the other hand, include documents which were composed or accumulated to serve the needs of some administration, whether of a kingdom, or a bishopric, or a private household. They differ from the literary sources in having been written for immediate utility, financial or legal, or else to establish legal title or privilege for the future. The thought that they might be useful some day justified their preservation. Historians never were so blind as to ignore records; but in the last eighty years there has been a growing awareness among medievalists of their incomparable value. It is some consequences of this 'record-mindedness' that I wish briefly to examine.

It has effected a revolution in our studies. Nowadays intelligent people in other walks of life often ask (at times a trifle querulously) why the historian no longer writes in the grand manner of Gibbon or the great Victorians. Some may suppose that the poor man's back and spirits have been broken by sheer weight of records; but this is not so. What has happened is more significant and more encouraging. The increase of accessible records and the accumulated scholarship of a century have together changed the content of history. We cannot be so sure as were our predecessors about the broad generalizations; more material and more critical work upon it have not only shown up their insufficiency but suggest that it is unprofitable to substitute others. In compensation for this disenchantment we are learning to see new relevance in a million

scraps for illuminating institutions, tracing action, and dis-
covering motive. It is an exciting pursuit and, for those who
think that comprehension should be prior to moral judgement,
is rewarding. So far, history has not travelled far along the new
path. 'Like all those [sciences] which have the human spirit for
their object' (and here I quote Marc Bloch) 'this newcomer in
the field of rational knowledge is also a science in its infancy.'
We might add that the infant history, having tried to run before
it could walk, must now cautiously learn to walk and keep its
balance. With all respect for the great historians of the past,
and in all humility, we must recognize that the increased resources of the medieval historian have imposed a new task
upon him. We are false to our calling if we fail to make use of
them as scientifically as we can.

I have said that the last eighty years have seen a great change
in the use of English medieval records. Eighty years ago
William Stubbs was occupying his professorial chair at Oxford.
Stubbs was the greatest of the nineteenth-century English
editors of chronicles; he was responsible for no less than
nineteen volumes of the Rolls series. But his *Constitutional
History* shows that he recognized all the importance of 'records'
for the history of institutions. He drew upon them as far as
they were available in print, in Prynne and Madox and Pal-
grave. After him came Reginald Lane Poole, James Horace
Round, and Thomas Frederick Tout—all Stubbs's pupils.
Frederic William Maitland and Paul Vinogradoff were of the
same generation, and James Tait was not much younger. With
them began a new concentration on legal, administrative, and
economic history. This concentration stimulated inquiry into
records; for in all these departments the essential raw materials
are charters, account-rolls, and the archives of the courts of
medieval England. As these were opened up, they revealed
further possibilities for the historian. Our splendid inheritance
of written record became far better known than ever before.

Publication of the records, either *in extenso* or in the form
of lengthy calendars and abstracts, proceeded much faster. To
mention only a few new enterprises: the Public Record Office
resumed (1891) the editing of chancery rolls; societies like the
Pipe Roll Society (1884) and the Canterbury and York Society

(1904) were founded to deal with certain classes of record; others, like the Oxford Historical Society (1884) and the Lincoln Record Society (1910), deal with particular regions.

The published record has helped to stimulate interest in the unpublished. Moreover, social changes and the effects of war have in this last generation raised in acute form the problems of preserving records. The British Record Society, the National Register of Archives, numerous local archive-offices and libraries have prevented much destruction; and the historian is under increasing obligations to the archivist. Nowadays, owners and solicitors and officials embarrassed by piles of paper are commonly ready to collaborate with archivists and librarians to preserve documents.

One could recount endless stories of choice medieval records which have come to light within our own recollection: Anglo-Saxon land-books found crumpled in a deed-box at Rugeley; missing leaves of a bishop's register lurking in the cellar of a Kentish mansion; the papal bull of canonization of St. Osmund of Salisbury covering Tudor court-rolls in Essex. It is significant that even documents which are of only slight importance command attention and are kept. The danger is not that which caused Sir Thomas Phillipps, in the early part of the nineteenth century, to give good prices for vellum: that charters and deeds would be destroyed 'in the shops of glue-makers and tailors'. It is more disconcerting that any piece of vellum becomes a prize for the dealer and the collector of antiquities. Hence the dispersal of collections which cease, once dispersed, to be intelligible and historically valuable. This, however, affects only a quasi-infinitesimal part of the medievalist's resources. They are mostly safe from all evils but fire and war.

What of the printing of records, which has advanced so notably during the last three generations? Editors have shown an understandable, if undue, bias towards those centuries from which the survivals are comparatively few and easy to read; but in general the published material has not been ill-chosen. Its value for historical studies is inestimable. Nevertheless, without reflecting upon the achievement of past and present editors of medieval records, one may say that we have only scratched the surface of the problem. The problem is, not how to make documents now unprinted legible to the largest possible number of people, but how to make the largest possible number of unprinted documents accessible and understandable to professional historians. This does not necessarily involve printing them.

It is high time to realize that all the medieval records of England, public and private, never will be and never can be published in the full and elaborate fashion which has been adopted in the past. So obvious a remark seems unpardonably commonplace; and yet we are often reluctant to consider the corollary: the pursuit of the best (that is, full publication), in a few instances, condemns to complete neglect whole categories of historical material. Some texts, indeed, seem to call inevitably for full publication, though we shall not go far before falling into disagreement about their choice. For the vast mass of our material we shall have to tolerate more summary treatment. Record offices and learned societies alike have to face this fact and consider whether they are using their resources to best advantage. It is a matter which does not only concern them. Local enterprise and local pride have done much in the past; but the popular term 'local records' is illogical and (apart from its value for local propaganda) mischievous. The materials for the history of a town or a village are materials for English history. It follows that the opening up of the records needs to be planned and to be subsidized more systematically than before. The State should be ready to encourage local enterprise with money, which could be distributed through the British Academy or some other channel.

Were it only a question of the cost of printing, one might argue that Her Majesty's Treasury could meet the case by spending a great deal more money on learned publications. More money is due from the State to scholarship, but the problem is not to be resolved so simply. The medieval material in the Public Record Office alone is so vast that no one of sound mind will believe that England can produce enough men and women qualified and willing to transcribe it all and prepare it for press; certainly not in the next hundred years, nor yet in two or three centuries. These tasks are for experts only and they are laborious. It is more fitting that those who can use the records should be given easier access to the originals. We must not be so immersed in the Middle Ages as to ignore the uses of the camera. And we must be content with less than the best. Historians of modern times have faced these facts squarely; so must medievalists.

This imposes an obligation. If it is not expedient to print documents *in extenso*, then there should be many more aids to the student in the shape of hand-lists, which may enable him to find the document he needs, and in the shape of guides to office practice and legal usage, which will teach him what his document is and will put it in its proper frame. Patterns are not lacking; but more money and more careful planning need to be put into the making of these tools.

If some great enterprises, under present conditions, will take many decades to complete, historians might at least get interim profit from unpublished work in progress. To illustrate my point: although the charters and writs of King Henry II may never be printed in full, one may reasonably hope for a *Regesta*, a calendar on the German model, of that king's acts; but not for many years. If this is undertaken, cannot the calendar, as it grows, be prepared with duplicate cards accessible to students in the British Museum or the Public Record Office? And cannot those cards be copied, by photography or other means, for deposit in libraries outside London? Such expedients are not unknown, but they are singularly slow in coming into fashion in England.

Then there arises the question of re-editing texts which were published imperfectly long ago. We shall never see a revised Rymer's *Foedera*, and we do not want one. But the book is there, with all its faults, indispensable for historians. Could we not have printed *corrigenda* in a handy form, to prevent the constant repetition of Rymer's errors? A new Kemble's *Codex diplomaticus aevi saxonici* is unlikely to appear in our lifetime; will not the experts in Anglo-Saxon England give us at least a printed critical bibliography of the essays and notes which have thrown light on this or that charter?[1]

All this talk of hand-lists and guides and card-indexes

[1] To meet this need the Royal Historical Society produced in 1968, in its

sounds mighty prosaic, but it touches the root of the matter.
For these things require to be done methodically and with
a clear view of what is needed most. It is an English habit to
distrust method—still more, methodology—and English historians like to claim 'amateur status'. But the medievalist who
has to do with records finds that he needs more than common
sense and diligence to extract their meaning. Records, like the
little children of long ago, only speak when they are spoken
to, and they will not talk to strangers. The student must understand their language: that is, their forms and formulas and legal
background, as well as the Latin or English or Anglo-Norman
in which they are written. In other words, he must study
palaeography and diplomatic and the institutions which the
records served. He must do so, moreover, not with the idea of
getting useful tips to solve the immediate problem, but with
the intention of learning sound principles of historical criticism.

Since England is backward in diplomatic study, it is important to be aware of what continental scholars have done for
the study of continental chanceries. There is no English equivalent to Harry Bresslau's *Handbuch der Urkundenlehre für Deutsch-
land und Italien*. Hubert Hall saw that it was needed fifty years
ago, but unfortunately his *Studies in English Official Documents*
(published here in 1908) failed to meet the need. No man could
write such a work until far more had been done to assemble
records on a reasonable system and to answer separately particular questions of administrative history; but these activities
imply a recognition of the general problem which has not been
very widespread in England.

An example will make my meaning clear. In 1903 a writ-
charter of King William the Conqueror was published in
facsimile by experts of the British Museum. It was again
reproduced in 1915, this time by experts of the Public Record
Office. Given their *imprimatur*, it was accepted by Round and
others as a genuine writ of William I. In 1927 Tait showed it
up as spurious. The lesson is this: the exposure of a forgery
which only came a quarter of a century after the first facsimile

'Guides and Handbooks' series, *Anglo-Saxon Charters: an Annotated List and
Bibliography*, edited by P. H. Sawyer. The first fascicule of a 'new Kemble',
published by the British Academy, has now appeared (1973).

edition (and which resulted then, not from applying diplomatic tests, but from a delicate and masterly use of other historical evidence) need not have been so tardy if the editors had possessed a catalogue of the acts of William I. They could then have seen that their document offended in half a dozen particulars against the common form which can be reconstructed from some two hundred writs of the Conqueror. In fact, a catalogue was produced by H. W. C. Davis in 1913 : *Regesta Regum Anglo-Normannorum*, volume 1, but the introduction to it is quite insufficient as a study in diplomatic. Nor has any guide to the usages of William I's chancery been published on the basis of Davis's *Regesta* from that day to this. It is to a Frenchman, the greatest son of the École des chartes, Léopold Delisle, that England owes the only elaborate treatment of the acts of a medieval king. Doubtless, the *Regesta* of Henry I, announced and eagerly awaited, will supply a long-felt need,[1] while work on the twelfth-century chancery which has been done in Cambridge during the last few years has at length applied to English material the sort of exact palaeographical analysis used long ago on the continent by Sickel and his school.[2] Others are approaching scientifically the voluminous records of the later Middle Ages concerning the royal courts of law and of estate management—to mention only two topics; but much more effort is required in this direction before we in England have assembled the critical apparatus necessary for using and testing our resources.

These remarks on technique lead me to consider other implications of our present record-mindedness for the study of medieval history. I will not stop to talk of the many circumstances which have conspired to stimulate interest in records; but it must be confessed that our record-mindedness has something of the extravagance of a historical fashion. We have to guard against an inordinate and exclusive respect for records,

---

[1] *Regesta Regum Anglo-Normannorum*, vol. ii: *Regesta Regis Henrici I 1100–1135*, ed. C. Johnson and H. A. Cronne (Oxford, 1956). See also vols. iii–iv (1968–9): *Regesta Regis Stephani . . . 1135–1154*, ed. H. A. Cronne and R. H. C. Davis, and *Facsimiles of English Royal Writs to A.D. 1100*, ed. T. A. M. Bishop and P. Chaplais (Oxford, 1957).

[2] T. A. M. Bishop, *Scriptores Regis: Facsimiles to identify and illustrate the hands of royal scribes in original charters of Henry I, Stephen, and Henry II* (Oxford, 1961).

contrasted with other historical material, and to suppress the notion that records are the one key to knowledge of the Middle Ages.

A generation ago people talked of the 'rage for the unpublished' which affected students of history. That is a mild distemper, still with us but seldom fatal, to which the young and the sentimental are specially prone. Nowadays, the more insidious disease is the 'rage for the authentic'. One sees a trace of it sixty years ago in Round's preface to his *Feudal England*, where he quotes approvingly a Belgian scholar who wrote of charters: 'Dans les chartes . . . tout est authentique, certain, précis, indubitable.' More recently, English archivists have declared that records, or archives, 'represent not what someone wishes us to believe, but the facts', and a distinguished historian claims that 'it is possible to reconstruct a coherent and convincing picture of the principal events of 1215 upon the basis of records of unimpugnable veracity'. These are large claims. Records represent 'the facts'! Are medievalists so naïve as to suppose that an official statement of 'the facts' may not contain the rankest misrepresentation, that the impersonality of the record-maker never conceals a biased selection of the facts? Are they certain that they can always discover the facts which lie deep embedded in the documents?

The contemporary chronicler, we properly insist, gives his own 'subjective' view, and his memory is fallible. These faults are human frailties which we easily recognize because we share them. By contrast, the record-maker (however honest) is serving his own ends or those of the people who pay him to write the record. His view is partial, in all senses of the word. The good clerk records what is useful, acceptable, expedient. It cannot be assumed that because he works to rule, therefore his record is infallible, still less that it is to be taken at its face value. Every historian knows that fictions were incorporated into medieval records, sometimes to deceive, sometimes as a matter of form, and sometimes from sheer carelessness.

The election of Wenzel IV of Bohemia as king of the Romans occasioned a famous piece of deliberate falsification. He was elected without having received papal approbation and in defiance of the pope's expressed views, on 10 June 1376;

but since his father, the Emperor Charles IV, judged it politic to seek the pope's formal approval, he wrote to Pope Gregory XI, after Wenzel had been both elected and crowned, a letter antedated to 6 March, asking for approval ostensibly in advance. The pope replied with a letter which maintained the fiction, dated 3 May. A tangled web of diplomatic misdating ensued. Such an episode as this can sometimes be clarified by reference to other sources; but at many points purely formal misrepresentation obscures the working of medieval government. To return to England for instances of this. There are the 'proofs of age', furnished by sworn witnesses for use in courts of law; much of the most vivid testimony to the date of baptism (the usual object of these inquiries) is palpably invented, or else borrowed from earlier cases. For a more serious example of misrepresentation, take the recent discovery that loans to the Crown in the fifteenth century were sometimes set down in the Receipt Roll of the Exchequer as being larger than in fact they were; the object being to conceal from contemporaries, as they effectively conceal from us, a usurious undertaking to pay interest on the loan.

Genuine records offer pitfalls in plenty, so I will not dwell on forgeries. From the early Middle Ages, along with many crude inventions, forgeries survive which were skilful enough to pass muster in those days and to puzzle scholars today. In Dr. Florence Harmer's corpus of Anglo-Saxon writs the authentic instruments outnumber the untrustworthy only by a fairly small margin.

Even the 'authentic' character of a record, which appeals to a lawyer and which an archivist must sometimes be at pains to preserve, is not the criterion of its value as historical evidence. The tendentious official account or the forgery, once recognized as such, will be valuable to the historian precisely because it is not objective or not authentic. It becomes more evidently a 'human record'. And the good historian, wrote Marc Bloch, 'is like the ogre in the story-book. Where he smells human flesh, there, he knows, he will find his quarry.'

All that I have said is really a plea for scientific treatment of records. Knowledge of possibilities implies knowledge of limitations. The danger is not that records will be used too much but that uncritical reliance will be put upon them because of the charm of the 'authentic'.

The consequence of record-mindedness for the study of literary sources is plain to see. In 1895 the official Rolls series came to the end of its publication of literary texts with volume ii of Henry of Knighton's chronicle; and from that day to this the critical study of medieval English historical narratives has made comparatively few advances. This is not to depreciate all the important work on the Anglo-Saxon chronicle or the light thrown upon some historians of the late fourteenth century and after. But these and other excellent works hardly make an abundant harvest for sixty summers. For the text of some chronicles and biographies we still go back to the noble but inconvenient folios of Roger Twysden and Henry Wharton. Some most notable collections of letters are only to be had in the century-old editions of J. A. Giles, as rare as they are inadequate. We have not built enough on the magnificent foundations laid by the great nineteenth-century editors, Stubbs, Luard, Liebermann. Happily there are some signs of a renaissance in these studies, indicated here in Cambridge by the appearance of new editors for John of Salisbury and a successor to Luard to deal with Matthew Paris.[1]

Medieval narratives stand today as much in need of good critical work as do the records; and the difference in method, like the difference in kind, can be exaggerated. The distinguishing of the genuine from the false, of the original from the copy, the dating and the determination of provenance—all these procedures are common to the two categories (if, indeed, one is justified in making the categories). What is certain is that the true historian, like a judge, gets his evidence wherever he can find it. Materials of all sorts and sizes are thrown into the balance. If I do not lay emphasis upon stout boots and pick and shovel, and the critical eye turned to the landscape and to man-made objects, it is not that I underrate the value of archaeological evidence to the medievalist. It is because I have

---

[1] *The Letters of John of Salisbury*, ed. W. J. Millor and H. E. Butler, revised by C. N. L. Brooke (1955) and *The Historia Pontificalis of John of Salisbury*, ed. Marjorie Chibnall (1956), both in 'Nelson's Medieval Texts'; and Richard Vaughan, *Matthew Paris* (1958), in 'Cambridge Studies in Medieval Life and Thought'.

limited this lecture to a consideration of the written word. Materials of all sorts, I repeat, come within the province of the historian. That is why a university, with its various disciplines and its museums and art galleries, ought to be a better training-ground for a historian than a record office.

The literary sources may help to save us from dangers which I believe to be very real just now. First, events are too often measured according to the bulk of records they leave behind; secondly, and related to this, historians tend to neglect conditions and developments which were not themselves productive of written record.

One has only to have taken part in a little committee work to know that momentous matters, even if they cause the most anxious and lengthy debate, often form no more than a tenth of the agenda; and their record may be correspondingly brief. So it was in the Middle Ages. The bulk of the record was disproportionate to the significance of the action. The intensive studies on the medieval parliament of England since Maitland published *Memoranda de Parliamento* in 1893 bear this out. A historian who takes up the same position as the maker of the records only sees half the view.

Liebermann once said that we see the early Middle Ages 'through clerical spectacles'. He meant, of course, to recall that nearly all the literary sources and the majority of records were the work of clerics and bear a special imprint. Looking at the records only, we may fancy we see the medieval world through the spectacles of the lawyer, the civil servant, or the bailiff. They are overwhelmingly records of crime, litigation, and the exploiting of large estates. Until late in the thirteenth century records of these sorts completely swamp those designed to serve other needs of a mainly illiterate society. And just as clerical spectacles have, among other things, encouraged historians to see the Middle Ages in terms of the ungodly and the godly, black and white, so if we don the lawyer's spectacles we see that over-systematic picture of feudal society which all historians now reject.

Here and elsewhere, historians have been tempted to think in terms of government and institutions which produce records rather than of people and communities which do not. The manor, for example, has its well-marked structure, seignorial and agrarian; but what were the lateral links in this small social group, and what held together the inhabitants of several manors in a single village? These questions are hard to answer. Historians have lately assembled sparse signs of the community of the vill in medieval England. They are suggestive of an existence outside the lord's court and boon-work and the agrarian routine, of folk who met in church and tavern and talked and acted together; neither ciphers nor 'economic men'. If we would learn more about them we must sometimes disengage ourselves from the institutions to search for traces of the less clearly recorded human groups. Not only lawyers and economists, but linguists and sociologists suggest questions which the historian can with advantage put to his sources. How profitable a change of approach can be is shown by Professor George Homans's book on *English Villagers of the Thirteenth Century*. Professor Owen Lattimore provides another instance when he points to the border populations dwelling on both sides of a frontier, which may sometimes be regarded together 'as a joint community that is functionally recognizable though not institutionally defined. It is not surprising' (he observes) 'that the ambivalent loyalties of frontier peoples are often conspicuous and historically important.' The makers of the records did not share our interests. Nevertheless, with judicious coaxing, they may be induced to tell of some of these things, and literary and archaeological sources may help us to keep a sense of due proportion.

I will pursue the matter no further. Large tracts of medieval history lie right outside my chosen topic. The history of philosophy, theology, and the natural sciences leaves little trace in the records of the Middle Ages. So also the history of letters. These are subjects in which knowledge progresses fast and Cambridge is taking a conspicuous part in the advance. Cambridge also has a long tradition of European historical studies which has continued and bears good fruit in the present generation. Though I have chosen a narrower framework for this lecture, I would not like it to be thought that the choice was made with an exclusive intention or out of purely insular interests. For I have been considering problems which are not peculiar to England, and a method and an attitude of mind which concern a wider field. The problem of how to use medieval records is the problem of how to enlarge our critical apparatus and how to interpret with judgement and humanity. So it is the concern of all. Everyone who teaches and learns about history in a university is at once producer and consumer. It is for him to do his own 'research'. That horrid word, by now well established in our academic jargon, should apply to the undergraduate's pursuits as well as to his teacher's. He need not be the first person to go to the source; he need not be drawing on it for the first time; but historical inquiry will only give its peculiar training to his mind if, from time to time, he makes a critical and fair-minded approach to the materials from which history is written. He will learn to appreciate the historical process not simply by reading smooth historical narratives but by practising the technique of the historian. The testing and analysing of sources should have for him the value that laboratory experiment has for the student of the natural sciences. History studied in this way never stales. That is why we can always learn from the best historians of the past and why the latest work is never definitive. Neither this generation nor any to come will so anatomize the past as to put historians out of business. 'History', it has been said, 'is a science of observation of the living, not of dissection of the dead.' So I conclude my remarks on records, in the words of a great scholar, Thomas Madox, written in 1711 and valid today: 'Although the Subject of the *English* Antiquities hath (as I said before) been pretty well cultivated of late Years; it is still capable of great improvements.'

2. The Letters of Pope Innocent III*

THE pope with whose letters this paper is concerned came to the pontificate in 1198 at the comparatively early age of thirty-seven or thirty-eight, and in the space of eighteen years (for he died in 1216) established a reputation throughout Latin Christendom which was surpassed by that of no other pope of the Middle Ages. He adjudicated between claimants to the Empire, made and unmade kings, and assumed the position of overlord and guardian in several states, including England. To an unprecedented extent the papal court became the chief court of appeal for the entire Church, and Innocent emphasized the Church's unity under his government by convening a General Council. For these reasons and others Innocent III is notable, and historians of each later age, whether attracted or repelled by his character and aims, have paid tribute to his greatness. They have indeed had little excuse for overlooking him, since the surviving records of his pontificate are very rich. His own letters are the most valuable source of all and the following remarks are concerned with the nature of the evidence which they provide.

To speak on this subject rather than on a specific part of it must seem to any informed person an audacious undertaking. For there are over 5,000 collected letters of the pope,[1] and many hundreds not collected. What can be said briefly about such a field for detailed study? Something may be said about the letters as a whole, to aid the interpretation of them in detail. They are constantly used by historians and not infrequently misunderstood. Viewed as a whole they raise

---

* A lecture delivered in The John Rylands Library, on Wednesday, 9 Jan. 1952, with some modifications and additions. First published in the *Bulletin of the John Rylands Library*, XXXV (1952–3), 23–43. For later writings on the subject, see the Additional Note below, pp. 37–8.

[1] i.e. calendared by Potthast. Those letters which survive in the papal registers (over 3,600 of them) are printed *in extenso*, with some others, in Migne's *Patrologia latina*, vols. ccxiv–ccxvii.

certain questions about their transmission, their authorship, their accuracy, and so forth; if we can approximately answer these questions we can assess the historical value of any single letter or group of letters more confidently.

No short account can describe the scope of these letters, which embrace all topics, ecclesiastical and political, moral and legal, with which the pope was concerned; they are addressed to almost all parts of Europe and the Mediterranean world; but a few examples will illustrate the extraordinary variety. Here is a handful of letters chosen at random.

The first[1] is written to 'the illustrious Miramolinus king of Morocco and his subjects, praying that they may attain knowledge of the truth and abide therein to their advantage'. This letter is to recommend the Trinitarian brethren who worked for the ransom and exchange of Christian captives among the Moors. Then there is a letter[2] to the archbishop of Vienne, the bishop of Geneva, and the abbot of Chassagne, ordering them to hold a judicial enquiry into the alleged enormities of the archbishop of Lyon. A third letter[3] is important for its light on the nascent university of Paris: it is addressed to 'the doctors of Holy Writ, of Decrees, and of the Liberal Arts, dwelling at Paris', and confirms a statute made by the *universitas magistrorum*.

To turn to another topic: not only did Innocent III claim sole authority to declare the canonization of saints; he also was called upon to pronounce on the authenticity of relics. Here, in full, is a letter which initiates proceedings in an affair of this sort:[4]

Innocent, bishop, servant of the servants of God, to his beloved sons the abbot and prior of St. Victor and Master G. Cornutus, canon of Paris, greeting and the apostolic blessing.

[1] Migne, ccxiv. 544.   [2] Ibid. ccxv. 1299.
[3] Ibid. ccxv. 1585.
[4] Ibid. ccxvi. 549. The protocol, or opening clause, does not appear in the register in full; likewise the endings of this and the next letter to be quoted are abridged in the register; they have been completed here according to common form.

Cf. Geoffrey de Courlon, *Le Livre des reliques de l'abbaye de St-Pierre-le-Vif de Sens*, ed. G. Julliot and M. Prou (Sens, 1887), for Archbishop Hugh's authentic record (1160) and his grant of some relics of S. Loup to St-Loup-de-Naud (pp. 288–90), and an agreement between the two abbeys, after litigation, for sharing the profits of a preaching tour, in 1432 (pp. 249 sqq.).

Our beloved sons the abbot and convent of Ste. Colombe of Sens in their complaint to us have represented that the entire body of S. Loup the confessor, archbishop of Sens, rests in their church together with his head, as appears clearly from the authentic record of Hugh, of happy memory, archbishop of Sens, who summoned certain bishops and assembled the clergy and people and exhibited to them all the body and the head. Nevertheless, they complain, the abbot and monks of St-Pierre-le-Vif of Sens, to the damage of the abbey of Ste. Colombe, cause their preachers to declare far and wide in the diocese that the head and certain limbs of the confessor are in a priory of theirs, St-Loup-de-Naud; and they complain that this is quite contrary to the truth. Since deceit should not be tolerated under the veil of piety, we order you by this apostolic letter on our authority carefully to admonish and effectively to induce the abbot and monks of St. Pierre to desist from this audacity, compelling them if need be, when you have enquired into the truth of the matter, by ecclesiastical censure without right of appeal. For it ill accords with either their well-being or their reputation that they should obtain alms by the preaching of lies. No letter is to prejudice truth and justice, should there be produced any such letter obtained from the Apostolic See. If all of you cannot attend to the execution of this, let two of you execute it notwithstanding. Dated at the Lateran, the 14th of March, in the fifteenth year of our pontificate.

Here the pope was acting as supreme judge. The next example[1] likewise illustrates his judicial omnipotence, but this time in the *forum internum*, where he assigns penance to the penitent:

To the archbishops, bishops, abbots, and priors to whom this letter shall come. The bearer of this letter, Robert by name, came to the compassionate Apostolic See and tearfully confessed his sin, a great sin indeed and a grave one. For when he had been captured with his wife and daughter by the Saracens, their chief, whom they call the Admiral, issued an order that, since a famine was imminent, all those prisoners who had children should kill them; and by reason of this order, this wretched man, urged on by pangs of hunger, killed and ate his daughter. And when on a second occasion another order went out, he killed his own wife; but when her flesh was cooked and served up before him, he could not bring himself to eat it. Appalled by the horror of such a crime, we have thought fit to enjoin upon him this penance: that he never hereafter on any

[1] Migne, ccxiv. 1063.

account eat meat, and that he fast every Friday on bread and water and likewise on the Monday and Wednesday in the Lent of Christmas and the Lent of Easter; and on other days of each Lent he is to fast devoutly and remain content with one dish of pottage, observing the same on the vigils of saints' days. He is to go about unshod, in a woollen tunic with a very short scapular, carrying a penitent's staff a cubit in length. He is to accept no more food from anyone than suffices for a day, and he is never to spend above two nights in the same place unless driven by necessity and unable to proceed because of illness or war or weather. In this way let him visit the shrines of the saints for three years; and when he comes to a church let him prostrate himself and not enter until he has received discipline with rod or whip. He shall persist always without hope of marriage. He shall never attend public sports. He is to say the Lord's Prayer a hundred times every day and bow the knee each time. At the end of three years let him return with this letter to the Apostolic See to seek mercy, and take pains to observe what shall then be enjoined upon him. You, therefore, brethren and children, show pity to the pitiful and in the time of his need reveal to him the fulness of your love. Dated at the monastery of Subiaco, the 3rd of September, in the fifth year of our pontificate.

This letter, remarkable though it is, records routine business. Here is a more exceptional letter,[1] addressed a few months after Innocent became pope to Octavian, cardinal-bishop of Ostia:

A few days before we left Rome an aged (and, we believe, a devout) priest came to our presence and in private declared that the blessed apostle Peter had appeared to him in a vision by night as he slept, saying: 'Go to Pope Innocent and tell him from me that I have loved him as a son from his birth and after raising him to various ranks I have at last placed him in my seat. On this account he ought to love the beauty and honour of my house and improve it with vigilant care. Let him know, then, that only a few altars in my church are consecrated; and so it happens that the divine mysteries are celebrated on unconsecrated[2] altars. Let him cause to be

----

[1] Migne, ccxiv. 336.

[2] *dissecratis.* This is an unusual, if not unique, use of the word in Latin. I am indebted to the Revd. Père Paul Grosjean, S.J. (Bollandist) for the suggestion that the priest who reported his vision thought, if he did not speak, in the vernacular, and that the pope adopted the word spoken to him. The context suggests that the meaning must be *unconsecrated*, not *desecrated* or *polluted*. On the other hand Dr. Michele Cerrati takes this to mean that Innocent 'fece riconsacrare' the altars (*Documenti e ricerche per la storia dell'antica Basilica Vaticana*, Studi e testi vol. 26

consecrated with due reverence those altars at least on which he knows the divine office is often celebrated.' Now when the same vision had been revealed once and then again to the priest, and he had not done as he was ordered, the apostle spoke at last a third time,[1] angrily saying: 'Because you have not hearkened to my command, I will take away from you your hearing.' Thenceforward he became so deaf that he could hear nothing. Crying bitterly and lamenting on this account, the pious man came to the shrine of St. Peter, asking with tears that he would take pity and restore him his hearing, for he would straightway fulfil his command. By God's mercy his prayer was heard, and he told us exactly what had happened to him. While, as the apostle says, we ought not to believe every spirit (1 John 4: 1), yet, since in a matter of this sort an angel of Satan would not transform himself into an angel of light (2 Cor. 11: 14) and since, when it would be proper to do what is proposed even if the revelation were untrue, it is better to show pious faith than rash incredulity, by this apostolic letter we bid you, brother, in whom we have full confidence, personally consecrate the altars of Saints Philip and James, Saints Simon and Jude, St. Gregory and St. Andrew, which are said to be unconsecrated, or else have them consecrated by others on our authority. For we believe that thereby the fruit of eternal reward will accrue to us.

As a final example, let me quote the letter addressed in May 1199 to all the ecclesiastical and lay princes of Germany.[2] It was written at a time when rival claimants for the crown of the Holy Roman Empire had been in the field for some months. The pope was keenly interested in the outcome, and was predisposed to Otto of Brunswick rather than Philip of Swabia, but he had not yet shown his hand. This is one of the earliest letters copied into the special *Register on Imperial Affairs*, which was

(Rome, 1914), p. 64, nn. 1 and 2). For the pope's use of the vernacular, see Tillmann, *Papst Innocenz III*, pp. 50, 154 and *Traditio*, xx (1964), 151, 161.

1 Visions commonly had to be repeated before action was taken. On another occasion Innocent acted on a command from the Virgin Mary, which was conveyed to him by one Master Rainer, after three apparitions to a companion of Rainer's in a hermitage outside Rome (Rad. de Coggeshall, *Chron. anglicanum* (RS), pp. 130–3; cf. H. Grundmann, *Deutsches Archiv*, xvi (1960), 447–50).
2 'Regestum domni Innocentii tertii pape super negotio romani imperii', ep. 2 (Migne, ccxvi. 997). This register has been sumptuously reproduced in facsimile by Wilhelm Peitz, S.J. (Biblioteca Vaticana, 1928); there is an elaborate critical edition by Friedrich Kempf, S.J. (Misc. Historiae Pontificiae XII. 21: Rome, Pont. Univ. Gregoriana, 1947) and a plain text by Walther Holtzmann (Bonn, 1947–8).

begun in the papal chancery in this year. The register contains some highly important statements of political theory and gives an excellent view of Innocent's diplomatic language and practice.

The degree of harmony which should prevail between Church and State is shown by Christ in His own person, Who is the King of kings and Lord of lords (1 Tim. 6: 15), a priest for ever after the order of Melchizedek (Heb. 5: 6), Who in the human nature which He had taken upon Himself came of both priestly and royal stock. To indicate this harmony, indeed, the most blessed Peter spoke to those who had turned to the faith of Christ, saying: 'Ye are a chosen generation, a royal priesthood' (1 Pet. 2: 9). And Christ is addressed in the Apocalypse: 'Thou hast made us unto our God kings and princes' (Apoc. 5: 10). For these are the two cherubim with faces turned to the mercy-seat which are described as looking one to another, with their wings joined (cf. Exod. 25: 18–20). These are the two marvellous and beautiful pillars placed by the gate in the porch of the temple, 'and a line of twelve cubits did compass either of them about' (1 Kings 7: 15–21). These are the two great lights which God made in the firmament of the heaven: 'the greater light to rule the day and the lesser light to rule the night' (Gen. 1: 16). They are the two swords concerning which the apostles answered: 'Behold, here are two swords' (Luke 22: 38). We refrain from expounding the meaning of all these texts and many more extracted from Holy Writ which expressly signify the harmony between Church and State, since the profit derived from this harmony makes it even clearer. For by this harmony the faith is spread and heresy confuted, virtues are implanted and vices cut down, justice is preserved and wickedness cast out; peace flourishes, persecution subsides. With the pacification of the Christian people the barbarism of the pagans is subdued, with the improvement of the State the liberty of the Church grows; the security of the body conduces to the salvation of the soul, and the rights of both clergy and people are preserved.

While all realms in which the name of Christ is worshipped regard the Roman Church as their mother, yet the Roman Empire ought to embrace her particularly closely and devotedly, so that she may be succoured by the Empire's defence and may herself contribute to the needs of the Empire. But he who is always envious of peace and quiet has now divided the Roman Empire, just as formerly he divided the Roman Church, and has sown such discord among you that you have presumed to nominate two persons as your kings. Divided among yourselves, you stubbornly adhere to them without considering how many and how great are the dangers which this brings not only to the Roman Empire but to all Christian people. See how the liberty of the Empire is diminished by this cause of dissension. Laws are annulled, authority is curtailed, churches are destroyed, the poor are afflicted, the princes oppressed, the whole land is laid waste and (what is worse) there is likely to ensure the slaughter of men's bodies and the imperilling of their souls. This division, also, in no small degree emboldens the enemies of the Christian faith against the faithful.

Therefore, we who have heard and learnt about these things are grieved at heart and troubled with great sorrow (cf. Gen. 6:6), for we do not (as some pestilent fellows pretend) aim at the ruin or abasement of the Empire; rather do we aspire to preserve and exalt it, since although some emperors have violently injured the Church, others have shown her manifold honours.

But we have hitherto waited patiently (cf. Ps. 39:1) to see whether you yourselves would be guided by wiser counsel and take pains to put an end to such ills or would have recourse to our aid, so that with your help this dissension might be allayed by us, to whom it belongs first and last to deal with this business. But because you have so far been negligent and idle we, who according to the words of the prophet (Jer. 1:10) are set by God over the nations and kingdoms to root out and to destroy, to build and to plant, anxious to fulfil the duties of our office, fervently admonish you all and exhort you in the Lord, ordering by this apostolic letter that you have the fear of God before your eyes and zeal for the honour of the Empire, lest its liberty perish or its authority be annihilated. Provide more diligently for it, lest by fostering discord you destroy the majesty of the Empire which ought to be preserved by your efforts. Otherwise, since longer delay is producing great danger, we shall arrange what we shall find to be expedient and shall take care to give the apostolic favour to him whom we shall consider to be supported by the greater zeal of his electors and his own superior merits.[1]

The great collection of letters of which the foregoing are samples cannot be understood without consideration being paid to their transmission. How have they come down to us?

---

[1] 'quem credemus maioribus studiis et meritis adiuvari': cf. R. W. and A. J. Carlyle, *Medieval Political Theory in the West*, v (1928), 205.

The answer is: partly in the Vatican Registers—that is, the file-copies made and preserved by the papal chancery—partly in the originals despatched or in copies made from the originals, preserved in all parts of Europe by the pope's correspondents. The registers of Innocent III have attracted the attention of many scholars in the past hundred years, from Léopold Delisle onwards.[1] Their researches have, among other results, established the twofold object of the registers—as memoranda for the pope and his clerks and as authentic record for the recipients of papal grants and mandates. This explains the absence of some letters from the registers. Apart from the fact that whole categories of letters went unregistered, the choice depended in some measure on the taste and habit of individual clerks rather than on a fixed office-routine. Any argument from silence is therefore precluded. Access to the register was readily allowed to petitioners in the Curia—indeed, too readily, as appears from Innocent III's letters[2] about an Hungarian cleric who was shown the register of Pope Alexander III so that he might inspect the copy of a letter, and who cunningly cut out and stole two leaves from the middle of a quire, leaving the binding thread untouched; the loss was only discovered later. The registers also provided a source for the decretal-collections prepared by canon lawyers: this meant that the enregistered copy of a letter might be touched up to produce a more satisfactory legal pronouncement. The mere fact of registration may be significant for an understanding of the background and import of a letter. Von Heckel pointed out[3] how a mere 'letter of justice'—normally a common form, not seen by the pope and not enregistered—came exceptionally to be entered because it introduced a new rule of law. Again, Fr. Kempf, investigating the dates at which the special registration of imperial business was started, dropped, and resumed, offers a valuable means of interpreting the pope's policy towards the imperial election.[4]

---

[1] L. Delisle, 'Mémoire sur les actes d'Innocent III', *Bibl. de l'École des Chartes*, xix (1857); for recent literature, see Additional Note, pp. 37–8 below.

[2] Migne, ccxiv. 494, 502.

[3] R. von Heckel, in *Hist. Jahrbuch*, lv (1935), 277–304, cf. lvii (1937), 86–93.

[4] Kempf, *Die Register Innocenz III* (Misc. Hist. Pont. ix. 18: Rome, 1945), pp. 45–65.

Then there are the letters which have survived only outside the papal archives. First of all, how is one to determine their authenticity? The letters in the register make it clear that forgeries of the pope's letters existed in plenty. In 1207 the bishop and dean of Paris referred to the pope a decretal lately alleged in court before them. The pope, in reply,[1] quotes the decretal in full and denounces it: it has certain parts consonant with the law, with which the forger has coloured his lies, but it is no *decretale*, rather a *concretale*. The canonist Bernardus Compostellanus puts on record[2] concerning a decretal ascribed to Innocent III that the pope had told him personally that it was not his, although it was not repugnant to the law. In several letters Innocent describes how he detected forgeries by personal examination of them. This suggests that there is room for diplomatic criticism in the strict Mabillonian sense: the applying of criteria to distinguish the true from the false. Fortunately enough authentic letters survive and enough is known of the practices of the papal chancery to permit the applying of fairly satisfactory tests.

It is equally important to determine concerning any authentic letter, however preserved, whether it reached the destination for which it was originally intended. This commonplace deserves a little attention. The pope quite often has to entrust to delegates in distant places letters which could be used, and should only be used, in certain circumstances.[3] Sometimes alternative forms were provided. Both forms or neither of them might be enregistered.[4] Or letters might be countermanded after they had been copied into the register, and the fact would not necessarily be noted.[5] Moreover, even if a letter

---

[1] Migne, ccxv. 1113–14. One part of the quoted decretal is found as a letter of Innocent III to the archbishop of Canterbury in the appendix to a decretal-collection in the Bodleian MS. Tanner 8. See W. Holtzmann in *Festschrift zur Feier des 200 jährigen Bestehens der Akad. der Wissensch. in Göttingen, 1951* (phil.-hist. Kl.), p. 144, and C. R. Cheney in *Traditio*, xv (1959), 480–3.

[2] *Sitzungsberichte d. Wiener Akad.* (phil.-hist. Kl.), clxxi (1914), ii. 116.

[3] Helene Tillmann, 'Ueber päpstl. Schreiben mit bedingter Gültigkeit im 12 u. 13 Jh.', in *Mitteilungen des oesterreich. Instituts für Geschichtsforschung*, xlv (1931), 191–200. The same procedure is found in the government of the centralized religious orders; a good example (A.D. 1210) may be seen in *Statuta ord. Cisterciensis*, ed. J. M. Canivez, i (Louvain, 1933), p. 374, no. 30.

[4] Cf. Migne, ccxiv. 490.

[5] Cf. *Studies . . . pres. to F. M. Powicke* (1948), p. 109, n. 3.

were delivered to a litigant or a petitioner, it might be inop-
portune to use the letter,[1] and since the addressee of a papal
mandate was seldom the person who procured the mandate
from the curia, the addressee would never see it. This is what
the monks of Christ Church, Canterbury told the pope in an
elaborately elegant letter[2] in 1200, when they were in the midst
of a lawsuit with their archbishop, Hubert Walter. They had
feared an unfavourable verdict from the pope's delegates
because, so they said, in England they could not get any good
barristers to oppose the archbishop (who was also the king's
chancellor); so they had obtained a letter from the pope dated
21 May 1200 revoking the commission of his delegates and
summoning the parties to be at Rome in November 1200.
But by the time the monks had obtained this letter (and the
getting of it must have taken two months at least), circumstances had altered. They had (according to their own story)
secured the services of skilled lawyers who had come to
Becket's shrine on pilgrimage from overseas, and thanks to
them the monks' prospects in the case before the delegates
looked brighter. Furthermore, the monks admitted that they
did not like the terms of the pope's letter of 21 May 1200,
which did not provide all the legal safeguards of his former
mandate. They therefore wrote to Innocent, asking him to
defer the action contemplated; and in the sequel they came to
a settlement under the arbitration of the original delegates.
Such incidents as this must have happened often. A few years
later, in December 1205, monks of Canterbury brought home
from Rome a letter-close addressed to King John on behalf of
their sub-prior as a candidate for the office of archbishop. But
by the time it reached England, the convent had repudiated
the sub-prior and the letter can never have been delivered to
the king. It is still in the archives of Christ Church, Canterbury.[3]
Clearly, we cannot assume that because a letter went out from
the Curia, it reached its destination.

Another critical question now arises. How accurate are the

[1] See what Archbishop Anselm told Paschal II in 1104 to justify withholding
papal letters to the king and queen of England (ep. 315, *Opp.*, ed. F. S. Schmitt,
v. 243).
[2] *Epistolae cantuarienses*, ed. W. Stubbs (RS), p. 510.
[3] See *BIHR*, xxi (1948), 233–8.

letters as narratives of the events which they describe? One
obvious reason why the historian finds in Innocent III's letters
an incomparable source is their lengthy narratives. It may be
a series of diplomatic *démarches*, such as the pope describes in
his letter[1] of 16 November 1202 to the Byzantine emperor; or
the various stages in a protracted lawsuit, as recounted in his
letter[2] of 4 June 1202 to the archbishop of Canterbury; or the
report of a violent assault upon a prelate, as graphically described in the pope's letter[3] of 21 June 1199 to the king of
Hungary. As regards the record of diplomatic events, we may
take it that when the pope gives a résumé of the letter to
which he replies, the résumé is correct; when he goes
beyond this to describe oral negotiations and discussion with
third parties, there is not the same prima facie case, and outside corroboration is usually lacking. The position is much
worse when we turn to letters recounting litigation and the
hardships suffered by petitioners. For here the narrative commonly precedes a mandate for delegates to act in a certain way
si res ita se habet, or *si ita est*, or with some other phrase antici-
pating the possibility that matters have been fraudulently represented to the pope. The common form, 'No letter is to
prejudice truth or justice' (quoted above in the letter concerning
the relics of S. Loup), points the same way. These phrases
only confirm what we know from other sources: that the pope
continually sent out orders based on *ex parte* statements. The
practice is commented upon with some asperity by Archbishop
Hubert Walter in 1198, in a letter[4] to Bishop John of Norwich:
'the lord pope, who is violently opposed to me, has denied
a hearing to my clerks who wanted to reply to each charge on
my behalf, and has straightway, without enquiry into the truth,
granted the monks a letter in which he orders me to demolish
the church of Lambeth'. This feature of papal letters should
warn us against taking all their statements about past events at
face value.

　　The letter to the princes of Germany quoted above raises
a much bigger problem, involving questions of style and
authorship: are the letters an accurate guide to the pope's

---

[1] Migne, ccxiv. 1123.　　　　　　　　　　[2] Ibid. ccxiv. 1026.
[3] Ibid. ccxiv. 643.　　　　　　[4] *Epist. cantuar.*, p. 395. Cf. below, p. 261.

sentiments and doctrines and policy? Without doubt they are commonly treated as such. Historians of the Church and of political theory construct from them a composite picture of the pope's theories of government. It is not always remembered that these papal letters were not for the most part set treatises on the nature of political authority or anything of that sort; they were occasional statements adapted to the correspondents and to the circumstances. Rarely will the pope feel called upon to deal so comprehensively with the doctrine of Church and State as he does in the letter 'Solitae benignitatis',[1] addressed to the Byzantine Emperor Alexius III. Nevertheless, these various casual statements have the advantage for historians that each letter shows the pope's response to a particular known situation and can be dated with far more precision than can most medieval treatises. That suggests, I may remark in passing, the desirability of studying the pope's letters with strict attention to chronology, to observe, if possible, developments in his ideas in the course of his eighteen-year-long pontificate.[2]

But this appraisal of individual letters cannot go on unless something is known about the manner of their composition. First, some remarks about the literary style. The diction of the pope's writing office, in his chancery, had developed through long centuries, retaining many ancient formulas and epithets. But it had changed markedly during the twelfth century in accordance with the newly established fashion of rhythmic prose. A style evolved (not, indeed, peculiar to the papal chancery) which was sonorous, balanced, smooth; but its practitioners could not be brief. Too often they produce so many words as to stifle the sense, and darkly convey quite ordinary sentiments in long, labyrinthine periods. The letters of Innocent III show these features in general.[3] For an understanding of them it is important to recognize that certain polite formulas are repeatedly used and are devoid of special

---

[1] Migne, ccxvi. 1182.

[2] Cf. Carlyle's discussion of a change in the pope's attitude to the imperial election between 1199 and 1202 (op. cit. v. 218-19).

[3] J. de Ghellinck considers that Innocent III's letters are a little better in this respect than those of his predecessors (*L'Essor de la littérature latine* (Brussels 1946), i. 67-8).

significance. For instance, a king—even when he is in the pope's bad books and is on the verge of excommunication—will be addressed and be referred to as the pope's most dear son in Christ. Similarly, the special prerogative love which the pope expresses for Sancho, king of Portugal, in December 1198 becomes less remarkable when we find the same preference expressed for the kings of Sicily, Jerusalem, England, and Hungary, in letters written within a few months of this one.[1] This does not convict the pope of insincerity: it merely shows that we must try to recognize the papal chancery's conventions. These conventions sometimes have a more positive significance. At a time when the pope was beginning to regard favourably Philip of Swabia, whom he had formerly rejected as a claimant to the imperial crown, the honorific *serenitas* creeps into a letter to Philip,[2] although the word was usually reserved for crowned heads: it shows more plainly than the rest of the letter the direction in which the pope was moving.

Innocent III issued a great many grants of familiar privileges, mandates appointing judges, and other routine letters, which do not show any marked change from earlier papal correspondence. They could be composed by any well-trained curial clerk.[3] But the letters (especially those in the registers) include many on political affairs, many judicial decisions, many exhortations to prelates to be zealous pastors and to the faithful laity to support Crusades. There are also many decretal letters which state the pope's opinion on points of canon law, and these often involved theological and moral considerations. Here the draftsman had more latitude, and he usually availed himself of it, adapting his manner to the subject in hand.

The letters were written in the name of Innocent III, but how many did he write himself? Can one distinguish between those which were his own composition and the letters composed by his chancellor and clerks? No scholar has worked to answer these questions with the care which was bestowed some years ago by Blaul and Caspar on the letters of Pope

[1] Migne, ccxiv. 419, 389–90, 417, 451, 473, and cxvi. 513, 515. Cf. ccxiv. 339 to the consuls of Milan.

[2] Reg. super negotio imperii, no. 143 (Migne, ccxvi. 1142).

[3] For this see the article of Professor G. Barraclough, 'Audientia litterarum contradictarum', in *Dict. de droit canonique*, i (1935), 1388.

Gregory VII,[1] when it seemed possible to attribute certain letters to that pope on stylistic and other grounds. It is commonly assumed that Innocent III has left the stamp of his own style and personality on many of the letters. The late Augustin Fliche characterized them by 'a studied style, full of imagery, fertile in antitheses, rich in reminiscences of the liturgy and of the Old and New Testaments, with passages from profane authors, notably Horace and Ovid, and with Scriptural comparisons which are sometimes rather forced'.[2] Such letters, indeed, there are and the probability that the pope wrote them is increased by stylistic likenesses with Innocent's theological works, written before he became pope. Moreover, the letters of Innocent's immediate predecessors do not show so markedly these features. The same school of rhetoric had produced their tropes, but they very seldom develop—as the Innocentian letters sometimes do—into a little theological or moral essay, serving as the preamble to a precise mandate or indulgence. An example will show this type of preamble. In 1206 Innocent had to complain that the English collectors of a tax for the Crusade, demanded six years earlier, had been negligent in their task. His letter[3] to two English bishops enjoining action begins as follows:

So deficient and unstable is human fragility and the downward path to evil so slippery and smooth, that if, disregarding the offence against God, men could work evil without temporal penalty or restraint, many would this very day be found culpable and evil-doing who are accounted firm in their faith and active in good works. Therefore, although by nature we are equal and formed out of the same lump, yet for the correction of this unsteadiness and weakness, by the organization of government, some men are made prelates over others, and by God's ordering are appointed to ranks of dignity and to the honours of pre-eminent station. In this way the censure of a superior may correct offences committed through the negligence or malice of subordinates, and thus, one being directed and confirmed in the path of rectitude by another, we may pass more safely to our fatherland, provided (as it were) with guides through

[1] Blaul in *Archiv für Urkundenforschung*, iv (1911), 113 sqq. and Caspar in *Das Register Gregors VII* (Mon. Germ. Hist., 1920), pp. xv–xvi. Cf. p. 33 n. 1.
[2] A. Fliche and E. Jarry, *Hist. de l'Église*, x: La chrétienté romaine (1950), p. 15.
[3] *EHR* lxiii (1948), 347–8.

the desert places of our earthly home and the valley of pilgrimage in which we dwell and abide in this life.

This is scarcely typical of the large extent to which the language of the letters echoes the Bible. In the letter to the princes of Germany which has been quoted there are twelve biblical parallels. The preamble to a letter of protection for a religious house[1] crams ten Scriptural texts (mostly Pauline) into the space of twenty short lines. Another letter[2] strings together three quotations from the book of Proverbs, thus: 'For you know by the teaching of Holy Writ that a father chastises the son in whom he delights (3: 12), and the stripes of a friend are better than the kisses of an enemy (cf. 27: 6), and reproofs of instruction are the way of life (6: 23)'. A biography of Innocent, in which Frederick Rolfe collaborated and which shows more than one Corvine characteristic, draws attention to the pope's exhaustive knowledge of the Scriptures—'as may be seen in his sermons, which, for ingenious and fecund stringing-together of texts, suggest the fine old-fashioned style of evangelicals of the mid-Victorian era'.[3] More or less ingenuity is displayed in the application of texts to unexpected ends. Sometimes the effect is banal, as: 'When the true Moses— that is, Christ—raises his hands—that is, gives help and solace —the victory goes to Israel—that is, the Church'. At other times texts are subtly glossed to show the nature of the pope's authority.[4] The most famous cases of this are the numerous references to Melchizedek, the priest-king, and to the texts concerning St. Peter.[5] Another instance[6] emphasizes the pope's judicial authority in the Church: 'Out of the mouth of Him who sat upon the throne issued a two-edged sword. This is the sword of Solomon which cuts both ways, giving to each his due. We therefore who, although unworthy, occupy by God's mercy the place of the true Solomon, wield the sword wisely when we decide according to the dictates of justice in legal

---

[1] Migne, ccxiv. 504. [2] Ibid. ccxvii. 365.
[3] C. H. C. Pirie-Gordon, *Innocent the Great* (1907), p. 209.
[4] See L. Buisson, in *Adel u. Kirche ... G. Tellenbach dargebr.* (1969), pp. 469–76.
[5] See K. Burdach, *Vom Mittelalter zur Reformation*, II i (1913), 240–62, and G. Martini, 'Regale sacerdotium', *Archivio della Società Romana di Storia Patria*, lxi (1938), pp. 1–166.
[6] Migne, ccxiv. 246, cf. ccxv. 195, 784.

fashion the questions ventilated in our court. For puzzling questions which arise and knotty points of litigation are referred to the Apostolic See so that when the merits of a case have been exposed by the statements of the parties, sentence may come forth from the Apostolic See, turning dubieties into certainties and bringing obscurities into the light; so that the dissension of litigants is appeased and justice protects and emulates her author.'

On the assumption that the letters were framed by the pope, scholars have seen in them traces of his education. He owed much to his Parisian studies in the Bible, where (as he himself tells us)[1] Pierre de Corbeil, a noted commentator, had been his teacher. His legal studies at Bologna[2] had certainly been of equal importance, and the letters commonly quote the canons contained in the *Decretum* of Gratian and refer occasionally to the civil law. Sprinkled through the correspondence are tags such as a law-student would recall, taken from the *Code* or *Digest* or elsewhere: 'Cum iuxta imperialis sanctionis auctoritatem ab omnibus quod omnes tangit approbari debeat', 'Non habet imperium par in parem', 'Cessante causa cessare debet effectus'. More than this, the structure of rescripts and their authoritative tone recall the imperial style of the civil law books. At other times the writer takes his tags from the abundant field of vulgar proverbs: 'Qui nimium emungit, elicit sanguinem';' Qui ferit primo, ferit tangendo, qui ferit secundo, ferit dolendo.'[3] Along with these features minor points emerge in a taste for parallels between words of similar sound (parachesis): thus, *affectus* and *effectus*, *servire* and *sevire*,[4] and for transpositions of epithets: thus, *fidelitas devota et fidelis devotio*, *non solum discretionis spiritum verum etiam discretionem spiritus*, *unitatis concordiam et concordie unitatem, culpabiliter durum et dure*

---

[1] Migne, ccxiv. 442–4. Cf. M. Maccarrone, 'Innocenzo III prima del pontificato', *Archivio della R. Deputazione Romana di Storia Patria*, lxvi (1943), 73–4.

[2] His teacher was Huguccio, for whom, in this connection, see A. Stickler, 'Der Schwerterbegriff bei Huguccio', *Ephemerides iuris canonici*, iii (Rome, 1947), 201–42.   [3] Migne, ccxvi. 101, 66; cf. ibid., 825 and ccxv. 694.

[4] Migne, ccxiv. 418, 377. Cf. 'Quia seculo senescente, in sua segnescit meditatione Maria', ibid. ccxv. 618. This feature of Innocent's style may result from his familiarity with St. Augustine's writings: see Mary I. Barry, *St. Augustine the Orator* (Washington, 1924), pp. 70–4 and C. I. Balmus, *Étude sur le style de saint Augustin dans les Confessions et la Cité de Dieu* (1930), pp. 294–5.

culpabilem.[1] These would not attract much notice were they not closely paralleled in Innocent's sermons and other treatises: for example, *O superba praesumptio et praesumptuosa superbia.*[2]

These characteristics, recurring in one letter after another, tend to the conclusion that Innocent himself drafted many of the letters. They encourage us to seek signs of the pope's character, although the letters are all official letters and the man is submerged in his office. The pope cannot but be pontifical. Pope Gregory VII had occasionally descended from the pontifical 'we' to a personal 'I'; Innocent III hardly ever does so.[3] Yet he was, if we may judge from his other writings and from the statements of contemporaries, a man of very strong personality, who joined to his high ideas of papal authority a keen sense of the obligations of priestly office and a deep Christian faith. Surely, if he himself drafted the letters, some sign of this would appear? Innocent's dominant personality and ready speech is recorded in some sharp and sarcastic retorts to those who pleaded in lawsuits before him.[4] The same personal note, tinged with impatience, seems to sound now and then in the letters, as when a correspondent is told that the pope cannot be in two places at once, or that, although he is God's deputy on earth, he has no power of divination. A letter to the distinguished scholar, Master Prepositinus, begins: 'Time was when we believed that wisdom governed the elderly and prudence adorned the learned'.[5]

Over and above these possible indications of temperament, the different facets of the pope's character are reflected with special intensity in some of the letters. The *Register on Imperial Affairs* shows his pretensions in the sphere of politics, the letters on the pope's accession are imbued with strong piety, a decretal letter to the bishop of Ferrara[6] gives what can only be the pope's own opinion on a christological question. Again,

[1] Migne, ccxiv. 265; ccxvi. 101, 884, 1140. Cf. ibid. ccxv. 574: 'dispensando dissimulat et dissimulando dispensat'.

[2] Ibid. ccxvii. 729, cf. 658, 705. This feature also finds a parallel in St. Augustine's writings: see Balmus, pp. 158–9.

[3] Migne, ccxv. 513–14, 517.

[4] e.g. *Chronicon abbatiae de Evesham* (RS), pp. 151–2, 160, 189; *Traditio*, xx (1964), 126.

[5] Migne, ccxiv. 319, 350; ccxv. 43. Cf. ccxvii. 276 (*Traditio*, xv (1959), 480).

[6] Ibid. ccxvi. 16–18. Cf. M. Maccarrone, *Studi su Innocenzo III* (1972), pp. 387–8.

it is difficult to believe that the anxious insistence on the pope's desire to maintain the rights of others and on his duty to answer before God for the wise and the unwise are common-places dragged into the letters by subordinate draftsmen. At the same time, we must squarely face the facts that there is no positive proof of the pope's drafting of any particular letter and that we cannot hope to distinguish clearly between those which he wrote and those written by high officials of the Curia who shared his views and his intellectual background, and acted under his orders and influence. Nor can we assume that the most eloquent or the most profound letters are necessarily those which the pope himself composed.[1]

A final remark about authorship must be made. Although internal evidence suggests that the pope may have taken a large part in all but the routine correspondence, many lawsuits in the Curia were entrusted to members of the pope's household,[2] and in these cases at least the narrative incorporated in the written judgment must usually have been worded by the auditor or his clerk. Further, when the pope had occasion (as in a bull of canonization[3]) to state facts or allegations brought forward by a petitioner, he commonly used the words of a written petition, even to the point of incorporating its turns of rhetoric and scriptural similes.

The richly figured style, studded with quotations from the prophets and apostles, is an embarrassment to those who wish to understand Innocent III's political theory—as may be judged from the controversy which still wages on this matter. Did the pope claim simply that the head of the Church possessed authority superior in nature to that of the head of the State, or did he claim that the temporal ruler derived his authority from the Church and that he, Pope Innocent, ruled over men's bodies as well as over their souls?[4]

---

[1] Cf. Caspar's judicious remarks, *Das Register Gregors VII*, p. xvi. Besides the references given above see, on the pope's style, Marie Florin, 'Innocenz III als Schriftsteller u. als Papst, ein Vergleich', *Zeitschr. für Kirchengesch.*, xlv (1927), 334–57, and Edelgard von Strube, *Innozenz' III politische Korrespondenz u. die religiöse Weltherrschaftsidee der Kurie* (Libau, 1936).

[2] e.g. Migne, ccxv. 1281, 1285.

[3] e.g. *Selected Letters of Pope Innocent III*, p. 30 n. 22.

[4] See for example E. W. Meyer, *Staatstheorien Papst Innozenz' III* (Bonn, 1919),

The question cannot properly be answered by quoting any single pronouncement of the pope. The language of symbolism which is invoked to describe the relations of *regnum* and *sacerdotium*—the two swords, the sun and the moon—sounds impressive but lacks precision. Then there are the favourite scriptural texts, such as 'Thou makest them princes in all the earth' (Ps. 44: 17 Vulg.; 45 : 16 A.V.), 'I have this day set thee over the nations', etc. (Jer. 1 : 10), and 'Ye are a chosen generation, a royal priesthood', etc. (1 Peter 2 : 9). If these texts were held to imply political dominion, then the pope was making the widest claims; but did he wish them to be interpreted in any but a spiritual sense? A recent exegetist, Monsignore Michele Maccarrone, calls attention to the recurrence of the most striking texts in the liturgy for the feast of SS. Peter and Paul. He argues that as they are in the liturgy invested with an exclusively spiritual meaning, so Innocent III put the same construction on the words.[1] But Innocent upon occasion quotes Horace and Ovid, and no one supposes that he always imports into the words the poets' meaning. Why then should we suppose that every phrase borrowed from the Bible or the liturgy carries with it, when used by this pope, its original meaning? Why should we suppose that he restricts himself to the interpretations of his predecessors or even that he employs the words in the same sense on each occasion? It is of the essence of the literary style which he practised that texts and similes and metaphors can be adapted to varying circumstances, do not always bear the same construction.[2] To interpret Innocent's utterances correctly it is not enough to search out the sources of his terminology. We must weigh his words with his deeds and consider how and when each important letter came to be written.

For however single-minded the pope was in seeking the regeneration of Christendom (following the royal road, deviating neither to the right nor to the left—as he for ever tells his

Carlyle, *Med. Pol. Theory*, vols. ii and v, Michele Maccarrone, 'Chiesa e Stato nella Dottrina di Papa Innocenzo III', *Lateranum*, N.S. vi. 3–4 (Rome, 1940 (1941)), Helene Tillmann, 'Zur Frage des Verhältnisses von Kirche und Staat in Lehre und Praxis Papst Innocenz' III', *Deutsches Archiv*, ix (1951), 136–81, and the works of Burdach, Martini, and Strube cited above.

[1] Maccarrone, 'Chiesa e Stato', pp. 10, 27–8, 30–1, etc.
[2] Cf. Strube, p. 121 and Martini, p. 136.

correspondents), where his work impinged on politics he was an opportunist. It was not only in discussing the imperial election that he proposed the three tests: *quid liceat, quid deceat, quid expediat*.[1] The same threefold question is raised on other occasions in his letters. And among his biblical texts he is fond of 'a time to keep silence and a time to speak' (Eccles. 3 : 7).

The chronology of the letters is of interest in this connection. Besides the fact that the most high-sounding and extensive statements of papal authority come from the first four years of the pontificate, it is noticeable that the *plenitudo potestatis*, which is prominent in the preambles to many comparatively unimportant letters in the early years, is far less often introduced into letters in later years. Within a week of the pope's consecration he informed the archbishop of Ravenna[2] that ecclesiastical liberty is nowhere better safeguarded than where the Roman Church has full power both in temporal and in spiritual affairs. The following year he praised the king of Armenia[3] for seeking the help of the Roman Church not only in spiritual but also in temporal matters. I do not think one often finds such language later. May it not be that the young pope, fresh from his legal studies, was more outspoken than the disillusioned statesman of the second decade? It no longer seemed expedient to harp continually on these themes in his public utterances, though the policy was unchanged. Perhaps the veiled, ambiguous style so often adopted for conveying the pope's political ideas was imposed by circumstances. The bull 'Etsi karissimus', by which Innocent condemned and annulled Magna Carta in August 1215, is anything but explicit. Historians and canonists are hard put to it to say precisely on what grounds Innocent justified this action.[4] But what, after all, did that matter? Diplomatic correspondence of this sort is framed not so much

---

[1] Reg. super negotio imperii no. 29 (Migne, ccxvi. 1025). Cf. ccxiv. 59 and ccxv. 1498. The phrase is used by Innocent's notary, Thomas of Capua (Emmy Heller, in *Archiv für Urkundenforschung*, xiii (1935), 288); another who used it was Abbot Guibert of Gembloux (Migne, ccxi. 1304). The contrasting of these three verbs is found in late classical latin (*Thes. ling lat.*, V. 2 fasc. xi, col. 1614). Prof. Ullmann kindly called my attention to St. Bernard's use of the contrast, *De consideratione*, iii, c. iv, § 15 (Migne, clxxxii. 767).

[2] Migne, ccxiv. 21, cf. 541.   [3] Ibid. ccxiv. 813.

[4] Cf. *Magna Carta commemoration essays* (Royal Hist. Soc., 1917), pp. 26–40, *EHR* xxxiii (1918), 263–4, W. Ullmann, *Medieval Papalism* (1949), pp. 71–5.

to expose the writer's thoughts as to explain his action without violent shock to public opinion.

And so we come to a related topic: the effect of these letters on the pope's correspondents. Church historians have been prone to treat the letters of Innocent III as evidence not only of his intentions but of his achievements. In the sphere of politics this is only true to a strictly limited extent. History written from the letters alone will be badly distorted. The occasions when kings and princes unwillingly did as they were told at the pope's bidding are not many. The duke of Bulgaria might be prepared to receive a crown from the pope, and King John might surrender England and Ireland to receive them back as fiefs of the Roman See: both thereby recognized the superiority of the pope. But in each case the sequel shows that the lay prince got the better of the bargain. King Philip Augustus not only answers curtly the pope's attempts to intervene in French politics, but mobilizes the nobles of France in defence of the lay power. The most striking of Innocent III's letters on political theory which found their way into the lawbooks—the decretals *Novit ille*, *Venerabilem*, and *Solitae benignitatis*[1]—bore little or no fruit at the time.

In the more strictly ecclesiastical business of appeals to Rome, there is often to be seen a wide gap between a mandate and its execution. Execution might be delayed because of political disorders or a royal prohibition. Doubts, real or feigned, might arise about the authenticity of the mandate; or any one of numerous exceptions might be pleaded against it. Ambiguities in the mandate might be beyond the powers of judges-delegate to solve, as when in 1200 a long wrangle between opposing counsel ended with the judges referring the 'verborum obscuritatem' to the pope. And the judges in this case were no less persons than Hugh, bishop of Lincoln, Eustace, bishop of Ely, and Samson, abbot of St. Edmunds.[2]

---

[1] *Extra*, 2, 1, 13 and 1, 6, 34, and Migne, ccxvi. 1182.

[2] *Epistolae cantuar.*, pp. 494–6, cf. p. 25. Walter of Contances, archbishop of Rouen, having taken legal advice, held up a case on the grounds that a papal mandate was 'contra ius commune ac tocius provinciae consuetudinem' (Migne, ccxvii. 276). An example of the temporary suppression of a papal letter for political and military reasons is recorded in the letter of Boniface of Montferrat to the pope, April 1203 (Migne, ccxv. 105).

In short, our conclusion on this matter must be that the efficacy of papal government under Innocent III cannot be measured simply by reading the papal letters and counting the cases in which the pope intervened.

It has been no part of my plan to make an estimate of Innocent III's character or achievements. These topics have arisen incidentally in a discussion of the letters. My remarks on the letters have tended in the main to diminish their face-value in one way or another. But criticism of this kind brings its compensations. Each letter becomes more significant when it is seen in its setting, when its phraseology is compared with that of other letters. And the correspondence as a whole becomes a surer guide to the apparent contradictions of Innocent's many-sided genius, and to the conflicts, the successes, and the failures of his pontificate.

ADDITIONAL NOTE

Since this lecture was delivered a great deal of important work on Pope Innocent III has been published. In 1954 Dr. Helene Tillmann published a substantial biography, *Papst Innocenz III* (Bonner Historische Forschungen, Bd. 3) and Fr. Friedrich Kempf, S.J. *Papsttum und Kaisertum bei Innocenz III* (Misc. Hist. Pont. xix, Rome). In 1972 Michele Maccarrone published *Studi su Innocenzo III*. Here I confine myself to mentioning books and papers specially concerned with the register of Innocent III, the transmission of his letters, and the processes of the papal chancery in his time. Among these the most notable is the critical edition, undertaken under the direction of Dr. Leo Santifaller, by the Austrian Historical Institute in Rome and the Austrian Academy of Sciences, Vienna: *Die Register Innocenz' III*. The first volume appeared in 1964 (Böhlau, Graz-Köln). This covers the first pontifical year and was edited by Othmar Hageneder and Anton Haidacher. An index by Alfred A. Strnad appeared in 1968. In connection with this edition the editors and collaborators have published various preparatory studies and later essays, which include: Helmut Feigl, 'Die Ueberlieferung der Register Papst Innozenz' III', *Mitt. Inst. österreich. Geschichtsforschung*, lxv (1957), 242–95; O. Hageneder, 'Die äusseren Merkmale der Originalregister Innocenz' III', ibid. lxv. 296–339 and 'Quellenkritisches zu den Originalregistern Innozenz' III', ibid. lxviii (1960), 128–39, and 'Ueber "Expeditionsbündel" im Registrum Vaticanum 4',

Römische hist. Mitteilungen, xii (1970), 111–24; A. Haidacher, 'Beiträge zur Kenntnis der verlorenen Registerbände Innozenz' III', ibid. iv (1961), 37–62; A. A. Strnad, 'Zehn Urkunden Papst Innocenz' III', ibid. xi (1969), 23–58. The arguments of Friedrich Bock, 'Studien zu den Originalregistern Innocenz' III', *Archival. Zeitschr.*, li (1955), 329–66 have been refuted by (among others) Friedrich Kempf, 'Zu den Originalregistern Innocenz' III', *Quellen und Forschungen aus ital. Archiven und Bibliotheken*, xxxvi (1956), 86–137. Dr. Edith Pásztor has written 'Studi e problemi relativi ai Registri di Innocenzo III', *Annali della Scuola Speciale per Archivisti e Bibliotecari dell'Università di Roma*, ii (1962), 287–304. Patrick J. Dunning calendared 'The letters of Innocent III to Ireland', *Traditio*, xviii (1962), 229–53 and M. P. Sheehy edited *Pontificia Hibernica: medieval Papal Chancery Documents concerning Ireland, 640–1261* (Dublin, 1962). C. R. Cheney and W. H. Semple edited, with English translation, *Selected Letters of Pope Innocent III concerning England* (Nelson's Medieval Texts, 1953); C. R. and Mary G. Cheney edited *Letters of Pope Innocent III concerning England and Wales: a calendar with an appendix of texts* (Oxford, 1967) and 'Additions and corrections' to this book in *BIHR* xliv (1971), 98–115. Anton Largiadèr edited *Die Papsturkunden des Staatsarchiv Zürich von Innozenz III bis Martin V* (Zürich, 1963) and *Die Papsturkunden der Schweiz von Innozenz III bis Martin V ohne Zürich* (2 vols., Zürich, 1968, 1970). Special studies have been devoted to Innocentian letters which survive in, or attached to, decretal collections: Stephan Kuttner, 'The Collection of Alanus, a concordance of its two recensions', *Rivista di Storia del Diritto*, xxvi (1953), 37–53, and 'A Collection of Decretal Letters in Bamberg', *Medievalia et Humanistica*, n.s. i (1970), 41–56; C. R. Cheney, 'Decretals of Innocent III in Paris, B.N. MS. Lat. 3922A', *Traditio*, xi (1955), 151–62, and 'Three Decretal Collections before Compilatio IV', ibid. xv (1959), 464–84, and 'An Annotator of Durham Cathedral MS. C. III. 3', *Studia Gratiana*, xi (1967), 37–68; C. R. and Mary G. Cheney, 'A draft Decretal of Pope Innocent III on a case of identity', *Quellen und Forschungen aus ital. Archiven und Bibliotheken*, xli (1961), 29–47. Giulio Battelli has published two volumes of P. M. Baumgarten's card-index of papal originals drawn from all parts of Europe and deposited in the Vatican Archives: *Schedario Baumgarten: Descrizione diplomatica di bolle e brevi originali da Innocenzo III a Pio IX* (vol. i, Città del Vaticano, 1965).

3. Papal Privileges for Gilbertine Houses*

ORIGINAL solemn privileges of the medieval popes are sufficiently scarce in England to make the discovery of substantial fragments worthy of remark. The seven fragments here described were brought to the writer's notice by Mr. F. G. Emmison, then County Archivist of Essex, and it was by his kindness that it became possible to identify and study them. They are rectangular fragments, in size ranging from 174 × 257 mm to 345 × 352 mm, and they have served for centuries past as covers for court-rolls of the Petres of Ingatestone. Despite misuse and mutilation, they are for the most part legible. They were identified as something extraneous and out of the ordinary when the seventeenth Lord Petre placed some of his family's muniments on deposit in the Essex Record Office.[1] Later investigations revealed among the Petre muniments three more Gilbertine fragments to add to the four originally discovered.[2] The seven may be briefly identified as follows:

1, 2, and 3 are quarters (top and bottom left hand, and bottom right hand) of a solemn privilege of Pope Alexander III in favour of the Gilbertine house of Alvingham, in Lincolnshire, issued in 1178.[3]

4 is a strip from the top right hand of a solemn privilege of Pope Alexander III in favour of the Gilbertine house of Malton in Yorkshire, of the same date.[4]

---

* First published, with a facsimile (reduced) of fragment 3, in *BIHR*, xxi (1946), 39–58; here revised in the light of later discoveries.

[1] See a brief notice of about 9,000 documents deposited in 1938, *BIHR*, xvii. 53–4 and xviii. 90.

[2] Nos. 2, 4, and 7 came to light between 1946 and 1954.

[3] Chelmsford, Essex Record Office, D/DP Q 1/3 (= 1), Q 1/4 (=3) and D/DP Q 1/11 (= 2). See below, p. 57.

[4] D/DP Q 1/5 (= 4), printed from a cartulary copy in *PUE*, i. 425–7 no. 154, cf. iii. 381 no. 249 note. Fragment 4 reads 'Langatun' for 'Langetun'.

5 is the top left-hand quarter of a solemn privilege of Pope Alexander III in favour of the Gilbertine house of Chicksands, in Bedfordshire, probably also issued in 1178.[1]

6 and 7 are the top right-hand quarter and a middle portion of a solemn privilege of Pope Celestine III or Pope Innocent III in favour of the Gilbertine houses of Watton and Malton, in Yorkshire.[2]

Other fragments of solemn privileges have come to light in the same collection, viz. a middle strip from a privilege of Pope Eugenius III (1151 × 1152) for the Austin priory of Southwick, in Hampshire,[3] and part of the right-hand side of a solemn privilege in which Pope Calixtus III on 1 January 1457 proclaimed the canonization of Osmund, bishop of Salisbury (d. 1099).[4]

There is no need to discuss at length the descent of these once magnificent documents to the menial service which they have been performing for so long in Lord Petre's muniment-room. If we glance at A. F. Pollard's article on Sir William Petre (d. 1572) in *D.N.B.*, we read that the founder of the family fortunes was 'one of the most zealous of the visitors' of monasteries, 1536–9; 'his great achievement was the almost total extirpation of the Gilbertines'; and 'Petre acquired enormous property by the dissolution of the monasteries'.[5] His clerks must have had ample opportunities for collecting

---

[1] D/DP Q 1/2 (= 5). See below, pp. 61–2.

[2] D/DP Q 1/6 (= 6) and Q 1/7 (= 7). See below, pp. 63–5.

[3] D/DP Q 1/1, printed in *PUE*, iii. 212–13 no. 81. Holtzmann's copy of the whole text comes from a nineteenth-century transcript of Southwick Register 3 (deposited Hants Record Office), fo. 8; an earlier text is in Southwick Reg. 1 (ibid.), fo. 14.

[4] D/DP Q 1/10, cf. *BIHR*, xxi. 40. The whole bull was printed from another text, with illustrative documents, by A. R. Malden, *The Canonization of St. Osmund* (Wilts. Record Soc., 1901). The Petre collection also includes several papal letters of grace, similarly misused: Nicholas IV for Kenilworth, 1290 (D/DP Q 1/8), Boniface IX for the abbot of St. Albans, 1395 (D/DP Q 1/9), Clement VI for Joan, widow of Robert fitzWalter, 1342–52 (D/DP M. 1173). I am obliged to Mr. K. C. Newton, County Archivist, for information about these documents.

[5] Petre himself took the surrender of Alvingham Priory, but he did not get the lands of this house or of the other Gilbertine houses which these fragments concern. See Rose Graham, *St. Gilbert of Sempringham and the Gilbertines* (1901), pp. 192 sqq. and F. G. Emmison, *Guide to the Essex Record Office* (1969).

waste parchment to cover their records at a time when title-deeds of papal origin were condemned.[1]

The seven fragments with which this note is concerned comprise parts of four documents, of which only two have been printed, both from incomplete copies. Their contents add something to our knowledge of the early history of the Gilbertine Order. This will be the first concern of the following pages, with particular reference to the headship of the Order after the retirement, or partial retirement, of St. Gilbert. We shall then consider the interest of the fragments for the study of papal diplomatic.

I

Of the transcripts which follow this note the first is the most satisfying, for with the help of the Alvingham cartulary it has been possible to reconstruct practically the whole of this privilege, to which fragments 1, 2, and 3 belong. The copy in the cartulary (Bodleian MS. Laud. misc. 642 fo. 2^v) is in the main faithful, but lacks the final protocol which includes the date. Fortunately, fragments 2 and 3 supply this part. The possession of a complete composite text of this privilege enables us to reconstruct with confidence the opening portions of the other privileges to which fragments 5, 6, and 7 belong. And since the papal chancery adhered very closely to precedent, this group of privileges can profitably be looked at as a whole. Fragment 4, for Malton, is of no textual value, for all of it is to be found in the cartulary copy printed by Holtzmann.[2] This copy, although it omits the subscriptions, has the merit of preserving the 'great date', which agrees in all particulars with the Alvingham fragments. Since both documents were issued on the same day, it is likely that the subscriptions were the same in both. No copy of the privilege for Chicksands has been found. We have to fall back on fragment 5, which provides less opportunity for reconstructing the whole original than no. 4. It has neither subscription nor date. But comparison with fragments 1–4 is instructive. By the time of Alexander III the

---

[1] Cf. below, p. 66.
[2] Previously quoted by R. Graham, op. cit., pp. 96–7.

papal chancery had achieved a regularity and elegance of calligraphy which it never surpassed in later days. These fragments are all excellent examples of the formal papal script of the time, seen at its best in privileges, with its elongated capitals, its lengthened ligatures, its long vertical ascenders. So well-established was the traditional style of writing that we must be wary of attributing too much to the hand of one scribe. It is, however, probable on palaeographical grounds that these five fragments were written by one hand. The angle of writing, the form of the 'tittle' abbreviation, the distended small 's', and the capital 'A', 'C', 'E', and 'L' are closely similar in all three documents. The most marked peculiarity appears in the small 'g', of which the bottom stroke is (after the manner of the time) brought back horizontally far beyond the rest of the letter; in all three documents the horizontal stroke of the 'g' has a loop made by a separate penstroke under the top part of the letter.[1] For each of these three privileges the parchment has been prepared for writing with lines ruled at a space thirteen millimetres apart. So great is the likeness in general that the different spellings 'adipisci' (fragment 1) and 'adhipisci' (fragments 4 and 5) may be disregarded. It is reasonable to conclude that these three privileges, for Alvingham, Malton, and Chicksands, were engrossed by the same hand and on one occasion. The proctors of the Gilbertines at Rome may well have sought simultaneous confirmations of the property and liberties of every house in the Order.[2] Since the constitution varied from house to house it was not easy to achieve precision in a privilege designed for the Order as a whole: the differences between the bulls for Malton and Alvingham demonstrate the difficulty. Therefore we may infer that the Chicksands privilege represented by fragment 5 was, like the others, dated 25 June 1178.[3]

The chief difference between the Malton privilege and the newly discovered documents results from the different conformation of the houses. Malton contained only canons and lay

---

[1] A looped 'g' is fairly common in papal chancery documents of this period (e.g. B.M., MS. Cotton Aug. ii. 136), but it is usually formed differently.

[2] As Rose Graham suggested many years ago, loc. cit.

[3] It is, of course, not unusual for closely related papal bulls to be dated a few days apart, and we must reckon with this possibility in the case of Chicksands.

brethren (*conversi*); Alvingham and Chicksands contained nuns. In Alvingham and Chicksands, indeed, the original founders did not envisage the presence of canons, though lay brethren are mentioned at Alvingham as servants of the nuns.[1] By 1178 canons had apparently been established in both places: at least, this seems the most natural interpretation of the clause: 'Statuimus quoque ut ordo . . .'. At all events, canons were in future to be installed, and installed in a position of considerable authority. This emerges from the clause: 'Adicimus insuper ut domui . . .'. It is also laid down, in terms which agree with the Malton privilege, that the lay brethren shall be obedient to the prior and canons. But the following clause in the Alvingham privilege naturally has no counterpart at Malton: it provides that the canons and lay brethren are to dwell at a distance from the nuns outside their enclosure, and makes arrangements for divine service as an exceptional occasion for bringing the sexes into proximity. Gilbert of Sempringham's Order had only gradually taken on its final shape, and these papal prescriptions of 1178 were making essential rules for the relations of the sexes within the Order.

Partly privilege, partly ordinance, these documents for Alvingham, Malton, and Chicksands seem to reflect both a petition from the Order to the pope and a papal enquiry into the Order's discipline. It is tempting to associate with them in point of date two general letters on behalf of the Order written by Alexander III to King Henry II and to the archbishops, bishops, and archdeacons of England respectively.[2] As Dom David Knowles has said, 'in default of any dating to these letters a wide field is left for speculation'; he would connect them with the letter of Alexander III to Gilbert of Sempringham written in the years 1167–9, when certain lay brethren of the Order had lately been in revolt.[3] But the chronology of the revolt, and of the inquiries set on foot by the pope, admits of

---

[1] *Mon. Ang.*, vii. 958a (no. 2) and 950. Cf. M. D. Knowles, 'The revolt of the lay brothers of Sempringham', *EHR*, l (1935), 466–87.

[2] *PUE*, i. 454 nos. 184–5.

[3] *EHR*, l. 473 and *PUE*, i. 368 no. 104. Dr. Raymonde Foreville, without reference to Knowles, reached the same conclusion: *Un Procès de Canonisation à l'aube du xiiie siècle (1201–1202): Le Livre de saint Gilbert de Sempringham* (Paris, 1943), pp. 103–4.

much doubt. Dom David has demonstrated that the critical episode occurred between 1165 and September 1169.[1] Evidence is wanting, however, that the pope treated the reports he received from England in support of Gilbert as a final settlement of the case. Admittedly, he wrote at latest on 20 September 1169 to Gilbert to protect him from any opposition to the exercise of his disciplinary power over his subjects and to confirm the exemption of the Order from local ecclesiastical authority. And this, as the pope explained, was called for by the recent dissension in the Order and the power of correction which had for the occasion been committed to certain local persons (that is, bishops). But this safeguarding of Gilbert's canonical rights did not settle, or even assume to be settled, the main points at issue. The Curia had not given judgement (so far as we know) respecting the charges that Gilbert had exceeded his canonical rights and that there had been serious moral lapses in the Order. That this was so is suggested by the letter to the pope written by Hugh, cardinal deacon of S. Angelo, legate of the apostolic see in England in the years 1175 and 1176.[2] The legate says that he has visited Sempringham and has formed the highest opinion of the nuns and of Gilbert; he denounces the former rebels, and begs the pope to receive kindly the petitions of Gilbert and his brethren and sisters. While the legate's words suggest that he had no instruction to visit Sempringham, the tone of the letter implies that the head of the Order still was looking for support in the Curia. Dom David Knowles finds difficulty in fitting this letter into his chronological scheme; but the events leading up to Becket's murder and the troubles which ensued might easily prevent what we may call 'the Sempringham Scandal' from being cleared up sooner to everyone's satisfaction. Cardinal Hugh, as Dr. Raymonde Foreville has observed, was the first legate *a latere* to enter England during Henry II's reign.[3] He held

---

[1] *EHR*, l. 468–9. Cf. Foreville, op. cit., pp. 86–8.

[2] Printed by Knowles, *EHR*, l. 483 (cf. pp. 468 n. 1, 473), Foreville, p. 108, *PUE*, iii. 361 no. 231. This letter only appears in one late manuscript of the Gilbertine collection of letters (Digby 36); I suppose it to be genuine, though both the pope's address and the cardinal's title are unusual.

[3] Foreville, *L'Église et la royauté en Angleterre sous Henri II Plantagenêt* (1943), p. 434.

visitations of churches and he took an opportunity to acquaint himself with the state of Sempringham. His report to the Curia is the latest statement of the case that we possess, and the next record of the Gilbertines at the Curia is contained in these three solemn privileges of June 1178. In the light of the preceding history, they appear to answer the Order's petition for a clear confirmation of its property and privileges after a period of uncertainty while, at the same time, they lay down disciplinary rules for the avoidance of scandal in the future.

II

The address clauses of these three privileges of 1178 have one interesting feature in common: all name Prior Roger.[1] Can it be that there were three persons of this name in charge of the three Gilbertine houses in this year? We cannot check this from other sources.[2] If it were so, it would be an extraordinary coincidence. On the other hand, we do know that at some time before St. Gilbert's death, he handed over the general administration of the Order he had founded to one Roger, an early disciple whom he had previously appointed to be prior of Malton.[3] Hitherto, the date of Gilbert's retirement has been unknown, nor has it been clear what was involved in the change: we are told that the saint continued until his death (in 1189) to take an active interest in the whole Order, and at some time after September 1186 he used his influence or authority to mitigate the rule about lay brethren.[4] Now a

---

[1] *Malton*: Dil. filiis Rogero priori b. Marie de Malton et reliquis fratribus canonicis et conversis tam presentibus quam futuris regularem vitam secundum instituta ordinis de Sempingham ibidem professis.

Alvingham: Dil. filiis Rogero priori et monialibus b. Marie de Alvingham et reliquis fratribus canonicis et sor. . . .

Chicksands: Dil. filiis Rogero priori et monialibus b. Marie de Chikesande et reliquis fra. . . .

[2] See D. Knowles, C. N. L. Brooke, and V. London, *The Heads of Religious Houses, England and Wales, 940–1216* (Cambridge, 1972). At pp. 201, 203 the privileges for Alvingham and Malton provide the evidence for Priors Roger in 1178 at both houses, 'evidently two different men'.

[3] *Mon. Ang.*, vii. pp. xvii* and xx* (after p. 945).

[4] Ibid., p. xx* and Foreville, *Procès*, pp. 82, 89. In a final concord in the king's court, 4 July 1188, the master of the Order of Sempringham is a party and is named 'frater Rogerus' (*Final Concords of the County of Lincoln*, ii, ed. C. W. Foster (Lincoln Record Soc., 1920), 331).

comparison of these three documents prompts the conjecture that all refer to the same man, Roger, prior of Malton, who had become manager of the whole Order and prior of all its houses, superior to the local priors.

But modern writers generally tell us that the head of the Order of Sempringham was called *Magister*,[1] and the matter needs clarifying. It is necessary to examine in some detail the titles used by the first few heads of the Order, St. Gilbert, Roger, and Gilbert II, as well as the titles by which other people addressed them.

St. Gilbert. Gilbert studied in his youth in the schools of France and earned the academic title of *magister*. 'Master Gilbert of Sempringham', or plain 'Gilbert of Sempringham', without mention of office, is what appears most often in the charter-material, whether as beneficiary or as witness.[2] The earliest sniff of a title of office seems to be in the agreement between the Orders of Cîteaux and Sempringham in 1164, where the witness-list has 'signum Gilleberti magistri'.[3] The title of office is more explicit in a Yorkshire charter dated 1170×1179, in which *magistro Gilberto priore ordinis de Sempingham* is the first witness,[4] and in a charter of William de Vesci in favour of Ormesby Priory, addressed to *fratri Gyleberto magistro ordinis de Semp'*.[5] One letter of Pope Alexander III addresses

---

[1] Rose Graham implied as much, although she referred once to 'the Master, or "Prior of All"' (op. cit., p. 52). Knowles writes that at a date later than 1147 Gilbert 'consented to assume the office and title of Master' (*Monastic Order in England, 943–1216* (Cambridge, 1940), p. 206). Foreville speaks of 'le titre même de maître de l'Ordre, que Gilbert de Sempringham garda jusqu'à la fin de sa vie' and suggests that this followed the example of Robert d'Arbrissel, founder of the Order of Fontevrault (*Procès*, p. xii). The alternatives to Master as title for the head of the Order are not discussed in *Heads of Religious Houses*.

[2] *Docts. . . . of the Danelaw*, ed. F. M. Stenton (Brit. Acad., 1920), p. 2; B.M. MS. Cotton Vesp. E. xx fo. 38; *Mon. Ang.*, vii. 966a (Mr.); *Early Yorks. Charters*, ed. W. Farrer and C. T. Clay (1914–65), i. 475 (Mr.), ii. 406 (Mr.), 408; iii. 39, 500 (Mr.), xii. 131 (Mr.); *Reg. Antiquissimum . . . of Lincoln*, ed. C. W. Foster and K. Major (Lincoln Record Soc., 1931–68), i. 250, 265, ii. 5, iv. 266 (Mr.); *Transcripts of Gilbertine Charters*, ed. F. M. Stenton (Lincoln Rec. Soc., 1922), pp. 17, 29, 35, 41, 62 (all Mr.), 4; *The Genealogist*, N.S. xv (1898–9), 159 (Mr.), 222 (Mr.), 223, xvi (1899–1900), 156 (Mr.); *Cal. of Charter Rolls*, iv. 403 (Mr.); Hist. Manuscripts Commission, *Report on the MSS. of Lord Middleton* (1911), p. 2 (Mr.).

[3] Followed by 'Signum Torphini prioris de Semplingham' and *signa* of seven other priors (*Cartularium Abbathiae de Rievalle* (Surtees Soc., 1889), p. 183).

[4] *Early Yorks. Charters*, ii. 503.

[5] Ibid. xii. 93.

Gilbert by name, and this gives him the title of *magister ordinis de Sempingham*.[1] In other letters the same pope addressed, apparently indifferently, the 'master and canons' and the 'prior and canons' of the Order.[2] A letter of King Henry II about Gilbert speaks of him as *prenominatus magister ordinis*, and the letter of Cardinal Hugh, the legate, describes him as *harum ancillarum dei caput et magister*.[3] A charter for the nuns of Ormesby (1160 × 1166) refers to Gilbert as *fundator religionis de Sempingham* and includes among the witnesses Albinus *capellanus magistri*.[4] In the next generation, when Gilbert's canonization was sought, the commendatory letters of the English prelates, headed by Archbishop Hubert, refer usually to Master Gilbert[5] and describe him as *primus ordinis de Sempingham institutor et fundator* or *rector* or *inventor*, and Innocent III adopted the first formula in the bull of canonization.[6] After the canonization Archbishop Hubert referred to Gilbert as *beatus Gilbertus magister ordinis de Sempingham*.[7]

Roger. The second head of the Order made a grant as *prior ordinis de Sempingham*,[8] and described himself thus in writing to the pope.[9] In 1201 he was given this title by the abbots who inquired into Gilbert's claims to sanctity and by the rural dean and parson of Chilwell.[10] A variant of this style shows that Roger, like the founder of the Order, had the training of a scholar: he was commonly called *magister R. prior ordinis*,[11] and in one document we find *magister Rogerus et conventus domus de Sempingham*.[12] In 1204 a final concord was made 'in the

---

[1] *PUE*, i. 368 no. 103 (1167 × 1169), preserved only in xiii-century copies.

[2] Ibid. i. 442 no. 171 (1170 × 1180) and 454 no. 184 (1159 × 1181, ? 1178).

[3] Foreville, *Procès*, pp. 106, 108; also printed in *EHR*, l. 483, 485. Bodleian MS. Digby 36, to which Knowles attaches more value than does Foreville, reads 'prenominatus magister G.', not 'prenominatus magister ordinis'.

[4] *Transcripts of Gilbertine Charters*, p. 42.

[5] Foreville, *Procès*, pp. 10, 11, 93, cf. 7, 9.

[6] Ibid., pp. 16, 18, 22, 23, 26, 33.

[7] Ibid., pp. 37, 39, 40.

[8] 1196 × 1198: *Reg. Antiquiss. Lincoln*, ii. 329.

[9] In 1201, Foreville, *Procès*, p. 29.

[10] Ibid., pp. 11, 66.

[11] *Reg. Antiquiss. Lincoln*, ii. 40; *Docts. . . . of the Danelaw*, pp. 10, 12, 54; *Mon. Ang.*, vii. 962*b*.

[12] *Reg. Antiquiss. Lincoln*, iii. 400. Cf. a charter for Sixle Priory, late Henry II or Richard I, which refers to the assignment of a grant by 'Magister R. de Sempyngham' (*Transcripts of Gilbertine Charters*, p. 22).

presence of Sir Roger, prior of the Order of Sempringham'
and the prior witnessed it as 'Master Roger of the Order of
Sempringham'.[1] On the other hand, the word *magister* was
applied to Roger's office by Archbishop Hubert, who twice
addressed him as *magister ordinis de Sempingham*.[2] Maybe the
clerks of the archbishop, then royal chancellor, learnt this
practice in the chancery, for *magister ordinis* is the title which
occurs in the surviving records of the royal chancery and the
Curia Regis.[3] But the papal chancery of Clement III and
Celestine III continued to waver, in addressing letters, between
magistro et canonicis et monialibus . . . ordinis and *priori et capitulo
ordinis*.[4] Innocent III used the titles *maior prior* and *summus
prior*.[5]

Gilbert II. Master Roger prior or *magister ordinis* died in
1204,[6] his successor died within six months, and with the
fourth head a third title appears. Gilbert II issued a charter as
rector ordinis and referred to Master Roger as *R. quondam rector
ordinis*.[7] But on other occasions, when he was acting on behalf
of individual houses of the Order, he assumed the title *magister
ordinis*;[8] and in at least three charters he styles himself *prior
ordinis*.[9] The papal chancery during the first half of the thirteenth

---

[1] *Yorks. Deeds*, vi (Yorks. Archaeol. Soc., Record series lxxvi, ed. C. T. Clay),
94.　　　　[2] Foreville, *Procès*, pp. 28, 36, cf. 39 (1201 and 1202).

[3] The confirmation charters of Richard I (13 Sept. 1189) and John (7 Sept.
1199), etc.: *The Genealogist*, N.S. xvi. 226–8; *Cartae Antiquae Rolls 1–10* (Pipe Roll
Soc., N.S. xvii, 1939), pp. 31–3; *Rot. Chartarum*, ed. T. D. Hardy (Rec. Com.,
1837), p. 18; *Rot. Lit. Claus.*, ed. Hardy (Rec. Com., 1833), i. 112*a*; *Rot. Lit. Pat.*,
ed. Hardy (Rec. Com., 1835), i. 166*b*; *Curia Regis Rolls*, ii. 34, 272, 295, 300, 302,
iii. 14, 30, 56, 224, 232.

[4] *PUE*, i. 546 no. 256, 548 no. 258 (both 1188) and 606–8 nos. 308–10 (all
1192). Cf. fragment 6 below, probably of Innocent III.

[5] C. R. and M. G. Cheney, *Letters of Innocent III*, nos. 345A, 376–7, 619.

[6] He died 23 Oct. 1204 and his successor, John, died 11 May 1205: 'Successio
magistrorum ordinis' in P.R.O. Transcripts 9/16 from Vatican MS. Barberini
xliii. 74.

[7] *Reg. Antiquiss. Lincoln*, ii. 330 (1213 × 1223). 'Institutor et rector' and
'fundator et rector' are titles applied to St. Gilbert in the commendatory letters
of 1201 (Foreville, *Procès*, pp. 18, 22, 26).

[8] *Reg. Antiquiss. Lincoln*, iii. 400 (1205 × 1223), v. 78 (1206 × 1209); *Early
Yorks. Charters*, ii. 426 (1205 × 1210).

[9] *Transcripts of Gilbertine Charters*, p. 95; *Docts. . . . of the Danelaw*, p. 312: in this
charter three witnesses are described as 'capellani magistri Gileberti prioris
ordinis de Simpingham'; *Chartulary of Fountains Abbey*, ed. W. T. Lancaster
(Leeds, 1915), i. 420.

century most often spoke of the *magister* in letters to the Order, but sometimes wrote to the *prior ordinis* or to the *superior prior*.[1] It is particularly significant that in the diocese of Lincoln, where the chief house and strength of the Order lay, the chancery of Bishop Hugh of Wells (1209–35) was inconsistent in its practice. As early as 1214 it used the title *magister*[2] but the documents entered in the episcopal register before 1223 refer instead to *prior ordinis* or *prior totius ordinis*.[3] Thereafter *magister* became the rule.

So far, we have ignored the Institutes of the Order printed in the *Monasticon*, which have frequent occasion to mention the head of the Order and come, in part, from St. Gilbert's own pen. This material is hard to use as evidence since, although the earliest recension has obviously been worked over and has received many additions, we cannot well distinguish the parts of different dates. But one fact leaps to the eye. The word *magister*, though common, is not the most common title of the head of the Order, and it nowhere occurs in a section which is demonstrably the work of St. Gilbert.[4] On the other hand, *summus prior ordinis* is occasionally used[5] and *prior omnium* is the commonest title. In sections where the text uses these terms the rubric reads *magister*. The inference is unescapable. At Sempringham, as in the chancery of the bishop of Lincoln, the title *magister* only triumphed over other titles relatively late.

This tedious inquiry points to the conclusion that St. Gilbert never said explicitly what title he and his successors were to bear. This is not surprising in the light of what we know about his character, his humility, his reluctance to proceed to holy orders, his desire to divest himself of responsibility by affiliation to Cîteaux.[6] The fact that he and his next

---

[1] *Calendar of . . . Papal Registers*, i, ed. W. H. Bliss, p. 57; *Registres d'Innocent IV*, ed. É. Berger (École franc. de Rome, 1884–1919), no. 1004 (and in *Mon. Ang.*, vii. 960, attributed to Innocent III).

[2] *Liber antiquus de ordinationibus vicariarum*, ed. A. Gibbons (Lincoln, 1888), p. 72.

[3] *Rotuli Hugonis de Welles* (CYS), i. 29, 103, 171, iii. 14.

[4] *Mon. Ang.*, vii. p. xxx* (after p. 945) gives the 'forma eligendi magistrum', but the date of this section is uncertain.

[5] Ibid., p. xxxi*: 'summus prior ordinis de Sempingham qui curam omnium gerit'. Cf. p. lxviii*.

[6] Cf. the remarks of Beatrice Lees on the title of *magister* in the Order of the

successor were both *magistri* in the academic sense in which it was applied in the twelfth century may have encouraged people to call them Masters of their Order; this was all the more likely because their constitutional position differed from that of most monastic heads. The rule of nuns may have had something to do with the choice of title. The founder of Fontevrault had taken the name of master, and in the twelfth and thirteenth centuries in England Benedictine and Cistercian nunneries were often put under the care of a secular or regular priest who was called *prior, rector, custos,* or *magister.* The titles seem to be interchangeable, but *magistri* are not uncommon.[1] The variety is certainly comparable to what has been noted in the Gilbertine Order. There, *magister* did not come into common use as a title of office until the thirteenth century and was not exclusively used until the century was far advanced. The head of the Order was originally often called *prior.*

It has seemed worth while to pursue this matter to the end for its own sake, but the reader will perceive the bearing of our conclusion on the papal privileges of 1178. It becomes easy to suppose that the *Rogerus prior* to whom each privilege was addressed is one man; and he was at once prior of Alvingham, Chicksands, and Malton, because he was 'prior superior' of these and the other houses of the Order. These privileges were presumably sought by the head of the Order, and if Roger approached Pope Alexander III as he approached Innocent III, he described himself as prior: hence the papal mode of address.

In the light of these documents we turn to the papal privilege for Watton and Malton (fragments 6 and 7), of which only two parts survive, probably comprising less than half of the original. The script suggests the time of Celestine III or Innocent III, and the lists of earlier popes, ending with Clement III, make Celestine III a possible grantor. If this were so, the activity of the Order in getting grants from the Curia in June and July 1192[2] would point to this for a probable date. But

Temple: *Records of the Templars in England in the Twelfth Century* (Brit. Acad., 1935), p. lxiii.

[1] Cf. above, p. 44 n. 1. *Magistri* appear at Greenfield, Leybourne, Stixwould, and Wykeham (Cist.) and Derby Kingsmead and Stainfield (Ben.): see *Heads of Religious Houses,* pp. 211 sqq. and Eileen Power, *Medieval English Nunneries* (Cambridge, 1922), pp. 228–36. [2] *PUE,* i. 603–8 nos. 305, 308–10.

Holtzmann doubted whether the versions of the well-known formulas 'Obeunte vero te' and 'Sane laborum' in fragment 6 could be assigned to Celestine, and proposed Innocent III.[1] In support of this, there is the reference to King Henry II and King Richard his son, which suggests that both are dead, and there is the confirmation to Watton of Langdale and its appurtenances, which is the subject of a charter of King John on 28 March 1200.[2] We cannot be quite sure of the reconstruction of the protocol, but the surviving parts of the text run on the same lines as a confirmatory privilege granted to the Order by Innocent IV some forty to fifty years later, on 8 February 1245, addressed 'dilectis filiis Roberto superiori priori ecclesie beate Marie de Sempingham atque successoribus canonice substitutis et reliquis fratribus canonicis atque sororibus tam presentibus quam futuris regularem vitam professis'.[3] The mention in our fragmentary address of two religious houses (. . . *de Wattona et de Maltona*) suggests that two heads of houses have been named in the missing part; but it is clear from the following words (*eiusque successoribus*) that only one head has been named. Again, it emerges from the clause 'Obeunte vero te' that the person addressed commands the obedience of all the communities of the Order. We may therefore suppose that this bull, like those of 1178, was addressed primarily to *Rogerus prior* as 'prior superior'. It is none the less strange that a privilege which apparently starts by confirming the named possessions of only two of the houses of the Order, Watton and Malton, becomes in its later part the vehicle for a confirmation of general liberties and ordinances of the Order. Like the variation of title which has been noted, it argues a stage of improvisation in the affairs of the Order during the headship of Master Roger.

If the foregoing arguments about title are valid, the privileges of 1178 serve another purpose in Gilbertine history: they provide a *terminus ante quem* for the succession of Roger prior of Malton to the effective headship of the Order. The privilege

---

[1] In private letters to me, dated 24 and 26 June 1947. If the privilege is Innocent III's, it may belong to the first months of 1202 (*Letters of Innocent III*, no. 1089, cf. nos. 375–7).

[2] *Mon. Ang.*, vii. 956; *Rotuli Chartarum*, p. 42.

[3] *Registres d'Innocent IV*, no. 1004; *Mon. Ang.*, vii. 960.

of 30 June 1169 for Malton Priory, on which that of 25 June
1178 was based, is addressed 'Gileberto priori ecclesie beate
Marie virginis de Malton eiusque successoribus canonice substituendis'.[1] This probably indicates that the founder was still
'prior superior', while Roger may have been already local prior
of Malton. Before June 1178 the situation had changed. From
the *Vita* we know that Gilbert retained some semblance of
authority and was consulted by his coadjutor on matters of
importance during the last years of his life;[2] but he must have
retired from effective mastership of his Order more than ten
years before he died, a centenarian, in February 1189. The
terms of the letter written by the legate, Hugh Pierleoni,
suggest that he was still in office in January or February 1176.[3]

III[4]

The Alvingham privilege, apart from its importance for the
history of the Gilbertines, interests the student of papal
diplomatic. Perhaps two hundred solemn privileges of Pope
Alexander III survive in continental libraries and archives,[5]
but probably there are not more than half a dozen in England.
The fortunate discovery of this one furnishes a little more
evidence for the study of the subscriptions of the cardinals.
These subscriptions are ranged under that of the pope himself,
with the bishops' names in the centre, the priests' on the left,
and the deacons' on the right. They form one of the most
picturesque and useful external features of original twelfth-
century privileges. For the form of the subscriptions, both in
the shape of the crosses and the character of the handwritings,

---

[1] *PUE*, i. 378 no. 112; cf. *Heads of Religious Houses*, p. 203.

[2] *Mon. Ang.*, vii. pp. xi–xii*, xiv*.

[3] Above, p. 44 n. 2. The cardinal subscribed privileges of 1178 (see below).

[4] This section owes much to the collection of photographs of privileges in
Austrian archives which Professor Galbraith kindly placed at my disposal. These
are my authority wherever I give no authority beyond 'JL'. I am also grateful to
Professor Galbraith for the loan of photostats of privileges in the British Museum
and Public Record Office.

[5] B. Katterbach and W. M. Peitz, 'Die Unterschriften der Päpste und Kardinäle
in den Bullae maiores vom 11. bis 14. Jahrhundert', in *Miscellanea F. Ehrle*, iv
(Studi e Testi, 40, Vatican, 1924), 177–274, refer to more than 80 originals in
Italian, German, Austrian, and Swiss archives. The volumes of Kehr's *Papsturkunden* enumerate many others.

shows marked individuality. Already the crosses have assumed quaint distinctive forms, but they are still like crosses. In the course of the thirteenth century they become more elaborate, and less like crosses.[1] And it has been established beyond doubt that each cardinal's subscription bears some mark of the cardinal's own pen. Just as the pope completed with his own hand the cross in the outer circle of the Rota and wrote the elongated 'E' which began the inscription 'Ego Alexander catholice ecclesie episcopus subscripsi', so each cardinal contributed a cross and a part, at least, of the following inscription; if he did not finish it himself, it was completed by his own clerk.[2]

The remaining fragments of the Alvingham privilege show lists of cardinals—a bishop, priests, and deacons—which agree with the subscriptions on a privilege of 1 July 1178 (also beginning with the familiar form, 'Quotiens illud a') in favour of the priory of St. Amand-lez-Thourotte, a dependency of St. Martin of Tournai.[3] The datary is the chancellor Albert, as in the Malton and Alvingham privileges, dated 25 June.

Turning to the list of cardinal deacons, we can establish with a fair degree of probability the authentic autograph of each cardinal, partly by inspecting the handwriting and the ink, partly by comparing with originals and facsimiles of other

[1] Examples are in Rymer, I. i. 152 (1218); F. Steffens, *Paléographie latine*, ed. R. Coulon (1910), pl. 91 (1234); W. Arndt and M. Tangl, *Schrifttafeln*, pt. iii (1903), pl. 91 (1263); G. Battelli, *Acta Pontificum* (2nd ed., Vatican, 1965), pl. 18 (1289), 22 (1307). The forms may be compared with the signs of notaries public.

[2] See the exhaustive work of Katterbach and Peitz (above, p. 52 n. 5), where the accompanying photographs of over a hundred subscriptions offer most convincing proof of the authors' main contention. The xiv-century chancery ordinance was already the rule: 'Quilibet cardinalis debet se subscribere manu propria cum signo crucis depicto vel alio signo si alio est usus' (M. Tangl, *Die päpstlichen Kanzleiordnungen 1200–1500* (Innsbruck, 1894), p. 303). As Kaltenbrunner observed in 1880, one may find subscriptions of a single cardinal written in one and the same day in different hands and inks; but the cross, with rare exceptions, was the cardinal's work (*Mittheilungen des Instit. für oesterr. Geschichtsforschung*, i. 387).

[3] *Papsturkunden in den Niederlanden*, ed. J. Ramackers (Abh. der Gesellsch. der Wissensch. zu Göttingen, Phil.-hist. Kl., 3 F. ix), i. ii (1934), no. 193. The same bishop and priests are named on an original privilege for the abbey of S. Pietro, Cremona, dated 10 June 1178, but this only contains the names of three of the cardinal deacons, Ardicio, Cinthyus, Hugo (*Acta Pontificum Romanorum Inedita*, ed. J. von Pflugk-Harttung (1881–6), iii. 262 no. 272).

originals. It so happens that the name which heads the list is
one which adorns papal bulls for nearly fifty years. Iacintus,
or Hyacinth, had belonged to the college of cardinals since
1144.[1] In his early days, he usually wrote his whole title on
solemn privileges, but in Alexander III's time he occasionally
left the inscription to be completed by a clerk and only
wrote the cross and 'Ego',[2] or cross and 'E'. As late as 1178,
the year of the Alvingham bull, he wrote as much as 'Ego
Iacintus cardinalis diaconus' on a privilege, but it is rare
to find his whole autograph signature in the last years of
Alexander III or in the following pontificates. The cross and the
'E' of 'Ego' are the only constants. These remain characteristic,
unmistakable. In the course of years, the cardinal's writing
becomes less stiff, more current, and in the end shows signs
of a shaky hand. But the cross is consistently formed with bold
serifs, with a mark like a semicolon in the bottom left-hand
angle, and with a dot surmounted by a dash, like the *punctus
elevatus*, in the top right-hand angle.[3] In 1191 Cardinal Hyacinth
became Pope Celestine III. Thereafter, the old man repeated
the same form of signature in completing the cross within
the rota. The Alvingham privilege has a well-formed cross
and a large capital 'E' written in a firm hand; the rest of the

---

[1] J. M. Brixius, *Die Mitglieder des Kardinalskollegium von 1130 bis 1181* (1912),
pp. 52, 104.

[2] So Katterbach and Peitz, loc. cit., p. 229. B.M. MS. Cotton Cleop. E. i fo.
123 is an original of Eugenius III (1147) in which the cardinal seems to have
written only the cross and 'Ego Iacintus' (see *Facsimiles*, First series (New
Palaeographical Soc., 1904), no. 46). In another privilege of the same year
Hyacinth seems only to write the cross and 'Ego': P.R.O., S.C. 7/15/38 (*Mon.
Ang.*, vii. 154).

[3] Katterbach and Peitz, loc. cit., pp. 222–3 and pl. 29, 34b, 38c, 39d, 44c, 45c,
47, 56, 57b, 59b. See also the privileges cited in the last note; Pflugk-Harttung,
Chartarum Pont. Roman. Specimina selecta (1885–7), pl. 82, 89, 90, 98, 121 no. 50,
123 no. 116; Battelli, op. cit., pl. 10; B.M. Add. Ch. 66715 (*Archaeologia Aeliana*,
N.S. xvi (1894), p. 271 pl. 17); P.R.O., S.C. 7/28/22 (Rymer, i. i. 37–8); and the
following, not published in facsimile: B.M. MS. Cotton Aug. ii. 124 (*PUE*, i. 494
no. 219), B.M. Egerton Ch. 113 (JL 16069), B.M. Harl. Ch. 75 A. 1 (JL 15696),
B.M. Add. Ch. 26066 (JL 14411), B.M. Add. Ch. 12833 (JL 14914), Westminster
Abbey Muniments no. 1508 (*PUE*, i. 551 no. 262), JL 8850, 9370, 10257, 10316–
17, 11630, 12814, 12959, 12961, 13009, 13376, 16440. The only exception I have
seen is B.M. Harl. Ch. 111 A. 2 (1156. *PUE*, i. 307 no. 62) which, despite a faulty
dating clause, is adjudged genuine by Holtzmann. Hyacinth's cross here has dots
and dashes in the top left hand and bottom right hand angles and a dot only in
the bottom left hand angle.

subscription is written in different ink and does not conform to the known examples from Hyacinth's hand.

Ardicio had subscribed to papal bulls since January 1157. Most of the other examples of his subscription which have been noted[1] begin with a cross which is embellished with a dot and a dash in each of its four angles. The Alvingham example, by contrast, has a plain cross with short serifs. On the other hand, the 'E' of 'Ego' in this privilege is unmistakably repeated in the example reproduced by Battelli.[2] In each case the rest of the subscription is probably by another scribe.

Cinthyus first subscribed in March 1158. Other examples of his subscription[3] show the plain cross with big serifs which we see in the Alvingham privilege. The form of the 'E' is similar in the examples of 1168 and 1177, with a heavily thickened downstroke. The form of the name is similar in most examples,[4] and the whole inscription is in a more angular, austere hand than is usual in these documents. It is possible that Cinthyus wrote the whole inscription himself. If so, we must attribute the irregularities and departure from the ruled line in the Alvingham privilege to the cardinal's advancing years or to some temporary cause. But a comparison of the facsimiles of a dozen originals shows at least four hands at work writing Cinthyus's name: the cardinal's clerks may be responsible for one and all. Without examining the original documents we can detect no change of ink and pen in the course of one subscription. So it may be that the cross alone is the autograph work of the cardinal.

Hugo Pierleoni was a much younger man than the preceding

---

[1] *Archaeologia Aeliana*, N.S. xvi. 271, pl. 17 (1157), B.M. Harl. Ch. 111 A. 5 (*PUE*, i. 340 no. 80), Harl. Ch. 83 A. 21 (*PUE*, i. 358 no. 97), MS. Cotton Aug. ii. 136 (*Mon. Ang.*, iii. 637), Battelli, op. cit., pl. 10, P.R.O., S.C. 7/28/22 (Rymer, I. i. 37), B.M. MS. Cotton Cleop. E. i fos. 118–21 (*PUE*, i. 516 no. 231), Pflugk-Harttung, *Specimina*, pl. 97, JL 11630, 12814, 14876, 15072, 15427. The first example has dots but no dashes; the third and fourth have no dots. JL 11630 (1169) copies the form of the preceding cross, which is Hyacinth's.

[2] The 'E' differs in other examples. P.R.O., S.C. 7/28/22, JL 14876, 15072, 15427 (1183–5) are all extraordinarily elaborate and elongated.

[3] B.M. Harl. Ch. 83 A. 21, Katterbach and Peitz, loc. cit., pl. 45c, Battelli, op. cit., pl. 10, P.R.O., S. C. 7/1/9 (Rymer, I. i. 27–8), B.M. MS. Cotton Aug. ii. 125 (*PUE*, i. 411 no. 139), Pflugk-Harttung, *Specimina*, pl. 90, JL 11630, 12740, 12814, 12959, 12961, 13009.

[4] JL 11630 spells the name 'Cinthius'.

cardinals, and first subscribed in March 1173. The Alvingham privilege shows a highly ornate cross followed by a fantastic capital 'E', and these are matched in documents six months earlier in date.[1] A change of pen seems to follow the cross and the 'E', so these may be the only autograph part of the subscription.

Rainerius subscribed first in July 1175, but no early examples of his signature have been examined. His cross is elaborate, with dots in the angles, circles at the ends of the four arms, and a comma under the right-hand extremity. In the Alvingham privilege the words 'Ego Rainerius' are plainly written by the same hand as the cross, but the line was completed by a clerk.[2]

Arduinus was a newcomer to the cardinalate when the Alvingham bull was written. The earliest trace of him noted by Brixius is dated 4 July 1178;[3] there is another subscription on 1 July,[4] and the Alvingham bull provides a slightly earlier example. This would be compatible with his creation in the ember week of Whitsun, according to the approved custom.[5] The cross in the Alvingham subscription is ornamented lightly by a dash in each of the top angles. This does not correspond with the crosses reproduced by Pflugk-Harttung from documents of later date.[6] Not enough examples have been found to pronounce on the handwriting of the subscription, but there is no clear change in the course of it.[7] One feature of this subscription deserves notice. It does not keep firmly on the ruled line, but rears above it at one point as if to avoid the elongated 'ALEXANDER' and the lofty ascending 'a' of the pontifical

---

[1] Pflugk-Harttung, *Specimina*, pl. 90. Cf. Katterbach and Peitz, p. 230. A subscription of Oct. 1173 shows an elaborate, but slightly different, form of cross and an initial 'E' from which the later form developed. A plainer cross with the fantastic form of 'E' is in JL 12814 (April 1177). Cf. Kaltenbrunner, as above, p. 53 n. 2.

[2] For three other examples, 1176–82, see B.M. MS. Cotton Aug. ii. 125 (*PUE*, i. 411 no. 139), JL 12740, Pflugk-Harttung, *Specimina*, pl. 96. In JL 13346 (1179) the cross has straight serifs instead of circles.

[3] Brixius, p. 60.

[4] Above, p. 53.

[5] 28 May–3 June 1178. Cf. Brixius, pp. 7–15 on the custom of creation of cardinals in the *Quatuor tempora*, or Ember weeks.

[6] *Specimina*, pl. 96, 121 nos. 1 and 2.

[7] Katterbach and Peitz, p. 234, point to a later privilege in which Arduinus only drew the cross.

anno in the date. Clearly the affixing of the date must have preceded, by however short a space of time, the subscription of this cardinal. The case is not without parallel. Subscription after dating is also suggested by the list of cardinal deacons on a privilege of Alexander III for the prioress and nuns of Wroxall, 10 June 1163. Here the deacons' subscriptions, having filled the space between 'Benevalete' and the dating clause, continue below the latter, so that '+Ego Manfredus diaconus cardinalis sancti Georgii ad velum aureum ss.' appears in the bottom margin, within an inch of the foot of the document.[1] This raises at once the questions: at what stage in the process of engrossment did a privilege receive its date? What determined its date? Of what value is the date for determining the movements of pope or cardinals?[2] These are not questions to be hastily answered; but the Alvingham privilege provides a shred of evidence which cannot be neglected.[3]

Fragments 1, 2, and 3: Privilege for Alvingham Priory[4]

ALEXANDER EPISCOPUS SERVUS SERVORUM DEI DILECTIS FILIIS ROGERO PRIORI ET MONIALIBUS BEATE MARIE DE ALVINGHAM ET RELIQUIS FRATRIBUS CANONICIS ET SOR*ORIBUS*[5] *TAM PRESENTIBUS*

[1] B.M. Harl. Ch. 83 A. 21. In printing this, Holtzmann overlooked the marginal subscription concealed by the fold (*PUE*, i. 360).

[2] Delisle maintained that 'les souscriptions prouvent qu'à la date du privilège les cardinaux qui souscrivaient résidaient à la cour pontificale' (*Mémoire sur les Actes d'Innocent III* (1858), p. 35). But this cannot be accepted without reserve. Brixius (op. cit., p. 15) cites examples of cardinals' subscriptions dated a short time after their death. For some of the problems see H. Bresslau, *Handbuch der Urkundenlehre* (2nd ed., 1912–31), ii. 463 n. 1 and authors there quoted, and ibid. 474–5. Cf. an example of inconsistent dating in *PUE*, ii. 151 no. 14 (1131).

[3] P. Herde, *Beiträge zum päpstl. Kanzlei- und Urkundenwesen im 13 Jahrhundert* (2nd ed., Kallmünz, 1967), p. 223, puts the writing of the 'great date' after that of the cardinals' subscription.

[4] Cf. above, p. 39 n. 3 and p. 41. The reconstructed passages in this and the following transcripts are indicated by italic type. The Alvingham privilege is reconstructed after the copy contained in Bodleian MS. Laud misc. 642 fos. 2ᵛ–3ʳ. The reconstruction of fragments 5–7 depends (except where otherwise noted) on the reconstructed Alvingham text. Various endorsements, xvi century and later, only indicate the use of these fragments as wrappers to the Petre muniments, and they are therefore not printed here.

[5] The remaining letters of this word are not clear: the word might possibly be 'conv*ersis*', which would agree with the formula of the Malton privilege; but 'sororibus' appears in the address of fragment 6 and of Innocent IV's privilege

QUAM FUTURIS REGULAREM VITAM SECUNDUM INSTITUTA ORDINIS DE SEMPINGHAM IBIDEM PRO-FESSIS IN PERPETUUM. Quotiens illud a nobis[1] petitur quod religioni et honestati convenire dinoscitur animo nos *decet libenti concedere et petentium desideriis congruum impertiri suffragium.* Eapropter, *dilecti in* domino filii, vestris iustis postulationibus clementer annuimus et prefatam ecclesiam, in *qua divino mancipati estis obsequio, ad exemplar predecessorum nostrorum felicis memorie* INNOCENTII, EUGENII, et ADRIANI, Romanorum pontificum, sub beati Petri et nostra protectione suscip*imus et presentis scripti privilegio communimus. Statuentes ut quascumque possessiones,* quecumque bona eadem ecclesia inpresentiarum iuste et canonice possidet aut in futurum conce*ssione pontificum, largitione regum vel principum, oblatione fidelium seu aliis iustis modis* prestante domino poterit adipisci, firma vobis vestrisque successoribus et illibata perman*eant. In quibus hec propriis duximus exprimenda vocabulis: locum ipsum in quo predicta* ecclesia sita est cum suis pertinentiis, ecclesias beate Marie et sancti Adelwaldi parro*chiales in Alvingham cum suis pertinentiis, ecclesiam[2] sancti Leonardi de Cokerington' cum suis* pertinentiis, ecclesiam de Kedingtun[3] cum suis pertinentiis, ecclesiam de Caletorp[4] cum su*is pertinentiis, ecclesiam omnium sanctorum de Neutuna[5] cum suis pertinentiis, grangiam de* Neutuna cum suis pertinentiis ex dono Roberti Walberti et Osberti filii eius, molendinum de Swinhop *et quicquid Synon de Chanci in territorio eiusdem ville vobis dedit et carta confirmavit,* grangiam de Cuninghesbi[6] cum suis pertinentiis, salinam unam in Kermun*d*torp, grangiam de *Caletorp cum suis pertinentiis. Statuimus quoque ut ordo sanctimonialium et sororum,* canonicorum et conversorum, atque rationabiles institutiones que nimirum The*o*baldi *Cantuariensis et Henrici quondam Eboracensis archiepiscoporum et venerabilis fratris nostri Rogeri[7] Eboracensis ecclesie nunc* archiepiscopi ac dilecti filii Gileberti primi patris vestri temporibus facte in eode*m loco constitute sunt, ibidem perpetuis temporibus inviolabiliter observentur.* Inhibemus quoque ne terras vel ecclesias aut aliquod aliud beneficium predicte congregationi *collatum liceat alicui personaliter dari nisi communi et generali assensu omnium predicte professio*nis sanctimonialium.

to the Order (*Mon. Ang.*, vii. 960*a*). The cartulary reads 'laicis' for 'sororibus', but this is certainly an error; probably the scribe had the formula of private charters in his mind: 'clericis et laicis, tam presentibus quam futuris'.

[1] Cartulary: 'a nobis illud'.
[2] Cartulary here expunges 'omnium sanctorum de Neutuna'.
[3] Cartulary: 'Kedington''.
[4] Cartulary: 'Calethorp'.
[5] Cartulary: 'Neutona''.
[6] Cartulary: 'Cuninghesby'.
[7] Supplied from *PUE*, i. 426, omitted in cartulary.

Sane laborum vestrorum, quos propriis manibus aut sumptibus *colitis, sive de nutrimentis animalium vestrorum nullus omnino decimas exigere presumat.* Libertates vero et immunitates, quas illustris rex Anglorum Henricus secundus *et Henricus rex filius eius ecclesie vestre cartis suis confirmaverunt,*[1] *ratas* perpetuo decernimus permanere. Preterea auxilia et universas indebitas et inconsuetas *exactiones ab archiepiscopis vel episcopis, archidiaconis seu decanis, aliisve omnibus ecclesia*sticis personis et maxime pro aliquo sacramento percipiendo in ecclesiis *vestris omnino fieri prohibemus, nisi tantum sinodalia et episcopalia, que de canonum* iure debentur. Paci quoque et tranquillitati vestre paterna sollicitudine providere vole*ntes auctoritate apostolica prohibemus ut infra clausuram loci vestri seu* grangiarum vestrarum nullus violentiam vel rapinam seu furtum facere, vel hominem capere *aut interficere audeat. Et si quis hoc ausu temerario presumpserit, censura ecclesiastica* percellatur. Adicimus insuper ut domui vestre, ad monialium et fratrum laicorum *integritatem et disciplinam servandam, secundum ipsius ordinis instituta, canonici vita* et moribus maturi, sicut necessarium visum fuerit, preponantur, quibus et animarum *cura pro dispositione prioris immineat, et totius domus cura in exterioribus com*mittatur, ut bona temporalia possint per eos ad subsidium monialium fideliter custodiri, et *ne aliquis possessiones vel alia bona inconsulto et contradicente priore usurpet, debent*[2] *at*tentius provideri. Laici vero conversi in omnibus priori et canonicis[3] subditi et obe*dientes existant, nec aliquam potestatem domus vel pecunie sibi usurpare presumant* nisi que a priore ordinate et *rationabiliter* ad tempus *fuerit eis iniuncta. Habitacula quoque canonicorum et conversorum ita sint a domibus monialium extra illarum septa remota par*iter[4] et disiuncta, ne ad invicem se videre valeant aut hinc inde audiri, nisi ad divinum *officium tantum complendum, cum manifesta* necessitas et certa ratio id fieri postulaverit, neque hoc sit[5] nisi sub presentia plurimorum. Altare vero in quo divinum monialibus celebratur *officium, lapideo pariete intercludatur* aut ligneo ita quod neuter sexus visione alterius perfruatur. Canonici autem in divinis officiis ubique sine ulla exceptione cum missas etiam monialibus celebrant servitium habeant clericorum. Moniales quoque in omnibus illum modum officii sui in ecclesia servent qui a dilecto in domino filio Gileberto primo priore[6] ordinis de Sempingham institutus et a beato Bernardo quondam Clarevallis

---

[1] Cartulary: 'confirmavit', cf. fragment 5.
[2] Cartulary: 'debeat'.   [3] Cartulary: 'canonici'.
[4] Fragment 2 (bottom left hand) begins with the letters 'iter' and fragment 3 (bottom right hand) begins with the word 'necessitas'.
[5] *Mon. Ang.*, vii. 961 reads 'fiat' for 'sit'.
[6] At other points the privileges all speak of Gilbert as 'primus pater'.

abbate nec non et aliis plerisque religiosis personis primo fuerat approbatus, scilicet non musice cantando sed honeste et moderate psallendo atque legendo. Preterea cum commune¹ interdictum terre fuerit,² liceat vobis clausis ianuis, exclusis excommunicatis et interdictis, non pulsatis campanis, submissa³ voce divina officia celebrare. Sepulturam quoque ipsius loci liberam esse decernimus, ut eorum devotioni et extreme voluntati, qui se illic sepeliri deliberaverint, nisi forte excommunicati vel interdicti sint nullus obsistat, salva tamen iustitia illarum ecclesiarum a quibus mortuorum corpora assumuntur. Decernimus ergo ut nulli omnino hominum fas sit prefatam ecclesiam temere perturbare aut eius possessiones auferre vel ablatas retinere, minuere, seu quibuslibet vexationibus fatigare, sed omnia integra conserventur eorum pro quorum gubernatione ac sustentatione concessa sunt usibus omnimodis profutura, salva apostolice sedis auctoritate et diocesani episcopi canonica iustitia. Si qua igitur in futurum ecclesiastica secularisve persona hanc nostre constitutionis paginam sciens⁴ contra eam temere venire temptaverit, secundo tertiove commonita, nisi reatum digna satisfactione correxerit potestatis honorisque sui careat dignitate, reamque se divino iudicio existere de perpetrata iniquitate cognoscat, et a sacratissimo corpore et sanguine dei et domini redemptoris nostri Iesu Christi aliena fiat atque in extremo examine divine ultioni subiaceat. Cunctis autem eidem loco sua iura servantibus sit pax domini nostri Iesu Christi, quatinus et hic fructum bone actionis percipiant et apud districtum iudicem premia eterne pacis inveniant. AMEN,   amen,⁵   amen.

[Rota] Ego Alexander catholice ecclesie episcopus
          subscripsi. Bene valete.

+Ego Hubaldus Hostiensis episcopus subscripsi.
+Ego Iohannes presbiter cardinalis sanctorum Iohannis et
    Pauli tituli Pamachii subscripsi.
+Ego Boso presbiter cardinalis sancte Pudentiane tituli
    Pastoris subscripsi.
+Ego Petrus presbiter cardinalis tituli sancte Susanne subscripsi.
+Ego Vivianus presbiter cardinalis tituli sancti Stephani in
    Celio Monte subscripsi.

---

¹ The contemporary Malton privilege and Innocent IV's privilege read 'generale' for 'commune' and 'suppressa' for 'submissa'.
² Cartulary: 'interfuerit' for 'terre fuerit'.
³ Orig. reads 'sub missa'.   ⁴ Cartulary: 'scient.'
⁵ The cartulary copy ends here.

+Ego Iacintus diaconus cardinalis sancte Marie in Cosmydyn subscripsi.

+Ego Ardicio diaconus cardinalis sancti Theodori subscripsi.

+Ego Cinthyus diaconus cardinalis sancti Adriani subscripsi.

+Ego Hugo diaconus cardinalis sancti Angeli sub-scripsi.

+Ego Rainerius diaconus cardinalis sancti Georgii ad velum aureum subscripsi.

+Ego Arduinus diaconus cardinalis sancte Marie in via lata subscripsi.

Dat' Laterani per manum Alberti sancte Romane ecclesie pres-biteri cardinalis et cancellarii vii kal. Iulii, indictione XIª, incar-nationis dominice anno Mº Cº LXXº VIIIº, pontificatus vero domni ALEXANDRI pape III anno XVIIII.

Fragment 5: Privilege for Chicksands Priory[1]

ALEXANDER EPISCOPUS SERVUS SERVORUM DEI DILECTIS FILIIS ROGERO PRIORI ET MONIALIBUS BEATE MARIE DE CHIKESANDE ET RELIQUIS FRA-*TRIBUS CANONICIS ET SORORIBUS TAM PRESENTIBUS QUAM FUTURIS REGULAREM VITAM SECUNDUM INSTITUTA ORDINIS DE SEMPINGHAM IBIDEM PRO-FESSIS IN PERPETUUM.* Quotiens illud a nobis petitur quod religioni et honestati convenire dinoscitur animo *nos decet libenti concedere et petentium desideriis congruum impertiri suffragium. Eapropter,* dilecti in domino filii, vestris iustis postulationibus clementer annuimus et p*refatam ecclesiam in qua divino manicipati estis obsequio, ad exemplar predece*ssorum nostrorum felicis memorie INNOCENTII, EUGENII, et ADRIANI, Romanorum pontificum, sub b*eati Petri et nostra protectione suscipimus et presentis scripti privilegio communimus.* Statuentes, ut quascumque possessiones, quecumque bona eadem ecclesia inpresentiarum ius*te et canonice possidet aut in futurum con-cessione pontificum, largitione regum vel principum,* oblatione fidelium seu aliis iustis modis prestante domino poterit adhipisci, firma *vobis vestrisque successoribus et illibata permaneant. In quibus hec propriis duximus exprimenda* vocabulis: ecclesiam de Chikesande cum suis pertinentiis, et quicquid in territorio eiusdem ville *habetis* . . . . . .

[1] D/DP Q 1/2.

Maldunia, et de Cameltonia, et Pontem qui supra aquam est sub
curia vestra, ecclesiam de Hagan*es* . . . . . . bosco et plano et omnibus
aliis suis pertinentiis. Quicquid iuris habetis in ecclesia de . . . . . .
suis pertinentiis, ecclesiam de Lincelade cum suis pertinentiis, ecclesiam de Coggapol cu*m suis pertinentiis* . . . . . . et confirmata, capellam
sancti Iohannis evangeliste in territorio de Swineheved cum suis
pert*inentiis* . . . . . . *ter*ritorio illo rationabiliter possidetis, et quicquid
habetis in Standunia, capellam sancti Th*ome* . . . . . . inde
factas et scripto confirmatas per capitulum de Chikesande et
personam matricis ecclesie . . . . . . pasturas et prata que habetis
in Muleworthe, grangiam de Chipenham, cum . . . . . . *Statuimus
quoque ut ordo sanctimonialium et soro*rum, canonicorum, et conversorum, atque rationabiles institutiones que nimirum Theobaldi
*Cantuariensis et Henrici quondam Eboracensis archiepiscoporum et venera-
bilis fratris nostri Rogeri Ebora*censis ecclesie nunc archiepiscopi ac
dilecti filii Gileberti primi patris vestri temporibus facte *in eodem
loco constitute sunt, ibidem perpetuis temporibus inviolabiliter observentur.*
Inhibemus quoque ne terras, nec ecclesias, nec aliquod beneficium
predicte congregationi *collatum liceat alicui personaliter dari nisi
communi et generali assensu omnium predicte profes*sionis sanctimonialium.
Sane laborum vestrorum, quos propriis manibus aut sump*tibus
colitis, sive de nutrimentis animalium vestrorum nullus omnino decimas
exigere* presumat. Libertates vero et immunitates, quas illustris rex
Anglorum Henric*us secundus*[1] *et Henricus rex filius eius ecclesie vestre
cartis suis confirmave*runt, ratas esse perpetuo decernimus. Preterea
auxilia et universas indebitas et inco*nsuetas exactiones ab archiepiscopis
vel episcopis, archidiaconis seu decanis, aliisve omnibus* ecclesiasticis
personis et maxime pro aliquo sacramento ecclesiastico percipiendo
in ecclesiis *vestris omnino fieri prohibemus, nisi tantum sinodalia et
episcopalia, que de canonum iure* debentur. Paci quoque et tranquillitati
vestre paterna sollicitudine providere volentes *auctoritate apostolica
prohibemus ut infra clausuram loci vestri seu grangiarum ve*strarum nullus
violentiam vel rapinam seu furtum facere, vel hominem capere aut
interficere *audeat. Et si quis hoc ausu temerario presumpserit, censura
ecclesiastica percellatur. A*dicimus insuper ut domui vestre, ad monialium
et fratrum laicorum integritatem et disciplinam servand*am, secundum
ipsius ordinis instituta, canonici vita et moribus maturi, sicut necessarium
visum* fuerit, preponantur, quibus et animarum *cura* pro *dispositione
prioris immineat, et totius domus cura in exterioribus committatur, ut bona
temporalia possint per eos ad subsidium monialium fideliter custodiri.* . . .

---

[1] Henry II's charter is printed by G. H. Fowler in Beds. Hist. Rec. Soc.
Publications, i. 118.

Fragments 6 and 7: Privilege for Watton and Malton Priories[1]

[*CELESTINUS* ot *INNOCENTIUS*] *EPISCOPUS SERVUS SERVORUM DEI DILECTIS FILIIS ROGERO PRIORI BEATE MARIE DE WATTONA*[2] ET DE MALTONA EIUSQUE SUCCESSORIBUS CANONICE SUBSTITUENDIS ET RELIQUIS FRATRIBUS CANONICIS ATQUE SORORIBUS TAM PRESENTIBUS QUAM FUTURIS REGUL*AREM VITAM* PROFESSIS IN PERPETUUM. *Quotiens illud a nobis petitur quod religioni et honestati convenire dinoscitur animo nos decet*[3] *libenti concedere et petentium de*sideriis congruum suffragium inpertiri. Eapropter, dilecti in domino filii, vestris iustis postulationibus clementer annuimus et prefatas ecclesias beate Marie de Wattona et *de Maltona,*[4] *in quibus divino mancipati estis obsequio, ad exemplar predecessorum nostrorum felicis reco*rdationis INNOCENTII, EUGENII, ADRIANI, ALEXANDRI, LUCII, et CLEMENTIS, Romanorum pontificum, sub beati Petri et nostra protectione suscipimus et presentis scripti privilegio com*munimus. Statuentes ut quascumque possessiones, quecumque bona inpresentiarum iuste et canonice possidetis au*t in futurum concessione pontificum, largitione regum vel principum, oblatione fidelium seu aliis iustis modis prestante domino poteritis adipisci, firma vobis vestrisque succes*soribus et illibata permaneant. In quibus hec propriis duximus exprimenda vocabulis: locum ipsum in quo predicta ecclesia beat*e Marie de Wattona sita est cum omnibus suis pertinentiis, villam de Wattona cum omnibus suis pertinentiis, ecclesiam de Daltona cum suis pertinentiis, et quicquid in eadem villa et . . . . . . de Houwalt cum suis pertinentiis, Ravenstaindala, cum ecclesia et suis pertinentiis, Langhedale cum suis pertinentiis, ecclesiam de Killingwic cum suis pertinentiis, et quicquid in eadem vil*la* . . . . . . s in Brunnebi, et in Eboraco, et in Feribi, et in Barve, in Punzwat, Kimou, Ettona, Schirna, Ruale, Hadlesei, Diffgelbi, Scharheburc, in Santona, in Driffeld, in Hohum, in Hot . . . . . . *cum* omnibus suis pertinentiis, et quicquid in eadem villa habetis, ecclesiam de Northun cum suis pertinentiis, ecclesiam de Wintringham

---

[1] D/DP Q 1/6 and Q 1/7. Calendared in *Letters of Pope Innocent III*, no. 1089. Cf. above, pp. 50–1.

[2] The reason for thus reconstructing the address is discussed above, p. 50.

[3] 'decet' in the Alvingham privilege of 1178 and elsewhere in examples of this formula; but the Malton privilege of 1178 (fragment 4) reads 'convenit' at this point.

[4] 'de Maltona' is required by the terms of the address and by the list of property given below.

cum suis pertinentiis, et quicquid in eisdem villis habetis . . .
. . . ecclesiam de Anacastra cum suis pertinentiis, et quicquid in
eisdem villis habetis et in Wilhebi, ecclesiam de Waledene cum suis
pertinentiis, et quicquid habetis in Muletorp, Brideshale, Kirkebi,
Hotun, Eboraco, Feribi, Neutun, Hovingham, Coltun et in
Scarheburc. Statuentes ut non liceat cuiquam religionem vestram
vel iura vel rationabiles institutiones a primo patre vestro Gileberto
scripto commendatas et predictorum antecessorum nostrorum
INNOCENTII, EUGENII, ADRIANI, ALEXANDRI, LUCII,
et CLEMENTIS, Romanorum pontificum et nostri auctoritate
scriptoque confirmatas, sine maioris et sanioris partis consilio et
consensu corrumpere vel mutare vel aliquid superaddere quod
predicte religioni vestre vel salubribus videatur institutionibus
obviare. Inter hec autem ista nominatim duximus exprimenda, ut
unum cellarium, una coquina, sub sanctimonialium et sororum cura
sit omnibus tam sanctimonialibus et sororibus quam canonicis et
fratribus et pecunia in auro et argento et pannis sub earundem
custodia existere debeat, atque omnis monachorum, canonicorum,
clericorum, et laicorum illicitus ingressus et accessus ad eas penitus
inhibeatur, quemadmodum in earum scripto salubri et rationabili
providentia distinctum esse dinoscitur et statutum. Obeunte vero
te nunc supradicte religionis magistro vel tuorum quolibet successorum, nullus eisdem congregationibus qualibet surreptionis
astutia seu violentia preponatur sed summus prior eligatur consilio
priorum ordinis et circatorum et assensu prepositarum, sicut in
vestris institutionibus continetur, cui soli omnes conventus domo-
rum profiteri et obedire secundum formam ordinis vestri censemus.
Omnis autem potestas abbatibus vel prioribus super hiis que ad
divinum cultum pertinent concessa in sibi subditos et divino cultui
mancipatos, tam in coronis faciendis quam in confessione ad
missam dicenda et benedictione ante evangelium danda, et ceteris
omnibus, superiori priori vestro qui preest universis congregationibus de Sempingham inconcussa permaneat. Inhibemus quoque ne
terras vel ecclesias vel aliquod aliud beneficium predictis congregationibus collatum liceat alicui personaliter dari nisi communi et
generali assensu omnium sive maioris et sanioris partis prefate
professionis canonicorum et sanctimonialium. Sane laborum vestrorum, quos propriis manibus aut sumptibus colitis, sive de nutrimentis animalium vestrorum a vobis sive ab aliis, pro eo quod illa
in custodia vel pastura sua habent, ubicunque sint, nullus omnino
decimas exigere vel extorquere presumat. Libertates etiam et immunitates quas illustris memorie rex Anglorum Henricus secundus

et Riccardus rex filius eius ecclesie vestre cartis suis confirmaverunt,[1] ratas perpetuo decernimus permanere. Prohibemus autem ut nulli vestrorum post factam in eodem loco professionem liceat ex eodem claustro discedere, discedentem vero absque prelati sui licentia nullus audeat retinere, sed nec alicui Cisterciensium ordinis liceat aliquem fugitivorum vestrorum retinere vel vobis illorum fugitivos recipere, contra autenticum scriptum inter vos rationabiliter factum.[2] Preterea, auxilia et universas indebitas et inconsuetas exactiones ab archiepiscopis vel episcopis, archidiaconis seu decanis, aliisve quibuslibet ecclesiasticis personis in vestris ecclesiis omnino fieri prohibemus, et maxime pro aliquo sacramento ecclesiastico percipiendo nisi synodalia tantum et episcopalia, que de canonum iure debentur, quibus tamen conventuales ecclesias vestras, contra id quod de ducentibus communem vitam in sacris canonibus est statutum nullius volumus improbitate gravari. Paci quoque et tranquillitati vestre paterna diligentia providentes, inhibemus ne archiepiscopus vel episcopus seu archidiaconus aut alia quelibet ecclesiastica persona hospitia vel procurationes seu tallias ab ecclesiis vestris contra antiquam et rationabilem consuetudinem exigere audeat. Sed nec priorem vestrum vel canonicos seu moniales aut aliquem de professis vestris suspendere, interdicere, vel excommunicare attemptet. Inhibemus etiam ut nulli ecclesiastice secularive persone infra parrochias ecclesiarum vestrarum monasterium monachorum, canonicorum, sanctimonialium, heremitarum, seu inclusorum capellas, altaria, et cimiteria liceat quomodolibet sine vestro et diocesani *episcopi assensu construere.*[3] ......

[1] For a charter of King Richard for the nuns of Sempringham, 13 Sept. 1189, see *The Genealogist*, n.s. xvi. 226.

[2] For the agreement, dated 1164, see *Cartularium Abbathiae de Rievalle* (Surtees Soc., 1889), p. 183.

[3] Missing words supplied from the copy in the Alvingham cartulary of a privilege of Innocent IV (attributed in *Mon. Ang.*, vii. 961 to Innocent III), addressed to 'Roberto superiori priori ecclesie b. Marie de Sempingham. . .'.

4. A Papal Privilege for Tonbridge Priory*

NOT many solemn privileges of the medieval popes for English beneficiaries survived the Reformation; but some were cut up then to do service as wrappers for account rolls and court books.[1] A note by Gladys Scott Thomson in her account of the records of Woburn Abbey belatedly called attention to a wrapper which encloses the ministers' accounts for that monastery for the thirtieth year of Henry VIII.[2] On examination this revealed a substantial piece of stiff, thick parchment, measuring about 241×345 mm., cut from the middle of the lower half of a solemn privilege. It contains twenty-eight ruled lines. The loss of the top half of the document means the absence of all proper names of the grantor, the beneficiaries, and their property. Had the whole of the bottom half survived, it would at least have shown the name of the pope, the subscribing cardinals, and the 'great date' common to privileges. Unfortunately, little of this part remains: the last letters of a pope's name ('-tius') and the titles and 'subscripsi' signs, but not the names, of the cardinal bishops of Ostia and Velletri and of Albano (in that order). That is all.

The handwriting provides a first clue, for it permits one to date the document within, say, twenty years of the year 1200; and the only pope '. . . tius' assignable to this period is Innocent III (1198–1216). Having established this much, one

---

* First published in BIHR, xxxviii (1965), 192–200.

[1] For some mutilated survivors see above, pp. 39–41. See also C. R. Cheney, 'Some features of surviving papal letters in England', in *Atti del III Congresso Internazionale di Diplomatica*, Rome, Sept.–Oct. 1971.

[2] 'Woburn Abbey and the dissolution of the monasteries', *Trans. Roy. Hist. Soc.*, 4th ser., xvi (1933), 129–60, at p. 158, referring to P.R.O., S.C. 6/Hen. VIII/30. Miss Scott Thomson connected the fragment tentatively with the surrender of Woburn's privileges to Dr. William Petre. As will be seen, Woburn was not the source; but Dr. Petre was concerned with the confiscation (and preservation) of papal privileges from other sources as well: see above, p. 40.

noticed next the peculiar form of SS used for 'subscripsi' by the bishop of Albano or his clerk. This closely resembled subscription-marks available for comparison of John, cardinal bishop of Albano, on original privileges of the years 1203, 1204, and 1207.[1] Since this bishop was junior to Octavian cardinal bishop of Ostia and Velletri from April 1199 until Octavian's death not later than 1206, and since the bishop of Ostia and Velletri takes precedence of the bishop of Albano in subscribing this privilege, internal evidence dates the fragment 1199 × 1206. A scrutiny of the remaining portion of text —about one-third or two-fifths of each of seventeen lines— produced no proper names, but it did prove that the privilege was granted to a house of regular canons, for it includes the right to instal some of their number in their parish churches. The range of possibilities was further narrowed by finding a clause which requires payment to the pope each year of an ounce of gold.

Considering the provenance of the fragment, it seemed highly probable that the privilege concerned an English monastery. At this point recourse to the late W. E. Lunt's *Financial Relations of the Papacy with England to 1327* settled the matter. For in his chapter on 'the census of exempt and protected monasteries' Lunt dealt exhaustively with the evidence in English and papal archives for these tributes to Rome. The total number of English tributary religious houses in the thirteenth century was small (seventeen). Among them only three were under obligation to pay 'an ounce of gold': these were the ancient Benedictine abbeys of Malmesbury and St. Albans and the priory of Austin canons at Tonbridge, Kent, in the diocese of Rochester.[2] Here was the quarry.

Lunt's prime authority for putting Tonbridge among the

[1] G. T. Clark, *Cartae et alia munimenta . . . Glamorgan* (4 vols., Cardiff, 1885–93), iii. 228, for Margam, 20 Nov. 1203; Potthast, no. 2212, for the church of St. Mang, Regensburg, 20 May 1204; G. Battelli, *Acta Pontificum* (Exempla scripturarum, fasc. iii, 2nd ed., Vatican, 1965), pl. 13, for St. Leucio, Todi, 13 Oct. 1207.

[2] An ounce of gold was equated by the papal collectors to one mark sterling, W. E. Lunt, *Financial Relations . . . to 1327* (Mediaeval Academy of America, 1933), p. 640. Lunt's second volume (published 1962), dealing with the years 1327–1534, discusses the census during this later period (pp. 55–66) but has nothing to add on the case of Tonbridge.

exempt tributary houses was a privilege of Pope Celestine III, dated 2 January 1192, printed by John Thorpe and Walther Holtzmann from the copy in a Rochester episcopal register.[1] Comparison with our text showed no departure from the terms of Celestine's privilege in the remaining words of the Innocentian fragment. That the one was the exemplar of the other was suggested by an unusual sequence of forms common to both. 'Paci quoque et tranquillitati vestre providere volentes' introduces the rule that professed brethren shall not go away without the prior's leave; whereas in privileges of this sort it is usual to find the phrase as an introduction to the next clause, relating to theft, robbery, arson, and bodily violence.[2] It seemed fairly safe, therefore, to reconstruct approximately the whole privilege of Innocent III around the fragment, by copying the terms of Celestine III's bull. Only the subscriptions of cardinal priests and deacons and the date were missing.

Support for this view comes from the Vatican Archives, despite the facts that the surviving chancery registers of Innocent III contain no privilege for Tonbridge and the cameral *Liber Censuum*, in its record of tribute due from English monasteries, makes no mention of Tonbridge. Tonbridge's liability contracted with Celestine III was not, Lunt suggests,

arranged in time to be incorporated into the original compilation of the Liber Censuum, and for some reason it was not added later. . . . The collectors, however, were informed of the obligation. They received census from the monastery during the fourteenth century, and Iterius de Concoreto had occasion in 1331 to excommunicate the prior and convent in order to force them to render the amount due.[3]

Also, in the surviving fourteenth-century table of contents of the lost register of Innocent III's fourth year is the entry: 'Priori [et fratribus] ecclesie beate Marie Magdalene iuxta

---

[1] *Registrum Roffense* (1769), pp. 666–8; *PUE*, ii. 458 no. 266; calendared by Charles Johnson, *Registrum Hamonis Hethe* (CYS, 1948), i. 18–19. Thorpe claimed to publish 'ex autographo' in the capitular archives of Rochester, but Holtzmann suggests that this (like other of Thorpe's references) is incorrect and that the text is that of Hethe's register.

[2] Cf. M. Tangl, *Päpstliche Kanzleiordnungen von 1200–1500* (Innsbruck, 1894, repr. Darmstadt, 1959), p. 232.

[3] Lunt, *Financial Relations . . . to 1327*, pp. 108–9.

Tuneburg confirmatio omnium iurium et possessionum que possidere dinoscuntur', followed by the note of five more letters in favour of the prior and canons.[1] This in turn may be connected with an entry in Arch. Vat. Indice 254, a series of notes from earlier papal registers prepared *c*. 1270 for the use of the Apostolic Camera, recording letters which concern tribute to the Roman church. Here we read, among notes on Innocent III's registers: 'In regestro quarti anni repperitur . . . ccxvi. c. Item quod prior et fratres sancte Marie Magdalene que est iuxta Tunebrugum ad austrum sita ad indicium etc. tenetur ad censum unius uncie auri. Licet omnibus'.[2] So we learn that the tribute to the Roman church provided for in the privilege of Celestine III was confirmed by Innocent III late in his fourth year (22 February 1201–21 February 1202), and the Innocentian text began with the same words as Celestine's: 'Licet omnibus'.

Lunt's researches permit more precision. In dealing with the privilege granted by Celestine III he remarked: 'a bull of Innocent III, dated 5 January 1201, leaves no doubt that it was Celestine III who received Tonbridge into the immediate ownership and protection of the apostolic see'.[3] For this he referred to a small roll among the ecclesiastical documents of the King's Remembrancer of the Exchequer,[4] which is the notarial record of evidences produced before the bishop of Norwich on 4 February 1297 to prove Tonbridge's claim to the church of Stradishall and the chapel or church of Denston, in Suffolk. Unluckily, the notary felt under no obligation to copy *in extenso* the documents that were produced by the proctor of Tonbridge:

quedam munimenta auctentica ostendit quorum clausulis aptis ad

---

[1] Arch. Vat., Reg. Vat. 8A fo. 153ʳ, printed by A. Theiner, *Vetera Monumenta Slavorum meridionalium Historiam illustrantia* (Rome, 1863), p. 62 no. 239; Pott. 1568. Cf. Pott. 1569–73.

[2] I owe the knowledge of this note to Dr. Anton Haidacher, who kindly sent information about the contents of the Indice 254 supplementing his valuable 'Beiträge zur Kenntnis der verlorenen Registerbände Innozenz' III', *Römische Historische Mitteilungen*, iv (1960–1), 37–62.

[3] *Financial Relations . . . to 1327*, p. 108 n. 8. The date in modern form is 5 Jan. 1202.

[4] P.R.O., E 135/15/17.

negotium de quo agebatur cum principiis et fine ipsorum instrumentorum cum bullarum et sigillorum auctoritate et munimine
utebatur idem procurator cum effectu, et dictus procurator huiusmodi instrumenta sana et integra, non abrasa, non abolita, nec in
aliqua sui parte vitiata, eidem patri ostendit, et copiam dictarum
clausularum inscriptis sibi tradidit, facta prius coram dicto patre
collatione, quarum defensionum et clausularum ut premittitur cum
provocationibus et appellationibus tenores tales sunt. . . .

All the notary gave, therefore, were abridgments of a charter
of Richard earl of Clare, a letter of Celestine III (19 December
1191), a privilege of Innocent III, two charters of Bishop
Thomas of Norwich, and a letter of proxy. The privilege of
Innocent III suffered particularly severe pruning. The copy
gives the protocol and preamble ('Licet omnibus') in full, but
only names the Suffolk possessions: 'the church of Stradishall
with a chapel and other appurtenances'. Three clausulae of
privileges follow ('Sane novalium', 'Interdicimus etiam', 'Liceat
quoque'), but none of those parts, except for the sanctions
clause, which leave traces in the fragmentary original. Nor are
the cardinals' subscriptions included. To make up for these
deficiencies the notary supplied the 'great date'; and this date
(5 January 1202) agrees perfectly with the position occupied
by the entry in the lost Vatican register, while the *incipit* agrees
with the note of that entry in Vatican Indice 254.

From three main sources, then, we can reconstruct almost
all of the privilege of Innocent III for Tonbridge. The text
printed below is formed in part from the abridged exemplification in the notarial instrument of 1297; this is filled out by
reference to the text of Celestine's privilege, and within this
framework the fragmentary original fits perfectly. By way of
justification for proceeding thus, it may be said that the preamble preserved in the exemplification of 1297 shows that in
1202 the chancery clerks had the previous privilege before
them; the practice of the time was, in such cases, to repeat the
same common forms; and wherever this can be tested on the
fragmentary original with regard to the last nine clausulae there
is exact correspondence. The only point at which new matter
may have been introduced is in the list of possessions: property
acquired between 1191 and 1201 may have been added to the

list in the former privilege. The lists of cardinal priests and cardinal deacons who subscribed in 1202 are irrecoverable.

The discovery of this privilege for Tonbridge Priory is important, not (as has been seen) because it contains anything new, but because it directs attention to Celestine III's grant in 1192, and this, although printed nearly two centuries ago, has been insufficiently examined. The Austin canons of Tonbridge have not attracted much notice from historians of monasticism. Dugdale's *Monasticon* has little to say about them. J. F. Wadmore, contributing a brief paper on Tonbridge Priory to *Archaeologia Cantiana*, xiv (1882), 326–43, opened with an apology: 'I trust I may not be deemed presumptuous in calling attention to the Priory of St. Mary Magdalene at Tonbridge for Canons Regular of the Order of St. Augustine, the history of which is more or less shrouded in obscurity, and its site forgotten.' Wadmore made considerable use of documents from Tonbridge Priory now in the Bodleian Library,[1] but he did not come to any clearly stated conclusion about the date of the priory's foundation and he did not dwell upon the privilege of Celestine III or draw out its implications. As regards the foundation, he apparently approved the date, latter years of Henry II, proposed by Dugdale and Tanner, on the assumption that the founder, Richard de Clare, was the lord of Clare who died *c.* 1136. J. H. Round made the same assumption when he wrote the account of this Richard de Clare in the *Dictionary of National Biography*, and he was followed by the editors of G.E.C., *Complete Peerage* (iii. 243). R. C. Fowler, writing on Tonbridge Priory in the *Victoria County History*, identified the founder correctly with Richard de Clare, earl of Hertford 1173–1217.[2] It is probable, from the terms of Celestine III's

[1] W. H. Turner and H. O. Coxe, *Calendar of Charters and Rolls preserved in the Bodleian Library* had been published in 1878. The section on Tonbridge Priory, pp. 110–41, calls for a good many corrections of detail.

[2] *Victoria History of the County of Kent*, ii (1926), p. 167. A lost letter of Innocent III, *c.* 5 Jan. 1202, ordered the archbishop of Canterbury and the bishop of Ely to find out whether Richard earl of Clare (i.e. Hertford) has built and endowed a house of canons, as he asserts, Theiner, p. 62 no. 243; Pott. 1572. In Nov. 1325 Edward II learnt by inquisition that Richard de Clare sometime earl of Hertford founded a priory in his manor of Tonbridge before the time of memory, *Reg. Roffense*, pp. 670–2; *Mon. Ang.*, vi. i. 394; *Cal. Close Rolls 1323–7*, p. 427; *Cal. Inquisitions Misc. (Chancery)*, ii (1916), p. 221 no. 886. J. C. Dickinson suggests

privilege, that this was obtained fairly soon after the foundation of the priory; and the earliest dated or dateable document to mention the priory seems to be the letter of this pope dated 19 December 1191.

Neither Fowler nor any other recent writer save Lunt seems to have considered the relations of the canons of Tonbridge with the pope and the English hierarchy. Yet the provision for annual census, made in 1192 and confirmed in 1202, is remarkable, to say the least. For Tonbridge paid tribute *ad indicium libertatis* and this implied exemption. Now Lunt points out that there were some 'monasteries paying census which were not exempt, just as there were exempt monasteries which did not pay census'.[1] But English Augustinian houses in either the tributary or the exempt class are scarce. No more than seven houses appear in papal records as tributary,[2] and in one of them, Royston, the provision for census in the privilege of 29 July 1192 apparently never took effect. Only two English Augustinian houses—neither of them tribute-paying—are noted by Mr. Dickinson as exempt: Waltham Abbey, where exemption presumably stemmed from the status of the earlier collegiate foundation as a royal chapel, and St. Botolph of Colchester.[3] There can be little doubt that Tonbridge should be added to their number. Not only was the privilege obtained at, or shortly after, the priory's foundation. It was confirmed ten years later by Innocent III, and census was still being paid in the fourteenth century. Moreover, the printed registers of Rochester and Canterbury confirm in a negative way the effectiveness of this payment *ad indicium libertatis*; for nowhere is there any sign that diocesan or metropolitan visited this house or that the diocesan confirmed the election of priors, and the historians of Tonbridge have produced no facts pointing to the exercise of the ordinary's jurisdiction.

foundation 'perhaps late *temp.* Henry II', *The Origins of the Austin Canons and their Introduction into England* (1950), p. 297.

[1] *Financial Relations . . . to 1327*, p. 88.

[2] These were Anglesey, Bodmin, Carlisle, Chacombe, Launde, Royston, Tonbridge. Only Bodmin, Carlisle and Launde were of even moderate wealth and consequence. Probably all but Tonbridge paid census *ad indicium protectionis*, which did not confer exemption.

[3] Dickinson, p. 162.

Tonbridge Priory seems to have been small and not among the wealthier Augustinian houses, though it played some part in the business of the Augustinian Provincial Chapters. When Wolsey dissolved it to endow his college, its disappearance caused momentary discontent in the neighbourhood but made no great stir. All this makes it the more surprising that an exemption so extensive was not, as far as we know, seriously contested. A lost letter of Innocent III, contemporaneous with his privilege to Tonbridge, ordered the archbishop of Canterbury and the bishop of Rochester not to presume to molest the canons;[1] this suggests that some attempted encroachment on their liberties had prompted the canons to seek confirmation of Celestine's privilege. But at no later date, apparently, did any acquisitive bishop of Rochester interfere. In the fourteenth century Bishop Hamo de Hethe's registrar made a copy of the privilege of Celestine III, and that was all. Perhaps the priory's immunity was less likely to be assailed because so unimportant a house constituted no serious threat to episcopal and metropolitan power. Perhaps it was aided by the support of the founder's family, the powerful house of Clare; for records of the thirteenth and fourteenth centuries witness to the permanent link between the canons and their patrons.

I. Letter of Pope Celestine III, 19 Dec. 1191, from P.R.O., E 135/15/17 m. 2, a copy made in 1297, possibly (though not obviously) abridged. Printed here since it is not noted in Jaffé-Loewenfeld's *Regesta* or *PUE*.

Celestinus episcopus servus servorum dei dilectis filiis Iohanni priori et canonicis Sancte Marie Magdalene de Tonebrig' salutem et apostolicam benedictionem. Cum ecclesia vestra specialiter ad ecclesiam Romanam pertineat comodis vestris libenter intendere volumus et paci vestre in posterum providere. Inde est quod vestris iustis postulationibus annuentes omne ius quod nobilis vir Ricardus comes de Clare in ecclesiis de Aldinge et Merewrth' et Stradeshulle habuit et eidem ecclesie vestre de assensu diocesanorum episcoporum ad usus vestros intuitu pietatis concessit vobis et ipsi ecclesie auctoritate apostolica confirmamus et presentis scripti patrocinio communimus. Nulli ergo omnino hominum liceat hanc paginam nostre confirmacionis infringere vel ei ausu temerario

---

[1] Theiner p. 62 no. 244; Pott. 1573.

contraire. Si quis autem hoc attemptare presumpserit, indigna-
cionem omnipotentis dei et beatorum Petri et Pauli apostolorum
eius se noverit incursurum. Dat' Laterani, x°iiii kal. Ianuarii pontificatus nostri anno primo.

II. Privilege of Pope Innocent III, 5 Jan. 1202, from the
fragmentary original in P.R.O., S.C. 6/Hen.VIII/30
(Wrapper), with some missing parts supplied from the
notarial abridgement of 1297 in P.R.O., E 135/15/17 m. 2,
completed from the corresponding privilege of Celestine
III (*PUE*, ii. 458 no. 266). The parts supplied from the
notarial copy are in square brackets, those from Celestine's
privilege are in italic type. In footnote references 1192 =
Celestine's privilege, 1297 = the notarial abridgement of
Innocent's privilege.

[INNOCENCIUS EPISCOPUS SERVUS SERVORUM DEI
DILECTIS FILIIS IOHANNI PRIORI ECCLESIE SANCTE
MARIE MAGDALENE QUE IUXTA TONEBRIG' AD AUS-
TRUM SITA EST EIUSQUE^a FRATRIBUS TAM PRESENTI-
BUS QUAM FUTURIS REGULAREM^b VITAM PROFESSIS
IMPERPETUUM. Licet omnibus existamus ecclesiis debitores,
illis tamen specialius adesse nos convenit que nobis et beato Petro
a Christi fidelibus offeruntur et speciali desiderant apostolico
privilegio communiri. Eapropter nobilis viri R. comitis de Clara
precibus inclinati prescriptam ecclesiam quam in fundo proprio,
quem beato Petro et ecclesie Romane obtulerat, fabricavit ad
exemplar felicis recordacionis Celestini pape predecessoris nostri in
ius beati Petri et specialem sedis apostolice protectionem suscipimus
et presentis scripti privilegio communimus; in primis siquidem
statuentes ut ordo canonicus, qui secundum deum et beati Augustini
regulam in eodem loco noscitur institutus, perpetuis ibidem temporibus inviolabiliter observetur. Preterea quascumque possessiones, quecumque bona eadem ecclesia in presenciarum iuste et
canonice possidet aut in futurum concessione pontificum, largitione
regum vel principum, oblatione fidelium, seu aliis iustis modis
prestante domino poterit adipisci, firma vobis vestrisque successoribus et illibata permaneant; in quibus hec propriis duximus exprimenda vocabulis :] *ecclesiam de Ealdynges cum capella de Brenchesleie et
cum omnibus pertinentiis earum,* [ecclesiam de Stradeshulle cum capella
et ceteris pertinenciis suis,] *ecclesiam de Mereworth' cum omnibus per-*

<hr>

^a eiusdem *1297.*   ^b regulariter *1297.*

tinentiis suis, decem marcas argenti de redditu manerii de Tonebrig',[c] *totam terram in bosco et plano que apellatur le Schases de Weteleston' et de Smocham et terram unam iuxta molendinum de Tonebrig' ad orientem et quater viginti porcos in foresta de Tonebrig' singulis annis quietos de pannagio et duos summarios libere et quiete singulis diebus ad portandum vobis ligna de nemore de Tonebrig', servitium et dominium de mesuagio quod fuit Algari ante portam castelli, unum cervum singulis annis in festo sancte Marie Magdalene per homines comitis capiendum, totam terram de Duding-burie cum pertinentiis suis que fuit Roberti de Greelle, totam terram de Hallo quam Acius tenuit, duas summas frumenti annuatim de Farlega, unum mesuagium iuxta barram in villa de Tonebrig', et sex denarios singulis annis de domo que fuit Agnetis iuxta pontem de Tonebrig', sex denarios in Roffa singulis annis de donatione Randulfi filii Dinat, terram que fuit Gilberti le filz iuxta portam vestram, terram de Wicehelendenne que fuit Willelmi ianitoris, et terram quam tenetis iuxta domum vestram que fuit eiusdem Willelmi.* [Sane novalium vestrorum, que propriis manibus vel sumptibus colitis, sive de nutrimentis vestrorum animalium, nullus a vobis decimas exigere vel extorquere presumat. Interdicimus etiam ut nullus archiepiscopus vel episcopus aut eorum officiales sine mandato Romani pontificis aut legati ab eius latere destinati in vos vel ecclesiam vestram vel clericos vestros in vestra maiori ecclesia ministrantes excommunicationis, suspensionis, vel interdicti sentenciam promulgare presumat; et[d] si factum fuerit, auctoritate apostolica irritum habeatur nec in ea pontificalem in aliquo exerceat potestatem, sed eandem ecclesiam sub iurisdictione Romani pontificis perpetuo manere censemus. Liceat quoque vobis pro dedicatione basilice vestre seu capellarum que infra eius septa habentur et consecratione altarium, institutione priorum, ordinatione canonicorum et clericorum vestrorum, pro crismate et oleo sancto et aqua episcopali atque aliis sacramentis ecclesiasticis que vobis fuerint necessaria, catholicum quem malueritis advocare vel adire episcopum, qui apostolica fultus auctoritate quod postulatur indulgeat[e] nec maliciose hoc denegare presumat.][f] *In parochialibus autem ecclesiis quas habetis liceat vobis quatuor vel tres ad minus de canonicis vestris ponere, quorum unus diocesano episcopo presentetur, ut illi curam animarum committat et ei de spiritualibus, vobis autem de temporalibus et ordinis observantia debeat respondere. Liceat quoque vobis clericos vel laicos liberos et absolutos e seculo fugientes ad conversionem recipere et eos in ecclesia vestra sine contradictione qualibet retinere. Paci quoque et tranquillitati vestre providere volentes,*

---

[c] *1192 spells the name* Thonebregge *throughout.*   [d] et *1297;* quod *1192.*
[e] indulgeat *1192;* indugeat *1297.*   [f] *1297 omits the following clauses.*

pro*hibemus ut ulli fratrum vestrorum post factam in eodem loco professionem fas sit absque prioris sui licentia de cl*austro vestro discedere; discedentem vero absque communium litterarum c*autione nullus audeat retinere. Constituimus insuper ut nullus infra ambitum locorum seu grangiarum vestrarum fur*tum vel rapinam committere, violentiam facere, ignem apponere, seu *hominem temere capere aut interficere audeat. Libertates preterea ab eisdem predecessoribus nostris per autentica privilegia eidem venerabili loco provida deliberatione concessas nos auctor*e deo ratas et inconvulsas in posterum volumus conservare.[g] *Obeunte vero te, nunc eiusdem loci priore, vel tuorum quolibet successorum, nullus e fratribus ibi qualibet surreptio*nis astutia seu violentia preponatur nec ad eiusdem loci regimen e*xtraneus assumatur, nisi forte, quod absit, in loco ipso idonea persona ad huiusmodi officium non possit repperiri, sed de con*gregatione ipsa et quem fratres communi consensu vel fratrum maior pars consi*lii sanioris secundum dei timorem et beati Augustini regulam*[h] *providerint eligendum. Sepulturam preterea ipsius* loci liberam esse decernimus, ut eorum devotioni et extreme voluntati qui se *illic sepeliri deliberaverint, nisi forte excommunicati vel interdicti sint, nullus obsistat, salva tamen iustitia illarum* ecclesiarum a quibus mortuorum corpora assumuntur. Decernimus[j] ergo ut [nulli omnino hominum liceat prefatam ecclesiam temere perturbare, aut eius possessiones[k] auferre vel ablatas] retinere,[l] minuere, seu quibuslibet vexationibus fatigare, sed omnia in-[tegra conserventur eorum pro quorum gubernatione ac sustentatione concessa sunt usibus omnimodis profutura,]*salv*a sedis apostolice auctoritate et diocesanorum episcoporum in aliis *ecclesiis vobis subiectis canonica iustitia. Ad indicium autem huius percepte a sede apostolica libertat*is unam unciam auri nobis nostrisque successoribus ann*is singulis persolvetis.*[m] [Si qua igitur in futurum ecclesiastica secularisve persona hanc nostre con-]stitutionis paginam sciens contra eam temere venire temptaverit, [secundo tertiove commonita nisi reatum suum congrua satisfactione correxerit, potestatis honorisque sui digni-]tate careat, reamque se divino iudicio existere de perpetrata iniquitate cognos-[cat, et a sacratissimo corpore et sanguine dei et domini redemptoris nostri Iesu Christi aliena fiat, atque in extremo ex-]amine districte ultioni subiaceat. Cunctis

---

[g] *The clause normally ends here with* conservari. *1192 continues*: et sicut ecclesia vestra in religionis observantia exstat eximia, ita nichilominus cum omnibus ad ipsam pertinentibus perpetuis futuris temporibus ab omni servitio libera ab omni mundiali strepitu maneat inconcussa; *but there is not sufficient space in the original for this.*

[h] *Thus 1192; in other privileges in this clause is added* libera voluntate.

[j] *1297 resumes here.*   [k] possessionem *1297.*

[l] *1297 adds* vel.   [m] *1297 omits* salva . . . persolvetis.

autem eidem loco sua iura servantibus [sit pax domini nostri Iesu Christi quatinus et hic fructum bone actionis percipiant et apud districtum i-]udicem premia eterne pacis inveniant. Amen. Amen. [Amen.]

[(Rota). Ego Innocen-]^ntius catholice ecclesie episcopus SS. Bene valete.^o

[+Ego Octavianus Ho-]^nstiensis et Velletrensis episcopus SS.

[+Ego Iohannes]^n Albanensis episcopus SS.^p

[Dat' Anagnie per manum Blasii sancte Romane ecclesie subdiaconi et notarii. Non. Ianuarii indictione quinta, incarnationis dominice anno millesimo ducentesimo primo, pontificatus vero domni Innocencii pape iii anno quarto.]

---

^n *Missing in original; omitted with the rest of the subscriptions from 1297.*

^o Bene valete *in the usual monogrammatic form.*

^p *Four ruled lines, blank, follow in the original. The lists of cardinal priests and cardinal deacons, which flanked the names of the bishops, are missing.*

5. Magna Carta Beati Thome: another Canterbury Forgery*

IN the *Concilia Magnae Britanniae et Hiberniae* of David Wilkins (1737) there stands under the year 1166 (i. 437–8) a document entitled: 'Charta Thomae Becket, Cant. archiepiscopi, de privilegiis Cantuar. ecclesiae'.[1] Wilkins printed it from a copy in the archiepiscopal register of William Courtenay (1381–96), fo. 46ᵛ, where it is included in the copy of an *inspeximus* by the prior of St. Gregory's, Canterbury, and the dean of christianity of the city, dated 1275, Thursday before the Purification (that is, 30 January 1276).[2] The charter of St. Thomas is printed also in J. A. Giles's edition of his Letters ((1845), i. 158), and again in the *Materials* edited by J. C. Robertson and J. B. Sheppard (RS, vii (1885), pp. 60–3), which makes use of Canterbury, Christ Church, Reg. A, fos. 38ᵛ, 61ʳ.[3]

This is a remarkable document which has in modern times attracted less attention than it deserves. Noticed briefly by local Canterbury historians, Nicolas Battely, J. Brigstocke Sheppard, and C. E. Woodruff,[4] it finds no mention in the standard histories of the archbishop or in extensive modern accounts of Christ Church, Canterbury and of the conflicts between the prior and convent and the archbishops. Yet, if its provisions are to be taken seriously, it is a fundamental source.

In a preamble Archbishop Thomas refers to the calamities which his conduct has brought upon the church of Canterbury

---

* Reprinted from *BIHR*, xxxvi (1963), 1–26.

[1] I wish to express my thanks to Professor V. H. Galbraith and Professor R. W. Southern, who kindly read this paper in draft, for valuable advice.

[2] The *inspeximus* also includes the confirmatory bull of Pope Gregory IX, 'Cum ecclesiam vestram', of 21 Jan. 1228 (below, p. 108).

[3] The text is, for convenience, printed below, p. 105.

[4] W. Somner, *Antiquities of Canterbury*, ed. N. Battely (1703), II. i. 104–5; J. B. Sheppard, in Hist. MSS. Comm., *8th Rept.*, app. i, p. 320*b*; C. E. Woodruff and W. Danks, *Memorials of Canterbury Cathedral* (1912), p. 103.

during seven years, and declares himself ready to expose his head and body to his persecutors in order to obtain its peace and security. The dispositions which follow in the charter may for convenience be numbered from one to twelve. (I) The archbishop places the church, its persons, lands, etc. under the protection of God, the Roman Curia, and himself, forbidding any to alienate the church's rights without the consent of the whole chapter of monks. (II) Is a perpetual anathema to bind all who harm the possessions or rights of the church or maliciously reveal the chapter's secrets. (III) No person of other profession or order is to be admitted to the chapter's secrets. (IV) The manors and possessions of the monks and the churches on them, with certain offerings called *exennia*, are confirmed. (V) The monks are confirmed in their right to appoint and remove their officials and servants. (VI) The monks may utter ecclesiastical censures against all malefactors. (VII) They may appeal to the apostolic see 'contra omnia gravamina'. (VIII) Anathema is pronounced on anyone who attempts to transfer the metropolitan see or the primacy elsewhere. (IX) Suffragan bishops of the church of Canterbury are not to be consecrated elsewhere than in the church of Canterbury, except by common consent of the whole chapter. (X) Chrism and oil for the province of Canterbury shall only be distributed from the cathedral church. (XI) The archbishop wishes and implores the monks to show all reverence and honour to the suffragan bishops and the abbots of the province, and the bishops to show their true love for the monks. Finally, (XII) the archbishop confirms the rights, revenues, and churches of his fellow-exiles and implores all to avoid doing them harm.

Like most of the authenticated acts of Archbishop Thomas, the charter bears no date. If we accept the reading of the preamble which appears in the printed editions and which speaks of the seven calamitous and anxious years of the church of Canterbury, there is no difficulty in assigning the charter to the year 1170, for Becket returned in the seventh year of his exile. To be sure, the word *septennium* is no better attested in the manuscripts than *sempiternum*, but it makes better sense and has much to commend it. In any case, the charter speaks of those who have shared the archbishop's exile and who, by implication, have returned to Canterbury. To the scribe of Lambeth MS. 1212, who copied it late in the thirteenth century, it appeared to be the martyr's last will, composed a few days before he died.[1] It has the air, indeed, of belonging, if not to the very eve of martyrdom, to the same month: Becket only arrived in England on 1 December. But what of the textual tradition?

Copies are in registers of Christ Church, Canterbury, composed in the time of Prior Henry of Eastry (1285–1331) and after, and in other documents among the muniments of the cathedral priory which are of no greater age.[2] Besides being copied into the archiepiscopal register of William Courtenay in the *inspeximus* already mentioned, of 30 January 1276, it appears in the register of the see contained in Lambeth MS. 1212, p. 258, and in Lambeth, Cartae misc. XIII. 6 (ii), written in 1286. The clause which calls down curses upon those who injure the church of Canterbury was copied with other anathemas early in the fourteenth century in a Worcester book, Bodleian MS. Rawlinson C.428, fo. 171ʳ*b*, and was invoked by archbishops of Canterbury from the time of Robert Winchelsey.[3] Is there, then, no trace of this charter, known in the later Middle Ages as Magna Carta Beati Thome, earlier than these late texts and quotations, all of them a hundred years after its reputed date?

There are highly significant traces. First, the clause (XI) which protects the prior and convent of Canterbury against the consecration of suffragan bishops of the province outside the cathedral church is cited at various consecrations of bishops from the time of Robert Grosseteste's consecration at Reading in June 1235.[4] Secondly, if a plausible conjecture of the late

---

[1] The rubric reads: 'Testamentum beati Thome martiris gloriosi conditum perpaucos dies ante mortem suam'.

[2] Canterbury, D. & C. Mun., Chartae antiquae, C. 204 and C. 120, m. 1, Reg. A, fos. 38ᵛ (formerly 45) and 61ʳ (formerly 68), Reg. I, fo. 85ᵛ, Reg. O, fo. 159ᵛ (formerly 359); also in Canterbury books elsewhere; B.M., Cotton MS. Galba E III, fo. 55ʳ Galba E IV, fo. 58ᵛ, Cambridge, St. John's College, MS. N 6, fo. [5ʳ] (formerly 14).

[3] Wilkins, ii. 313*b* (1309); *Reg. H. Chichele*, ed. E. F. Jacob (CYS, 1937–47), iii. 104 (1414); *Reg. T. Bourgchier*, ed. F. R. H. Du Boulay (CYS, 1956), p. 16 (1454).

[4] 'Cauciones' by bishops consecrated elsewhere, and by the prelates officiating at their consecration, were carefully preserved by the monks of Canterbury.

Canon C. E. Woodruff be accepted, this was the document of which a spurious original was exposed in the time of Archbishop Edmund, in 1237.[1] But before we consider these indications (which come, after all, sixty years after Thomas's death), the form and substance of the charter had better be examined, especially in relation to the history of the cathedral priory from Archbishop Thomas's time to Archbishop Edmund's.

As regards form, caution is necessary. We do not know enough about the secretarial arrangements of Archbishop Thomas and possess too few of his administrative letters to be sure that his clerks achieved or even desired consistency, and Dr. Saltman's study of Archbishop Theobald's acts should discourage dogmatism.[2] For Becket about two hundred letters, preserved as records of his dispute with King Henry II, are assembled in the *Materials for the History of Thomas Becket*.[3] But none of these survives in original, and only a handful of them are formal administrative acts. Other indubitable charters and mandates of the archbishop probably do not number forty, of

Some may be seen in Canterbury, D. & C. Mun., Chartae antiquae, C. 120 (a fifteenth-century roll), and a longer series, ibid., Reg. A, fos. 62ʳ (formerly 69)–77ʳ; some are in Reg. I, fo. 98 and Reg. O, fo. 185ʳ. 'Cauciones' given by Archbishop Stephen Langton in 1215, 1226, and 1227 do not mention St. Thomas's charter (*Acta Stephani Langton*, ed. Kathleen Major (CYS, 1950), pp. 21, 114, 121). For the 'caucio' of Robert Grosseteste see below, p. 95. Of later documents which mention the charter of St. Thomas, examples are the letter of Archbishop John Pecham on the occasion of consecrating Richard Swinfield, bishop of Hereford, in 1283: 'Cum beatus Thomas martir ... et nichilominus beatus Eadmundus ... statuerint consecrationes suffraganeorum ... in ipsa ecclesia ... celebrari debere' (Canterbury, Reg. I, fo. 98ᵛ), and the licence of the prior and convent of Christ Church in similar terms for Griffin, elect of Bangor, to be consecrated elsewhere in 1307: 'Licet beatus Thomas martir inclitus ... et nichilominus beatus Eadmundus ... statuerint consecrationes suffraganeorum ... in dicta ecclesia nostra ... celebrari debere' (Cambridge, Univ. Libr., MS. Ee. 5.31, fo. 106ᵛ). For later references see *Reg. H. Chichele*, i. 111 (1429) and Somner, ii, i. 105 (1443), ii, ii. 45 (1509).

[1] 'Some early professions of canonical obedience to the see of Canterbury', *Trans. St. Paul's Ecclesiological Soc.* vii (1916), 161–2.

[2] A. Saltman, *Theobald, Archbishop of Canterbury* (1956), pp. 181–232.

[3] Edited by J. C. Robertson and J. B. Sheppard in vols. v–vii (RS, 1881–5) of the *Materials for the History of Thomas Becket* (hereafter cited as *Materials*). Professor Raymonde Foreville, 'Lettres "extravagantes" de Thomas Becket, archevêque de Canterbury', *Mélanges d'histoire du moyen âge dédiés à la mémoire de Louis Halphen* (Paris, 1951), pp. 225–38 (hereafter cited as *Mélanges*) counts 194, without reckoning letters written in his name by his clerks, John of Salisbury, Lombard of Piacenza, and Herbert of Bosham (p. 226 n. 6).

which four only are originals. Diplomatic criteria are consequently hard to apply. Nevertheless, it is possible to arrive at conclusions about some common habits—if not invariable rules—of Thomas Becket's chancery. It is worth while deducing these for comparison with Magna Carta.

Apart from acts of which the original title and address are omitted or abridged, an overwhelming majority of those ascribed to Thomas Becket use the title: *Thomas dei gratia ecclesie Cant.* (or *Cant. ecclesie*) *minister humilis* (or *humilis minister*), with or without the addition of the dignity of *apostolice sedis legatus*, bestowed on Thomas in April 1166. In the non-administrative letters, some such epithet as *exsul miserabilis* occasionally supplements or replaces *minister humilis.*[1] A comparatively small minority of the non-administrative letters (which survive only in copies) have the title: *Thomas dei gratia archiepiscopus Cant. et apostolice sedis legatus.*[2] These two main forms are so overwhelmingly numerous as to cast grave doubts on any letter which begins with other words.[3] In no certainly genuine administrative act did this archbishop use the primatial style, *totius Anglie primas.*[4] As regards title, then, Magna

[1] *Materials*, vi. 471, 640, vii. 17, 183, 187.

[2] Ibid. v. 232, 234, vi. 181, 193, 541, 542, 558, 560, 561, vii. 45, 50, 97, 100, 104, 107, 110, 256, 258, 307, 320, 324. The letter to the subprior and monks of Christ Church at vi. 589 inserts 'totius Angliae primas' after 'Cantuariensis archiepiscopus'.

[3] Cf. Saltman, pp. 181–2 for the common confusion between the acts of Theobald and those of Thomas. He points to four certain acts of Theobald with the title *Cant. ecclesie minister humilis*: the archbishop's will, one act in favour of Christ Church, and two in favour of Dover Priory. See also *The Letters of John of Salisbury*, ed. W. J. Millor and others, i (1955), p. 71 (no. 7, formerly no. 36), p. 166 (no. 105, formerly no. 43).

[4] Cf. C. R. Cheney, *English Bishops' Chanceries 1100–1250* (Manchester, 1950), p. 65. *Materials*, vi. 589 uses the primatial title (cf. above, n. 2). Because of the concurrent evidence of the originals and the majority of copies of acts which can be certainly assigned to Thomas, one is led to credit his chancery with some degree of consistency in this matter. For this reason I am disposed to reject all administrative acts containing the primatial style. This involves attributing to Theobald nos. 9–12 of the series which Mlle Foreville ascribes to Thomas (*Mélanges*, pp. 232–4). Mlle Foreville accepted the name of Thomas in these copies before Dr. Saltman had published his work on Theobald, which shows so many genuine acts of Theobald ascribed in cartularies to Thomas. I should also tentatively ascribe to Theobald the following which are not included by Dr. Saltman in his collection, on the grounds that they describe the archbishop as primate: Salisbury, D. & C. Mun., Liber evidenciarum C, p. 125; Lambeth MS. 241, fo. 37ʳ; B.M., Add. MS. 40725, fo. 19ᵛ and Cotton MS. Tib. E. v, fo. 228ᵛ;

Carta, which reads *dei gratia archiepiscopus et apostolice sedis legatus*, agrees with some twenty-two letters of the collected correspondence, but not with any of the administrative *acta*.[1] Coming to the form of address used by the archbishop in his charters, indulgences, etc. which call for a general address, we find that Thomas, like Theobald, uses *omnibus* (or *universis*) *sancte matris ecclesie filiis* or a closely similar formula, sometimes qualified with *ad quos presentes littere pervenerint*. Compared with other productions ascribed to Archbishop Thomas, Magna Carta is unique in its address: *omnibus ad quos presens scriptum pervenerit*. Nor does the greeting of Magna Carta agree with the plain *salutem* which is most common in the administrative letters (though *salutem et patris benedictionem* and *salutem et benedictionem* are both found in copies, each once).[2] The text of Magna Carta is loosely constructed, and does not conform very closely to the usual pattern of Thomas's *acta*. The flowery preamble accords ill with the commonplace form of notification which follows; and the various sentences of malediction, confirmation, and exhortation do not hang together happily. 'Huius confirmationis nostre paginam' is an inexact description of the foregoing clauses. Certainly no one would maintain that stylistically the charter makes a harmonious whole. At several points the phraseology is unexpected. It is a strange coincidence that Thomas should in his lifetime speak of risking 'capud et corpus persecutoribus', when his body and the crown of his head were so soon to become separate objects of veneration. Then, again, he places the church of Canterbury under the protection of the Roman Curia,[3] when *apostolica sedes* or *ecclesia Romana* would seem more natural expressions. Such inelegancies

G. Oliver, *Monasticon Exoniense* (Exeter, 1846), p. 41. It is, of course, possible in any of these nine cases (as also in *Materials*, vi. 589) that the original title of an act of Archbishop Thomas has been retouched by a copyist.

[1] It should not be necessary to underline the fact that at Canterbury in the next hundred years a forger would have much of the collected correspondence at his disposal but few, if any, of Thomas's administrative *acta*.

[2] *Materials*, v. 261 (cf. Saltman, p. 407) and Lambeth MS. 241, fo. 36ᵛ.

[3] The term *Curia* is used in Becket's correspondence less to represent the majesty of papal power than to indicate the court in which the business of Christendom was transacted, and the term is often used when the archbishop is is dissatisfied: 'Non est mihi propositum ulterius vexandi curiam: eam adeant qui praevalent in iniquitatibus suis' (*Materials*, vii. 280, cf. pp. 282, 284, 291).

as the repetition of 'aliquo integumento vel causa' and of 'molestiam', and the phrase 'cum restitutione ablatorum condignam ecclesie faciat restitutionem' in the *sanctio*[1] do not inspire confidence. The final *apprecatio*, 'amen', is unusual in Thomas's acts which, when unwitnessed, usually end with 'Valete'.[2] It might be argued, against these objections, that in the troubled last month of Thomas Becket's life, to which this charter must be assigned, some hastiness and lack of care in drafting was to be expected. But Becket had his secretarial staff about him at the time; expert draftsmen were not wanting.

If the formal features of Magna Carta do not enable us to pass a final verdict on the document, they are at least sufficiently irregular to make us alert to notice any other marks of falsity. At the present stage in the enquiry the presumption is that this is not—at least, not in all its details—a genuine act of Archbishop Thomas. An examination of its contents takes us much further.

In scrutinizing the contents one must bear in mind two facts. First, after the early years of Thomas Becket's pontificate, the archbishop had little contact with the cathedral community until the last month of his life, and since the archbishop did not enjoy his usual revenues or exercise his usual jurisdiction, the opportunities for disagreement which existed under normal conditions were diminished. In other words, the occasion did not arise for many such confirmations, concessions, and compromises as we find among the *acta* of Archbishop Theobald. Secondly, the immense prestige of the martyr in the generation following his death, and the advantage which the community of Christ Church was quick to derive from it, meant that his name was invoked whenever the liberties of the church of Canterbury seemed to be in danger. To quote Stubbs: 'the martyrdom of St. Thomas, which, if it was an offering at all,

---

[1] The *sanctio*, with its curse and blessing, is not known in any other document of Becket, but such clauses were probably not standardized (cf. Saltman, pp. 212–13). *Acta* of Becket with curses occur in Lambeth MS. 241, fo. 36ᵛ (preceded by blessing), *Cal. Charter Rolls, 1327–41*, p. 395; *Mon. Angl.*, iv. 269 (= Bodleian Libr., Bucks. charter 73); Hampshire Record Office, Southwick Priory Register III, fo. 4ᵛ.

[2] 'Amen, Valete' appears at the end of the copy in Lambeth MS. 241, fo. 36ᵛ as in twelve of Theobald's *acta* (Saltman, p. 223).

was certainly an offering for the immunities of the whole of the clergy, was looked on as the redemption of the church of Canterbury'.[1] In the great collection of *Epistolae Cantuarienses*, recording the disputes between Archbishops Baldwin and Hubert and their cathedral community, the monks' letters abound in references to 'libertates pro quibus gloriosus martyr Thomas occubuit'.[2]

The conditions of the archbishop's return to Canterbury in December 1170 might explain why he was moved to produce a general confirmation of privileges for the community to which he was restored. Even if the form of Magna Carta is peculiar, there is nothing anachronistic in those clauses which protect with anathema the possessions and rights of the church of Canterbury (I, II, VI). The appeal to the monks and bishops to live on good terms with each other (XI) was not inappropriate, and it would be natural for the rights of Thomas's companions in exile to be safeguarded (XII). Clause VIII, which speaks of enemies who threaten to remove the metropolitan and primatial see from Canterbury, recalls the accusations made against Gilbert Foliot of London in Thomas's last years.[3] But, having said this, we have indicated all that does not fall under suspicion. Not only was the pontificate of Thomas devoid of particular incidents which would give rise to most of the remaining clauses: one and all provided matter for very violent disputes between archbishop and convent in the days of Archbishops Baldwin and Hubert. Had the martyr the gift of prophecy? Those disputes, from 1186 to 1200, are recorded with incomparable fullness in the 557 letters of *Epistolae Cantuarienses* and elsewhere; yet nowhere in the legal disputations and the rhetorical appeals of the monks, during these years, is there one single suggestion that the monks could produce in support of their claims a charter given less than thirty years before by the martyr who had become their patron saint.

---

[1] *Epistolae Cantuarienses*, ed. W. Stubbs (RS, 1865), p. xxxi (hereafter cited as *Ep. Cant.*).

[2] e.g. ibid., p. 505.

[3] Becket's letter (*Materials*, vi. 591) suggests that Foliot sought to establish a third metropolitan see in London; but John of Salisbury and other Becketian sources accuse him of aiming to supplant Canterbury (A. Morey and C. N. L. Brooke, *Gilbert Foliot and his Letters*, pp. 151–2).

The only 'confirmation' by St. Thomas they allege is his head.[1] The argument *ex silentio* must always be applied cautiously, but there are some occasions when it is compelling. And to this argument from the letters we may add the statement of the monk-historian Gervase. Archbishop Thomas, says Gervase, 'so long as he lived, did nothing in prejudice of the convent, but showed the monks affection and every favour. . . . He promised indeed that he would honour them more than any of his predecessors; but he was prevented by his martyrdom, and God fulfilled more gloriously what His champion had promised.'[2] Gervase, be it remembered, joined the community of Christ Church while Thomas was archbishop, and wrote his history between about 1188 and 1210.

Clause IV offers a striking example. Here, in confirming the manors and other possessions pertaining to the monks, the archbishop specifies the *exennia* as theirs. These were the offerings made from the monks' manors at Christmas and Easter, and in the time of Theobald they were paid to the archbishop. In the time of Thomas's exile the monks had apparently contrived to get them, instead of the royal custodian of the see; but when in later years the destination of the *exennia* was disputed, it was not Thomas but his successor, Richard, who was remembered as having given the monks their legal title. Gervase says of him: 'villarum etiam nostrarum exenia non abstulit sed concessit, quae etiam tunc temporis ecclesia habuit, cum tempore exilii Sancti Thomae tyrannus ille Randulfus del Broch ex praecepto regis exulantis custodiret episcopatum'.[3] Again, in his Life of Archbishop Richard, Gervase says: 'exenia quoque reddidit conventui quae de quibusdam villis monachorum solebant sed iniuste archiepiscopo deferri'.[4] Considering that one of the first complaints raised

---

[1] 'Libertates et privilegia quae beatissimus dei martyr noster Thomas adhuc recenti sanguine cerebri in lapidibus ecclesiae rubricavit' (*Ep. Cant.*, p. 444). 'Quod nos urget acrius, in contentionem iuris ecclesiae nostrae libertates evocantur, pro quibus gloriosus martyr Thomas occubuit. Qui videns ecclesiasticae libertatis dignitatem infirmari, studuit eam in statum debitum revocare, et in eius confirmationem caput proprium allegavit' (ibid., p. 505).

[2] *Hist. Works of Gervase of Canterbury*, ed. W. Stubbs (RS, 1879–80), i. 48 (hereafter cited as Gervase).

[3] Gervase, i. 49.

[4] Ibid., ii. 399.

against Archbishop Baldwin was the charge of levying the *exennia*, it is incredible that the writers of the *Epistolae Cantuarienses* should make no reference to Thomas's grant, if Magna Carta were known to them. They content themselves with saying that Baldwin acts contrary to 'scriptis antecessorum suorum authenticis' and 'contra iuris formam et antiquam antecessorum suorum consuetudinem'.[1] The churches on the monks' manors, which are likewise confirmed to the monks by clause IV of Magna Carta, have a similar history. The monks in dispute with Archbishop Hubert in 1198 claimed that the convent had possessed the patronage until the time of Archbishop Theobald. 'The Blessed Thomas', they said, 'wanted to make a composition with the convent about the churches, but impeded by exile and prevented by death he was unable to do so.' It was, in fact, Archbishop Richard who gave back the churches of Eastry, Monkton, Meopham, and Eynsford, as chronicled by Gervase, noted in the Canterbury Martyrology, and confirmed by Pope Alexander III.[2]

Clause VIII, on the threatened transfer of the metropolitan see, has been noted above as compatible with the date 1170, in view of the fears entertained in the archbishop's entourage about the ambitions of Gilbert Foliot. But when it is read in conjunction with the next clause, which safeguards the rights of the prior and convent of Canterbury in episcopal consecrations, it seems to reflect the fear of the monks that the archbishop of Canterbury himself may make another church his metropolitan and primatial see. There is no contemporary evidence that Thomas gave rise to this fear. But within a generation the efforts of Baldwin and Hubert to establish a collegiate church, first at Canterbury and then at Lambeth, caused such a fear, which rapidly amounted to an obsession with the monks of Christ Church. Their dismay led them to produce every possible argument to obstruct the archbishops' intention; yet they never suggested that their blessed martyr had foreseen and specifically guarded against the nefarious doings of his

---

[1] *Ep. Cant.*, pp. 115, 150, cf. p. 94.

[2] Gervase, i. 48, ii. 399; *Ep. Cant.*, p. 557; *PUE*, ii. 364 (1178), cf. p. 370 (1179). And see Richard's charters, Canterbury, D. & C. Mun., Reg. C, fo. 140ʳ (Hist. MSS. Comm., *8th Rept.*, app. i, p. 328*a*); Lambeth, Cartae misc. XIII. 15; B.M., Add. MS. 6159, fo. 287ᵛ; etc.

G

successors by a written threat of anathema.[1] It is noteworthy that they repudiated the report put about by Archbishop Baldwin that his desire to establish a prebendal church dedicated to St. Thomas was in line with an expressed intention of St. Thomas to found such a church, dedicated to St. Stephen.[2]

Clause IX is intimately connected with clause VIII. The monks wished all suffragans of Canterbury to be consecrated in the metropolitan church. It is doubtful whether this was a live issue in 1170. In the next century it will be claimed at different times that what Thomas's charter confirmed was 'de iure communi'[3] and 'ex antiqua consuetudine Cantuariensis ecclesie',[4] but both propositions are doubtful. In Gratian's *Decretum* one reads (Dist. 51, c. 5): 'Episcopus autem conprovincialis ibi consecrandus est ubi metropolitanus elegerit; metropolitanus autem non nisi in civitate metropoli.' As for the practice of the province of Canterbury in the century after the Norman Conquest, thirty-nine of the recorded consecrations of archbishops of Canterbury and their suffragans took place at Canterbury; twenty-three are recorded elsewhere, and for eighteen the place is unrecorded. While this does not point to a consistent tradition over the whole period, it does appear that none of the six consecrations which were celebrated between 1152 and 1169 took place outside the cathedral church; and the monk Gervase reports of Archbishop Thomas 'duos interea sacravit episcopos in ecclesia Cantuariensi'.[5] Recent custom, then, was in favour of such a rule in 1170; but there

---

[1] The fears of the monks are expressed fully in *Ep. Cant.*, pp. 534–7. An obvious place to refer to Magna Carta cl. VIII occurs on p. 537, but it is not mentioned. Nor does the 'Processus negotii' (pp. 520–30) refer to it. See also Gervase, i. 37, for a statement of the intentions behind Archbishop Baldwin's acts, as interpreted by the monks.

[2] *Ep. Cant.*, pp. 7–8, 17, 248, 421, 556. Geoffrey Ridel, bishop of Ely, formerly archdeacon of Canterbury, recalled Archbishop Thomas saying that he wished to do so (p. 19). The monks denied it (pp. 44–5, 119) and produced two monk-chaplains of the martyr who said that they had never heard him speak of it (p. 135).

[3] *Registres de Grégoire IX (1227–41)*, ed. L. Auvray, etc. (École française de Rome, 1896–1955), no. 2840 (20 Nov. 1235). Cf. below, p. 95.

[4] Ibid., no. 4045 (18 Jan. 1238).

[5] Gervase, ii. 392. The numbers of consecrations at Canterbury given here and farther on are based on W. Stubbs, *Registrum Sacrum Anglicanum* (2nd ed., Oxford, 1897).

is no reason to suppose that the monks, even if in 1170 they valued the custom, felt that it was in danger. Such apprehension was likely to arise as relations between archbishop and monks deteriorated, and when the archbishops were pursuing their plans for a collegiate church. And this is precisely what happened. Apart from Magna Carta, clause IX, the first mention of this rule about consecrations comes from the period of the great lawsuit.[1] In 1191 the papal legate, it is said, was persuaded that consecrations should not take place elsewhere than in the church of Canterbury.[2] Moreover, in this period the proportion of consecrations celebrated outside the cathedral church rises markedly. Between 1169 and July 1214 only twelve bishops are known to have been consecrated in Christ Church; in four cases the place is unrecorded; in thirty-four the ceremony was celebrated elsewhere.[3] If the charter of St. Thomas was at hand to justify the monks' claim, it is strange that it was not, so far as we know, cited.

These are the more significant clauses, but others must be mentioned because they fit into the pattern formed by the rest. Clause III, which objects to the sharing of capitular secrets[4] by others than monks of Christ Church, has no discoverable relevance to the days of Archbishop Thomas; but the admission of the archdeacon of Canterbury to the chapter-house became a matter for regulation under his successor, as it had been under Theobald.[5] The promise in clause V to allow the monks freedom to appoint and dismiss officials and servants recalls that trouble arose in the time of Baldwin, who appointed a cellarer and sacrist in 1187.[6] The right conferred on the monks by clause VII to appeal to the apostolic see 'contra

---

[1] *Ep. Cant.*, pp. 325, 327–8, 413. Cf. I. J. Churchill, *Canterbury Administration* (1933), i. 285. The account by Gervase of the consecration abroad of Waleran of Rochester (1184) suggests that the monks of Christ Church were already sensitive on this point (Gervase, i. 306–7); but the full and probably earlier account in the *Domesday Monachorum* (ed. D. C. Douglas (1944), p. 107) suggests that the place of consecration was not the main issue: moreover, the evidence for earlier practice was the oral witness of nine old monks, not any charter.

[2] Gervase, i. 487.　　　　　　　　　　　　　　　[3] In four cases at Rome.

[4] Cf. Gervase, i. 355 (1187).

[5] Saltman, p. 258; *PUE*, ii. 409 (1181).

[6] *Ep. Cant.*, pp. 89, 92–3, 291, 299–300, 316. In their complaint on p. 94 the monks refer to the charters of Theobald and King William and King Henry, but not to any charter of Archbishop Thomas. Cf. *PUE*, ii. 447 (8 Apr. 1187).

omnia gravamina' hardly seems to be a matter within an archbishop's competence: it was, in fact, conferred on the monks by
the pope in 1179.[1] The provision in clause X that chrism and
oil for the province shall only be distributed from the church
of Canterbury recalls Baldwin's action in 1187 when he consecrated chrism at London.[2]

The cumulative effect of these facts is overwhelming. The
clauses examined raise issues which were not likely to appear of
great moment in 1170: but they were so intensely felt by the
monks of Christ Church during the last years of the twelfth
century that any relevant prescriptions by the Blessed Thomas
would have been welcome. Not only did Magna Carta find no
mention among the muniments cited in the great lawsuit; the
monk Gervase tells us that Thomas intended to do good to
the community but was prevented by his martyrdom.[3] The
conclusion is irresistible that Magna Carta was not cited then
because it did not then exist. It is a forgery, forged by a later
generation of Canterbury monks, with ambitions, fears, and
grievances unconnected with St. Thomas. The rhetoric of their
forebears might encourage thirteenth-century monks of Christ
Church to assert in documentary form the privileges for which
Thomas was deemed to have died. In the letters of the great
lawsuit which were available to them, they might read how he
had rubricated their liberties and privileges with his blood on
the stones of the church;[4] and Pope Innocent III took up the
same metaphor in the course of Langton's election: St. Thomas,
he said, wrote a special privilege for Christ Church, as it were,
in his blood.[5]

The process of undermining the claim of Magna Carta Beati
Thome to be an authentic act of Archbishop Thomas has at
the same time suggested that it was not produced in the great
lawsuit of 1186–1200. When, then, was it fabricated? What
later circumstances might have produced such an invention?

---

[1] *PUE*, ii. 379. Cf. Gervase, i. 35, *s.a.* 1186: 'miserabiles monachi compulsi
sunt ab omni gravamine sedem apostolicam appellare'.

[2] *Ep. Cant.*, p. 29.   [3] Above, p. 87.

[4] Above, p. 86 n. 1.

[5] 'Qui privilegium speciale pro ipsa [ecclesia] quasi sanguine suo scripsit'
(Migne, ccxv. 1048; Pott. 2940, to the prior and convent; repeated in the letter
to the king, Migne, ccxv. 1046; Pott. 2937).

The latter years of Hubert's pontificate (1201–5) did not provide a particularly suitable occasion. If Magna Carta had been composed between Hubert's death and Stephen Langton's election, it would have asserted, we may be sure, the monks' sole right to choose their archbishop, for the suffragans were claiming to participate; but the subject is not mentioned.[1] Thereafter, the monks were probably preoccupied by other matters until Langton gained possession of the see in 1213. During the next fifteen years Langton's behaviour might encourage the monks to strengthen their claims respecting the consecration of suffragans; for a survey of the consecrations celebrated by Langton shows that he only consecrated four suffragans in his metropolitan church (none of them after 1219), as compared with fifteen whom he consecrated elsewhere.[2] But apart from this, there seems to have been no reason why the monks should be apprehensive of Langton's intentions, no suggestion of plans for a rival collegiate church, of appropriation of conventual revenue, of intrusion of seculars into capitular business.[3] The chroniclers do not point to any discord between this archbishop and his cathedral community.

It is therefore surprising to find an indication of Magna Carta in a document dated within Langton's lifetime: nothing less than a confirmation of the charter by a papal letter of 21 January 1228. When in 1276 the prior of St. Gregory's and the dean of christianity of Canterbury inspected Magna Carta, they also inspected this confirmation by Pope Gregory IX. We do not know in what form the documents were presented for inspection: the prior and his colleague do not assert that they bore seals, or say how they determined their authenticity.

[1] The pope ruled against the suffragans, 20 Dec. 1206 (Migne ccxv. 1043); they raised the issue again when Walter of Evesham was elected in Aug. 1228 (Roger Wendover, *Flores historiarum*, ed. H. O. Coxe (Eng. Hist. Soc., 1841–4), iv. 171).

[2] The 'caucio Pandulphi legati de consecratione episcopi Londoniensis', addressed to the prior and convent, undertakes that the fact that he has caused Bishop Eustace to be consecrated elsewhere shall not prejudice them, or their church, or their archbishop: it does not mention St. Thomas (Canterbury, D. & C. Mun., Reg. A, fo. 63ᵛ).

[3] In 1236 the monks complained that Archbishops Stephen and Richard Wethershed, like Edmund, interfered in the appointment of officials and servants (below, p. 97).

They may not have insisted on seeing 'originals'. Be that as it may, the *inspeximus* would—if we had the original of it— provide the earliest extant texts of both documents.[1] The papal confirmation of 1228 does not in so many words recite the text of Magna Carta, though a few years later the method of inspection was adopted by the pope in confirming charters of Archbishop Anselm and King William II for Canterbury.[2] Instead, it provides a fairly complete précis of the charter's clauses, introduced by the words: 'Vobis sane insinuantibus intelleximus quod idem martir . . . certa edidit instituta, et confirmavit . . .', etc. From this formula we cannot be sure that the pope was actually shown Magna Carta, in original or in copy; for although *insinuare* could technically refer to the production of a document in court, it could have a more general sense, equivalent to the French *enseigner*.[3] Another doubt arises. This is the one extant letter in a whole dossier of Gregory IX's letters concerned with the privileges of Canterbury which is not in the papal register. It was surely a strange lapse on the part of the monks' proctors in 1228 if they procured so valuable a bull and failed to pay for its registration? Apart from this fact, and the unusual form in which the confirmation is cast, the letter has another feature which, though of itself hardly worth remark, must, in view of these other points, be taken into account: the address reads 'dilectis filiis priori et conventui ecclesie Christi Cantuariensis'. The title is familiar enough in

[1] Above, pp. 1, 2. It should be observed that the *inspeximus* does not survive in original. A copy of the papal letter of 21 Jan. 1228 is in Lambeth MS. 1212, p. 259 with the significant note: 'Istam non habemus sed monachi habent'; it is also copied into the archiepiscopal register of Thomas Arundel, vol. i, fo. 10^r (Lambeth) and in several registers at Canterbury: Reg. A, fo. 46^r, Reg. I, fo. 47^r (formerly 60), Reg. O, fo. 160^r (formerly 360); also in Lambeth, Cartae misc. XIII. 6 (ii). For text see appendix, p. 108.

[2] 1 July 1236: *Reg. Grégoire IX*, nos. 3233–5; *CPL*, i. 155. Copies are in Lambeth MS. 1212, p. 255.

[3] See the full text below, p. 108. Copies of valuable or fragile muniments were sometimes sent to Rome in place of originals: *Historians of the Church of York*, ed. J. Raine (RS, 1879–94), ii. 204; *Historia et cartularium monasterii S. Petri Gloucestrie*, ed. W. H. Hart (RS, 1863–7), iii. 10–17; *Historiae Anglicanae Scriptores X*, ed. R. Twysden (1652), col. 1833, 1867; *Ep. Cant.*, pp. 96, 417. For the meaning of *insinuare* cf. Lyndwood's gloss on a canon of Archbishop John Stratford: 'Insinuatione. id est apud acta iudicis publicatione vel transumptione' (*Provinciale*, 3, 13, 6 (ed. 1679), p. 181*a*). In the preambles to papal letters of this period the word seems to refer simply to the presentation of a written petition.

letters of the time, for example in those of Archbishop Edmund and the legate Otto; but the words 'ecclesie Christi' were seldom used in letters emanating from the chancery of Pope Gregory IX.[1] It is arguable that since the letter only exists in late copies, the familiar words crept in through the carelessness of a Canterbury scribe, just as some copies of genuine charters of Henry I received the addition 'dei gratia' to the king's title; but this is not particularly plausible when one remembers that in this copy we are dealing with a formal *inspeximus* of the papal bull. Doubt arises, therefore, whether the papal bull is genuine and whether, if forged, it was composed in 1228 or at some later date. An apparently authentic document of 1229[2] at first sight speaks in favour of authenticity. It is letters patent of Robert Bingham, certifying that he has been consecrated bishop of Salisbury at Wilton because of his infirmities, that

in confirmatione domini pape Gregorii noni quam indulsit predicte Cantuariensis ecclesic monachis perspeximus contineri quod non nisi in ecclesia Cantuariensi eius suffraganei consecrentur, sicut ex ipsa confirmatione manifestius apparet,

and that therefore the consecration was only celebrated at Wilton with the consent of the monks and without prejudice to their church. If the letter of Pope Gregory IX which was shown to the officiating bishops in May 1229 was the confirmation of 21 January 1228 now in question (whether or not it was

[1] There are four in Gregory IX's register: nos. 1807 (9 Feb. 1234, for St. Martin's, Dover), 3232 (1 July 1236), 3303 (23 Aug. 1236, addressing the prior of Christ Church with others), and 3430 (9 Jan. 1237); no. 1652 (22 Dec. 1233) is 'capitulo Cant.' and no. 5307 (8 Nov. 1240) 'capitulo ecclesie S. Trinitatis Cant.'. Honorius III, who on one occasion addressed the prior and convent 'ecclesie Christi Cant.' (3 Dec. 1220), a few days later (in connection with the translation of St. Thomas) addressed them as prior and convent 'ecclesie S. Thome Cant.' (18 Dec.: *Regesta papae Honorii III*, ed. P. Pressutti (Rome, 1888–95), nos. 2813, 2884).

[2] B.M., Add. Ch. 16354, folded at foot, with slit for sealing double queue. Fourteenth-century endorsements include: 'Cautio R. Sar' episcopi de consecratione sua extra Cant' de assensu nostro'. The ceremony took place on 27 May 1229, performed, as stated in the preamble, by Bishops Jocelin of Bath and William of Worcester on a commission from Master Richard, the elect of Canterbury. Similar *cauciones* of the officiating prelates and of the dean and chapter of Salisbury were copied with this in Canterbury, D. & C. Mun., Reg. A, fo. 66ʳ and Chartae antiquae, C. 120, m. 2.

genuine), it bears witness to the existence before May 1229 of Magna Carta in some form or other.[1] But if Magna Carta existed in 1229, it is strange that we should hear no more about it for six more years, and that when, on 20 November 1235, the monks obtained papal confirmation of their say in the consecration of suffragans, they did not cite Magna Carta, as they did three years later.[2] If Magna Carta did not exist in 1229, it is hard to see how the papal letter shown to the bishops in May can have been the existing confirmation of 21 January 1228. They may have been shown a genuine letter of the same date or a forgery; it may have been an original or a copy. There was no need for it to be so elaborate as the existing bull or for it to mention St. Thomas: it merely had to safeguard the monks' say in the consecration of suffragans. To Jocelin of Bath, one of the officiating bishops, there would be nothing strange in this. Had not he been obliged to recognize the rights of the prior and convent when he was consecrated at Reading in 1206?[3]

The evidence for the existence of Magna Carta in 1227[4] or in 1229 is so inconclusive that the inquiry must be pursued to find more certain traces. In passing, we may remark that on 20 July 1231 Gregory IX granted the prior and convent of Canterbury, at the king's request, that notwithstanding lapse of time, they might use certain privileges and indults, given by popes and by their archbishops, which because of impediments they had not used. This grant was renewed by the pope on 3 January 1236.[5] By the time of this renewal Edmund of Abingdon was archbishop (consecrated on 2 April 1234).

---

[1] Even if the papal letter of 21 Jan. 1228 was genuine, it does not follow that the pope had actually seen Magna Carta or that an 'original' of that document had been composed at this date; but the substance of its terms must already have been thought out to provide the material for the papal letter.

[2] See below, pp. 95, 98.

[3] Hist. MSS. Comm., *8th Rept.*, app. i, p. 320*b*.

[4] i.e. before it could be used in Rome to obtain a confirmation on 21 Jan. 1228.

[5] *Reg. Grégoire IX*, nos. 694, 2892; *CPL*, i. 128, 149. Copies are at Canterbury: D. & C. Mun., Reg. A, fo. 38ʳ (formerly 45) and Reg. I, fo. 55ʳ. This recalls Eadmer's story about the intensive search of the Christ Church archives undertaken in 1120, which led to the 'discovery' of the primacy privileges produced at Rome in 1123 (see R. W. Southern, 'The Canterbury forgeries', *EHR*, lxxiii (1958), 217–24). Perhaps a similar search was being undertaken with similar 'discoveries' in view.

Metropolitan and monks were once more involved in unhappy wrangling, of which a monastic partisan has written a long account in continuation to Gervase of Canterbury.[1] Here it is unnecessary to re-tell the whole story; but it is significant that the subjects of dispute in the early stages (between 1234 and 1238) revived the issue of the time of Baldwin and Hubert, and that this time, unlike the previous occasion, the authority of St. Thomas was invoked.

In June 1235 Edmund alarmed the prior and convent of Christ Church by consecrating Robert Grosseteste as bishop of Lincoln and Hugh as bishop of St. Asaph, at Reading instead of Canterbury.[2] The monks got a written pledge from the archbishop that this was only permissible with their assent.[3] They went further, and on 20 November 1235 got confirmation of their right, with special reference to this incident and to Edmund's pledge, from Pope Gregory IX.[4] The indult makes no reference to the pope's earlier confirmation (21 January 1228) of St. Thomas's charter, and does not mention St. Thomas, but asserts the convent's right 'de iure communi et indulgentia speciali ab apostolica vobis sede concessa'. But if the monks' proctor at the Curia or the papal chancery clerks did not see fit to refer to St. Thomas's charter, the monks had evidently impressed Robert Grosseteste with the fact of its existence. The *caucio* which he gave on the occasion of his consecration reads :[5]

Quia in carta gloriosi martiris Thome auctoritate domini pape

---

[1] Gervase, ii. 130–85, cf. Stubbs, ibid. i, pp. xx–xxi. See a modern account in W. Wallace, *St. Edmund of Canterbury* (1893), ch. xviii, and for a shorter and more recent statement, C. H. Lawrence, *St. Edmund of Abingdon* (Oxford, 1960), pp. 164–8.

[2] See Grosseteste's letter, written beforehand to the archbishop, dwelling on the unnecessary offence this would give to the monks of Canterbury (*R. Grosseteste . . . Epistolae*, ed. H. R. Luard (RS, 1861), pp. 54–6; cf. F. S. Stevenson, *Robert Grosseteste* (1899), pp. 114–17).

[3] Canterbury, D. & C. Mun., Reg. A, fo. 62ʳ (formerly 69), Reg. I, fo. 97ʳ (formerly 110), Reg. O, fo. 185ʳ (formerly 387), Chartae antiquae, C. 120; Lambeth, Reg. T. Arundel, vol. i, fo. 10ʳ; B.M., Add. MS. 6159, fo. 288ʳ.

[4] *Reg. Grégoire IX*, no. 2840 ('Cum sicut asseritis'); *CPL*, i. 149. Also in Canterbury, Reg. A and Chartae antiquae, C. 120 and in Lambeth, Reg. T. Arundel as above, n. 3. For text see appendix.

[5] Canterbury, D. &. C. Mun., Chartae antiquae, C. 120, m. 1 (a 15th-century roll). Wharton apparently saw the original *caucio* with Grosseteste's seal attached: his transcript is in Lambeth MS. 582, p. 62.

Gregorii noni confirmata, sicut ex ipsa confirmatione plenius apparet, specialiter hec perspeximus contineri quod suffraganei Cantuariensis ecclesie alibi quam in ecclesia Cantuariensi cui tenentur ex professione et debita subiectione nullatenus consecrentur, nisi de communi assensu totius capituli monachorum Cantuariensium, nos non nisi de predictorum monachorum assensu requisito et per venerabilem patrem nostrum Edmundum dei gratia Cantuariensem archiepiscopum obtento munus consecrationis ab eodem et a venerabilibus fratribus nostris videlicet I. Bathoniensi, R. Saresbiriensi, R. Londoniensi, H. Eliensi, R. Herefordensi apud Rading' obtinuimus. In cuius rei testimonium sigillum nostrum huic scripto apponi fecimus.

It is to be noted that Grosseteste uses the very words of clause IX of the charter; on the other hand, he does not say that he has seen the charter, but implies that he is persuaded of its contents by the confirmation of Gregory IX. The Great Charter is indeed elusive!

What prompted the monks' next move is unknown, but within a month of obtaining the papal indult regarding consecrations they got a papal mandate to judges delegate to hear their action against Archbishop Edmund for the recovery of what they claimed as their rights in the advowsons and *exennia* of the monastery's manors.[1] In the course of this case the charter of St. Thomas emerges unquestionably from the earlier obscurity. Royal writs of prohibition enabled Edmund to evade the formal process in the court of the judges delegate, and at long last an agreement between the parties was reached out of court in December 1237.[2] The archbishop had made some concessions, but the arrangement provided for ratification of the terms by pope and king.[3] Whether either of the parties had come to agreement in perfect good faith is questionable. The archbishop immediately set out for Rome, accompanied by the archdeacon of Canterbury, Simon Langton, his monk-chaplain Eustace, and clerks. Representatives of the

[1] The mandate (Viterbo, 22 Dec. 1235) to the abbots of Boxley, St. Radegund's (Bradsole), and Lessness is not in the papal register. It is included in the judges' report printed from Canterbury, D. &. C. Mun., Chartae antiquae, A. 168 in Wallace, p. 488.

[2] Printed by Wallace, pp. 495–8. Texts are in Canterbury, D. & C. Mun., Reg. A, fo. 174ᵛ and Reg. E, fo. 63ᵛ.

[3] Gervase, ii. 131.

prior and convent also went, apparently to reopen their case against the archbishop.[1] They had reason to be nervous, for Edmund's actions during his long sojourn in the Curia threatened their pretensions at various points. On 14 April 1238 he obtained an indult to consecrate bishops outside Canterbury when urgent need required, notwithstanding the grant which he had made to the monks and which the pope had twice confirmed.[2] On 17 May 1238 the pope informed the legate Otto, in England, that the archbishop had asked permission to found a collegiate church and endow it, and that the proctors of Christ Church opposed it, saying that they had other muniments at home, besides the award of 1200 recorded in the register of Innocent III.[3] Battle was being joined on the old issue.

But it is time to see how Magna Carta comes into the litigation. If it was available, it was bound to be a major weapon in the monks' armoury. It was alleged in the monks' *libellus*, when they sued before the judges delegate for advowsons, *exennia*, etc., in 1236. This document, drawn up before 10 May 1236, complained against the archbishop

quod cum [prior et conventus] liberam habere debeant potestatem ponendi et amovendi officiales et servientes suos tam intus quam extra, vos et predicti predecessores vestri [Stephanus et Ricardus] iniuste impedivistis eos, in eorum grave preiudicium, quominus predicta potestate uti possent, silicet ponendi pro voluntate sua tres officiales et eosdem amovendi, videlicet sacristam, celerarium, et camerarium, item tres servientes, videlicet duos ianitores, silicet unum ecclesie et alterum curie, et senescallum in aula, et sic veniendo

---

[1] The proctors' objections are reported in a papal letter to the legate Otto, 26 May 1238 (*Reg. Grégoire IX*, no. 4363; *CPL*, i. 174); cf. letter of 8 Nov. 1240 (*Reg. Grégoire IX*, no. 5307; *CPL*, i. 192).

[2] *Reg. Grégoire IX*, no. 4339, not printed; *CPL*, i. 173. Texts are in Lambeth MS. 1212, p. 260, Lambeth, Reg. T. Arundel, vol. i, fo. 10ʳ, Cambridge, St. John's Coll. MS. N. 6, fo. [4ᵛ]. The pope had renewed his confirmation as recently as 28 Jan. 1238 (*Reg. Grégoire IX*, no. 4045, misdated 'xv kal. Feb.', not printed; *CPL*, i. 167; Lambeth, Reg. T. Arundel, vol. i, fo. 10ʳ); for texts, see appendix. The letter of 14 Apr. was followed by a complementary grant that the archbishop might wear the pallium when consecrating bishops outside the province of Canterbury (26 May 1238: *Reg. Grégoire IX*, no. 4361, not printed; *CPL*, i. 174; Lambeth MS. 1212, p. 265).

[3] *Reg. Grégoire IX*, no. 4345; *CPL*, i. 173. For the award of 1200 see *Ep. Cant.*, p. 517 (cf. Pott. 1386).

contra cartas et concessiones predecessorum vestrorum et precipue contra cartam sancti Thome martiris.[1]

A trace of the charter in the Curia is also found during these years, in January 1238, when the privilege concerning consecration of suffragans is said to be claimed by the monks 'ex antiqua consuetudine Cantuariensis ecclesie et speciali concessione beati Thome martiris vestri archiepiscopi', and as confirmed by Archbishop Edmund.[2] This is in marked contrast to the silence about St. Thomas in the earlier papal confirmation: in 1235 the same claim had been made 'de iure communi et indulgentia speciali ab apostolica vobis sede concessa'. Both the *libellus* of May 1236 and the papal confirmation of 28 January 1238 are best explained on the supposition that Magna Carta was in existence. Part of it had apparently been quoted by Grosseteste in June 1235, but the absence of a reference to it in the papal confirmation of 20 November 1235 suggests that it was not ready to be taken to Rome when that confirmation was sought: it was at that time quietly incubating at Canterbury.

The supposition that 1235–6 was the time of its manufacture is strengthened by a scandal which arose in Canterbury in 1237–8 over a forgery. This affair is reported briefly by Matthew Paris, and with more detail by the continuator of Gervase.[3] Their accounts are supplemented and corrected by several papal letters, by a letter from the archbishop's officials to the papal legate, Otto,[4] and by a badly damaged record of an enquiry conducted by order of the legate in February 1238.[5] Making allowance for incompleteness and bias in these sources, we can form some ideas about the emergence of Magna Carta; but no certainty. When people implicated in a fraud tell their story we cannot accept it with full confidence.

[1] Wallace, p. 488, from Canterbury, D. & C. Mun., Chartae antiquae, A. 168, which I quote.

[2] See p. 97 n. 2.

[3] M. Paris, *Chronica majora*, ed. H. R. Luard (RS, 1872–83), iii. 492–3 and *Historia Anglorum*, ed. F. Madden (RS, 1866–9), ii. 411, and more sketchily in his 'Vita Edmundi', ed. C. H. Lawrence, in *St. Edmund of Abingdon* (1960), pp. 254–5; Gervase, ii. 130–3.

[4] See Lawrence, p. 163, from P.R.O., S.C. 11/159.

[5] Canterbury, D. &. C. Mun., Chartae antiquae, A. 227. I am indebted to Dr. William Urry, who discovered this fragment, for kindly bringing it to my notice.

In the course of the years 1236–7, when the prior and convent of Canterbury were suing the archbishop before judges
delegate, a monk of Christ Church, Ralph of Orpington,
revealed to the archbishop that he had been concerned in
forgery.[1] The forgery related to a charter of St. Thomas, which
we believe to be Magna Carta. According to Brother Ralph, he
had been called in by the prior, John of Chetham, to help in its
production after the sacrist and keeper of muniments, Brother
Simon of Hartlip, had an accident with a genuine original
charter of St. Thomas. Simon, when he eventually confessed
to a part in the fraud,[2] told the chapter that messengers from
Rome had brought back to him charters which had been sent
there for preparing the monks' lawsuits. He picked up the
charter of St. Thomas carelessly, and inadvertently tore the
document from the seal. Much concerned at the mishap, he
told the prior. The prior, as one ignorant of the law, guided by
monastic simplicity, advised that the charter be copied word
for word. The two then asked Brother Ralph of Orpington to
use his skill in attaching the rewritten charter to the original
seal. When the archbishop heard Brother Ralph's story, he was
apparently on the point of leaving Canterbury, and he declared
sentence of excommunication on any who should dare to forge
any charter or privilege or use a forgery and who did not
confess their fault within eight days.[3] Although the prior was
present, his monastic simplicity did not allow him to regard
himself as guilty, and he continued to celebrate the divine
office with a clear conscience. Before the archbishop left for
Rome, he apparently obtained from the prior his version of the
affair and proceeded to absolve both the prior and Brother
Simon. They swore that they had not used the rewritten charter
and that the rewriting was unknown to the rest of the community, and they destroyed it. All this had happened before the
archbishop set out for Rome late in December 1237. He took
with him, as far as the abbey of St. Bertin, the expert on seals,
Brother Ralph, but for whose confession he would have known
nothing of the forgery. But the vindictive prior secured
Ralph's return to Canterbury, where he was thrust into prison,

---

[1] Ibid.   [2] Gervase, ii. 131.
[3] Canterbury, D. & C. Mun., Chartae antiquae, A. 227.

and (according to the continuator of Gervase) got leave after a fortnight to betake himself to Melrose Abbey, where he assumed the Cistercian habit. This caused Robert of Abingdon and the archbishop's official to appeal to the legate on Ralph's behalf,[1] and led the archbishop to get papal authority to forbid the prior and convent to punish monks who revealed excesses of their fellow-monks to the archbishop when he held inquiry.[2]

While the archbishop pursued his dispute in the papal Curia during the early months of 1238, the forgery at Canterbury was brought to the knowledge of the whole community. On 20 February Albert, chancellor of Cologne, came down with a commission from the legate to enquire into the business and report.[3] Prior John and Brother Simon told their artless story. The rest of the community vowed that this was the first they had heard of the forgery, and that it had not been used in any litigation or business transaction.

But the frauds of the prior had not been fully exposed. Archbishop Edmund's complaints in the Curia resulted in a papal commission to the legate Otto (22 May 1238),[4] which ordered him to make a thorough examination of the muniments of the church of Canterbury, to assign to the archbishop those which concerned him, and to the prior and convent those which concerned them. Those of common interest were to be held by the archbishop.[5] Forgeries, certain or suspect, were to

---

[1] Lawrence, p. 163.

[2] 14 May 1238: *Reg. Grégoire IX*, no. 4340, extracts only printed; CPL, i. 173. Copied in Lambeth MS. 1212, p. 260 with the note: 'Item habetur duplicata de regestro sub bulla Gregorii decimi infra.' Printed from Canterbury, D. & C. Mun., Reg. A, fo. 32ᵛ (formerly 39), where dated 'ii id.', with wrong date (2 Nov.) by Wallace, p. 499, and discussed by him, pp. 282–3.

[3] Canterbury, D. & C. Mun., Chartae antiquae, A. 227. This visit was presumably prompted by the letter of Robert of Abingdon and the archbishop's official.

[4] *Reg. Grégoire IX*, no. 4371; CPL, i. 174. An abridged, undated version in Gervase, ii. 132. The legate also had to enquire about the archbishop's proposal for a collegiate church at Maidstone, under a commission of 17 May 1238 (above, p. 97).

[5] Duplicates were to be shared. The archbishop was to provide the prior and convent with copies of other documents of common interest, when convenient. The bi-lingual charter of Henry I confirming to Archbishop Anselm the temporalities of Canterbury (*Regesta Regum*, no. 840), existed in quadruplicate. One (Lambeth, Carte misc. XI. 1), which found its way to the archbishops' archives, has the endorsement: 'Detur archiepiscopo quia repertum est duplicatum/ii

be sent under seal to the pope. This brought the legate, with the archbishop, to Canterbury in autumn 1238. Otto's inquiry confirmed the guilt of the prior and the sacrist in the matter of St. Thomas's charter and uncovered another scandal. For when the archbishop asked to see a privilege of Pope Alexander III which he said he had entrusted to the prior's predecessor, John of Sittingbourne, it could not be found. The monks hesitated, until at length Brother Bartholomew of Sandwich admitted that he had burnt it; and the reason for the burning is given by Matthew Paris.[1] Prior John of Chetham, it seems, 'pietate minus discreta', had secretly erased in this document what was detrimental to the convent's interests and had added favourable words; and because the erasures were bound to be found out and would give the community a bad name for forgery, the privilege was burnt. Whether Matthew Paris's explanation is the right one or not, it provides a reason for the burning of the bull, and that it was burnt there is no doubt. As a result of the legate's enquiry, John of Chetham resigned the priorate into the legate's hands; his resignation was accepted and he went off at once to become a Carthusian monk. Simon of Hartlip likewise transferred 'ad arctiorem ordinem', and Bartholomew of Sandwich was sent by the legate to stay at Westminster Abbey until further orders.[2] We do not know what caused the legate to act so severely as this. Maybe the confessed destruction of a papal privilege counted for more than an allegedly innocent renewal of an archbishop's charter. Be that as it may, it was a drastic purge applied to the convent. Years later, after Archbishop Edmund's death, the convent of Christ Church thought fit to get from the pope a recognition that only three had been implicated in the rewriting and sealing of the privilege of St. Thomas ('in spiritu simplicitatis') and that the rest of the community was blameless. 'As they are ennobled by the glory

quadrupl.'. Another surviving original (B.M. MS. Cotton ch. vii. 1) is endorsed: 'Ista quadruplicata est Anselmo archiepiscopo Latine et Anglice', and this note was copied in the list of the archives of the see in Lambeth MS. 1212. A third original survives in B.M. Campbell ch. xxix. 5. Cf. 'Table of Canterbury Archbishopric Charters', ed. I. J. Churchill (*Camden Miscellany*, xv (Royal Hist. Soc., 1929)), p. 1.

[1] Gervase, ii. 133; M. Paris, *Chronica majora*, iii. 492–3.
[2] Gervase, ii. 133–4.

of the martyr', wrote the pope, 'it is not right that their good fame should be traduced or their innocence suspected.'[1]

Although this incident of the forgery clearly bears on the origin of Magna Carta, it does little more than offer a series of alternatives, which must now be stated and examined: either the 'carta Sancti Thome', which is said to have been rewritten word for word, was Magna Carta or it was not; either Prior John of Chetham and Brother Simon destroyed their handiwork utterly or they left behind them at least a copy of it; either they had an original, genuine or forged, which (as they asserted) they copied or they invented their 'rewritten' charter; and if they had an exemplar, either they made an exact copy or they introduced interpolations. Balance of probability favours the identification of the forged charter of 1237 with Magna Carta. No other charter of Thomas Becket is known which could have profited the monks at this juncture, and Magna Carta would give them what they wanted. It seems unnecessary to predicate another charter. The one difficulty in making this identification seems to lie in the statement of Albert of Cologne that the prior and Brother Simon destroyed their handiwork. If it was destroyed, how came it to be inspected in 1276? Our reply to this must depend in some measure on our estimate of the contemporary judgement on the prior and his accomplices. If their pose of monastic guilelessness was accepted by the authorities, the latter would suppose that the forgery was a matter of form, that the irregularly sealed document embodied a genuine text of St. Thomas. They would be willing, and indeed anxious, for other copies to be preserved. But, in fact, the prior was apparently convicted of fraudulent intention in the doctoring of the papal bull, and his judges may well have been suspicious about the charter of Thomas: certainly their judgement on all the offenders was severe. It is perhaps most probable that the prior and his accomplices failed to reveal the manufacture of more than one copy and that in this way one survived.[2]

---

[1] 5 Mar. 1241: *Reg. Grégoire IX*, no. 5388; *CPL*, i. 194. Printed from Canterbury, Reg. A, fo. 68ᵛ by Wallace, p. 499, whose translation of the last sentence (p. 281) is adopted here. Dom Wilfrid's account of the incident confuses the burnt bull of Alexander III with the charter of St. Thomas (p. 280).

[2] One may recall with what complacency a Cistercian abbot of Meaux re-

Supposing the forgery to be Magna Carta, was it invented in 1235–6 or at an earlier date? Here, again, there can be no certainty. The most important clauses of Magna Carta are indicated, it has been seen, in a papal letter of 21 January 1228. That would settle the matter if the letter were above suspicion. But the letter is open to suspicion, and the stubborn fact remains that in the next seven years our sources are silent on the subject of any privilege given by St. Thomas. The argument from silence is very strong here; and we must admit that the man who could forge Magna Carta would be capable of forging the confirmation of Pope Gregory IX. It may be that the forgery incubated over several years, and that the papal letter of 20 July 1231 and its renewal on 3 January 1236, which permitted the prior and convent to produce hitherto unused muniments, are signs that the forgery was on its way. The document may have existed in draft long before the bold spirits were found who would try their hand at making an 'original'. Too little is known of medieval forgers in general and of the habits of Canterbury forgers in particular to admit of certainty; there seems to be no compelling reason for implicating anyone but John of Chetham and his accomplices.

The intriguing questions remain whether the forgers had actually removed a genuine seal of Archbishop Thomas from a genuine document and whether they were working on, and adding to, a genuine grant of much more limited scope. As was remarked at the beginning of this article, parts of Magna Carta are unexceptionable. But whether these parts are traces of an authentic act or merely evidence of the ingenuity of the forgers (thinking to add an air of verisimilitude by introducing, for example, a reference to the fellow exiles)[1] we cannot say. Enough doubtful matters have been raised.

corded how, when the first abbot, Adam, surrendered certain title-deeds to Archbishop Roger of York to be burnt, and received compensation in money for what was relinquished, duplicate deeds were kept back by the monks, *ut deus disposuit*, for production on a later day ('cartae autem originales . . . duplices habebantur: . . . una carta originalis de donatione Henrici archiepiscopi et alia de confirmatione capituli in monasterio nostro, ut deus disposuit, fuerant reservatae.' *Chronica monasterii de Melsa*, ed. E. A. Bond (RS, 1866–8), i. 94–5).

[1] The martyr's kinsmen were remembered for a long time at Christ Church; allowances were being made for some of them in 1222 (see Hist. MSS. Comm., *5th Rept.*, app. i, p. 431*b*, where dated 1221).

Confining our conclusions to what is probable, even though not susceptible of absolute proof, the evidence which has been produced seems to establish that Magna Carta Beati Thome was forged in the interests of the monks of Christ Church long after Thomas Becket's death. It was not available to them in the great lawsuit which occupied the last years of the twelfth century and it only emerged clearly into the light of day in the time of Archbishop Edmund. As soon as it was produced it was discredited by the confession of one of the forgers. Put away and forgotten or discreetly suppressed, it was brought out a generation later, and from 1276 onwards was recopied and quoted in the later Middle Ages. It is by no means the most notable of the forgeries for which the monks of Christ Church, over the centuries, were responsible. Compared with the primacy documents forged in the twelfth century[1] and the plenary indulgence forged in the fourteenth,[2] it is historically of slight importance. But equally it is evidence of the incurable corruption which infected splendid, wealthy, and jealous monastic communities like Christ Church. 'Holy Father', said Archdeacon Simon Langton to Pope Gregory IX in 1238, 'there is not a single sort of forgery that is not perpetrated in the church of Canterbury. For they have forged in gold, in lead, in wax, and in every kind of metal.'[3] His outburst was understandable. Those who did these things and condoned them had no common sense of honesty. There is peculiar irony in the manufacture of Magna Carta Beati Thome for the purpose of defeating Archbishop Edmund, for the archbishop was in his lifetime devoted to the cult of St. Thomas, and later on the hagiographers drew constant comparisons between Edmund the confessor and Thomas the martyr.

[1] Southern, *ubi supra*, pp. 193–226.

[2] Raymonde Foreville, *Le Jubilé de Saint Thomas Becket du xiii* au xv* siècle (1220–1470)* (Paris, 1958), pp. 10–11, 131, 136–7. Equally significant, though less far-reaching in their claims, are the Canterbury forgeries of title-deeds which have been discussed by Florence Harmer, *Anglo-Saxon Writs* (Manchester, 1952) and by T. A. M. Bishop and P. Chaplais, *Facsimiles of English Royal Writs to A.D. 1100 presented to V. H. Galbraith* (Oxford, 1957). The erasure and rewriting of which Matthew Paris speaks in connection with the privilege of Pope Alexander III (above, p. 101) is reminiscent of the clumsy tampering with writs of Edward the Confessor and William the Conqueror.

[3] Gervase, ii. 132.

APPENDIX

The text of the charter of St. Thomas which follows is based upon Lambeth, Cartae misc. XIII. 6 (ii) [= M], from the archiepiscopal archives, written in 1286, and it has been fully collated with all other texts so far noted: at Lambeth, MS. 1212 (register of the see), p. 258 [= L], and Reg. W. Courtenay, fo. 46ᵛ [= W]; at Cambridge, St. John's College, MS. N. 6, fo. [5ʳ] (formerly 14) [= N]; at Canterbury, D. & C. Mun., Reg. A, fo. 38ᵛ (formerly 45) [= A], Reg. A, fo. 61ʳ (formerly 68) [= B], Reg. I, fo. 85ᵛ [= J], Reg. O, fo. 159ᵛ (formerly 359) [= O], Chartae antiquae, C.120, m. 1 [= C], Chartae antiquae, C.204 [= D]; at the B.M., Cotton MS. Galba E. iii, fo. 55ʳ (formerly 54) [= E], Cotton MS. Galba E. iv, fo. 58ᵛ [= G].¹ Each text has many errors and an indication of all variants seems neither necessary nor useful. Variants are shown where the M reading is plainly at fault or where other texts give readings which are at least equally plausible.

The four papal letters are all printed from the texts in Lambeth, Reg. T. Arundel, vol. i, fo. 10ʳ. They have been collated with the other texts cited above, but these provide no significant variant.

Punctuation and capitalization of the manuscripts have not been retained, and the use of *c* and *t* is normalized.

---

*Carta beati Thome martiris de libertatibus ecclesie Christi Cantuariensis*ᵃ

Thomas dei gratia Cantuariensis archiepiscopus et apostolice sedis legatus omnibus ad quos presens scriptum pervenerit salutem et benedictionem.

Preteritorum casus temporumᵇ iccirco litterarum memorie commendantur ut per transacta mala vel presentia futura cautius valeant evitari. Ad omnium igitur notitiam volumus pervenire quod sancta Cantuariensis ecclesia, a cuius uberibus coaluimus, que nos auctore deo licet indignos in id quod sumus promovit, in odium capitis nostri multis calamitatibus et anxietatibus variis usque in septenniumᶜ pressa est, quod tota fere novitᵈ latinitas, et adhuc minis et

---

¹ The last two MSS. were used by Giles (see above, p. 78), but described by him as Galba A. iii and iv.

ᵃ *Title in* M, *which continues*: qui fuit cancellarius H. regis secundi quando data fuit carta de ecclesia Dovor' ecclesie Christi Cantuar'.   ᵇ *om.* temporum M.
ᶜ in septennium CEGW, *om.* in M; in sempiternum ABJLNO; ad sempiternum D.   ᵈ tota fere novit ACDJLNW, *reading* tuta B; fere novit tota M; fere tota novit EG.

dampnis innumeris cotidie fatigatur. Que cum sol esse soleat occidentis et in nostris temporibus eius obfuscata est claritas, quodlibet tormentum sed et mille mortis genera, si tot occurrerent, libentius exciperemus in domino quam sustineremus sub dissimulatione hiis diebus mala que patitur. Nos itaque, licet parati simus pro pace ipsius et indempnitate capud et corpus persecutoribus exponere, et ne pereat vel quid modicum perdat perire, quicquid de nobis contingat, indempnitati tamen eius*e* prospicere volentes in futurum, (I) ipsam ecclesiam cum omnibus personis, terris et tenementis*f*, pertinentiis et proventibus, libertatibus quoque et dignitatibus suis, sub dei protectione et curie Romane et nostra ponimus, prohibentes ex parte dei sub perpetuo etiam anathemate ne quis iura Cantuariensis ecclesie absque consensu totius capituli monachorum Cantuariensium aliquo integumento vel causa alienare presumat. A seculis enim inauditum est quod aliquis Cantuariensem ecclesiam leserit et non sit contritus aut correctus a Christo domino.[1] (II) Raptores igitur et alienatores possessionum, dignitatum et rerum detentores, consentaneos quodque et participes, et quicunque secreta capituli malitiose revelaverit alicui homini*g* usque ad condignam satisfactionem perpetuo anathemate condempnamus. (III) Nec volumus pati ut aliquis alterius professionis vel ordinis secretis capituli misceatur. (IV) Ea quoque specialiter que ad dilectos filios nostros monachos eiusdem ecclesie pertinent, videlicet villas, possessiones earundem*h* villarum et possessionum ecclesias, et exennia cum pertinentiis et proventibus, sicut in suis continetur munimentis,*j* eis inperpetuum confirmamus. Terras etiam et ecclesias pensionales, iura quoque et libertates, et res et quicquid habent vel habituri sunt, eis concedimus et confirmamus. (V) Officialium quoque suorum et servientium ponendi vel amovendi, omniumque que ad eos pertinent, tam intus quam extra, liberam concedimus et confirmamus inperpetuum disponendi libertatem, sicut eis melius et utilius visum fuerit de communi consilio capituli sui, quatinus sicut easdem habemus in possessionibus nostris secundum cartas regum libertates, similem habeamus in portionibus potestatem, salva nobis et suc-

---

[1] Cf. 'Quis enim a seculis in sanctorum sedem, ecclesiam Cantuariensem, tam immaniter insurrexit et non est precipitatus ex alto' (*Materials*, vi. 592).

---

e tamen eius BJMNO; tamen ipsius DEGL; tamen causam ipsius A; tam ipsius C; tanquam ipsius W.   *f* *add* suis CDEGLW, *and corr. in* N.   *g* homini BCJMNOW; hominum ADEGL.   *h* *add* -que ACDEGLW *and corr.* in N.   *j* monumentis M.

cessoribus nostris regulari disciplina. (VI) Adicimus ad hec auctoritate qua fungimur et indulgemus ut in malefactores ecclesie, si semel et secundo commoniti noluerint emendare, suspensionis, excommunicationis, et anathematis ferant sententiam; (VII) et ut liceat eis omni tempore contra omnia gravamina sedem apostolicam appellare. (VIII) Et quia minantur adversarii quod sedem metropolitanam vel primatus Anglie que a tempore beati Gregorii pape[k] per sanctum Augustinum in Cantuaria statuta est alias velint transferre, sub perpetuo prohibemus anathemate ne quis hominum aliquo integumento vel causa unquam[l] hoc attemptare presumat. (IX) Prohibemus etiam[m] ne episcopi Cantuariensis ecclesie suffraganei[n] alibi consecrentur quam in ecclesia Cantuariensi cui tenentur ex professione et debita subiectione, nisi de communi consensu totius capituli monachorum Cantuariensium. (X) Nec crisma vel oleum[o] per Cantuariensem provinciam dividendum aliunde quam ab ecclesia Cantuariensi aliquo tempore percipiatur. (XI) Volumus etiam et obsecramus in domino ut monachi Cantuariensis ecclesie suffraganeis eiusdem ecclesie, episcopis scilicet et abbatibus, omnem reverentiam exhibeant et honorem; ipsi quoque episcopi monachos Cantuariensis ecclesie in vera que deus est diligant caritate. Dignum siquidem est et consensum rationi ut qui eidem ecclesie Cantuariensi[p] debita tenentur ex professione simul et subiectione veram adinvicem observare debeant dilectionem, salva nobis et successoribus nostris debita reverentia et auctoritate. (XII) Clericis quoque et laycis qui coexules nostri facti sunt et participes laboris, omnia iura sua,[q] redditus, et ecclesias confirmamus, et obsecramus in domino ne quis eis iniuriam vel molestiam faciat. Si quis autem hominum huius nostre confirmationis[r] paginam infringere, vel ecclesiam Cantuariensem in aliquo vexare vel diminuere voluerit, vel dilectis filiis nostris monachis aliquam inferre voluerit molestiam, eternam dei et nostram habeat maledictionem nisi ante mortem cum restitutione ablatorum condignam ecclesie fecerit[s] restitutionem. Omnibus autem diligentibus et foventibus eam dei omnipotentis optamus gratiam, et sanctorum omnium qui in ecclesia Cantuariensi requiescunt societatem et nostram donamus benedictionem. Amen.[t]

---

[k] om. pape ACDEG; del. pape corr in N.   [l] vel causa umquam ACDEGJLW, -um erased in E; om. BMNO and add vel umquam in margin, corr. in N.   [m] etiam CDEGJLW, om. BMO; insuper A, interlined (? original hand) in N.   [n] add vel abbates DEG.   [o] olium M.   [p] eccl. Cant. AEGJM, transp. BCDLNOW.   [q] om. sua BMNO, interlined in B.   [r] confirm. nostre M.   [s] faciat M.   [t] om. Amen D: word erased before Amen in N.

Bulla concernens certas libertates ecclesie sancte Cantuariensis[1]

Gregorius episcopus servus servorum dei dilectis filiis priori et conventui ecclesie Christi Cantuariensis salutem et apostolicam benedictionem.

Cum ecclesiam vestram pro beati Thome martiris reverentia qui eam suo pretioso sanguine consecravit speciali diligamus affectu, eo libentius ipsam super hiis que in ea martir ipse constituit vel concessit eidem debemus et volumus confovere quo favore maiori digna sunt facta ipsius martiris et sincerius diligimus prefatam ecclesiam et eundem martirem devotius veneramur. Vobis sane insinuantibus intelleximus quod idem martir contra alienatores, raptores, et illicitos detentores iurium, possessionum, dignitatum, et aliorum bonorum ipsius ecclesie certa edidit instituta; et confirmavit ipsi ecclesie possessiones et villas cum exenniis et aliis pertinentiis earumdem, iura quoque, libertates, et alia bona sua; Cantuariensibus etiam monachis assumendi sibi servitores et removendi eos libertatem indulsit; atque constituit ut non nisi in Cantuariensi ecclesia suffraganei consecrentur, specialibus constitutionibus editis super libertatibus ipsius ecclesie conservandis. Nos ergo, vestris precibus inclinati, quod super hiis ab eodem martire provide factum est, sicut in eius litteris continetur, auctoritate apostolica confirmamus et presentis scripti patrocinio communimus. Nulli ergo omnino hominum liceat hanc paginam nostre confirmationis infringere vel ei ausu temerario contraire. Siquis autem hoc attemptare presumpserit, indignationem omnipotentis dei et beatorum Petri et Pauli apostolorum eius se noverit incursurum.

Dat' Laterani, xii kal. Februarii pontificatus nostri anno primo [21 January 1228].

Bulla concernens consecrationes episcoporum Cantuariensis provincie[2]

Gregorius episcopus servus servorum dei dilectis filiis priori et conventui Cantuariensi salutem et apostolicam benedictionem.

Cum sicut asseritis et in litteris venerabilis fratris nostri E. Cantuariensis archiepiscopi dicitur contineri consecrationes episcoporum Cantuariensis provincie in ecclesia Cantuariensi de iure communi et indulgentia speciali ab apostolica vobis sede concessa debeant celebrari, et nuper dictus archiepiscopus contra id veniens, de vestro tamen assensu, consecrationem venerabilis fratris nostri Lincolniensis episcopi suffraganei sui apud ecclesiam de Radinges propter loci vicinitatem duxerit celebrandam, vobis auctoritate presentium

---

[1] For other texts see p. 78 n. 2 and p. 92 n. 1.
[2] For other texts see p. 95 n. 4.

indulgemus ut nullum vobis ex consecratione predicta imposterum preiudicium generetur. Nulli ergo omnino hominum liceat hanc paginam nostre concessionis infringere vel ei ausu temerario contraire. Siquis autem [. . . etc.].

Dat' Viterbii, xii kal. Decembris pontificatus nostri anno nono [20 November 1235].

Bulla ut absque consensu capituli extra ecclesiam Cantuariensem nullus suffraganeus consecretur[1]

Gregorius episcopus servus servorum dei dilectis filiis priori et conventui Cantuariensi salutem et apostolicam benedictionem.

Cum a nobis petitur quod iustum est et honestum tam vigor equitatis quam ordo exigit rationis ut id per sollicitudinem officii nostri ad debitum perducatur effectum. Significastis siquidem nobis quod ex antiqua consuetudine Cantuariensis ecclesie et speciali concessione beati Thome martiris vestri archiepiscopi est obtentum ut suffraganei eiusdem ecclesie sine assensu Cantuariensis capituli alibi quam in Cantuariensi ecclesia non debeant consecrari; et nichilominus venerabilis frater noster Edmundus Cantuariensis archiepiscopus id idem vobis et ecclesie predicte concessit, prout in ipsius litteris inde confectis dicitur plenius contineri. Vestris igitur precibus grato concurrentes assensu, quod super hoc a predictis archiepiscopis pie ac provide factum est vobis et eidem ecclesie auctoritate apostolica confirmamus et presentis scripti patrocinio communimus. Nulli ergo omnino hominum liceat hanc paginam nostre confirmationis infringere vel ei ausu temerario contraire. Siquis autem [. . . etc.].

Dat' Laterani, v kal. Februarii pontificatus nostri anno undecimo [28 January 1238].

Bulla ut archiepiscopus alibi quam in sua Cantuariensi ecclesia necessitate interveniente suffraganeos poterit consecrare[2]

Gregorius episcopus servus servorum dei . . venerabili fratri archiepiscopo Cantuariensi salutem et apostolicam benedictionem.

De omnipotentis gratia sedi apostolice concessum esse dinoscitur ut membrorum eiusdem iustis desideriis et favorem benevolum et provisionis oportune remedium largiatur. Ex parte siquidem tua fuit propositum coram nobis per te monachis ecclesie Cantuariensis

---

[1] See above, p. 97 n. 2. Other texts (all dated 'v kal. Feb.') are in Canterbury, D. & C. Mun., Reg. A, fo. 62[r] (formerly 69), Reg. O, fo. 185[r] (formerly 387), and Chartae antiquae, C. 120, m. 1.

[2] For other texts see p. 97 n. 2.

fuisse concessum et a nobis etiam confirmatum quod perpetuis futuris temporibus in ipsa dumtaxat consecrare tuos suffraganeos tenearis. Verum cum observantia concessionis huiusmodi propter varietatem accidentium sicut asseritur absque discrimine non possit aliquando pervenire, nos arbitrantes debitum ut super hoc favorem nostrum sentias gratiosum, fraternitati tue quod eisdem suffraganeis alibi quam in ecclesia memorata cum necessitas id urgens exposcerit, non obstante concessione predicta, consecrationis beneficium libere largiaris auctoritate presentium concedimus facultatem. Nulli ergo omnino hominum liceat hanc paginam nostre concessionis infringere vel ei ausu temerario contraire. Siquis autem [. . . etc.].

Dat' Laterani, xviii kal. Maii pontificatus nostri anno duodecimo [14 April 1238].

6. Textual Problems of the English Provincial Canons*

I

THE field of legislation which I intend to survey consists of laws published by the archbishops of Canterbury and the archbishops of York between the years 1070 and 1518, applicable to England or to one of its two ecclesiastical provinces. I cannot claim to have made a thorough survey: the field is too wide. But even an incomplete study of the textual problems may have value for comparative purposes and may suggest lines of criticism to follow in approaching the medieval legislation of other provinces of the Church. Many of the problems will be familiar to legal historians who work in quite different fields.

For the first hundred years of this long span of four and a half centuries the juristic character of local legislation was perhaps a trifle vague. From the mid twelfth century onwards there can have been no doubt about its subordinate status. In the classical period of the canon law which began with Gratian, provincial legislation had its recognized place; and it was a humble place. It would (to borrow Frederic William Maitland's words) consist of 'statutes which are merely declaratory of the *ius commune* of the Church, statutes which recall it to memory, statutes which amplify it and give to it a sharper edge'.[1] The bulk of

---

* A paper read at Venice in Oct. 1967 and first published in *La Critica del Testo* (Atti del 2° Congresso internazionale della Società Italiana di Storia del Diritto, Florence, 1971), i. 165–88.

[1] *Roman Canon Law in the Church of England* (1898), p. 19. Cf. Stephan Kuttner, 'Methodological problems concerning the history of the canon law', *Speculum*, xxx (1955), 545; 'Even where such councils were presided over by a papal legate they had only an ancillary function. They would implement the common law by filling out details and by re-enforcing it in its local application. In the canonistic theory of the late thirteenth century, finally, particular statutory legislation was assimilated to local custom, with all the consequences arising, e.g. from the distinction of *consuetudo contra* or *praeter* or *secundum legem* and the doctrine of the

these laws is composed of miscellaneous enactments, which mainly concern either the discipline of the clergy or the relations of the civil government with the Church. There is also, particularly in the early period, a certain amount of general pastoral instruction, and in later times some liturgical rules.[1] All told, it does not add up to a very impressive volume. In the year 1504 it was possible to print a large proportion of the total output in the province of Canterbury (indeed, all that was then known) in the space of sixty-eight small quarto pages.[2] And it may be emphasized at once that the province of York produced very little by comparison with Canterbury's legislation. York, while jealously asserting its independence, followed the lead of Canterbury in many respects; and in 1462 it went so far as to accept such previous legislation of the southern province as was not repugnant to York canons.[3] Almost all the legislative material for both provinces known to exist is in print somewhere or other; but it must be confessed that for printed texts we very often have to rely on the defective editions of the seventeenth and eighteenth centuries, and that modern historians who trust what Mansi reprinted from Wilkins are likely to be led seriously astray.

From the point of view of textual history a fairly sharp distinction can be drawn between the earlier and the later laws,

relative effect of a new papal law upon each of these.' See also *EHR*, l (1935), 202–3.

[1] But the contrast should not be overstressed: the canons of Westminster (1175) contain liturgical rules, and there is didactic material in the canons of Lambeth (1281).

[2] *Constitutiones legitime seu legatine regionis anglicane . . . necnon et constitutiones provinciales . . .* (Paris, 1504). Later editions are more useful: there are two general collections, those of Spelman, 2 vols. (1639–64) and Wilkins, 4 vols. (1737). The laws as arranged and glossed by William Lyndwood were last printed in the edition of his *Provinciale* at Oxford, 1679. The provincial laws between 1205 and 1313 are critically edited in F. M. Powicke and C. R. Cheney, *Councils and Synods, with Other Documents relating to the English Church*, vol. 2, in two parts (Oxford, 1964) [= *C. & S*]. An annotated list of English Church Councils 602 × 603 to 1536 is given in F. M. Powicke and E. B. Fryde, *Handbook of British Chronology*, 2nd ed. (Royal Hist. Soc., 1961), pp. 545–65.

[3] See below, p. 178. For borrowings by one French province from another see J. Gaudemet, 'Aspects de la législation conciliaire française au XIIIᵉ siècle,' *Revue de Droit Canonique*, ix (1959), 316–40, at p. 329. See also his remarks in F. Lot and R. Fawtier, *Histoire des Institutions Françaises au Moyen Âge*, iii (1962), 317: 'Ainsi se constitue, au moins sur certains points, une législation disciplinaire qui tend à devenir commune à toutes les églises du Royaume.'

although it is a distinction which falsifies the course of conciliar history in one important detail. If we look at the *Pro-*
vinciale—the collection of provincial canons put together by
the English canonist, William Lyndwood, in 1430—we find
that he purported to include nothing earlier than the canons of
the Council of Oxford of 1222. He (or the lawyers of the fourteenth century on whom he relied) seemingly regarded the
Fourth Lateran Council as the limit of legal memory so far as
English provincial canons were concerned. To do so was to
omit more than half a dozen councils which had legislated for
the English Church or one of its provinces between the
Norman Conquest and 1215. The omission was justified in the
sense that later lawyers had no use for and did not copy
eleventh- and twelfth-century English canons. These went out
of circulation (at the latest) after the Council of Oxford of
1222. But there is one important exception: some of the
provincial canons of Westminster of 1175 were repeatedly
copied in the fourteenth and fifteenth centuries as canons of
Archbishop Richard, '1065'—an impossible date. Lyndwood
included them in his *Provinciale*. He assigned them, not to the
Archbishop Richard of 1175, but to a later archbishop, Richard
Wethershed, 1229–31. The textual historian, then, must distinguish on the one hand nearly all the eleventh- and twelfth-
century canons which, whatever influence they may have had
in their own day, did not fall into the hands of later lawyers and
submit to contamination and false ascription. On the other
hand there are the canons of 1175 together with the legislation
of three centuries after the Fourth Lateran Council; this was all
repeatedly copied, extended, embellished. That in itself produced a crop of new textual problems. But the post-Lateran
period presents another new difficulty: the material includes
various decrees, statutes, and constitutions (for all these names
are used) which cannot be assigned to any council and which
may not have been uttered in a council. A good many of them,
we discover, will not stand up to criticism. They prove to be
sailing under false colours and must be labelled *spuria*, or at
least *dubia*.

II

The problems which confront an historian who wants to use this legislation vary according to the period. They also vary according to the original procedure employed by the legislators for uttering and distributing their canons and constitutions. I use the word 'canon' for the laws made in councils, and reserve the word 'constitution' for any statute which is not explicitly fortified with the assent of the archbishop's suffragans;[1] and I shall concern myself first with canons. The best way to appreciate the pitfalls in the existing texts is to see what evidence of procedure can be squeezed out of them or drawn from other sources, such as letters about councils and narratives in chronicles. It must be admitted that the older printed editions do not give much help.

Facts about methods of drafting and authorizing canons are unfortunately scarce. The historian is bound to raise more questions than he can answer. Who prepared the agenda for a council? What amount of discussion preceded the drafting of the canons? At what point did an authoritative text take shape? What arrangements were made for making copies of it? What legal right, if any, had the bishops in a council to withhold consent to the proposed legislation? Did other clergy besides the bishops have any rights in the matter? Did assent imply authorization?

Questions of counsel and consent are not central to my subject, though they are not wholly irrelevant to the history of the texts. I shall not attempt to measure the precise authority accorded to participants in councils.[2] I must make another

---

[1] The words *statuta* and *constitutiones* are in fact found far more often in English medieval sources than the word *canones*, to cover all sorts of councils, including ecumenical. Yet *canon* was a recognized word for the act of a council (see the common gloss on Gratian, D. 18 c. 1). It is convenient to use the term in order to avoid confusion with non-conciliar legislation.

[2] See *EHR*, l (1935), 199–202 and E. W. Kemp, *Counsel and Consent* (1961), especially pp. 47–8. These questions are examined at length, in relation to French records, by Professor Richard L. Kay in his dissertation: *The Making of Statutes in French Provincial Councils, 1049–1305* (University of Wisconsin, 1959 Ph.D.). Dr. Kay did not concern himself with the actual preparation and transmission of texts. More recently he has examined fully the thirteenth-century provincial councils of Rouen, in 'Mansi and Rouen: a critique of the conciliar collections', *Catholic Historical Review*, lii (1966), 155–85.

disclaimer. These questions of procedural history invite comparison with other forms of medieval legislation: the early synodal acts of the Roman Church, capitularies of the Carolingians, and the statutes of the English kings in the later Middle Ages. But this comparison would lead too far afield. I only want to remark in passing that the English conciliar activity between the eleventh and the sixteenth century embraced various traditions for which parallels can be found in the history of legal systems, where German customs of public utterance contrast with sophisticated Roman methods of record. Oral pronouncement and carefully elaborated written canons represent differing theories of legislation: these determined the various ways of perpetuating the laws.[1]

Evidence of procedure for the Norman period begins with Archbishop Lanfranc's council at London in 1075.[2] In or after this council an official synodal act in the ancient style was drawn up (and happily survives in its original form).[3] It begins with the date and place of the assembly, names Archbishop

---

[1] On the synodal acts of the Roman church from the end of the fifth century onwards see briefly H. Bresslau, *Handbuch der Urkundenlehre* (2nd ed., Leipzig, 1912–31), i. 74–5, 194–5. For a Frankish synodal act of comparable form (Council of Narbonne, 589) see *Concilia Galliae, 511–695* (Corpus Christianorum, Series Latina, CXLVIIIA, 1963) ed. C. de Clercq, pp. 253–8. See also Bresslau, ii. 190–1, 225, 252–3, 395. For the capitularies see F. L. Ganshof, *Recherches sur les capitulaires* (Paris, 1958), pp. 18–21, 37–52. For English royal statutes see H. G. Richardson and G. O. Sayles, 'The early statutes', *Law Quarterly Review*, l (1934), 201–23, 540–71 (and separately, London, 1934).

[2] Records of other councils in William I's reign do not give any useful evidence: such legislation as survives from them (1070, 1072) is in the form of brief *capitula* (Wilkins, i. 365, cf. H. Böhmer, *Kirche und Staat in England und in der Normandie* (Leipzig, 1899), p. 63 n.). I do not think that the liturgical *ordines* for councils provide very safe evidence for the subject of this paper; but they indicate the practice of securing the signatures of bishops on written *acta*.

[3] Wilkins, i. 363–4. A pseudo-original, or *copie figurée*, survives in Cambridge, St. John's College MS. 236. My friend Mr. T. A. M. Bishop kindly points out that this is not an authenticated original but a contemporary copy from one. It is in a known Canterbury hand, probably that of one of Lanfranc's chaplains; it was written to be laid up in the Canterbury archives to which it later belonged, as witnesses the endorsement. According to the *Acta Lanfranci*, the archbishop set down the proceedings of this council in writing (*litteris commendavit*) at the request of many persons (C. Plummer, *Two of the Anglo-Saxon Chronicles Parallel* i. (Oxford, 1891), 289). For a detailed study of the Cambridge manuscript and of the council, see C. N. L. Brooke, 'Archbishop Lanfranc, the English Bishops, and the Council of London of 1075', *Studia Gratiana*, xii (1967: *Collectanea Stephan Kuttner* ii), 39–60.

Lanfranc as president, and specifies other bishops present. It describes the discussions which arose about the order of seating in council and records the decision taken. Then come regulations for monks, based on the Rule of St. Benedict and other sources. Ancient authorities are cited to justify the transfer of English episcopal sees from villages to towns; other transferences are said to have been deferred for consultation with the king. Next come six short disciplinary canons, mostly framed on the authority of papal 'decrees' and ancient canons. The document ends with a long list of witnessing bishops and abbots (+*Ego* . . . *subscripsi*).[1] Although this throws no light on the discussions which preceded the framing of the canons, it shows the way in which old law books were being used for guidance and authority. The emphasis on consent and subscription is significant; so is the apparent wish to put into circulation an authentic text of the synodal acts. One cannot help wondering whether the disciplinary canons received this formal publication less for their own sake than because of their association with matters of precedence and administrative order. These matters were very much in the mind of Archbishop Lanfranc. The same form had been adopted a few years earlier to record the decision on the primatial right of Canterbury *vis-à-vis* York;[2] and the endorsement of the acta of 1075 reads: 'Concilium Willelmi regis et Lanfranci archiepiscopi apud London de primatu Cantuariensis ecclesie et regulis ecclesiarum.'

The next piece of evidence on procedure concerns the national council which Archbishop Anselm of Canterbury held at Westminster with thirteen bishops in 1102. Eadmer, monk of Canterbury, who was also the secretary and biographer of St. Anselm, preserves for us the draft of a synodal act,[3] a draft which was not completed. It is formed on the same

---

[1] In St. John's College MS. 236 the subscriptions are not autograph.

[2] The synodal acts of the councils of Winchester and Windsor in 1072 are preserved in Canterbury, D. & C. Mun., A.1 and A.2, printed Wilkins, i. 324–5. The subscriptions of A.2 (which omits the passage referring to the second council (*Ventilata est* . . . *Pentecostes*) as well as a very large number of witnesses) have the air of being autograph signatures.

[3] Wilkins, i. 382–3; Eadmer, *Historia Novorum in Anglia* (RS, 1884), pp. 141–4; William of Malmesbury, *Gesta Pontificum* (RS, 1870), pp. 118–21.

pattern as those of 1072 and 1075, beginning with the date and place and description of those present. It records first the deposition of nine abbots and then adds thirty brief ordinances, sometimes reduced to very few words: 'Ut archidiaconi sint diaconi. Ut decime non nisi ecclesiis dentur.' The document, as preserved by Eadmer, is not completed by the subscriptions of the assembled prelates, and this fact is explained by three of Anselm's letters, written shortly afterwards. The first is addressed to William, archdeacon of Canterbury.[1] It deserves quotation in full:

I do not wish to send the decisions elaborated from the council's articles (*sententias capitulorum concilii expositas*) to you or to anybody at present. For when they were set forth in the council they could not be fully and perfectly recited, being brought forward suddenly without the necessary forethought and proper discussion. So there are some things which seem to need adding, and some perhaps ought to be altered; and I do not wish to do this without the consent of my fellow-bishops. I want, therefore, to draft them and show them to the bishops as soon as we meet, before sending them, framed and elaborated (*dictatae et expositae*), round the churches of England. But I am sending you the headings of the topics on which we spoke there, so that you may act according to what you can recall we decreed on those topics.

Writing to Archbishop Gerard of York, Anselm said:[2]

I am only sending you the articles (*capitula*) of the council, for I do not want to circulate copies of the decisions elaborated from them (*sententiarum eorum expositiones*) until they have been approved by the judgement of yourself and of the other bishops who were present in the council.

Replying to an inquiry from Archbishop Gerard in another letter, Anselm advised him to enforce what had been decided (*statuta*) by common consent in the council, and continued:[3]

Regarding those matters which we did not deal with in the council

[1] *S. Anselmi Cantuariensis Archiepiscopi Opera Omnia*, ed. F. S. Schmitt (1938–61), iv. 169 no. 257 (quoted in *EHR*, l (1935), 208 from Migne, clix. 94–5 where, for *nolo facere*, read *volo facere*).

[2] *S. Anselmi Op. Omnia*, iv. 165 no. 253.

[3] Ibid. iv. 168–9 no. 256. In December 1104 Paschal II, presumably prompted by Anselm, urged Henry I to publicize and put into effect 'constitutiones que ad coercenda vitiorum contagia sinodali apud vos sunt promulgate consensu' (*PUE*, i. 225 no. 6).

(for we could not do everything that was needful at once), such as the confiscation of prebends sold before the time of the council and the like, since these matters concern not only you and me and our churches but also many others, and since people disagree over them, I think it fitting for us to wait and make a definite decision (*sententiam certam statuamus*) by common counsel of us and our fellow bishops next Christmas.

Here we seem to have evidence that an ecclesiastical council might be presented with proposals, or *capitula*, articles for discussion, which formed the basis of interim decisions.[1] The council might disperse before a final draft was prepared. The archbishop who had presided might defer the preparation of the final draft to another meeting of bishops.[2]

We come down to the latter part of the twelfth century and the provincial council of Westminster of 1175 before finding any other statement about the procedure of legislation in a council. On this occasion the archbishop of Canterbury promulgated to the bishops and abbots assembled in council a series of canons (*certa capitula*) which he ordered to be inviolably observed, judging those to be 'transgressors of the sacred canons who should presume to contravene the statutes of this holy synod'. The nineteen chapters which follow include fourteen based on texts to be found in the *Decretum* of Gratian (including two *paleae*); three, and perhaps four, of the rest were taken from recent decretal letters directed to English addressees.[3] The selection had presumably been made before the council by advisers of the archbishop of Canterbury, whose

---

[1] The student of English constitutional history will recall the document entitled *Capitula que barones petunt et dominus rex concedit* which preceded Magna Carta in 1215.

[2] In this instance the outcome was deferred because of Anselm's departure from England in 1103. Eventually, in 1108, Anselm held another council which elaborated, and stopped up holes in, the original *capitulum* about married clerks which Archbishop Gerard had found inadequate.

[3] The chapters of doubtful origin are nos. 6 and 9. The text is in the *Gesta Regis Henrici*, now attributed to Roger of Howden (RS, 1867), i. 84–9 and in Howden's later chronicle, *Chron. Rogeri de Hoveden* (RS, 1868–71), ii. 72–7. Another text, imperfect, is in Gervase of Canterbury's chronicle (*Hist. Works*, (RS, 1879–80), i. 251–5). The text from the *Gesta Henrici* is in Wilkins, i. 476–9. On the use of the canons by the canonists see C. N. L. Brooke, 'Canons of English church councils in the early decretal collections', *Traditio*, xiii (1957), 471–80; cf. ibid. xvii (1961), 546.

familia included the well-known canonist Gerard Pucelle, Peter of Blois, and other *iurisperiti*.[1] The archbishop's chancellor, Brother Benedict of Canterbury, recited the canons in the council at his master's bidding. If the account given by Gerald of Wales may be trusted, there was no antecedent discussion, and when Bishop Bartholomew of Exeter spoke of certain points which called for emendation the chancellor shouted him down.[2] Debate, it seems, was not expected or wanted. There is no sign that a formal synodal act was drawn up afterwards to provide an authentic record of the canons and of the other doings of the council. The text of the canons with their preamble was preserved (with some variants) by two chroniclers and in the canonical *Collectio Belverensis*.

A few provincial councils of the thirteenth century have left records which throw light on methods of legislating. Two provincial councils of Canterbury were held in the year 1257. The May meeting discussed clerical grievances against the Crown, and came to no decision; but for the second council, in August, the archbishop prepared agenda which incorporated some of the May *gravamina*. This provided a basis for discussion and resulted in agreed *articuli*, or resolutions.[3] But still the prelates hesitated. The council had discussed delicate questions about the encroachments of civil government on ecclesiastical liberty. It was recommended that the resolutions should be further discussed and that those encroachments by the lay power should be distinguished which could not be overlooked without the imperilling of souls.[4] The next year, 1258, when the clamour for reform of the country's civil government reached a climax in the making of the Provisions of Oxford, the churchmen brought under review the material they had

[1] S. Kuttner and E. Rathbone, 'Anglo-Norman canonists of the twelfth century', *Traditio*, vii (1949–51), 301–2. See also C. Duggan, *Twelfth-century Decretal Collections and their Importance in English History* (1963). I leave out of account thirty-seven brief *capitula* entitled *Concilium Ricardi Cantuariensis* found in a decretal collection, B.M., MS. Cotton Claud. A. iv fo. 191ᵛ (Wilkins, i. 474). This has sometimes been thought to be a draft of canons of 1175 (*EHR*, l. 388, *Traditio*, xiii. 472 n. 8, Duggan, op. cit., p. 92); but the connection with 1175 is doubtful: sixteen of the thirty-seven chapters do not correspond to anything in the canons of 1175.

[2] *Giraldi Cambrensis Opera* (RS), vii. 59.

[3] *C. & S.* ii. 532 and 534.   [4] Ibid. ii. 536.

considered in the councils of 1257. This seems to have taken place in a council held in June 1258, first at Merton and then at Westminster. This time the resolutions were incorporated in a formal set of elaborate *constitutiones* which, like the far distant and long forgotten canons of 1075, were framed in a document which the assembled bishops attested. In 1075 they signed with their own hands or purported to do so; in 1258 they had their seals attached.[1]

When the prelates drew up their sealed *constitutiones* at Westminster in June 1258 they reserved to themselves the power of adding, subtracting, changing, and correcting, as should seem fit.[2] In spite of the formal recital in the council it is noticeable that the draftsmen used the terms *providemus* and *ordinamus*, never *statuimus* or *constituimus*. The terms used perhaps carried an implication of provisional, temporary measures. For, three years later, in May 1261, a council at Lambeth worked over these 1258 provisions and ordinances and produced a much revised version. Here the operative word is regularly *statuimus*. These statutes or canons of 1261 were recited at the end of the council and, like the provisions and ordinances of 1258, received the seals of those bishops who were present by way of authentication.[3] The intention was plainly to improve on and supersede what had been done in 1258.

The next council to legislate for the province of Canterbury was that held by Archbishop John Pecham at Reading in 1279.[4] The evidence shows that the new archbishop had prepared a long discourse on the state of the Church. In it were inserted earlier legatine and provincial canons and two papal constitutions, together with several new enactments designed to clarify or strengthen the existing laws. All this (or most of it) was recited and discussed in the council; and the archbishop in conclusion required his ordinances and additions (*ordinata vel adiecta*) to be read twice a year in the general chapters of all archdeaconries. But the practice of 1258 and 1261 was not repeated. There was no solemn authentication of the new material by the seals of the bishops. This is all the more interesting because a separate ordinance issued in the council

[1] *C. & S.* ii. 568–85.   [2] Ibid. ii. 585.
[3] Ibid. ii. 660–85.   [4] Ibid. ii. 828–51.

received this treatment: a condemnation of clerks who disturbed the peace of the university of Oxford bore the seals of
the archbishop and twelve suffragans.[1] Nevertheless, the 'additions and declarations', extracted unchanged from the original
discourse, did come into general circulation.

Two years later, in October 1281 at Lambeth, John Pecham
held another council, which was responsible for important
legislation.[2] This time there is no indication of the method of its
drafting. The canons were said to be recited at the end of the
council, but the bishops did not authenticate them with their
seals. The next year (1282) Archbishop John Pecham and his
suffragans held a council at the Old Temple, London, designed
to settle among other things the disputes between them over
the jurisdiction of the Court of Canterbury.[3] After much discussion a draft ordinance, drawn up in the archbishop's name, was
placed before the council; but it is unlikely that this secured
approval or was officially published. Pecham, it seems, did not
regard the terms of the ordinance as final; and in it he expressed
his willingness to reopen the matter at the next council. The
archbishop's registrar, in copying it years later, noted that
although it had the approval of the archbishop *et suorum*, it was
not sealed and had not been sent out *ad alios* [*episcopos?*].[4]
Nevertheless, at least one copy reached the hands of the
bishop of Worcester's registrar, and Pecham complained that
unauthorized versions circulated.

A long time elapses before we find any more evidence about
the drafting and publication of canons. In November 1328
Simon Mepham of Canterbury summoned his bishops and
other prelates and proctors to a provincial council at St. Paul's,
London, on 27 January 1329. His mandate of summons
required the bishops, before setting out for the council, to
deliberate with their clergy and inquire searchingly about
grievances and shortcomings which ought to be reformed by
the council's efforts. We know that the clergy of the diocese of
Salisbury met for the purpose, and some complaints of the
Exeter clergy were forwarded to the council by Bishop John

---

[1] Ibid. ii. 829 and 851–3.   [2] Ibid. ii. 886–918.
[3] Ibid. ii. 921–39.   [4] Ibid. ii. 932 n. b.

de Grandisson, who sent excuses for his own absence.¹ The canons of the council, as promulgated, bore some signs of these local preparations. Moreover, they seem to have been issued, if not immediately, very soon afterwards, in an authentic version. For the council rose on 10 February 1329; and by 8 March the bishop of Salisbury was able to tell the *locum tenens* of the dean of Salisbury and the archdeacons and other officials of the diocese that he had received the canons under the archbishop's seal. He transmitted to them a copy of the canons (which were also copied into his register). He ordered them to be published and expounded in churches throughout the diocese at convenient times, special emphasis being laid on those canons of which contraveners incurred the greater excommunication.²

With Simon Mepham's successor, legislation takes a more protracted course. Archbishop John Stratford of Canterbury held a council at London in October 1341 which considered canons 'for the preservation of the liberty of the Church and the reform of morals', according to the well-informed chronicler Adam Murimuth. A year later another council revised the earlier draft and greatly enlarged the scope. But publication did not immediately follow. It was not until May 1343 that Stratford sent a definitive series of canons to his suffragans, publishing them with the statement that they had been accepted in the recent council (presumably that of 18 October 1342) and naming the bishops who were witnesses. Why this published series included none of the canons drafted in October 1341 and revised in October 1342 we cannot say. Texts of them came into circulation, were often cited by lawyers with respect, and were included by Lyndwood in his *Provinciale*.³ This practice of deferring the publication of canons agreed in a council is seen in the northern province a few years later. Archbishop John Thoresby of York seems to have promulgated canons in a provincial council—undated—but published them under his seal, dated at his manor of Bishopthorpe on 29 September

---

¹ *Registers of Roger Martival, Bishop of Salisbury* (CYS), ii bis (1972), 596–7; *Reg. John de Grandisson, Bishop of Exeter*, ed. F. C. Hingeston-Randolph, i (1894), 448.

² *Reg. R. Martival*, ii bis, 598–9.

³ *EHR*, l. 415–17; Wilkins, ii. 675–8, 696–702, 702–9.

1367. A modification introduced in a later council—also un-dated—is recorded.[1] Again, in the south, Archbishop Thomas Arundel held a provincial council at Oxford in 1407 which approved an important enactment on heresy. But for one reason or another the canon was only 'published' at a council held in St. Paul's Cathedral, London, in January 1409. It was finally sent out by the archbishop under seal, to the bishop of London for transmission to the other suffragans, on 13 April 1409.[2] Similar instances of delay occur later in the fifteenth century. On 23 July 1463 there were published in a council held by Archbishop Thomas Bourgchier two canons which had been drawn up and recited in a council of 1462. A text of these canons occurs in a Canterbury Cathedral register with a note (presumably written during the intervening months): 'Iste constituciones non sunt adhuc publicande, ideo rogo vos ne videantur a multis.'[3]

III

From these signs of procedure, so infrequently recorded, we can at least surmise what probably happened or what may have happened on other occasions, and what sorts of documents conciliar proceedings left behind them. Written agenda or a draft of proposed canons might be prepared in the arch-bishop's secretariat before the council began.[4] In the assembly of bishops these might be revised, and different drafts might take shape in writing before the council ended. At the end of the council the bishops might be asked to put their seals to

---

[1] Wilkins, iii. 70, 72. But the evidence for the textual history of what is printed under Thoresby's name still requires elucidation.

[2] Wilkins, iii. 306, 311, 314.

[3] Wilkins, iii. 585–7 and *Registrum Thome Bourgchier Cantuariensis archiepiscopi*, ed. F. R. H. Du Boulay (CYS, 1957) pp. 108–11 and 108 n. 1. The canons were promulgated again in the convocation of Canterbury, 10 Feb. 1484 (Wilkins, iii. 616).

[4] In 1404 the archbishop of Canterbury invited the registrar of Worcester to draft a 'constitutio provincialis ad orandum pro episcopis defunctis', which he did—in flowery language. We do not know whether the draft was used; it was preserved by the registrar, Master Gilbert Stone, in his letter-book (MS. Bodley 859 fo. 41ᵛ) with the note that it was *rudi modo concepta de mandato reverendissimi patris domini Thome Arondell archiepiscopi*. See also *C. & S.* ii. 934 and 1137.

a final version, or the business might be reserved for further discussion (as in 1102, and 1257, and 1341).

Moreover, the general agreement reached in council might not be the last stage in the law-making. We know something—thanks in a great measure to the work of Professor Stephan Kuttner—of the way in which the canons of medieval general councils were elaborated after the councils were over. Already in 1215 the canons of the Fourth Lateran council, though drawn up beforehand in the Curia, were subjected to a certain amount of revision. Canon 71 (*Expeditio pro recuperanda Terra Sancta*) was published separately after the council in a form different from that which had circulated while the council was sitting and which is preserved in part by the chronicler Roger Wendover.[1] Later in the thirteenth century a final publication of the canons of a general council was always delayed. At Lyon in 1245 and 1274 Innocent IV and Gregory X promulgate their canons; but this is only 'a preliminary stage, subject to alterations and additions, until the final text of what the pope wishes to be regarded as legislative work of the council is released in the form of a topical collection, by "publication" to the universities'. And 'what had taken only a few weeks at Lyon, 1245, and a few months in 1274, was to drag on for years after the Council of Vienne. While the post-conciliar commission charged with revising and completing the decrees was engaged in its task, unauthorized versions had already been put in circulation.'[2] Beyond question the pope could by his own authority modify canons which he had promulgated 'sacro

---

[1] S. Kuttner and A. García y García, 'A new eyewitness account of the Fourth Lateran Council', *Traditio*, xx (1964), 115–78, see 133–4, 156, 174–8. Wendover may likewise have obtained access to a draft, and not the final version, of Magna Carta 1215, as recently suggested by J. C. Holt, 'The St. Albans chroniclers and Magna Carta', *Trans. Royal Historical Soc.*, 5th series xiv (1964), 67–88 at p. 85.

[2] S. Kuttner, 'The date of the Constitution *Saepe*', *Mélanges Eugène Tisserant*, iv (Studi e Testi, 234, 1964), 428–9. See for the whole matter Kuttner, *L'édition romaine des conciles généraux et les actes du premier concile de Lyon (Miscellanea Historiae Pontificiae*, iii, no. 5, Rome, 1940); idem, 'Die Konstitutionen des ersten allgemeinen Konzils von Lyon', *Studia et Documenta Historiae et Iuris*, vi (Rome, 1940), 71–110; idem, 'Conciliar law in the making: the Lyonese constitutions (1274) of Gregory X in a manuscript at Washington', *Miscellanea Pio Paschini*, ii (*Lateranum*, N.S. xv. 1–4, 1949), 39–81; Ewald Müller, *Das Konzil von Vienne* (Münster, 1934), pp. 387–404.

approbante concilio'.[1] The authority of an archbishop to modify canons approved in his provincial council was less clearly defined by the law;[2] but such modification was certainly practised.

The chief difficulty for the modern student confronted with a text which purports to be provincial legislation is to determine what stage in the genesis of a canon his text represents. Without clear evidence he must not assume that he has the final enactment before him. The archbishop's clerks kept the agenda which had been laid before the bishops, or even preliminary drafts of agenda. Prelates carried away from councils their imperfect, heavily corrected, copies of draft canons. The canons agreed provisionally in one council remained in circulation after they had been emended in another council or revised by the legislator on his own authority. The student of English provincial canons seldom has the good fortune to find an authenticated 'original'. British Museum, Cotton charter xvi. 29, with the canons of Lambeth, 1261, is perhaps the only survival. Even so, we do not know how these 'originals' came to be written: whether the archbishop's clerks supplied the bishops with official copies during or after the council, or whether it was incumbent upon all diocesans to make their own clerks take copies from an authentic 'master' version.[3] During the fourteenth century a procedure came to be often adopted for diffusing copies of canons and constitutions which provided guarantees of survival and of accuracy. The archbishop's chancery dispatched copies, in covering letters, after the council was over, to all the suffragan bishops; or else the bishop of London, as dean of the province of Canterbury, received a copy for transmission. By the mid fourteenth century the registrars of most English dioceses recorded important correspondence in official registers, and most of these survive. Consequently, we may look for quasi-authentic texts in episcopal registers; they are generally encased in a copy of the archbishop's letter commanding publication. A text of comparable authority is contained in British Museum Cotton

---

[1] See John Andreae, in the common gloss to *Clement.*, proem, *ver.* de cetero.
[2] Cf. *EHR*, l. 200–1 and Lyndwood, *Provinciale*, 5, 5, 3 *ver.* Condentis (p. 298*a*).
[3] *EHR*, l. 210–12.

charter xv. 12. This is a sealed letter patent of 1 April 1398 addressed by Robert Braybrooke, bishop of London, to the dean of his cathedral. It includes a letter of Roger Walden, archbishop of Canterbury, to the bishop, dated 8 March 1398, in which the archbishop reminds the bishop of the decisions of 'the last convocation of the clergy of our province of Canterbury celebrated on 2 March in your cathedral church of St. Paul, London'. The decisions consist in the first place of a canon on the observance of feast-days of St. David and others, and, secondly, of a resolution to meet a papal demand for an aid. The bishop of London is instructed to publish the decisions and require their execution in his diocese and to pass on the orders to all the archbishop's other suffragans.[1]

But not all the decisions of councils are so well reported. We are still left with a great many problematic texts on our hands, especially from the period before the middle of the fourteenth century. Even when texts are nearly contemporaneous with the councils they concern, even when they are found in reputable archives, they cannot always be treated as authentic legislation. The general problem can be best explained, in the light of what has already been said about procedure, by selecting three manuscripts as examples.

The first is an official archive. In the episcopal register of Godfrey Giffard, bishop of Worcester, copied among documents of April and May 1281, are three short paragraphs entitled: 'Statutum domini . . archiepiscopi de monialibus et de episcopis in excommunicationis sententiam incidentibus. . . .'[2] When they are compared with canons 17, 18, and 25 of the Council of Lambeth (October 1281) they appear to be trial shots at legislation on the same topics. They may well have been drafts brought home from London by the bishop of Worcester in May 1281, when he had met other bishops and when a council of some sort had taken place.[3] Another short text (not found in the Worcester register) confirms the supposition that the canons of Lambeth were not invented

---

[1] Printed in Wilkins, iii. 234–6 from a text addressed by the bishop of London to the archdeacon of London, dated 15 Apr. 1398. Cf. *EHR*, l. 211–12.
[2] *C. & S.* ii. 1124–5, nos. ix–xi; cf. ibid., 1119 and *JEH*, xii. 20–1.
[3] *C. & S.* ii. 886.

suddenly in October 1281; this text looks like a still earlier version of Lambeth c. 17 and 18 on peccant nuns. Two more texts described in the manuscripts as Pecham's may also be drafts of canons of Lambeth.[1] The Worcester registrar saved and copied various other documents from other ecclesiastical councils, in 1282, 1285, 1286, and 1295. Some of them consist of draft ordinances, one is preliminary agenda, entitled: 'Articuli super quibus deliberandum est ab episcopis.'[2] Not all can be readily identified.

My second example comes from British Museum MS. Harley 52. This volume, which contains the Pecham texts found under the year 1281 in the Worcester register, has not equal authority as an episcopal muniment; but its contents are of great interest and suggest that the compiler—about the middle of the fourteenth century—had access to official archives out of which he assembled documents of a provisional character together with authentic legislation.[3] Harley 52 contains canons of Oxford (1222), Lambeth (1261), Reading (1279), Lambeth (1281), London (1342–3). To take the latest first: a normal version of the canons sent out by Archbishop John Stratford in May 1343 is preceded by a lengthier document. This combines the draft canons of 1341, as revised in 1342 (but including the chapter *de bigamia* then omitted) with sixteen chapters published by the archbishop in May 1343 scattered among the rest in an unusual sequence and without the clause announcing publication.[4] It looks like all the material that was assembled for consideration in October 1342, both new and old, both that which was finally published and that which was allowed to circulate without formal publication. The same manuscript shows equal comprehensiveness in recording the Council of Reading (1279). It preserves a fuller version than is found anywhere else of the proceedings of Archbishop John Pecham and his suffragans.[5] Basically, this is elaborate agenda, rather than a record of

---

[1] Ibid. ii. 1119–21, nos. i and iii.

[2] Ibid. ii. 977, cf. 932, 934, 936, 969, 1136.

[3] Some of the contents connects the volume with the diocese of Salisbury: see Cheney, *English Synodalia of the Thirteenth Century* (Oxford, 2nd ed. 1968), pp. 59, 73–5, and *C. & S.* ii. 58, 364. It may have been the property of an episcopal or archidiaconal official.

[4] *EHR*, l. 416–17.

[5] *C. & S.* ii. 829–30.

what actually happened in the council. Maybe the bishops were provided on arrival in the council with copies of all that the archbishop proposed to say. But the maker of the Harleian version has revised certain introductory remarks. Thus, other manuscripts of the agenda conclude chapter I with the words: 'Quibus propositis legatur consilium Octoboni . . . Quo perlecto, dicet archiepiscopus vel aliquis eius nomine in hec verba subscripta. . .;' but Harley 52 reads: 'Hic lectum fuit consilium Octoboni . . . Quo perlecto, subiunctum fuit . . .' The same tense is preserved until the end of chapter 5. From then onwards no change is made to the subjunctives of the agenda, but notes are added which show that the author was present at the council or else had inside information about what happened in it: 'Istud lectum fuit seorsum inter fratres secrete' (c. 7) and 'Istud capitulum non fuit coram episcopis recitatum' (c. 9). These two chapters and several other appear in other manuscripts which contain substantial traces of the agenda; but they were not among the eight chapters which the bishop of Worcester's registrar chose to copy and which a contemporary clerk of the royal Exchequer wrote in his register under the title: 'Processus domini Iohannis . . . in congregatione sua Radingie.' In both the Worcester and the Exchequer manuscripts, as in most of the later texts, all else—of the highest interest to historians—has been discarded. The Harleian manuscript, fortunately for us, does not distinguish between the provisional and the final legislation either in 1279 or in 1342–3.

A third manuscript illustrates what might happen in the circumstances of the councils which Archbishop Boniface of Canterbury held in 1258 and 1261. It will be recalled that the *provisions* drafted and circulated in 1258 formed a basis for the canons of 1261, but that in the process of revision much was discarded and much added. An early fourteenth-century manuscript from St. Augustine's Abbey, Canterbury (now Cambridge, Corpus Christi College MS. 271 part II), preserves a good text (fo. 84r) of the finally approved canons of 1261; but this is immediately preceded (fo. 79r) by a version which can only be shortly described as intermediate between the provisions of 1258 and the approved canons of 1261.[1] It begins

[1] For an analysis of the differences see *C. & S.* ii. 665–6.

with the preamble of 1258. In passages of the canons where the wording of the provisions was modified, this version preserves sometimes one form of words, sometimes the other. Towards the end come three short chapters which have no parallel in either the provisions or the canons. The version concludes incongruously with part of the preamble of 1261; this was perhaps the last part to be re-drafted. The whole thing looks like a copy of disorganized notes, taken down during the council of 1261 and left unrevised when the final stage of re-drafting was reached. Nor does Corpus Christi MS. 271 represent the only version to show the draftsmen at work and their task uncompleted. A dozen other manuscripts of the fourteenth and fifteenth centuries combine in different ways elements of 1258 and 1261, with forms of wording which can only be explained as discarded experiments.[1] Anybody who has served on a committee for drafting knows how many half-erased, interlined trials and errors go into the waste-paper basket. Those who attended medieval provincial councils were not careful to destroy their rough notes.

I have chosen these examples to illustrate the textual problems because they provide relatively simple patterns. Documents can be readily identified as agenda or intermediate drafts when, as in these instances, a reliable text of antecedent documents or the final legislation is at hand for comparison. I need not insist on the interest of making this comparison. By doing so we may hope to penetrate the minds of the legislators and to discover the changes which they made in their texts through force of circumstances. But it is worth insisting that for many English provincial canons no well-authenticated texts are known. This is where the most difficult problems arise. One case is to be found in the Harleian manuscript (52) from which I have already drawn instructive examples. Besides its records of the proceedings of 1279 and 1342–3 (described above) this contains a slightly unusual version of the canons of Oxford of 1222. There is no known authentic text of these canons. All that we can do is to examine the seventy or so copies which are known and note how far there is a general consensus among texts of reputable origin. MS. Harl. 52 contains a chapter found only in

[1] Ibid. ii. 666 n. 2.

three other manuscripts. One of the three, Cambridge, Gonville & Caius College MS. 44 (of unknown provenance) is
probably the earliest of all our copies. The other two come
from Chichester Cathedral and Merton Priory (in the diocese
of Winchester) respectively. The unusual chapter which these
four manuscripts contain is very short: 'Item volumus ut in
ecclesiis religiosorum et in prebendariis [*aliter* prebendatis]
secundum formam generalis concilii vicarie [*aliter* vicarii]
ordinentur.' This has been printed in the latest edition as c. 14
of the Council of Oxford; but it is hard to resist the conclusion
that it has no right to be there.[1] It appears, to be sure, in relatively early manuscripts from various sources and is unlikely to
be a later spurious invention; but it is absent from sixty other
texts. Its brevity, and its use of *volumus* instead of the usual
word of command, *statuimus*, suggest that it is the remnant
of an earlier draft. Perhaps it was an article on the agenda
which met with resistance from the regulars and the cathedral
chapters and which, as a result, was never translated into
legislation; only in the revising of some few drafts did it escape
cancellation.[2]

It is difficult enough to reconstruct the business brought to
a council by studying the discrepant texts of its proceedings.
We have also to reckon with another kind of evidence. Notes
or recollections of rejected drafts may have survived independently of the texts of canons. Discussion in the council might
lead to general agreement on matters which nevertheless found
no expression in the canons, or might fail to be put on record
because opinion was divided. Those who attended the council
might carry away different recollections of what the council
had resolved. For example, two topics which recur in English
diocesan statutes of the thirteenth century may have been
debated in the provincial council at Oxford in 1222: the evils
attendant upon the convivial parties called scotales, and the
observance by the laity of *festa ferianda*. My reason for hazard-
ing the guess is this. Some twenty-five years after the council,
statutes for the bishopric of Winchester declared that 'accord-

---

[1] *C. & S.* ii. 110 and cf. 102 n. 1.
[2] Minor variant readings peculiar to texts ABC may be explicable in the same
way: e.g. p. 112 c. 21 n. k, p. 113 c. 25 n. o, p. 114 c. 28 n. z, p. 120 c. 44 n. b.

ing to the Council of Oxford . . . all those are excommunicated who organize or participate in scotales'.[1] Is this due to a reminiscence of a rejected section in the imposing Oxford list of general excommunications? It is only a straw in the wind, but it seems to tend that way. The evidence that the Council of Oxford contemplated legislating about *festa ferianda* is equally slender, but it cannot be ignored. The earliest editors of *Concilia* (Crabbe, Surius, and others) printed a text of the Oxford canons for which no manuscript authority has been found. It is peculiar in containing (c. 8) a long list of feast-days which in its present form cannot go back to such an early date as 1222. But the anachronisms in it do not dispose of the matter. For a late thirteenth-century manuscript probably from Christ Church, Canterbury (Cambridge, Corpus Christi College MS. 337) has a list of *festa ferianda* which is annotated at one point *secundum consilium Oxonie* (fo. 37ʳ). At least this shows that in the thirteenth century a council of Oxford was supposed to have regulated the observance of feast-days.[2] Maybe the council of 1222 debated the matter and decided to leave it for synodal regulation in each diocese.[3]

IV

In the cases which I have been considering the texts record, in however distorted a form, what happened in certain provincial councils. They may give an unwarranted currency to items which had been discussed and had been explicitly rejected or transformed by the legislators. But at least they have some link with reality. Besides these, there are cases in which the canons of a council acquired accretions which we cannot ascribe to any genuine tradition. They are the work of later copyists, who have joined texts which were originally separate. They are due to nothing but misunderstanding or carelessness. This is the case in an early manuscript of the canons of Westminster, 1200. It is the only text of these canons apart from that found in the contemporary chronicle of Roger of Howden, and it enlarges Howden's series with five more chapters. But

---

[1] *C. & S.* ii. 416 cf. 605.   [2] *BIHR*, xxxiv. 123–5.
[3] Ibid. 119–21.

an inspection of these additions shows them to be cast in the form of diocesan statutes; probably they emanated from one of Canterbury's suffragans not long after 1200.[1] A more complicated story lies behind the text which Wilkins printed in his *Concilia* from a fourteenth-century manuscript under the title: 'Statuta legenda in concilio Oxoniensi edita per dominum Stephanum Cantuariensem archiepiscopum.' This appendix to the well-authenticated canons of Oxford (1222) appears in ten related but distinct forms, in more than thirty manuscripts. It does not always have the same title. In the form in which it is associated with the Council of Oxford it is an unofficial compilation of much later date. This compilation was based on a set of synodal statutes, for an unidentified English diocese, composed about the years 1222–5. Only in the fourteenth century did it come to be tacked on to the text of the Oxford canons in certain manuscripts; and there was no authority for this.[2] It was not genuine provincial legislation at all; but it eventually passed as such and was glossed by William Lyndwood in his *Provinciale*.[3] Students of the early decretal collections will not fail to see in these instances a parallel to the process by which canons of English councils of 1143 and 1175 were tacked on to the genuine canons of Reims, 1148, and of Tours, 1163, and so acquired more elevated status.[4]

These *Statuta legenda* attributed to the Council of Oxford are representative of a large class of *spuria* which occur in the comprehensive collections of provincial law written during the fourteenth and fifteenth centuries. Some fifty or more of these volumes survive. They had mostly been written by professional scribes, presumably to be sold by stationers to students and practitioners of the law. The compilers and copyists were not much interested in the historical background of their texts. Ascriptions were often wildly inaccurate. So, when Lyndwood came in the year 1430 to compose a systematic *Provinciale* in five

---

[1] *EHR*, l. 389; Cheney, *From Becket to Langton* (Manchester, 1956), p. 143.

[2] *EHR*, l. 395–8, subject to corrections in *EHR*, lxxv. 18–23 and *C. & S.* ii. 139–54.

[3] See below, p. 170. The manuscripts available to Lyndwood led him to ascribe the statutes to an imaginary second council of Oxford held in 1322 by Archbishop Walter Reynolds.

[4] *Traditio*, xiii (1957), 471–80.

books, on the model of the Gregorian decretals, among the canons of two centuries he could not distinguish the genuine from the spurious. In adding his glosses to the texts he was at pains to note discrepancies of attribution in the manuscripts. Sometimes he expressed doubts. But his historical equipment was inadequate, and on at least one occasion he tacitly suppressed one faulty ascription only to substitute an ill-conceived conjecture of his own.[1] Forty-eight out of the 240 chapters of the *Provinciale* were not provincial legislation: twenty per cent! A high proportion of the *spuria* are found on examination to be statutes of diocesan bishops of the province. The entire series of canons attributed to Archbishop Edmund of Canterbury (1234–40) was extracted from the synodal statutes of Richard Poore of Salisbury (1217–28), long after the death of both these prelates. An isolated statute of another thirteenth-century bishop of Salisbury masqueraded as a canon of Stephen Langton, or Boniface of Savoy, or Robert Winchelsey.[2] Another statute, assigned by Lyndwood to Archbishop Boniface, and elsewhere to Archbishop Robert Winchelsey, is attributable to Bishop Peter Quinel of Exeter, 1287.[3] More examples could be quoted.

This treatment of diocesan statutes as provincial canons had some practical consequences. Not only were they more widely diffused. A lengthy gloss by Lyndwood points to the fact that, if these rules were given provincial quality, their enforcement would enlarge the competence of the archbishop's court—a court over which Lyndwood himself presided from 1417 until at least 1431. For metropolitan jurisdiction extended to the punishment of cases in which provincial canons had imposed penalties.

The archbishop, [wrote Lyndwood] can make a provincial canon or constitution touching the whole province, and by that constitution the subjects of the suffragans are bound, provided they are aware of it (unless their ignorance of it is crass or supine) . . . so that, if anyone should incur the penalty of such a constitution who is not of the archbishop's diocese but is a subject of his suffragan, in this

[1] For this and the following sentences see below, pp. 167–73.
[2] *JEH*, xii. 31 and *C. & S.* ii. 550.
[3] *JEH*, xii. 32 and *C. & S.* ii. 1026.

case not only the bishop can absolve his subject from such a sentence, but also the archbishop . . . Since therefore the archbishop can absolve one who incurs the penalty of a provincial constitution, so also he can punish a delinquent against such a statute.[1]

In fifteenth-century manuscripts documents of diocesan origin continued to appear as provincial canons, and passed as such into the printed editions.

After the critical study of English diocesan statutes in recent years it has become possible to identify many of the spurious provincial canons for what they really are. We still find it difficult to trace a good many items in the late medieval collections to their source. These are usually the isolated chapters which concern the obligations of parishioners to rectors and vicars of churches; in one case the constitution regulates the wages of stipendiary priests. They claim the parentage of one archbishop of Canterbury or another, but the texts of individual constitutions do not always agree on an author. They are not always assigned to a provincial council. It is possible that they are genuine archiepiscopal constitutions but that they were not ever brought before a council for ratification. In some manuscripts the titles of certain texts provide a clue to origin. The constitution is said to be *facta in visitatione metropolitana.*[2] This would allow for informal utterance and might explain the variety of versions. As an archbishop proceeded on visitation (and the archbishops of Canterbury were vigorous in visiting from the time of Archbishop Boniface (1245–70) onwards) he discovered what were local needs and local customary rules in matters of tithe, repair of church fabric, and so forth. He might content himself with recalling the clergy to the enforcement of diocesan statutes on these subjects which they already possessed. Or he might direct their attention to the statutes of a neighbouring diocese which he had lately seen. Or he might make special injunctions, reiterating and elaborating the common law of the Church, and might repeat these injunctions in one diocese after another. Something of the sort certainly went on in the time of Archbishop Robert Winchelsey. On 18 May 1301, after a visita-

---

[1] *Provinciale*, 3, 23, 10 *ver. Competentem* (pp. 239–40). Cf. F. W. Maitland, *Roman Canon Law in the Church of England*, p. 36.
[2] *JEH*, xii. 21 and *C. & S.* ii. 1382, 1385, 1387, 1391.

tion of Bristol, he addressed his mandate to the local dean, forbidding fixed payments at baptisms, and various other abuses. In 1303, after a visitation of London, he wrote to the bishop's official about tithes wrongfully withheld from London rectors. These were not provincial constitutions in the ordinary sense, but they brought a body of rules to the notice of the clergy of a diocese, or archdeaconry, or deanery, by the arch-bishop's authority.[1] Some of the miscellaneous material which found its way into the law books may have originated in this fashion; but the textual history varies from item to item. Each must be considered on its merits, and much of it remains dubious.[2] In the new edition of *Councils & Synods, 1205–1313* the editors felt justified in publishing—with *caveats*—under the name of Archbishop Robert Winchelsey only seven of the twenty texts ascribed to him in various manuscripts. And they published those seven constitutions there 'mainly because in each case the attribution to Winchelsey, whether well-founded or not, rests upon a continuous agreement in the later Middle Ages to respect them as authoritative pronouncements of this archbishop.'[3] In other words, the historical evidence does not prove that they were all published by Winchelsey.

V

The textual problems of the 'Winchelsey' constitutions under-line the need to scrutinize Lyndwood's *Provinciale* closely before it is used. His collection was not, strictly speaking, an official collection, like those issued by some metropolitans on the Continent in the fourteenth and fifteenth centuries or like the *Provinciale* of York, issued by Archbishop Thomas Wolsey in 1518.[4] But the reputation of the author and the popularity of the collection canonized its contents, just as the contents of the great unofficial canon law collections—both before and after Gratian—were canonized. As Gabriel Le Bras said: 'Burchard

[1] *JEH*, xii. 22–3.
[2] Ibid., pp. 14–32 *passim* and *C. & S.* ii. 1382–93.
[3] *C. & S.* ii. 1382.
[4] Cf. *EHR*, l. 216–17, and below, pp. 168–9.

of Worms re-baptized some hundreds of fragments. Without modifying anything else he thus created councils and decretals.'[1] The efforts of Lyndwood pale into insignificance when compared with the transformations which a Burchard or a Gratian effected in composing a common law of the Western Church. The fact remains that Lyndwood determined what should be the provincial law of the English Church after his day,[2] and the law which he approved was even applied in the post-Reformation Church of England. For Lyndwood the textual problems were far harder than they are for the modern student, equipped as he is with catalogues of manuscripts, microfilm copies, and countless aids to scholarship. Lyndwood was drawing upon the enactments of the preceding two centuries as he found them set out in recent books. Although he deplored the deficiencies of the texts on which he relied,[3] he took them all. When their terms did not fit their ascription he did his best to adjust the wording of the statute to the title. Thus, a constitution on tithes attributed to Archbishop Robert Winchelsey suggests by its form a mandate from a bishop or an archdeacon rather than a provincial law; so Lyndwood introduces into the text the words *per nostram provinciam*, to add an air of verisimilitude to the ascription.[4] When Lyndwood is confronted with two related versions of Archbishop John Pecham's canon on the eucharist—one of which is the approved canon of the Council of Lambeth (1281) whereas the other we believe to be a draft or an earlier superseded enactment—he conflates the two.[5] His

[1] G. Le Bras, *Histoire du Droit et des Institutions de l'Église en Occident*, tome i: *Prolégomènes* (1955), 67, cf. idem, 'De vita et de suppliciis auctoritatum. Notes sur les épreuves des textes canoniques au premier millénaire', *Studi in onore di Ugo Enrico Paoli* (Florence, 1956), pp. 453–7, and 'Les apocryphes dans les collections canoniques', *La Critica del Testo* (Atti del 2° Congresso internazionale della Società Italiana di Storia del Diritto, Florence, 1971), i. 371–91. A further metamorphosis noted by Charles Munier explains some false ascriptions in Gratian: 'Des capitulaires épiscopaux ou des décisions conciliaires ont été transformés en textes patristiques, parfois dans le but de leur conférer une plus grande autorité.' (*Proceedings of the 3rd Intern. Congress of Med. Canon Law* (Vatican, 1971), p. 45).

[2] Not only did the *collection* made by Lyndwood acquire a quasi-official standing; his gloss was alleged as authoritative by a proctor in an English case in the Rota in 1512. I owe my knowledge of this to the kindness of Dr. Michael Kelly.

[3] *Provinciale*, sig. *2 verso, in his dedication of the book to Henry Chichele, archbishop of Canterbury.

[4] *C. & S.* ii. 1389–90 note r.

[5] Ibid. ii. 894, 1118–20.

gloss is occasionally wide of the mark because he treats a synodal statute as a provincial canon.[1]

Lyndwood's *Provinciale*, like the recent manuscripts on which he doubtless relied, and the great printed editions of the *Concilia* which depended mainly on texts of the same sort, provide a guide to the provincial law of the English Church as it was in the first half of the fifteenth century. They are of use to the historian of legal practice at the end of the Middle Ages. But they cannot safely be used to trace the earlier history of the legislation they contain. The ascriptions are unreliable, *spuria* and *dubia* pass as *genuina*, drafts and proposals appear on equal terms with duly promulgated laws. The historian of law is, or should be, concerned with the evolution of the enactment as well as with the final *textus receptus*. He must use the English *Provinciale* and *Concilia* circumspectly, for they obscure many problems. He cannot accept all their texts at face-value, and must embark on textual criticism. Laborious though it is, this is not a pursuit which is far removed from the main path of historical inquiry, fit only for a few dull scholiasts. By investigating the textual problems the legal historian is led to central themes: the theory and practice of lawmaking through the centuries.

---

[1] Below, p. 173.

7. Statute-making in the English Church in the Thirteenth Century[*]

THE material of this paper may seem to professional canonists to be small beer, and I shall not concern myself with this local legislation as producing or illustrating great legal principles. I claim no competence as a lawyer. My remarks are simply the result of protracted collecting and examination of texts; and I can offer no complete survey, no ready answer to all the most interesting questions which the material prompts. It may be possible to shed a little light here and there on the questions why legislation occurred, what were the circumstances of composition, how the statutes were promulgated and transmitted.

Gabriel Le Bras, describing broadly the classical age of the canon law, observes: 'pendant un demi-siècle, de 1227 à 1277, le droit canon parviendra au sommet de sa course.'[1] It is of course no accident that this fits my subject. In the local legislation of the English Church, if you widen this period by about twenty years—say 1214–87—you have most of the more enduring laws, legatine, provincial, diocesan, produced in the councils and synods. To indicate the contents very briefly. Two legates a latere, Otto and Ottobuono, celebrated councils in 1237 and 1268 and published canons which formed the background of administration in the English Church for the rest of the Middle Ages and beyond. Three archbishops of Canterbury, Stephen Langton, Boniface of Savoy, and John Pecham, in four provincial councils (Oxford, 1222, Lambeth, 1261 and 1281, and Reading, 1279) provided other laws adapted to English needs; and their influence, like the authority of the

* First published in *Proceedings of the Second International Congress of Medieval Canon Law, Boston College, 12–16 August 1963*, ed. Stephan Kuttner and J. Joseph Ryan (Monumenta Iuris Canonici, Series C: Subsidia, vol. i. Città del Vaticano, 1965).

1 *Histoire du Droit et des Institutions de l'Église en Occident*, publiée sous la direction de Gabriel Le Bras, I: *Prolégomènes*, par G. Le Bras (Paris 1955), p. 161.

legatine canons, extended to the northern province of York. (York, throughout the thirteenth century, produced no independent provincial legislation.) At the level of the diocese, many English bishops made determined efforts to discipline and instruct their flocks through the medium of synodal statutes and pastoral letters. We see a great flowering, from a short series of diocesan statutes put out by Stephen Langton at Canterbury in 1213 or 1214 to the elaborate and lengthy set issued by Peter Quinel of Exeter in 1287. Between these we can assign to fifteen dioceses some thirty-two texts.[1]

I shall not dwell upon the legatine and provincial canons, but descend at once to the diocesan statutes of the thirteenth century, which present their own textual problems and points of interest. And the textual history has a wide historical interest: what evidence does it provide that the statutes were copied, read, understood, observed? The question of the observance of a law tends to induce in a legal historian the reaction of an ostrich. It is much easier (though not always easy) to measure the intention of the legislator than to determine the success of his efforts.[2] Was the law untimely and fruitless? Or did it become a dead letter at some later stage? In the case of our diocesan statutes the problem is particularly hard. Few complementary records survive to throw light on the operation of the law; and even if some of the prohibitions failed in their effect or fell into desuetude, the statutes also provided precepts and elementary instruction which had an educative value irrespective of sanctions and a constant contemporaneity.

English diocesan statutes offer no virgin field to the modern scholar. More than half of this legislation was printed more than two hundred years ago by David Wilkins, in *Concilia Magnae Britanniae et Hiberniae* (London, 1737) and passed thence

---

[1] The English sees numbered 17. In addition four Welsh sees were subordinate to Canterbury, and Whithorn, or Galloway, in Scotland was obedient to York. I do not include in the 32 texts mandates on particular topics, occasionally issued with synodal approval, such as those on Pentecostal processions at Exeter and Chichester or those on the revenues of deceased ecclesiastics at Wells and Hereford.

[2] A. H. M. Jones uttered words of warning about the use of legal enactments as historical evidence by modern historians of the Roman Empire: *The Later Roman Empire 284–602* (Oxford, 1964) i, p. viii.

into Mansi's *Amplissima*. Students have used these printed texts as sources for medieval ecclesiastical and social history. But the fashion in which the statutes were edited has militated against their proper use. They have been misunderstood and underrated, largely because the material could not be looked at as a whole. And this is because only part of it is accessible—and then only in a corrupt form—in the *Concilia*. The rest that is known appears in the edition of *Councils and Synods of the English Church*, planned by the late Sir Maurice Powicke.

Let me illustrate with one or two examples how the state of the printed texts has baffled modern students. These examples will help to introduce and explain certain features in the making and transmission of the statutes. The statutes of Robert Grosseteste, the great bishop of Lincoln, are preserved in far more manuscripts than any other statutes; but Wilkins disguises them as 'a sermon in the synod of Simon Langham, bishop of Ely,' assigned to the year 1364, whereas the correct date is *c.* 1239. This had the effect of making Gasquet and others post-date the evidence which the statutes provide by a century and a quarter. It also meant that when genuine statutes of Ely came to light, incorporating Grosseteste's statutes, their editors never thought of looking to Lincoln for their prototype.[1] Again, Wilkins printed an important set of statutes for the diocese of Winchester as the work of Bishop Henry Woodlock, 1308. Canon Deedes re-published them as the work of Bishop John of Pontoise, twenty years earlier. They can be shown to come from another Bishop John, twenty years earlier still. But not only this. Much of the substance of these Winchester statutes agrees with others which were current in the mid thirteenth century in another southern diocese, Wells, and in the north of England in York and Carlisle. They illustrate the constant borrowing which went on, the repetition (with a modicum of retouching) from diocese to diocese. It is not wise to cite these statutes without trying to track them to their source. The first scholar to use the Carlisle statutes (the Revd. James

---

[1] Cf. C. R. Cheney, *English Synodalia of the XIIIth Century*, 2nd ed. (Oxford, 1968), pp. 136–8 and *C. & S.* ii. 515–23. Details of statutes mentioned in the text above without footnote references will be found in *C. & S.* The numbering of certain statutes as, e.g. Salisbury I and II, follows the practice of that work.

Wilson, in 1905) did not know the others of the same family. Consequently he looked for, and thought he had found, characteristics of 'northern ecclesiastical life and morals' in injunctions which were, so far as we know, framed for the southern diocese of Wells before being repeated verbatim in the northern province. To establish lines of filiation is, indeed, a delicate process. Time and again in Wilkins' *Concilia* the correct relationship is turned back to front. Statutes of Durham, treated as the source of statutes of Richard Poore of Salisbury, are in reality the Salisbury statutes re-issued by Poore at Durham twenty years later. Statutes of York are dated 1306 by Wilkins, who derives them from Chichester statutes of 1289, when in fact they are more than fifty years older than, and the source of, the Chichester statutes. A statute on ornaments ascribed to Archbishop Walter Gray of York, *c.* 1250, certainly originated in the southern province long after his time; it would be extremely unwise—indeed, wholly unjustifiable—to treat it as evidence of the normal furnishing of churches in the diocese of York in the mid thirteenth century.[1]

We now have many more statutes than Wilkins knew. With internal evidence of date and by comparison of the various sets of statutes with one another, a lot may be learnt about the way in which certain series first came into existence. It is a commonplace that medieval ecclesiastical legislators borrowed much, and so helped to diffuse a common custom and discipline within certain limits. M. Gaudemet has recently remarked on the phenomenon in French provincial canons;[2] the work of Iakub Sawicki for Poland and Sigurd Kroon for Sweden show how much the bishops in these countries modelled their statutes on the legislation of France and Germany. When the English statutes are assembled we can get information of the same kind about diffusion and influence. So I turn first to chronology and grouping.

Before the thirteenth century, so the evidence suggests, there

---

[1] Cf. C. R. Cheney, 'So-called Statutes of Archbishops John Pecham and Robert Winchelsey', *JEH*, xii (1961), 18–19.

[2] See above, p. 112 n. 3. Examples of borrowing between French dioceses and provinces are noted by J. Gaudemet in *Revue de Droit Canonique*, ix (1959), 329.

was not much formal diocesan legislation in any region of north-west Europe, though its purpose may have been partly achieved by the oral delivery in synod or chapter of general injunctions. This may be the meaning of a clause in the charter by which Count Alan the Red of Britanny founded Swavesey Priory, Cambridgeshire, before 1086: 'when the archdeacon shall celebrate a synod a monk shall attend for one day . . . to hear *praecepta ecclesiastica.*'[1] In the mid twelfth century Pope Lucius II ordered priests in the diocese of Bayeux to attend their synod and carefully receive *praecepta synodalia* and pass them on to their parishioners.[2] Late in the twelfth century, in 1186, Bishop Hugh of Lincoln 'in his synods ordered that all his subjects, both clerical and lay, in virtue of their obedience should inviolably observe these decrees.'[3] Eight short precepts and prohibitions follow in the chronicler's text, introduced with the words 'Precepit ne. . .'. This might be a reporting of oral pronouncements, and it may be that the title of Odo de Sully's Paris statutes, *Prohibitiones et praecepta*, is a reminiscence of the practice of oral delivery.[4]

The main topics of English diocesan statutes of the thirteenth century, as with continental statutes of the later Middle Ages, may be roughly divided into (1) rules for the discipline of ecclesiastical officials and beneficed clergy, (2) guidance on the nature and administration of the sacraments both for the clergy and the laity, and (3) definitions of the duties of parishioners in matters of tithe, offerings, and so forth. Legislation of this sort is found in canons uttered by Hubert Walter, as legate at York in 1195, and as archbishop of Canterbury at Westminster in 1200. Archbishop Hubert is most often remembered for his services to the royal government of the Angevins and for the

[1] *Early Yorkshire Charters*, iv, ed. C. T. Clay (Yorks. Archaeol. Soc. Record Series, Extra series, 1935) 1.

[2] *Antiquus Cartularius ecclesiae Baiocensis* (*Livre Noir*) ed. V. Bourrienne (Soc. de l'Histoire de Normandie 1902–3), i. 198 (1144). The priest of the peculiar of Bayeux in the diocese of Lisieux was told to attend the bishop's synod 'praecepta tantum auditurus' (ibid. i. 113, cf. 163, 201, 203, 208, 216, 241).

[3] *Gesta Regis Henrici II Benedicti abbatis* ed. W. Stubbs (RS) i. 357.

[4] Cf. 'precepta' of Bishop Roger of Cambrai, 1181 × 1191, *Bull. Med. Canon Law*, n.s. ii (1972), 7–15. The term 'precepta et prohibitiones' is once used in English diocesan statutes of the thirteenth century: those of London II, which borrow extensively from Odo de Sully (*C. & S.* ii. 655, cf. 633).

secular side of his conduct; it is therefore of interest (though not necessarily surprising) that he should head the list of thirteenth-century prelates who worked for better education and better discipline among the clergy. His canons were preserved by chroniclers and others and were used, it seems, by later legislators. (I say 'it seems' because, here as so often, one cannot preclude the possibility of a lost common source.) Who drafted Hubert's canons we cannot say, nor can we name any evident source apart from the Third Lateran Council.

The next identifiable series has more obvious and interesting connections. Statutes printed by Martène from a Corbie manuscript now lost can be shown, by comparing the variants of a text in the flyleaves of a Bury St. Edmunds manuscript at Pembroke College, Cambridge, to be diocesan statutes for Canterbury of Archbishop Stephen Langton in 1213 or 1214: in the period between the summons to the Fourth Lateran and its meeting and between Langton's return to England as archbishop and the raising of the Interdict on England which had lain on the country since March 1208.[1] These statutes, although in some passages they copy Hubert Walter's canons, take us back at once to an academic circle at Paris in the first decade of the thirteenth century. Parts seem to be derived from the legatine canons uttered by Langton's friend Cardinal Robert Courson a few months before; and although there is no verbal borrowing from Odo de Sully, bishop of Paris, the archbishop can hardly have been uninfluenced by Odo's *Prohibitiones et precepta*, which came to be a model for many statutes of the didactic sort throughout northern Europe. These Canterbury statutes are the first of an English group which can be associated with Paris. Shortly after the Fourth Lateran, between 1217 and 1219, Richard Poore, bishop of Salisbury, issued what was one of the most extensive and most influential series of English diocesan statutes. Poore had been at Paris with Langton and Courson; his statutes draw on those of Odo de Sully and Langton; recensions revised after 1222 also use Langton's provincial canons of Oxford. When Poore was translated to Durham in 1228 he took his statutes with him to

[1] C. R. Cheney, 'The Earliest English Diocesan Statutes', *EHR*, lxxv (1960), 2–18.

the northernmost diocese of England; parts, at least, found their way to Scotland.[1] It is worth noting that throughout Poore's pontificate at Salisbury, the sub-dean of the cathedral church was Master Thomas of Chobham, author of a *Summa de Penitentia* which provided the same sort of teaching as is found and desiderated in the synodal statutes, though in a much more extended and systematic form.[2] At about the same time as Poore first produced his statutes, William of Blois, bishop of Worcester, issued a short series (1219). While this shows that the idea of issuing synodal statutes was 'in the air', it does not owe any of its provisions to Langton, Poore, and their circle.

A few years pass and then, between about 1224 and 1230, some seven more sets of diocesan statutes appear: Canterbury, Coventry, Exeter, Winchester, and Worcester are represented, and two more sets cannot be located.[3] Langton at Canterbury and William of Blois at Worcester naturally reiterate and amplify their earlier statutes; Exeter (I) and the unidentified statutes consist, like Canterbury (II), largely of quotations from Canterbury (I) and Salisbury (I). Winchester (I) and Coventry, although they cover much of the same ground, do not slavishly follow the prescriptions of their contemporaries. This group as a whole shows that there was wide interest in the issue of statutes, not confined to any particular section of the episcopate: the bishops concerned include men with curial background like Peter des Roches and William Briwere, and those who had been trained in academic life, Langton, Poore, and Stavensby. They have interests in common, but there are not many signs of mutual influence apart from the Canterbury–Salisbury nexus.

The third group I date tentatively 1239–47. It is more remarkable for its interconnections. If the first group owed much to the influence, prospective and retrospective, of the Fourth Lateran Council, and the second group much to the stimulus given by Langton's provincial council of Oxford

[1] Wilkins, i. 608.

[2] F. Broomfield, *Thomae de Chobham Summa Confessorum* (Louvain, 1968) and see below, pp. 187–8.

[3] It is possible that the Coventry statutes are a few years later. I do not count the reissue by Poore of his Salisbury statutes at Durham. This probably occurred soon after his translation to the northern diocese in 1228.

(1222), this third group, which followed the legatine council of London (1237), may well have been prompted by the efforts of Cardinal Otto to reform both secular and regular clergy during his legation in England between 1237 and 1241.[1] As happens often, we can hardly ever put exact dates to the statutes in this group: only Walter de Cantilupe's statutes of Worcester (III) are precisely dated, 26 July 1240. But where there is verbal identity between statutes of different dioceses we evidently have to reckon not merely with the holding of ideas in common but with personal friendships, common counsel, and the movement of individual officials and dignitaries from one diocese to another. This being so, it is reasonable to observe that despite the wide limits of date which must theoretically be allowed to various sets of statutes in this group, all of them could in fact have been issued within the years 1239–47.[2] Robert Grosseteste, Walter de Cantilupe, William Raleigh, Richard de Wich, Hugh Northwold, Robert Bingham, Nicholas Farnham, Fulk Basset, Walter Gray: these are the prelates responsible for the statutes of the years after 1239. All, with the possible exception of Walter Gray, the aged archbishop of York, were friends of Robert Grosseteste, bishop of Lincoln. Some of their statutes show heavy dependence upon his. At Ely, the Lincoln statutes were first re-issued with only slight modifications. Norwich also took them over, making many additions. The Norwich series was taken by their author, William Raleigh, to Winchester, when he was translated thither, and Raleigh's statutes provided material for Fulk Basset at London. Some statutes went farther afield; for it can be shown that statutes for the diocese of York not only were taken to Chichester, in the southern province, but also crossed the Irish Channel to the archdiocese of Dublin.[3]

[1] For whose activities see D. M. Williamson (Mrs. Owen), 'Some Aspects of the Legation of Cardinal Otto', *EHR*, lxiv (1949), 145–73.

[2] I used to suppose that the statutes of Cantilupe, dated 1240, were the earliest of this group; but closer examination has convinced me that Robert Grosseteste preceded him in issuing his pastoral instructions *c.* 1239, the fruit of his experience in diocesan visitations undertaken soon after he became bishop of Lincoln.

[3] See C. R. Cheney, 'A Group of Related Synodal Statutes of the Thirteenth Century', *Medieval Studies Presented to Aubrey Gwynn, S. J.*, ed. J. A. Watt, J. B. Morrall, and F. X. Martin, O.S.A. (Dublin, 1961) pp. 114–32.

The pervasive influence of Grosseteste must not be allowed to obscure the fact that all these bishops incurred large debts to earlier legislators. Clearly, the habit of statute-making turned prelates into collectors. They quote the recent legatine canons of Otto, as was natural; but for much of the sacramental teaching and other matters they draw on Odo de Sully's statutes, Langton's and, above all, Poore's. They make mosaics out of their predecessors' work.

This propensity to make mosaics leads one to remark how few of the series reveal any sense of form or sustained care in classification. If an arrangement of subjects under the headings of the seven sacraments is sometimes attempted, it generally breaks down. One borrowed statute overlaps with another, or uses a different word for the same thing. Thus the London statutes, dealing with the sacrament of baptism in the words of Exeter (I), order that water used for baptism shall not be kept *in baptisterio* for more than seven days; they provide elsewhere, in a passage drawn from Odo de Sully, for the renewal of the *fontem benedictum* every eighth day.[1] The juxtaposition of the two words for font occurs first in the statutes of Salisbury (I), where *fontes* comes in a quotation from Paris and *baptisterium* in the very next chapter from Canterbury; the conflate passage, containing both words, was repeated unmodified in half a dozen later statutes. Elegance of composition, in short, is not to be looked for, either now or later in the thirteenth century, though there are examples of fine writing of an inflated sort.

The work of Grosseteste and his colleagues was perhaps the high spot in the statute-making of the century: nothing on this scale is found later; but a short burst of activity happened with the next generation of bishops, probably between the years 1257 and 1262. Political affairs were then bringing prelates frequently together, and it was a time favourable to the interchange of ideas and programmes and records. So we find statutes for Salisbury (IV), Wells, Winchester (III), Carlisle, and York (II), all intimately connected. Late in the century, in 1287, Peter Quinel, bishop of Exeter, issued a new series longer than any of his predecessors' and comprehending most of the topics they cover. The compiler seems to have

---

[1] *C. & S.* ii. 635, 641.

known much of the earlier legislation, but as a rule he was at pains to reword his statutes. It is permissible to think that Archbishop John Pecham's canons in the Council of Lambeth (1281) may have acted as a stimulus, though there is no verbal borrowing.

The thirteenth-century statute-making thus falls into a few short periods, and the contents of the various series point to personal contacts between the legislators. To establish which personal contacts mattered most is beyond possibility. One can only say that bishops responsible for related statutes can often be discovered to have been meeting and co-operating in some way or other. Their officials and clerks, who may have been the actual draftsmen, had equal opportunities to meet in the course of their duties; and, just as bishops were sometimes translated, the officials sometimes moved from one diocese to another. The association of Langton and Poore with Courson in Paris has been noted.[1] Poore, we have seen, took his statutes from Salisbury to Durham when he was translated, and Raleigh took his from Norwich to Winchester. As a royal servant Raleigh was associated with Gilbert Basset,[2] whose brother Fulk he consecrated as bishop of London in 1245: Fulk's statutes borrow a good deal from Raleigh's. Then there is the group of related statutes for Salisbury (IV), Wells, and Carlisle. The Wells and the Carlisle statutes, almost identical, can both be dated in 1258 or 1259. Textual examination shows that the Salisbury statutes preceded them, and these, being attributed to Bishop Giles of Bridport, cannot be earlier than 1257. Now on 14 April 1258 the bishop of Salisbury and the bishop of Bath and Wells met at Bermondsey to consecrate Robert de Chaury as bishop of Carlisle. The connection is obvious. Finally, the connection between the statutes of York (I) and Chichester (II) may be explained by the fact that Archbishop Walter Giffard of York had an official, Master Gilbert of St. Leofard, who became bishop of Chichester.

Material traces of these contacts and borrowings are to be found in the muniment book of Salisbury into which was copied in the thirteenth century the only known text of

---

[1] *EHR*, lxxv (1960), 2–18, esp. 14 n. 3.
[2] Matthew Paris, *Chronica majora* ed. H. R. Luard (RS), iii. 381–2.

Winchester (II), and in that of Durham cathedral which contains the statutes of York (I and II).[1] Quite apart from the
interest of would-be legislators in the statutes of their colleagues, there was the practical need and legal obligation of
ecclesiastical corporations possessed of churches and tithe in
other dioceses to be acquainted with the rules and customs
which prevailed there.[2]

One fact emerges very prominently from analysis of the
available material, a fact quite obscured by Wilkins's errors and
omissions: the copying of the practices of the southern province of Canterbury in the northern province of York. The
laws of the three northern dioceses of York, Durham, and
Carlisle include comparatively few regulations which cannot
be found in practically the same words at an earlier date in the
south; they record only a handful of discrepant customs. This
predominant influence of the larger and wealthier province of
Canterbury is matched in the history of the provincial canons
and of the ordinances of the Benedictine general chapter;[3]
it is matched, too, in the behaviour of the clergy in respect of
taxation. York usually follows the lead of Canterbury in fact,
however jealously it nurtures provincial sentiment.

By way of introduction to the textual problems presented by
the manuscripts, a word should be said about the authority on
which the statutes were brought into existence. It seems that
a synod gave a bishop no more authority to legislate than he
possessed independently of it.[4] Some of his enactments needed
the assent of his cathedral chapter, and examples of such assent
occur in the synodal statutes;[5] but at least two bishops,
Stavensby of Coventry and Grosseteste of Lincoln, issued

---

[1] Salisbury, D. &. C. Muniments, Liber evidenciarum C; Brit. Mus., MS.
Lansdowne 397. Cf. *C. & S.* ii, Index of MSS.

[2] Cf. the association of London statutes with what appears to be a Norwich
list of feast-days: C. R. Cheney, 'Rules for the Observance of Feast-Days in
Medieval England', *BIHR*, xxxiv (1961), 127–9, and *C. & S.* ii. 655–6.

[3] Cf. C. R. Cheney, 'Legislation of the Medieval English Church', *EHR*,
l (1935), 216, and p. 112 above.

[4] Cheney, *English Synodalia*, 44–5.

[5] *C. & S.* ii. 197 (Hereford), 384, 552 (Salisbury), 497 (York), 500 (Norwich).
Cf. the preamble to statutes of Bishop Thomas of Breslau, 1290: 'presentibus et
expressum consensum prebentibus his nostris fratribus . . .' (*Concilia Poloniae*, ed.
J. Sawicki, x (Wrocław, 1963), 333–4, cf. 340–4).

statutes without reference to a synod. If the authority of the synod was occasionally invoked in such terms as 'presentis synodi auctoritate', it is doubtful whether this meant more than the 'synodali diffinitione', and the like, that we meet elsewhere. The *approbatio* of a synod was commonly claimed. Probably in every case of statutes approved in a synod the bishop's clerks had prepared them beforehand. This would not exclude the possibility of later modification, suggested maybe by the bishop's subjects. An interesting thirteenth-century note in a Devonshire cartulary appears to have been intended for recital in a synod of Walter Bronescombe, bishop of Exeter (1258–80). The note reads: 'And we order that the synodal statutes of Bishop William our predecessor be inviolably observed until we shall have reformed them in certain chapters, having reached a definite decision upon them after consulting the clergy and laity.'[1]

In what condition and to what extent have these statutes survived? Answers to these questions are needed if we are to evaluate the material for historical purposes. Of thirty-two sets of statutes a dozen survive only in single manuscripts. Among the remainder, each preserved in more than one copy, those of Lincoln head the list with about twenty-five manuscripts, Exeter (II) comes next with twelve copies, and a few others have four, five, or six. As regards date, half the sets of statutes, although published in the thirteenth century, are only known in fourteenth-century copies. Twenty-two of the sets, although published in the thirteenth century, were still being copied in the fourteenth century, some in the fifteenth. On the other hand I know of no early printed editions, such as we find in some French dioceses where, even when no manuscript survives, fourteenth-century statutes were printed in the fifteenth and sixteenth centuries.[2] Does the explanation lie in the nature of the English book-trade, or must it be sought elsewhere?

---

[1] *C. & S.* ii. 227.

[2] e.g. statutes of Albi (1340) were printed in 1499, 1528, and 1553; see André Artonne, 'Les statuts synodaux diocésains français', *Revue d'histoire de l'église de France*, xxxvi (1950), 179; and see further A. Artonne, L. Guizard, and Odette Pontal, *Répertoire des Statuts Synodaux des Diocèses de l'Ancienne France*, 2nd ed., 1969. Professor Iakub Sawicki's work shows the importance of the early printing press in the history of Polish synods.

Be that as it may, the facts noted about the manuscripts are significant.

Surviving copies are scarce. That could mean either that they were much read and fell to bits, or that they circulated little, were seldom copied, little known, and therefore deserve less attention from historians. The fact that a high proportion of the manuscripts comes from the later centuries shows that the former explanation is probably the right one. The statutes *were* much read and there *has* been enormous wastage. A parallel may be seen in Grosseteste's pastoral works: not one thirteenth-century copy of his *De decem mandatis* is listed by Professor Harrison Thomson. But the survival of late manuscripts also shows something else: the thirteenth-century statutes would not have been copied later if others had been issued which rendered them out of date. These late copies tell against any extensive statute-making in the fourteenth century the products of which might be presumed lost. In other words, the chief period of activity in England was the thirteenth century. Now this is of interest, because in France and other continental countries there were new compilations in plenty later in the Middle Ages. In England, by contrast, there are few new comprehensive series of synodal statutes in the fourteenth century. The ecclesiastical authorities seem to have been satisfied with what was already available.[1] When a fourteenth-century bishop had to make a general announcement or order he sent a separate mandate on the subject to his archdeacons for circulation in the deaneries. For example, the bishop of Winchester sent a letter on 15 July 1317 to his archdeacons: 'ad monendum omnes rectores Wintoniensis diocesis quod non reponant fructus suos alibi quam in solo ecclesiastico'.[2] Mandates of this sort were numerous throughout the century and, like this one, were often copied into the registers of the bishops

---

[1] A bishop might formally require the observance of a predecessor's statutes, as at Wells in 1342 (Wilkins, ii. 711), but there is little sign of this procedure. It is more usual to find fourteenth-century bishops invoking particular chapters of their predecessors' statutes: *C. & S.* ii. 491 notes 4 and 5, 496 notes 1 and 3, 600 note 4.

[2] *The Registers of John de Sandale and Rigaud de Asserio, Bishops of Winchester*, ed. F. J. Baigent (Hants Record Soc. 1897) 41. In effect this elaborated and added a sanction to one chapter of the Winchester statutes of Bishop John Gervais (1262 × 1265) (*C. & S.* ii. 712). See further, Cheney, *English Synodalia*, pp. 43–4.

who issued them. It is less common to find bishops sending out comprehensive instructions, though in 1361 Archbishop Simon Islip sent out a handbook on the seven deadly sins and their species and the ten commandments, to be copied by the clergy of the diocese of Canterbury; and in 1367 Archbishop John Thoresby of York copied and commented upon the chapter 'De informatione simplicium sacerdotum' of Archbishop John Pecham's provincial canons of Lambeth (1281).[1]

I have spoken of the number of thirteenth-century statutes and the number of the manuscripts of the statutes. The state of the surviving texts is also highly instructive. But in order to understand that, we must first observe what arrangements were originally made for the diffusion of the statutes. The most comprehensive early orders are those of Richard Poore at Salisbury. He orders that the archdeacons cause rural deans to have his statutes transcribed and corrected, and the deans are to cause other priests to have them by the next Michaelmas. An order based on this is issued by Fulk Basset at London. At Winchester, Peter des Roches orders that 'every archdeacon or dean, when he celebrates a general chapter, have the synodal statutes recited . . . and under pain of suspension these synodal statutes are to be written down in every church, lest anyone be able to excuse himself by ignorance.' At Worcester each parish priest is told to bring the statutes to synod with him, and when they are recited in synod he must be able to answer questions about them distinctly and clearly and to read them when called upon. Richard de Wich of Chichester ordains that all priests with cure of souls should have the statutes 'in libellis suis', to render account for transgression of any of the precepts. Other statutes follow the same pattern, and it is in compliance with injunctions of this sort that inventories of church property contain 'statuta synodalia'.[2] We find like arrangements in France. The bishop of Angers orders archdeacons to see that priests have the statutes; those who have no copies may obtain

---

[1] Cf. W. A. Pantin, *The English Church in the Fourteenth Century* (Cambridge, 1955), p. 212.

[2] Cheney, *English Synodalia*, pp. 45–6, and see later visitations of Exeter, as recorded in the register (edited by F. C. Hingeston-Randolph) of Bishop Walter de Stapeldon (pp. 130, 133, 337, 368).

them at their own expense from two sworn clerks of the bishop's court, who are named.[1] French statutes, too, order priests to produce in synod their own copies, not copies borrowed for the occasion (just as English archdeacons had to look out for incumbents who borrowed books and vestments from their neighbours to make a good showing at visitation time). In Breslau, Bishop Thomas in 1279 ordered his clergy to exhibit written copies of constitutions in their churches, near the altar, on a wooden board.[2]

Despite the punishment threatened in the English statutes against parish priests who fail to get and produce copies of the statutes, the rules were not observed perfectly. In 1330 visitations in the diocese of Exeter discovered 'sinodus deficit' in two churches as against three which possessed 'synodus cum summula' and a fourth which had the 'summula'.[3] In 1342 visitations in the same diocese revealed that six churches had 'sinodus falsus et defectivus' and the like.[4] Copies were still in the hands of parochial clergy in the fifteenth century, and a clerk of Exeter diocese left his *synodus* to the chapel of the Blessed Virgin Mary, Culmstock, in 1412;[5] but it is uncommon to distinguish among existing texts copies which demonstrably belonged to parochial incumbents.[6] B.M. MS. Add. 48344 is probably the *libellus* of some thirteenth-century priest of the diocese of London and contains London statutes, but it has no

[1] This and other prescriptions are quoted by Olga Dobiache-Rojdestvensky, *La vie paroissiale en France au XIIIe siècle* (1911), p. 56; cf. Cheney, *English Synodalia*, pp. 46–8. A treatise on synods, seemingly French, late in the 13th century, speaks of assemblies of clergy in the deaneries at which the presidents ought to enquire whether synodal statutes and mandates are observed (Vatican, Bibl. Apost., cod. Burghes. 176 fo. 162va. Another text of the work is in Paris, B.N. MS. lat. 16682).

[2] *Concilia Poloniae*, x. 333.

[3] *Register of John de Grandisson, Bishop of Exeter*, ed. F. C. Hingeston-Randolph (London and Exeter, 1894–9), i. 570, 572, 575–8.

[4] *EHR*, xxvi (1911), 110, 112, 120.

[5] *Register of Edmund Stafford, Bishop of Exeter*, ed. F. C. Hingeston-Randolph (London 1886), p. 399.

[6] For France there are manuscripts of statutes (Bib. Nat. MSS. lat. 1541, 1555, 1597) of which *ex libris* inscriptions show that they belonged to parish churches in the dioceses of Avignon and Nantes; but most of the texts of the statutes of Odo de Sully are of a different character: these may now be studied in the edition by Odette Pontal, *Les statuts synodaux français du XIIIe siècle*, tome I (Coll. des. docts. inédits sur l'histoire de France, série in 8o, vol. 9), Paris, 1972.

explicit mark of provenance. More often the texts owe their survival to the fact that they were handsome 'fair copies', forming part of a more substantial library, of an ecclesiastical official or a religious house.

English bishops were not content to arrange for copies of their statutes to be multiplied. They provided that in subsequent chapters of archdeaconries and deaneries the statutes should be publicly recited. Quinel of Exeter required priests to learn his *Summula* by heart, and a generation later his successor was trying to enforce the rule on parsons at their institution.[1] Cantilupe of Worcester required the public reading by a priest in chapter of some part of his statutes and of a tract on penance. 'When a difficulty arises in them,' he enjoined, 'let it be explained; and where the reader at one chapter leaves off, let another reader begin at the next chapter; and no reader is to be forewarned, but let the president of the chapter hand out what is to be read.' The need to explain (*exponere*) was continually stressed.[2] At Wells and Exeter it was envisaged that the parochial clergy would expound some at least of the statutes to the laity in the vernacular. In the fourteenth and fifteenth centuries John Pecham's statute 'De informatione simplicium sacerdotum' appeared in English translation and with an English commentary, and statutes for the archdeaconry of London were translated into English. But, naturally, not all was suitable for lay consumption. Oxford, New College MS. 207 has chapters extracted in the fourteenth century from statutes of Salisbury: they have marginal notes: 'non oportet dici laycis', 'non oportet exponi laycis'.[3]

References to corrected copies of the statutes and to the bringing of copies to synods point to additions and alterations

---

[1] *C. & S.* ii. 1077 and note 1; cf. ibid. 626 (Wells, 1258?): 'quasi cordetenus colligant'. At Albi in 1230 the clergy were told to read the synodal statutes twice a week, in lieu of reciting the seven penitential psalms; they were to bring their copies to synods and have them at hand when the archdeacon commented upon them; see L. de Lacger, 'Statuts synodaux inédits du diocèse d'Albi du xiiiᵉ siècle,' *Revue historique de Droit français et étranger*, 4ᵉ série, vi (1927), 427.

[2] *C. & S.* ii. 321 (Worcester), 435 (Durham), 496 (York), 1089–90 (Chichester). Gavanti, in seventeenth-century Italy, held that the statutes should be written in Latin, but might be glossed in the vernacular when read in synod (Cheney, *English Synodalia*, p. 11 n. 5).

[3] *C. & S.* ii. 366.

published in successive assemblies. This evidently was a common procedure. It explains the disorderly state of most of our texts and the doubts about their authorship. In such a process of compilation an original core of statutes, fairly shapely at first, would receive correction and addition, announced orally in synod after synod to the owners of copies. Such parish priests as were present would do their best to delete and interline. A whole new statute might be inserted at an appropriate point in the original text, as the president directed; but if there were not room for it there, it might join others to form an appendix at the end of the series.[1] The variation of pattern is not peculiar to this form of legislation. Dr. David Daube, in his *Studies in Biblical Law*, devotes a chapter to 'Codes and Codas', dealing with the practice of tacking on new rules to existing codes, illustrated from the Lex Aquilia and the Pentateuch.[2] The process of retouching synodal statutes can hardly ever have been done with complete accuracy. Our manuscripts reflect the consequences, though in a blurred fashion. When more than one manuscript of a set of statutes survive, the process is often evident, even if the details are obscure; for the manuscripts seldom contain all the same material. But even in statutes for which we only have a single manuscript, and that a late and a neat copy, we may with care detect the same features. The statutes of Richard de Wich for Chichester are written continuously by one hand in one manuscript, which comes from Chichester cathedral; but one chapter (c. 36) is apparently misplaced, and in two places a chapter appears to be the revised version of the chapter it follows, which ought to have been cancelled when the revised version was added to the exemplar of our only text. In other words, an existing text commonly presents statutes in a form in which they were never published. It is, as often as not, an incomplete conflation.

Along with these confusing features we must reckon with the facts that those who first copied the statutes seldom felt the need to indicate the author or time of composition, and those who copied them in later generations were, as a rule, ignorant and uninterested. Of Grosseteste's statutes fifteen manuscripts

---

[1] Cheney, *English Synodalia*, pp. 47–8.
[2] (Cambridge, 1947) ch. 2, pp. 74–101.

are without any mark of authorship, whereas only eight ascribe them to Grosseteste; one other ascribes them to Simon Langham, bishop of Ely,[1] one to Robert Winchelsey, archbishop of Canterbury. Statutes of Durham (II) are ascribed to Nicholas Farnham in one manuscript and to Walter Kirkham in another. The manuscripts of our earliest diocesan statutes, Canterbury (I), and the only known manuscript of the statutes of Carlisle have no titles. The circumstances of issue and copying explain not only the terribly corrupt state of certain statutes and the many errors of ascription (which seriously affect their evidential value), but also the great wastage of copies, and, indeed, the probable total loss of some statutes. Texts were written into priests' *libelli* in scores; and these unattractive little books, made more repulsive by use and frequent emendation, offering no inducement to later generations to preserve them, have perished in scores. It is a point to be remembered.

The omissions and errors of arrangement in our manuscripts at least suggest that the statutes were read and used. But what of the verbal errors in the texts? To take one example, what of the errors common to the only two known texts of the statutes of Wells, both written in the fourteenth century, long after the time (1258?) of issue? They are both contained in large, imposing volumes along with provincial and legatine canons, evidently prepared for the use of ecclesiastical lawyers. The amount of emendation required by these two texts, as revealed by a comparison with the sources and derivatives of the statutes, is prodigious. Neither of the scribes can have tried seriously to make sense of what he copied. Since they have many errors in common and since neither copied from the other, we must assume that yet a third corrupt copy lay behind them. A few errors, indeed, must go back to the copy which served as an archetype for the Carlisle derivative, since our Wells and our Carlisle texts occasionally err together.[2] Copying was mechanical and error was inveterate. The manuscripts seldom show signs of correction. Nobody seems to have minded.

Contemplation of the texts, indeed, makes one wonder whether the statutes were ever read with understanding or

---

[1] A thirteenth-century text with a fifteenth-century title.

[2] *C. & S.* ii. 592 note e, 595 note k, 598 note d, 610 note x, 612 notes f and m.

ever copied with care. Was the copying in later centuries mere formalism or antiquarianism? These gloomy reflections may be lightened somewhat if we leave the texts themselves and look elsewhere for traces of their impact on the Church. At least some parts of them influenced some people, for passages from them are quoted here and there, particularly in anonymous anthologies of didactic material.[1] The most striking and probably the most influential piece of borrowing is to be seen in the bulky writings of William of Paull (de Pagula): his *Summa Summarum* and *Oculus Sacerdotis* quote a good deal from thirteenth-century statutes of Salisbury, besides copying *in extenso* a tithe statute of doubtful origin.[2] Again, some of the statutes were torn from their context and circulated, origin forgotten, without title or with a spurious ascription. This is particularly true of statutes which bore upon the obligations of layfolk to pay tithes or mortuaries or other dues to the clergy. I have called attention elsewhere[3] to the amount of material which William Lyndwood, in 1430, put into his *Provinciale* under the names and metropolitan authority of archbishops of Canterbury who had had nothing to do with its promulgation. Before Lyndwood's time lawyers and stationers of the fourteenth century had been responsible for gathering together with the genuine provincial legislation these extracts from diocesan statutes of Salisbury, or Wells, or Exeter. We only possess one manuscript (mid-fourteenth-century and hitherto unpublished) of the synodal statutes of Robert Bingham for Salisbury, but his pronouncement on tithe appears in a dozen other places, sometimes ascribed to archbishops, to Stephen Langton or Boniface of Savoy or Robert Winchelsey, or else to the legate Otto, or even to Pope Innocent IV. By a similar process a synodal statute of Exeter, concerning trees in churchyards, came to masquerade in the statute-book as a royal statute of 25 Edward I.[4]

---

[1] B.M. MS. Harl. 106 is a good example, of the fifteenth century.

[2] For William see Leonard Boyle, O.P. 'The *Oculus sacerdotis* and Some Other Works of William of Pagula', *Trans. Royal Hist. Soc.* 5th series, v (1955), 81–110. Cf. *C. & S.* ii. 888 and notes. See also Boyle, 'The *Summa Summarum* and Some Other English Works of Canon Law', *Proceedings of the Second International Congress of Medieval Canon Law* (1965).

[3] 'William Lyndwood's Provinciale', below, pp. 167–73.

[4] *C. & S.* ii. 365, 1009.

This study of the condition and extent of survival confirms the impression got from the textual history of the provincial canons, different though that history is. The absence of authentication, the blind copying of corrupt nonsense, the acceptance of the spurious and the dubious, throw a cold light on the methods by which the hierarchy and the ecclesiastical lawyers accumulated a corpus of local laws. This, however, need not prevent us from deriving profit from a critical study of the statutes. Although they may, like so much of the evidence for medieval history, represent unattained ideals, they can be made to show what sort of instruction thirteenth-century prelates thought necessary and desirable for their clergy and people; and a comparison of the various statutes will show the extent to which custom varied from diocese to diocese, and the way in which it was transmitted from one diocese to another. But that is another story which cannot be touched on here.[1]

[1] Cf. 'Aspects of diocesan legislation', below, pp. 185–202.

8. William Lyndwood's *Provinciale**

FEW English canonists of the later Middle Ages made any mark as authors, and none has been esteemed so highly as William Lyndwood (*c.* 1375–1446). Chancellor of the archbishop of Canterbury, official of the Court of Canterbury, prelocutor of the clergy in convocation, an archdeacon and, late in life, a bishop, Lyndwood had ample experience of the workings of the canon law in England. When, having assembled in the *Provinciale* the constitutions put out by successive archbishops of Canterbury, he commented upon them, he brought to the task the learning of a doctor of both laws, well read in all the continental decretalists; civilians and theologians also appear in his gloss and he cites approvingly 'Richardus Hampole in prologo Psalterii sui'.[1] Among the English canonists he was, Maitland suggests, 'pre-eminently learned and pre-eminently able'.[2] As a legal commentary his gloss is far superior to that of the canon of Lincoln, John Athon or Acton, who had in the previous century glossed the legatine constitutions of Otto and Ottobuono. Thomas Fuller thought the *Provinciale* 'a worthy Work, highly esteemed by forraign Lawyers: not so particularly Provincial for England, but that they are usefull for other Countries, his Comment thereon being a Magazine of the Canon-Law.' He opined that the *Provinciale*, '(though now beheld by some as an Almanack out of date) will be valued by the judicious whilst Learning and Civility have a being'.[3] Edmund Gibson[4] testifies to the

---

* First published in *The Jurist*, xxi (1961), 405–34.

[1] *Provinciale*, 3.14.1 *ad ver.* Psalteria (p. 184*a*). The edition to which references are given here and below is that printed at Oxford, by H. Hall for R. Davis, 1679, small folio. This has two appendixes, separately paginated: the legatine constitutions of Otto and Ottobuono with the gloss of John Athon, and the provincial constitutions in their (presumed) order of publication.

[2] F. W. Maitland, *Roman Canon Law in the Church of England* (1898,) p. 6.

[3] Thomas Fuller, *The Church-History of Britain* (1655), ii. 176.

[4] Edmund Gibson, *Codex Iuris Ecclesiastici Anglicani* (1713), pp. vii, xii–xiii. The *Codex* reprints many of Lyndwood's texts and some of his commentary. For

influence of 'our learned commentator Lyndwood' upon later generations of English lawyers. So it is no wonder that Lyndwood has been the object of study in recent times: biographical details have been brought together,[1] Maitland has commented brilliantly and at length upon the significance of Lyndwood's gloss,[2] and English ecclesiastical historians who wish to cite the provincial constitutions have tended to take Lyndwood as their authority. All this both removes the necessity to discuss the man or his work in general and makes it desirable to look closely at the composition and contents of the *Provinciale*. What led Lyndwood to compose it? What texts were available to him? What use did he make of them? These are the questions with which this study is concerned.

I

Lyndwood's object in composing the *Provinciale* is set out plainly in the author's dedication to his master, Henry Chichele, archbishop of Canterbury. At the archbishop's instance, he had read and considered for a long time the statutes of the archbishops of Canterbury (including those of Chichele himself), published in councils of the province. He found in them far too many in a state of disorder, some corrupted by bad scribes, others which led to confusion by the prolixity of their preambles, others of uncertain authorship, and many of temporary or no importance. He cut out the superfluous (he says) and chose the more useful, and collected them, somewhat abridged,

the bearing of the provincial constitutions which Lyndwood glossed on the post-Reformation Church of England cf. *EHR*, l (1935), 194–5.

[1] See especially the article in *Dictionary of National Biography* by J. M. Rigg (1893) and A. B. Emden, *Biographical Register of the University of Oxford to A.D. 1500* (Oxford, 1957–9) ii. 1191–3. Lyndwood has been ignored by the compilers of the *Dictionnaire de Droit Canonique*.

[2] *Roman Canon Law*, especially chapter I on William Lyndwood, originally published in *EHR*, xi (1896). The sharp attack upon this by Arthur Ogle, *The Canon Law in Mediaeval England: an Examination of William Lyndwood's Provinciale, in reply to the late Prof. F. W. Maitland* (1912) was ill-conceived, perverse, and misleading. A more valuable general criticism is that of J. W. Gray, 'Canon law in England: some reflections on the Stubbs–Maitland controversy', in *Studies in Church History*, vol. iii, ed. G. J. Cuming (Leiden, 1966), 48–68. Cf. B. Z. Kedar, 'Canon law and local practice', *Bull. Med. Canon Law*, N.S. ii (1972), 17–32.

under appropriate titles after the model of the books of Decretals. This task he completed before he went on a diplomatic mission to Portugal from March to September 1422. In 1423, having returned to his duties as official of the Court of Canterbury, he decided to gloss these statutes with the idea of equipping himself better, through a study of the fundamental laws and canons, to deal with the legal cases and the business in which he was constantly involved. He realized that despite the merits of the constitutions, many prelates and judges and their subjects in the province of Canterbury neglected to observe them, and he thought that they would be better known and studied if they were more clearly presented. He therefore proffered his work to the archbishop for the good of the English Church, submitting it to correction if he had offended against the truth of divine, canon, or civil law. In a note at the end of the gloss, the author states that he reached the end of his work on the eve of Whitsun, 3 June 1430.[1]

The first task of Lyndwood, then, was to compress into the framework of the *tituli* of the Gregorian Decretals (so far as his material allowed) the provincial legislation at his disposal.[2] In this form it comprised about 240 chapters, and at the head of each chapter Lyndwood named the author. Towards the end of his gloss (5.15.2) he enumerated the 'constitutiones quas habemus in regno Angliae',[3] beginning with those of Archbishop Stephen Langton, 1222. He included in his collection the greater part of the laws of the archbishops from Langton to Chichele, together with some documents of questionable origin which will be discussed below. The omissions can be explained by the fact that some constitutions were

---

[1] The elaborate index of contents is dated 25 Jan. 1434 ('festo Conversionis sancti Pauli a.d. 1433'): sig i² verso. The dating clause states that William Lyndwood ('de Tilia Nemore') compiled the index; but perhaps *compilata* should be *compilatum* to agree with *librum* rather than *tabula*.

[2] He has only 75 titles, compared with the 185 Gregorian titles (Maitland, *Roman Canon Law*, p. 37), and the artificiality of his pattern is seen in lib. 1, tit.11 'De officio archipresbyteri' (p. 54) which copies the title of *Extra*, 1.24. It treats of the duty of parish priests to teach their flock, although elsewhere in his glosses Lyndwood equates the archpriest (not a common person, though not unknown, in England) to the rural dean. The *tabula* does not index 'archipresbyter'.

[3] Below, p. 162 n. 3.

little more than repetitions of earlier ones,[1] while others dealt with out-of-date[2] or trivial topics.

In collecting and re-arranging the old laws of the province Lyndwood was but doing what had been done in other provinces of the Latin Church in the fourteenth century. A much-travelled man, he may well have known some of the earlier compilations.[3] At the very time he was writing, at the other end of Europe, Archbishop Nicholas of Gniezno published (1420) a collection of provincial statutes in five books 'sub certis et consuetis titulis'.[4] These continental compilations were all issued by metropolitan authority. Lyndwood's, by contrast, was originally and remained an unofficial book, despite the author's statement to Chichele that he was 'vestrae paternitatis reverendissimae hortamentis instigatus.' But Lyndwood went further than the continental compilers when he supplied an ample gloss. This made up, to some extent, for the inadequacy of a mere *Provinciale* as a textbook for prelates and practitioners in the law, by copious reference to the *ius commune* and its commentators. He had in mind, so he says, the less well-informed and well-equipped students, who presumably had no access to large libraries and needed a gloss not only to discuss the law but also to define the terms.[5] On

---

[1] e.g., the constitution of Lambeth (1281) against pluralities is omitted because that of Reading (1279) is included. The reiteration of Winchelsey's decree on stipendiary priests by Courtenay and Chichele (cf. below, p. 168 n. 7) did not need to be added to the original version.

[2] The legislation of Stephen Langton and Boniface respecting the Jews was of no practical use in the fifteenth century, and was omitted.

[3] Cf. *EHR*, l (1935), 216–17, and Th. Gousset, *Les Actes de la Province ecclésiastique de Reims* (Reims, 1843), ii. 534–75 for Reims (*c.* 1330); J. D. Mansi, *Ampl. Collectio Conciliorum* (Venice, 1759–98), xxv. 297–350 for Mainz (1310) and xxvi. 75–106 for Prag (*c.* 1346) follow the pattern of *tituli* of the *Corpus Iuris Canonici*. Mansi xxvi. 23–74 for Florence, *c.* 1346, is arranged in five books.

[4] *EHR*, l (1935), 217 n. 1, and see Jakub Sawicki in *Studia Zródoznawcze*, i (Warszawa, 1957), 193 and tab. ix–xi, and in *Ztschr. der Savigny-Stiftung für Rechtsgeschichte, kan. Abt.*, xlvi (1960), 402–4.

[5] *Provinciale*, 2.2.1 *ad ver.* Commenta (p. 95a): Quia non solum sapientibus sed insipientibus (ut loquar cum apostolo Ad Rom. I) debitor sum, et praesens opus non praecipue nec principaliter viris scribo scientia literarum praeditis sed potius simpliciter literatis et pauca intelligentibus, quorum labor ut plurimum magis assuescit in inspiciendis constitutionibus provincialibus quam aliis ecclesiae constitutionibus generalibus, propterea, ad faciliorem harum constitutionum intellectum qui ex verborum expositione et eorundem significatione resultare potest, ad maiorem utilitatem simplicium in hoc opere studere volentium,

points of law it was his task (to borrow Maitland's words) to discuss 'the edicts issued by a non-sovereign legislator. He has to consider whether and how they can be harmonized with a large body of law which that legislator has no power to repeal or to override. The archbishop may make for his province statutes which are merely declaratory of the *ius commune* of the Church, statutes which recall it to memory, statutes which amplify it and give to it a sharper edge. He may supplement the papal legislation; but he has no power to derogate from, to say nothing of abrogating, the laws made by his superior.'[1]

The texts which Lyndwood assembled illustrate the historical growth of the English Church over two hundred years, but he collected them as documents of living law, and studied them as such. His readers in the fifteenth century were no more interested in the circumstances in which the constitutions of Oxford (1222) were issued than they were interested in the date and original significance of a twelfth-century text in *Extra* or a third-century text in the *Digest*.[2] To use Lyndwood as a guide to the law of any time but his own is a task of some delicacy.

II

Where did Lyndwood find the provincial constitutions which he undertook to gloss? Near the end of his work he obligingly sets out in chronological order 'the constitutions we have in the realm of England'[3] (with sublime indifference to the legislation of the province of York, if not in sheer ignorance of it). First comes Stephen Langton in the Council of Oxford, 1222; then come the legate Otto, 1236 (*sic*); Archbishop Boniface, 1260 (*sic*); the legate Ottobuono, 1268; John Pecham at Reading, 1279, and at Lambeth, 1281; Robert Winchelsey, 1305; Walter

sic ut patet, procedere dignum duxi, aliqua iuxta verborum proprietates ad utilitatem eorundem studentium interserens quae ex ipsarum constitutionum sententia sumi seu alias convenienter tractari minime potuissent.

[1] *Roman Canon Law*, p. 19.

[2] Cf. F. de Zulueta on the Bartolists: 'What mattered most to the law student was not the meaning of a text of Ulpian or Papinian to its author, but the meaning attached to it by doctrine and practice, in short what Accursius and Bartolus said it meant' (*Don Antonio Agustín* (Glasgow, 1939), p. 34).

[3] *Provinciale*, 5.15.2 *ad ver.* Minime (p. 319): 'Constitutiones quas habemus in regno Angliae'.

Reynolds, entitled Oxford II, 1322; Simon Mepham, 1328 (*sic*); John Stratford, 1342; Simon Islip, 1361 (*sic*); Simon Sudbury, 1378; Thomas Arundel in the Council of Oxford, 1408 (*sic*); Henry Chichele, 1415. He adds: 'Constitutionum vero Edmundi et Richardi archiepiscoporum datas non scribo, quia datam alicuius earundem non vidi certam; verum tamen est quod Richardus immediate successit Stephano praedicto, et Richardo successit Edmundus.' Under these ascriptions was included almost all that Lyndwood brought into his compilation. Since he had undertaken a *Provinciale*, he did not give the texts of the legatine canons of Otto and Ottobuono, who legislated for a wider area, but he referred to these often in his commentary, using the edition glossed by John Athon *c.* 1340.[1] He did not shrink from introducing two secular pronouncements: the writ *Circumspecte agatis* (1286)[2] and a part of the royal replies to the *Articuli cleri* (1316).[3]

The provincial constitutions in the *Provinciale*, as already remarked, include nearly everything of importance from Langton to Chichele. Had Lyndwood been doing an historian's task, he might have looked back beyond Langton: from Lanfranc to Hubert Walter a dozen English councils had issued constitutions, and Lyndwood had access to libraries where texts of these constitutions lay lurking. But Lyndwood was a lawyer, not an historian.[4] In general he did not wish to penetrate behind the texts which were usually cited.[5] From

---

[1] It was Athon who led him to give a wrong date to Otto's Council of London, 1237; see *Provinciale*, appendix I p. 5, proem *ad ver*. statuenda.

[2] For the date and nature of the document see E. B. Graves in *EHR*, xliii (1928), 1–20. See Lyndwood's note, *Provinciale*, 2.2.2 (p. 96): 'Excerpta ex responsionibus regiis'; he gives no date but notes 'non est constitutio provincialis sed emanavit a decreto domini regis, quomodo videlicet iustitiarii sui missi in dioecesi Norwicensi . . . se quoad clerum . . . abstinerent ab infrascriptis.'

[3] *Provinciale*, 3.28.7 (p. 268): 'Ex responsionibus regiis', without date; arts. 9, 15, 16. The articles are in *Stat. Realm* (Record Comm.), i. 171–4 and in *Sel. Documents of Eng. Constitutional Hist. 1307–1485*, ed. S. B. Chrimes and A. L. Brown (London, 1961), pp. 19–23.

[4] His list of constitutions was introduced in a gloss simply to show that the severity of a constitution of Archbishop Boniface was later mitigated by the legate Ottobuono.

[5] Maitland (*Roman Canon Law*, p. 5 n. 3) remarked on Lyndwood's exceptional citation of the out-of-date *Compilatio I* and *Compilatio III*, quoting *Provinciale*, 3.2.1 *ad ver*. beneficiati (p. 126).

his list, and from the existing manuscripts of constitutions, we infer that in the fourteenth century there had grown up a customary 'limit of legal memory' so far as provincial legislation went. The Council of Oxford, 1222, coming soon after the Fourth Lateran Council, 1215, seemed a good starting-point. William of Paull (Pagula) and John Athon do not go behind Langton in their citations. Little earlier legislation of national, legatine, or provincial councils was now copied; and if it was copied, lawyers took no account of it.[1] The one important exception to this generalization will appear shortly. Because Lyndwood had the practical object of helping lawyers to understand and use the current texts, it is *a priori* unlikely that he sought for his texts in out-of-the-way places. If there was a *textus receptus*, that was what he wanted. But there was none. Unfortunately, from Langton's day to Lyndwood's, provincial constitutions had been published and preserved without safeguards of authentic texts. Not until 1350, in Archbishop Simon Islip's time, did it become usual to enter an authentic copy of a provincial constitution in the archbishop's register,[2] and by then the greater part of the legislation which interested Lyndwood had been issued, and floated round the courts and consistories in a variety of corrupt versions.[3]

Collections were put together by stationers and students of law who were little interested in the circumstances in which the constitutions had been issued. The bigger the collection, the more useful it was; and early isolated texts of the thirteenth-century councils, still to be found occasionally in cathedral libraries and muniments, were probably little regarded by the lawyers. Their chosen reference-books were 'omnibus volumes'. A volume put together in 1400 was more desirable than one of 1300. The bad currency tended to drive the good out of circulation. Comparatively few surviving collections resemble each other so closely that we can be sure that one was copied directly or indirectly from another of them;[4] even a rough

[1] See above, p. 113.
[2] The registers of Islip's two predecessors, Mepham and Stratford, are missing, and may have contained the constitutions of these archbishops, 1329 and 1342–3.
[3] See *EHR*, l (1935), 211–13.
[4] Lambeth MS. 778 is almost certainly descended from B.M. MS. Harl. 3705, Holkham Hall MS. 226 from Cambridge, Corpus Christi Coll. MS. 84.

grouping of families is made difficult because of textual 'contamination': for instance, two manuscripts may agree in peculiar variants of the constitutions of Oxford, 1222, whereas their texts of Lambeth, 1261, belong to widely different traditions. The writers were eclectic as collectors and careless as copyists. The disparaging remarks of Lyndwood concerning the state of the texts[1] are justified by these collections. About fifty-three manuscripts of the fourteenth and fifteenth centuries, of various merit, are all that survive of the immense number which must have been written in the course of two hundred years for the use of canonists in the universities and the courts. In general, the earlier the manuscript the more trustworthy its ascriptions, if not its texts. Some of the later collections are wildly wrong. Lyndwood's dated list of constitutions gives clear indications that he took the constitutions from these tainted sources.

It is tempting to search the existing collections for the one which provided Lyndwood with his texts; but the search is vain. We do not find in any single manuscript *all* the constitutions which appear in the *Provinciale*, under the ascriptions which Lyndwood gave them. This is not really surprising, for Lyndwood must have had ample opportunity to browse among books. If he was not particularly historically-minded, he was undoubtedly diligent in comparing texts of constitutions which he found in current use; and he tells us in so many words that he has drawn from several sources: 'Ascribitur Iohanni Stratford, non tamen habetur in pluribus libris.'[2] 'Haec est constitutio Roberti Winchelsey Cantuariensis archiepiscopi secundum aliquos libros, secundum alios est Bonifacii, vel alias est constitutio communis episcoporum congregatorum apud Merton' in communi concilio, prout vidi in uno libro valde antiquo.'[3] Comparison of his list with the existing manuscript collections explains how he came to make mistakes of date and ascription, and shows, if not the actual manuscripts he used, the types or families of manuscripts.[4] It is indeed

---

[1] See above, p. 159, and *EHR*, l (1935), 218–21.
[2] *Provinciale*, 2.1.4 *ad ver*. Excussis (p. 90*a*).
[3] Ibid. 1.16.5 *ad ver*. Quoniam (p. 191*b*).
[4] On one of Lyndwood's chapters on tithe, ascribed to Robert Winchelsey (3.16.6, p. 199; cf. below p. 168), he notes: 'vidi tamen unum librum manus

possible that with much labour one might discover some remains of Lyndwood's library of provincial laws, but it is doubtful whether the labour would be justified, and where so much has been destroyed, the likelihood that these particular manuscripts have survived is small.[1]

III

It is time to see what Lyndwood made of the ascriptions which he found in the texts before him. We can then look at his editorial method in handling the texts themselves. To begin with there are those constitutions for which, he says, he has found no certain date. His manuscripts gave him the names of Archbishops Richard and Edmund, and he says categorically that these are Richard Wethershed (1229–31) and Edmund Rich (1234–40). A glance at the manuscripts is enough to destroy the basis of the first identification. The constitutions which Lyndwood gives as Richard Wethershed's are to be found in two manuscripts of the first half of the fourteenth century under an ascription to 'the council celebrated at Westminster in the time of Archbishop Richard, A.D. 1065'.[2] This impossible date is a corruption of A.D. 1175, when Archbishop Richard of Dover held his council at Westminster and when these constitutions, among others, were published.[3] But Lyndwood's grouping of Richard's and Edmund's constitutions was not fortuitous, and shows that he did not depend for the former on our fourteenth-century texts. His source was more corrupt. Apart from twelfth-century texts, the only other known copies of the constitutions of Westminster, 1175, are

antiquae ubi intitulatur et ascribitur Othobono, quondam in Anglia apostolicae sedis legato.' The title occurs in one of the twenty surviving texts: Bodleian MS. Ashmole 1146 fo. 42ᵛ, a fourteenth-century collection of the see of Chichester (cf. G. R. C. Davis, *Medieval Cartularies of Great Britain* (London, 1958), p. 28).

   [1] See *EHR*, l (1935), 217–18, 390 and below, Section V.
   [2] Lambeth MS. 171 fo. 9ʳ, Bodleian MS. Rawlinson C. 428 fo. 111ᵛ, from Worcester Cathedral Priory. The Bodleian MS. is probably derived from Lambeth 171.
   [3] Wilkins, i. 476–9, and see *EHR*, l (1935), 385–8 and C. N. L. Brooke, 'Canons of English Church Councils in the early Decretal Collections', *Traditio*, xiii (1957), 471–80. The Worcester MSS. (above, n. 2) omit c. 8.

some fifteen texts, all written *c.* 1400 or later, almost all bearing the date '1065',[1] all omitting certain chapters (of which none appears in the *Provinciale*), and all contained in 'omnibus volumes' of provincial constitutions. In almost every one of these late manuscripts, the volume containing 'Richard at Westminster, 1065' also contains 'provincial constitutions of St. Edmund, archbishop of Canterbury'.[2] Lyndwood must have known a text of this sort. He had enough historical sense to reject the date 1065, though he was unable to assign the constitutions to the correct Richard. As for the 'provincial constitutions of St. Edmund', he had no means of knowing that this ascription was unauthorized (so far as *we* know) by any early manuscript. Yet he entertained doubts; for while he comments unequivocally on twelve chapters: 'Constitutio quae est Edmundi', elsewhere he says: 'Dicitur fuisse Edmundi', 'Attribuitur Edmundo archiepiscopo', 'Intitulatur Edmundo in quibusdam libris'.[3] Doubts were well justified. Everything points to the fabrication of this series long after Edmund's death out of the genuine synodal statutes of Bishop Richard Poore of Salisbury, from which they were extracted verbatim.[4]

The error of date which Lyndwood made in assigning Archbishop Boniface's Council of Lambeth to the year 1260,

---

[1] Exceptions are noted below.

[2] Antwerp, Musée Plantin-Moretus 104 fo. 193ᵛ (Richard), fo. 195ʳ (Edmund). Cambridge, Univ. Libr. Add. 3575 fo. 314ᵛ (R. undated), fo. 316ʳ (Edmund); Gg. 6.21 fo. 52ʳ (R), fo. 53ʳ (E). Cambridge, Corpus Christi Coll. 84 fo. 192ᵛ (R), fo. 25ᵛ (E). Cambridge, Peterhouse 51 pt. ii fo. 36ᵛ (R), fo. 27ᵛ (E); 84 fo. 159ᵛ (R. date cut out), fo. 160ʳ (E). Cambridge, Trinity Coll. 1245 fo. 118ᵛ (R), fo. 119ʳ (E). Dublin, Trinity Coll. E. 2.22 (no. 526) p. 155 (R. dated 1366), p. 156 (E). Hereford, Cath. Libr. P. vii. 7 fo. 122ᵛ (R), fo. 133ʳ (E). Holkham Hall, 226 p. 60 (R), p. 62 (E). London, B. M. Cotton Otho A. xvi (lost) fo. 127ᵛ (R), fo. 128ᵛ (E); Harl. 335 fo. 66ʳ (R), fo. 44ᵛ (E). Lambeth 538 fo. 147ᵛ (R. dated 1066), fo. 150ʳ (E). Oxford, All Souls Coll. 42 fo. 221ᵛ (R), 235ʳ (E). Oxford, Balliol Coll. 158 fo. 179ᵛ (R), fo. 180ʳ (E). This family of manuscripts is represented in print in *Constitutiones legitime seu legatine* (Paris, 1504), fo. 142ᵛ (R), fo. 143ʳ (E).

Bodleian MS. Rawlinson C. 100 fo. 145ʳ and Philadelphia, Free Libr. MS. Carson 4 fo. 93ʳ also have 'Edmund'; both MSS. may originally have contained 'Richard 1065' as well.

The Worcester MSS. of 'Richard' (above, p. 166 n. 2) do not have 'Edmund'

[3] *Provinciale*, pp. 71, 26, 160, 204, 28.

[4] *EHR*, l (1935), 400–2 and C. R. Cheney, *Eng. Synodalia of the xiii Century*, 2nd ed. (Oxford, 1968), pp. 65–7 and above, p. 133.

instead of 1261, cannot be charged against the family of manuscripts which contains 'Richard' and 'Edmund'. This includes the constitutions of Lambeth, but in a spurious late conflated version, usually bearing the correct date. Lyndwood's text is far closer to the genuine constitutions of 1261, even though it is contaminated to a slight extent by reminiscences of the version of 1258.[1] In a group of texts (mostly late fourteenth-century or after) which share some of these characteristics there are four which bear the date 1260.[2] Lyndwood assigned to Boniface another chapter in the *Provinciale*, on the holy-water clerk,[3] and noted that it was ascribed in some books to Archbishop Boniface and in some to Robert Winchelsey. Surviving manuscripts are indeed found with these ascriptions, but both must be rejected: this is in fact a diocesan statute of Exeter of the year 1287.[4]

Lyndwood's dating of Archbishop John Pecham's councils (Reading, 1279, and Lambeth, 1281) calls for no comment: these dates are correct, as they are found in most of the sources. He also ascribes to Pecham five other constitutions which were at hand in the collections of his own day. The manuscripts did not state the occasion of their issue; while Lyndwood takes them at their face-value as genuine provincial legislation, they cannot be accepted as such without doubts and qualifications.[5]

With the ascription of a whole series of constitutions to Archbishop Robert Winchelsey in 1305 Lyndwood advances upon extremely unsafe ground. It has been shown elsewhere that for most of these texts the attribution is wrong[6] and that few, if any, were formal provincial legislation.[7] Lyndwood was

---

[1] For the varieties see *EHR*, l (1935), 402–6, and *C. & S.* ii.

[2] Cambridge, Caius Coll. 38 fo. 101ᵛ; Cambridge, Pembroke Coll. 131 fo. 75ᵛ; Brit. Mus. Harl. 3705 fo. 13ᵛ (and its copy, Lambeth 778). Cf. *Provinciale*, 3.13.3 *ad ver.* de Lambeth (p. 167*b*): 'Hoc concilium Bonifacii celebratum fuit a.d. 1260 secundum aliquos libros quos vidi.'

[3] *Provinciale*, 3.7.2 (p. 142).

[4] See C. R. Cheney, 'The so-called Statutes of John Pecham and Robert Winchelsey for the Province of Canterbury,' *JEH*, xii (1961), 32. For the ascription to Boniface in late MSS. of a conflate version of his constitutions see, e.g. Bodleian MS. Selden supra 43 fo. 50ᵛ.

[5] See *JEH*, xii (1961), 21.

[6] Ibid., p. 23. The texts given by Lyndwood are nos. 1, 6, 8–10, 14, and 17 in the series described on pp. 23–32.

[7] The constitution on stipendiary priests may be a genuine pronouncement of

misled by the collectors who had been busy in the generation before him. Of seven chapters which he ascribed to Winchelsey, one belonged to Archbishop Boniface,[1] one comes from synodal statutes of Wells (?1258),[2] one is abridged from a synodal statute of Salisbury (1257),[3] one is of unknown origin.[4] In one instance Lyndwood may actually have been instrumental in procuring the authentic stamp of metropolitan authority for a decree of Winchelsey which had been informally uttered; for he was prelocutor of the lower clergy in convocation in November 1419, when Archbishop Henry Chichele 'ad peticionem cleri quandam constitutionem provincialem per Robertum Wynchelse predecessorem suum editam que sic incipit: Capellani stipendiarii . . . ad totam provinciam Cantuariensem extendi et omnes artari declaravit et pronunciavit.'[5]

The next series of constitutions in Lyndwood's list was bound to confuse a fifteenth-century editor, for they existed in variant forms and under various ascriptions. Because Lyndwood found them entitled 'Oxford II' and dated '1322', he rejected the ascription which he found elsewhere to Archbishop Simon Mepham (1328–33) and assigned them to Walter Reynolds, archbishop from 1313 to 1327.[6] Among the

Winchelsey's and was in any case re-issued as an official decree for the province by Archbishops William Courtenay (Wilkins, iii. 213) and Henry Chichele (*Reg. H. Chichele*, ed. E. F. Jacob (CYS), iii. 59).

[1] See *JEH*, xii (1961), 27–8. Lyndwood noted the alternative ascription (above, at p. 165).

[2] *Provinciale*, 3.16.5 (p. 191); see *JEH*, xii (1961), 28, nos. 9–10.

[3] *Provinciale*, 3.14.2 (p. 184); see *JEH*, xii (1961), 31, no. 17. Lyndwood himself noted (*ad ver.* Tria) that he had included the same statute in an ampler form under an attribution to Simon Langham (*Provinciale*, 1.3.1): this is the Salisbury statute (*C. & S.* ii. 567), which is elsewhere attributed to Stephen Langton or Simon Islip (cf. *EHR*, l (1935), 398–400). No manuscript of the statute has been found with the ascription to Langham (see below, p. 171).

[4] *Provinciale*, 3.17.7 (p. 199). See below, p. 176 n. 2.

[5] Above, p. 168 n. 7, and *JEH*, xii (1961), 23–5. The decree of Winchelsey is distributed among four titles of the *Provinciale*: 1.14.1 (p. 69), 2.6.3 (p. 110), 3.23.9 (p. 237), 5.16. 6 (p. 330); cf. *C. & S.* ii. 1382–5.

[6] *Provinciale*, 5.15.2 *ad ver.* Minime (p. 319): 'Walteri Raynold quae intitulantur Oxon. 2 et in quibusdam libris ascribuntur Simoni Mepham, sed erronee: nam data illarum constitutionum est a.d. 1322 . . .' Cf. ibid. 1.4.4 (p. 32): 'Haec constitutio cum caeteris eiusdem datae sive temporis in quibusdam libris intitulatur Simoni Mepham archiepiscopo Cantuariensi; et forsan movit sic scribentes, quia haec constitutio cum aliis eiusdem temporis facta est iuxta quotationem communem a.d. 1322 et intitulatur Concilio Oxon. 2. Sed verum est secundum

numerous manuscripts which survive, fifteen (all of the fifteenth century) ascribe the constitutions to Archbishop 'Stephen' Mepham at Lambeth; others associate them with Stephen Langton and the Council of Oxford, 1222;[1] but in Cambridge, Caius College MS. 38 fo. 111ʳ, we find a late fourteenth-century text entitled: 'Incipiunt alia constitutio Oxon' II celebrat' a.d. m° ccc° xxii', and an imperfect copy of a similar text in Cambridge, Pembroke College MS. 131 fo. 87ʳ is entitled: 'Concilium apud Oxon' secundum celebratum ibidem a.d. m° ccc° vicesim'. It was upon a text of this sort that Lyndwood relied.[2] But he was certainly wrong. These so-called provincial constitutions of Oxford 1322 are all descended from synodal statutes of an unknown English diocese probably composed between 1222 and 1225.[3]

Lyndwood's use of Simon Mepham's genuine constitutions presents no problem.[4] Those of John Stratford which he gives are drawn both from the series (*inc.* 'Quam sit inhonestum . . .') which we believe to have been brought up at the provincial council of London in October 1342 and from the final series (*inc.* 'Sponsam Christi . . .') issued on the authority of that council in the following May.[5] He was uncertain about the dates,

cronicos quod anno praedicto sedit in ecclesia Cantuar' archiepiscopus Walterus cognomento Raynoldus, cui successit Simon Mepham a.d. 1323 [*recte* 1327].'

   [1] See the version in Wilkins, i. 593–7; cf. *C. & S.* ii. 139–54.
   [2] He did not include all the constitutions, for the good reason that he had drawn from other sources texts which were very similar to some of them. The appendix to the *Provinciale*, 1679, contains (p. 39) the selection which Lyndwood gave, under the ascription to Walter Reynolds in the Council of Oxford, 1322, and Wilkins reproduced this text under the same date and title (ii. 512–13). No manuscript containing this selection alone has been found: it was probably composed from the *Provinciale* by the editor of 1679 and has no independent authority. The fuller version was printed by Wilkins (i. 593–7) from a text which was associated with the Council of Oxford, 1222.
   [3] For a discussion of all the varieties see C. R. Cheney, 'The Earliest English Diocesan Statutes', *EHR*, lxxv (1960), 18–23.
   [4] The year '1328' in all manuscripts stands for the historical date 27 Jan. 1329.
   [5] Wilkins, ii. 696, 702. For this view of their character see *EHR*, l (1935), 415–17 and above, p. 122. That Lyndwood was not using a conflation of the two series (e.g. B.M. Harl. 52 fo. 93ʳ, cf. *EHR*, l (1935), 416 n. 9) is shown by his gloss on *Provinciale*, 3.22.4 (p. 222*a*): 'Haec est constitutio Iohannis Stratford, non tamen contenta inter constitutiones eiusdem quarum exordium sic incipit: Sponsam Christi'; cf. 3.6.4 (p. 140*a*), 3.4.4 (p. 133), 5.14.4 (p. 313), 5.15.7 (p. 323), 3.7.3 (p. 143).

assigning no place or time to the series 'Quam sit inhonestum'.[1] This is strange, because most of the existing texts of 'Quam sit inhonestum' are dated precisely at London, 10 October 1342, and these are found in collections of the type used by Lyndwood.[2] While he dates the series 'Sponsam Christi' 1342 in his list of constitutions, in other places he gives the year 1343 :[3] he may have been confused by variation in the manuscripts he was using, for of the forty or so surviving texts a few give the date 1343.[4] For the constitutions of Archbishop Simon Islip on feast-days and on stipendiary priests Lyndwood had authentic copies at hand in the archbishop's register. Why he assigned the date 1361 is hard to understand; for the correct date, 1362, appears both in the register and in other copies, authentic and unauthentic.[5]

But it was not in Simon Langham's register that Lyndwood found the constitution on mortuaries, or burial-fees, which he ascribed to that archbishop;[6] indeed, it is found in no manuscript under this name. Many of the late 'omnibus volumes' attribute it to Stephen Langton or Robert Winchelsey or Simon Islip, and it may well be that the canonist corrected the name from Stephen Langton to Simon Langham to admit of

---

[1] *Provinciale*, 3.6.4 *ad ver.* Concilio (p. 140*a*): 'De isto concilio aliquid certum in registris vel chronicis non reperi, videlicet quo tempore vel sub quo fuerit celebratum'; cf. 2.2.4 *ad ver.* Concilio (p. 98*b*).

[2] They include most of the manuscripts cited above as containing 'Richard, 1065' and 'Edmund'. Cambridge, Univ. Libr. MS. Gg. 6.21 fo. 46ᵛ is dated 20 Oct. 1342, Lambeth MS. 538 fo. 135ʳ 10 Oct. 1344; Oxford, Brasenose Coll. MS. 14 fo. 183w is dated at the end 1344.

[3] *Provinciale*, 1.2.2 *ad ver.* editae (p. 17*b*): 'secundum quotationem quam ego vidi a.d. 1343'; cf. 1.2.3 *ad ver.* constitutiones (p. 18*a*). In his list, 5.15.2 (p. 319*b*) he gives the date 1342.

[4] Cambridge, Univ. Libr. MS. Ii.3.14 fo. 203ᵛ; Bodleian MSS. Bodl. 794 fos. 149ʳ, 150ʳ, Selden supra 43 fo. 73ʳ (marginal correction); Oxford, Brasenose Coll. MS. 14 fo. 153ʳ. Cambridge, Corpus Christi Coll. MS. 84 fo. 34ᵛ (whence Holkham Hall MS. 226 fo. 82ʳ) and B.M. Harl. 335 fo. 70ᵛ read 'm ccc xlii aliter iii' and so reads the printed edition, *Constitutiones legitime* (Paris, 1504), fo. 134ᵛ.

[5] *Provinciale*, 2.3.3 (p. 101) and 3.23.10 (p. 238). Printed from Lambeth, Register of Simon Islip, fos. 186ᵛ, 188ᵛ in H. Spelman, *Concilia, Decreta, Leges . . .*, ii (1664), 609, 610. For other versions of the constitution on feast-days see C. R. Cheney, 'Rules for the Observance of Feast-days in Medieval England', *BIHR*, xxxiv (1961), and for that on stipendiary priests see *Reg. S. de Sudbiria, London* (CYS), i.193.

[6] *Provinciale*, 1.3.1 (p. 19).

his ascription of a related document to Robert Winchelsey.[1] But all these attributions are wrong; the so-called 'Langham' is actually a synodal statute of Giles of Bridport, bishop of Salisbury (1257), and the 'Winchelsey' document nothing but an abridged version of the same.[2]

Three out of the four chapters of the *Provinciale* which are ascribed to Archbishop Simon Sudbury, dated by Lyndwood 1378, give rise to doubt. The constitution on stipendiary priests is unquestionably genuine and may have been abridged by Lyndwood from the text in Sudbury's archiepiscopal register;[3] but the others,[4] which all relate to the confessional, are only described as provincial constitutions of Sudbury in a group of fifteenth-century manuscripts.[5] Here they form part of a series, mainly made up of excerpts from the synodal statutes of Richard Poore for the diocese of Salisbury (1217–1221). These three chapters are all from Poore[6] and all three, oddly enough, are among the 'Edmund' statutes with which Lyndwood was well acquainted. Whether they were ever issued by Sudbury remains doubtful.

Lyndwood's use of Archbishop Thomas Arundel's Oxford constitutions against heresy calls for no lengthy comment. He had them at hand in the register of the archbishop.[7] Like-

[1] *Provinciale*, 3.4.2 (p. 184). This is implied by his gloss near the end of 1.3.1 *ad ver*. Interpretatione (p. 22*b*).

[2] See *EHR*, l (1935), 398–9 and *JEH*, xii (1961), 31.

[3] *Provinciale*, 3.23.11 (p. 240). Printed in full from the register in Spelman, *Concilia*, ii. 626; Wilkins, iii. 135.   [4] *Provinciale*, 5.16.14–16 (pp. 342–5).

[5] Cambridge, Caius Coll. MS. 38 fo. 121[ra]; Cambridge, Peterhouse MS. 51 pt. ii fo. 38[ra]; B.M. MSS. Harl. 335 fo. 88[v] and Harl. 3705 fo. 101[r]. The Cambridge MSS. give the date 1378, the Harleian MSS. give respectively 1328 and 1278. The Harleian texts are described and discussed in an unpublished D.Phil. thesis by W. L. Warren, 'Simon Sudbury' (Bodleian Libr., Oxford, 1956), appendix C, pp. 506–29. While they are derived in large part from the statutes of Richard Poore they also contain traces of the earlier synodal statutes of Canterbury, 1213–14 (*EHR*, lxxv (1960), 2–18).

[6] Chapters 35–6, 34, 37 in the edition in *Salisbury Charters and Documents*, ed. W. D. Macray (RS, 1891), pp. 141–2.

[7] Lambeth, Register of Thomas Arundel, vol. ii fo. 10[r], whence printed in Spelman, *Concilia*, ii. 662–8 and Wilkins, iii. 314–19. The constitutions were issued originally at Oxford in 1407, but were finally published (as the enregistered text shows) in the London council of '14 Jan. 1408' (i.e., 1409): hence Lyndwood's date, 'Oxford, 1408', which is found in some manuscripts (e.g. Bodleian, MS. Selden supra 43 fo. 89[v] (*corr*. 'alias vii°'), cf. 95[r]) and in *Constitutiones legitime* (Paris, 1504), fo. 152[ra].

wise for the constitutions of his master, Chichele, authentic copies must have been available to Lyndwood; if the date which he gives (1415) is not correct for all of them, he probably considered that it was unnecessary to be precise.[1]

IV

This analysis of the *Provinciale* reveals that 48 of its 240 chapters were not provincial legislation. Having regard to the state of the collections which were current in Lyndwood's day, it was natural that he should go astray. Usually he accepted the ascriptions which he found, and his attempts at criticism of them were not happy: neither the changing of 'Richard, 1065' to Richard Wethershed nor of 'Stephen Langton' to Simon Langham was justified, although neither of the original titles was right. Here and there Lyndwood showed caution (for instance, when he doubted whether 'Langham's' statute was a provincial constitution), but he was not keenly aware of historical facts, which concerned him less than points of law. As Maitland remarked, he was capable of blaming John Pecham for ignoring a decree of Boniface VIII issued several years after the archbishop's death.[2] Lyndwood's failure to understand the circumstances in which his texts had originated explains, in W. T. Waugh's view, his ill-conceived glosses on Pecham's constitution against pluralities.[3] Again, failure to recognize that the 'Edmund' constitutions were diocesan statutes accounts for his inappropriate gloss on *testes synodales*.[4]

[1] The records of the convocation of Oct. 1414 are lost (*Reg. H. Chichele*, i. cxliv), but Professor Jacob remarked that the constitution 'De clericis bigamis' (*Provinciale*, 3.3.2) was probably issued then. It was sent to the bishop of London 23 Oct. 1414 (*Reg. Robert Rede*, ed. C. Deedes (Sussex Record Soc., 1908-10), i. 160-1) and was published at Paul's Cross 28 Oct. 1414 (Bodleian MS. Selden supra 43 fo. 95ᵛ); it appears among documents of Nov.–Dec. 1414 in *Registrum R. Mascall*, ed. J. H. Parry (CYS), pp. 120-1. The other two chapters, on feasts, in the *Provinciale* (2.3.4-5, p. 103) were dated respectively 14 Jan. 1415 (i.e. 1416) and 17 Dec. 1416 (*Reg. H. Chichele*, iii. 8 and 28).

[2] *Provinciale*, 3.19.8 *ad ver.* cum socia (p. 212*b*): 'Maxime cum I. Peccham auctor huius constitutionis bene noverat constitutionem illam Bonifacianam'; cf. Maitland, *Roman Canon Law*, p. 28.

[3] 'Archbishop Peckham and Pluralities', *EHR*, xxviii (1913), 630-5.

[4] *Provinciale*, 5.1.1 *ad ver.* Duo vel tres (p. 277*b*); cf. *EHR*, l (1935), 204-5. John Johnson spotted what was the matter: 'This constitution increases my suspicion

It is worth stopping to notice what happened when customary rules and synodal statutes came to be treated as provincial constitutions. Not only did they obtain a wider publicity; a lengthy and learned gloss by Lyndwood shows that in the opinion of the official of Canterbury they enlarged the competence of the archbishop's court. The metropolitan jurisdiction extended to the punishment of cases in which provincial constitutions had imposed penalties. 'For the archbishop,' says Lyndwood, 'can make a provincial canon or constitution touching the whole province, and by that constitution are bound the subjects of the suffragans, if only they are aware of it unless their ignorance of it is crass or supine . . . [cf. *Sext* 1.2.2] . . . so that, should anyone incur the penalty of such a constitution who is not of the archbishop's diocese but is a subject of his suffragan, in this case not only the bishop can absolve his subject from such a sentence, but also the archbishop. . . . Since therefore the archbishop can absolve one who incurs the penalty of a provincial constitution, so also he can punish a delinquent against such a statute.'[1] This deserves to be remembered when we observe how Lyndwood contributed to give metropolitan authority to some dubious documents.

With what consideration did he treat the actual texts before him? Here any opinion must be expressed cautiously, for we have not identified the manuscripts he used or discovered the autograph of his work. None the less, it is reasonable to call attention to certain points in his text which differ from all known manuscripts of the constitutions, and to see in them the evidence of re-touching. In one instance Lyndwood went so far as to conflate two texts to make one. Among the miscellaneous statutes attributed to John Pecham is one on the custody

that the archbishop intended all these rules for his own diocese only. If as L. supposes, this constitution related to the whole province, certainly some notice would have been taken of the suffragan bishops, and the informers directed principally to denounce their excesses to the primate. All L.'s difficulties on the text of this constitution vanish on supposition that it concerns the diocese of Canterbury only' (*A Collection of All the Eccles. Laws . . . of the Church of England* (London, 1720), vol. ii, *s.a.* 1236). A second edition was produced by John Baron (Oxford, 1850–1), but Johnson's discerning criticism has been generally neglected.

[1] *Provinciale*, 3.23.10 *ad ver.* Competentem (pp. 239–40); cf. Maitland, *Roman Canon Law*, p. 36.

of the Host which appears to lie behind c.1 of the Council of Lambeth (1281) on the same subject. Whether it was a mandate previously issued by Pecham on visitation, or a draft brought to the Council of Lambeth for discussion, or a statute proposed in an earlier council, we cannot say; but the similarities of wording are close and the only substantial difference is that the undated text requires fortnightly, not weekly, renewal of the reserved Host. Lyndwood, we infer, had both texts before him and produced a conflation for which no existing manuscript, outside the *Provinciale*, vouches. It was not, in the circumstances, a heinous offence.[1] A fairly innocuous case of verbal emendation which probably had no manuscript support is to be seen in the constitution of Archbishop Boniface on tithe, which Lyndwood attributes to Winchelsey.[2] In the *Provinciale* the mandatory words read: '*Volumus et statuimus* quod in cunctis ecclesiis per *Cantuariensem provinciam* constitutis uniformis sit petitio decimarum.' The manuscripts of the constitution, under its various ascriptions, commonly read: '*Volumus* quod in cunctis ecclesiis *per archiepiscopatum nostrum* [or, *per archidiaconatus*] uniformis sit petitio decimarum.' Lyndwood glosses the word *provinciam* in his text: 'Aliqui libri hic habent *Archiepiscopatum*, sed haec dictio *Archiepiscopatum*, in quodam concilio provinciali tento in ecclesia Sancti Pauli London' sub domino Henrico Chicheley archiepiscopo Cantuariensi, de consensu prelatorum et totius cleri fuit subducta, et loco eius posita haec dictio *Provinciam*, me tunc existente praelocutor ipsius cleri.'[3] Lyndwood may have made a similar change tacitly in the constitution of Winchelsey, 'Presbiteri stipendiarii,' which was ratified by Chichele in 1419. Here Lyndwood's *in provincia nostra* is in contrast to the *in archiepiscopatu nostro* of the manuscripts.[4] At a later point in this same constitution

---

[1] *Provinciale*, 3.25.2 (p. 248); Wilkins, ii. 48; *C. & S.* ii. 1119–20. Lyndwood's version orders weekly renewal of the Host.   [2] Ibid. 3.16.5 (p. 192).

[3] Lyndwood was prelocutor in convocations held at St. Paul's in 1419, 1421, 1424, 1425, 1426. Lyndwood may refer here to the meeting of 1419; cf. above, p. 169.

[4] *Provinciale*, 3.23.9 (p. 237). Cambridge, Caius Coll. MS. 38 fo. 124ᵛ and B.M. MS. Harl. 3705 fo. 67ʳ read *in archiepiscopatu vel provincia nostra*. Like Lyndwood they omit 'inmiscendo se ut prius in divinis' after 'incurrant'; but they omit other words present in the *Provinciale*, which shows that Lyndwood did not take his text from these manuscripts. Cf. *C. & S.* ii. 1382–5.

Lyndwood's 'Decernimus etiam ut presbyteri huiusmodi infra nostram provinciam celebrantes intersint' is an enlargement of the words in the manuscripts: 'debeant interesse'.[1] In yet another chapter ascribed to Winchelsey Lyndwood makes the mandate binding upon 'omnibus et singulis rectoribus . . . per nostram provinciam constitutis'; but these words are not found in any manuscript of the constitution; all read at this point: 'vobis omnibus et singulis'. The constitution was not Winchelsey's and was probably a diocesan statute to which Lyndwood gives the form of a law for the whole province.[2]

A few other phrases, which appear to be Lyndwood's own additions to the texts, were added with a different object. They do not emphasize or enlarge the authority of the law; they give a twist to its substance and a point to Lyndwood's gloss. Thus, all known manuscripts of Winchelsey's decree on the obligations of parishioners say that the expense of repairing chancels shall fall on the rector or vicar. The *Provinciale* adds: 'seu ad quos pertinent', and this enables Lyndwood to refer to customs in certain London churches whereby the laity repair the chancels.[3] Simon Islip's constitution on feast-days (1362) requires abstention 'ab universis popularium operibus',[4] but Lyndwood substitutes the word *servilibus* for *popularium*, to bring the order into line with canonical rules about *opera servilia*.[5] Again, the Council of Oxford, 1222, specifies the dress to be worn by the officials of bishops and of archdeacons in consistory. Lyndwood, by reading *officiales ipsorum archidiaconorum*, justifies the distinction he draws in his gloss between the officials of bishops and those of archdeacons, and claims the superior status of dignitary for the former.[6]

All told, the wilful inaccuracies of Lyndwood in reproducing the old legislation were few. If he occasionally took liberties with his texts, he seldom perverted the sense seriously. In his

---

[1] B.M. MS. Cotton Faustina A.viii fo. 117ᵛ reads: 'Iurent predicti presbiteri quod debeant interesse'; cf. *JEH*, xii (1961), 24–5.

[2] *Provinciale*, 3.17.7 (p. 200); cf. *JEH*, xii (1961), 30.

[3] Ibid., 3.27.2 (p. 253*b*); Cf. *C. & S.* ii. 1387–8.

[4] Spelman, *Concilia*, ii. 609, *Provinciale*, appendix II, p. 57.

[5] *Provinciale*, 2.3.3 (p. 101); cf. Lyndwood's glosses in 1.11.1 *ad ver*. Caeremoniis (*in fine*) and Canonicis institutis (pp. 56–7). Lyndwood omits Good Friday from the list of holidays.

[6] Ibid. 3.1.1 *ad ver*. Officiales archidiaconorum (p. 119*a*); cf. *C. & S.* ii. 116.

glosses he sometimes showed tendencies regrettably common among medieval canonists : to point obvious morals, to dodge crucial issues, and to wander into repetition and irrelevancy. But he was always supported by both sound learning and wide experience. He knew equally well the commentators on the common law of the Church and the peculiarities of English custom. And because his texts were not the utterances of a supreme legislator, but of inferior authority, he could upon occasion criticize them freely, saying when they failed to conform with the common law and when they had lapsed through desuetude. This makes the *Provinciale* a legal textbook of unusual interest.

V

Our survey of Lyndwood's sources and of the way in which he used them is completed, without the pretension of being an exhaustive survey. It is tempting to go on to raise questions connected with the transmission of his book; but it is too soon to answer them. This section is added to the foregoing study simply with the object of indicating in a general way the sort of material which exists and which needs scrutiny and analysis. The list of manuscripts in the appendix is provisional.

If we inquire what fortune Lyndwood's book enjoyed in the next hundred years, a satisfactory answer is hard to come by. Lyndwood himself did what he could to ensure its perpetuation. His will, dated 22 November 1443, which desired that his body should rest in St. Stephen's Chapel, Westminster, contains the following clauses :

Item, volo quod liber meus quem compilavi super constituciones provinciales reponatur in cathenis et inferratus sit, ut salvo et secure custodiatur, in superiori parte capelle sancti Stephani predicte vel alias in vestiario eius capelle, ut quociens opus fuerit pro veritate scripture primarie eiusdem pro correccione aliorum librorum ab eodem tractatu copiandorum recurri poterit dum sit opus. Item, volo quod copia eiusdem libri quem ut prefertur compilavi et pro maiori parte scripsit Thomas Hetham remaneat penes eundem Thomam iure proprio, ut ex copia eiusdem locanda possit aliquid lucrari in recompensam laboris sui.[1]

[1] Lambeth, Register of John Stafford, fo. 143ʳ; the whole will is printed from

Lyndwood died on 21 October 1446 and it must remain doubtful whether the careful provision he had made for his *Provinciale* was carried out. For an inventory copied into the Chancellor's Register at Oxford in August 1448 implies that Lyndwood's *Provinciale* 'in quaternis manu domini' was then in the possession of one of his executors, Master Ralph Drew, or Dreffe, at Oxford.[1] Its later fate is unknown; a book in quires has less chance of survival than a book in stout binding. Whether Thomas Hethman made profit from allowing his manuscript to be copied is likewise unknown. A study of the existing manuscripts might possibly throw light on these matters.

Not much memorable legislation emanated from the fifteenth-century archbishops of Canterbury after Lyndwood's day,[2] and in 1462 the provincial council of York accepted such previous legislation of the southern province as was not repugnant to the constitutions of York;[3] so Lyndwood's systematic collection was of permanent value, useful in both provinces, even without its gloss. In fact, a large proportion of the known manuscripts and of the printed editions contain the five books of constitutions without the commentary, or with only some small excerpts from it. The gloss made it a bulky and expensive volume and the surviving folio copies must have been written for rich book-buyers. But a serviceable little octavo was enough to contain the constitutions, and with its familiar arrangement in five books and its index of tituli it would provide a handier tool than the old collections arranged in order of councils without regard to subject-matter.

Glossed and unglossed, the *Provinciale* is only known to survive in about fifty-five manuscripts,[4] and it is impossible to

this source in *Archaeologia*, xxxiv (1852), 419 and translated by A. Ogle, *The Canon Law in Mediaeval England*, pp. 197–204. A seventeenth-century copy is in Bodleian MS. Rawlinson D. 817 fo. 217.

[1] *Registrum Cancellarii Oxoniensis 1434–69*, ed. H. E. Salter (Oxford Hist. Soc., 1932), i. 164; cf. A. B. Emden, *Biog. Reg. of the Univ. of Oxford to A.D. 1500* (1957–9), i. 594.

[2] Manuscripts of the *Provinciale* sometimes contain, at the end, additional constitutions of Chichele (especially that for the augmentation of vicarages, 1439 (Wilkins, iii. 286)) and one or two later documents.

[3] Wilkins, iii. 580, 663; cf. *EHR*, l (1935), 216 n. 3.

[4] See the appendix below.

estimate what percentage this represents of the copies made in the first hundred years. Lyndwood's name only rarely appears in medieval library catalogues of monasteries and colleges.[1] Collections designed for serious study of canon law would prefer the great glossators of the *Corpus Iuris* to Lyndwood and the small beer of provincial legislation. So when in 1469 Thomas Kent, doctor of both laws, bequeathed his law books to form a library for the use of official, dean, examiners, advocates, and proctors of the Court of Canterbury, the twenty-eight works included no Lyndwood and no provincial constitutions.[2] But if Kent's library was of the academic sort, those to whom he left it can hardly have avoided using Lyndwood's work. When records of the pre-Reformation courts christian have been more thoroughly examined, some slight evidence of this may be forthcoming. A careful survey of wills would almost certainly discover copies of the *Provinciale* in the hands of church dignitaries and ecclesiastical lawyers.[3]

The exiguous evidence of the manuscripts is explained by the record of printed editions. The whole work, with Lyndwood's glosses, and the index dated 1433, was produced in a splendid folio of 350 leaves by the Oxford printing press, not many years after it was first installed, at some unknown date in the 1480s.[4] This was not only one of the first dozen books

[1] The University Library, Cambridge, possessed a 'Lynwode' in 1473 (H. Bradshaw, *Collected Papers* (Cambridge, 1889), p. 45, no. 222). Exeter Cathedral possessed the 'Liber Provincialis W. Lynwood', in two volumes, in 1506 (G. Oliver, *Lives of the Bishops of Exeter* (Exeter, 1861), p. 366). Some of the copies in the Syon library early in the sixteenth century were of printed editions (T. 15, T. 27, T. 72); one or two other items described as 'Constituciones provinciales' may possibly conceal a manuscript copy of Lyndwood's collection: T. 16, T. 32, T. 71 (*Catalogue of the Libr. of Syon Monastery, Isleworth*, ed. M. Bateson (Cambridge, 1898), pp. 189, 191, 195). Two copies of 'Constituciones provinciales' were at Corpus Christi College, Cambridge, early in the sixteenth century (Corpus Christi Coll. MS. 232 fo. 13ᵛ). [2] Emden, *Biog. Reg. Univ. Oxford*, ii. 1038.

[3] Nicholas Carent, dean of Wells, bequeathed a Lyndwood to the cathedral library in 1467 (*Somerset Medieval Wills*, ed. F. W. Weaver (Somerset Record Soc. 1901), p. 211). In 1499 Bishop Richard Fox presented to the collegiate church of Bishop Auckland (dioc. Durham), with other books, 'Constituciones secundum usum Cantuariensis provincie cum glosa Willelmi Sherwode in pergameno' (*Reg. of R. Fox, Durham*, ed. M. Howden (Surtees Soc., 1932), p. 95). It is conceivable that William Sherwode or Shirwood, doctor of canon law, who died in 1482, wrote a gloss upon the constitutions; but it is improbable, and the name is probably here written in mistake for Lyndwood.

[4] A. W. Pollard and G. R. Redgrave, *S[hort-] T[itle] C[atalogue of Books printed*

printed at Oxford: it was bigger than any book to be printed
there in the next hundred years, and it was one of the first
law books of any sort to be printed anywhere in England.
The English common lawyer of the fifteenth century had no
large or comprehensive work in print, only Littleton on tenures
and a handful of recent statutes and year-books. The printing
of Lyndwood's book surely testifies to the large demand
a publisher might expect and at the same time it accounts for
the subsequent destruction of many manuscript copies. But
the Oxford edition was too heavy and too costly[1] a volume to
meet all needs. Shortly before the end of the century Wynkyn
de Worde produced Lyndwood's five books of *Constitutiones
Provinciales* without his gloss, in a small octavo, at Westminster
'in domo Caxston', 31 May 1496 (*STC*, 17103). A re-setting
came from the same printer less than three years later, 15 April
1499 (*STC*, 17104). Probably in the same year Richard Pynson
dedicated to John Warham, archbishop of Canterbury, an
edition based on the 1496 edition and soon afterwards produced
another with some few documents added (*STC*, 17105–6).[2] In
the sixteenth century continental printers entered the market,
and the Short Title Catalogue enumerates eight more editions,
some containing the gloss, printed at Paris, Antwerp, and
London between 1501 and 1534. A hundred years after its
first appearance Lyndwood's work must have been circulating
in a very great number of copies.

Thereafter the demand probably declined. An edition without the gloss was published in 1557 (*STC*, 17114), and then no
other appeared for a century after the Reformation. Another

in England . . . 1475–1640] (Bibliographical Soc., 1926), no. 17102. See Falconer
Madan, *The Early Oxford Press* (Oxford Hist. Soc., 1895), pp. 3–4, 240, 258-9
and pl. iv. For the description of two settings of certain leaves see [G. Chawner],
A List of the Incunabula in the Libr. of King's Coll. Cambridge (Cambridge, 1908),
pp. 52–3. The date is given tentatively by the bibliographers as 1483. At least
twenty-two copies survive.

[1] Its price is not known. The edition of which John Dorne, the Oxford book-
seller, sold two copies in 1520 at half a mark apiece was probably the smaller
Paris edition of 1506 (*STC*, 17109): *Collectanea*, first series (Oxford Hist. Soc.,
1885), pp. 108, 124.

[2] Antonio Zatta enriched Mansi, *Ampl. Collectio*, xxxi (Venice, 1798), with
the whole unglossed *Provinciale*, coll. 367–458, taken from a copy of *STC*,
17106. He described it as 'Provinciale Anglicanum vetus anno circiter 1509
editum'.

edition of the texts, with the addition of the legatine canons of Otto and Ottobuono, appeared at Oxford in 1664, under the title *Provinciale Vetus Provinciae Cantuariensis*, edited by Robert Sharrock, D.C.L.[1] Finally, in 1679, a comprehensive small folio was published at Oxford, which added to the glossed *Provinciale* the legatine canons with the gloss of John Athon, and the provincial constitutions in their presumed chronological order, with sundry other documents. The publishers claimed that in preparing their edition three printed editions and three manuscripts had been used, but did not particularize about their sources. Marginalia refer to an Eton manuscript of the *Provinciale* which may be identified as Eton Coll. MS. 98.[2]

Do surviving manuscripts or printed editions preserve Lyndwood's work in its original form? Did the author himself revise it after ending his gloss with thanks to the Almighty on the eve of Whitsun 1430? No answers to these questions can be made until the texts have been thoroughly examined. Bearing in mind the painful fate of Gratian's *Decretum* and Bracton's *De legibus Angliae*, he would be bold who expected to find a single archetype, discernible in the existing texts. Lyndwood, it has been seen, left two copies with which he was satisfied, but we do not know what happened to them, and probably other copies already existed when Lyndwood made his will. A superficial survey of some of the manuscripts suffices to show that the sequence of texts sometimes varies and a text is sometimes inserted which does not appear in the *textus receptus* of 1679.[3] Various additions are made in the midst or at the end

---

[1] 1630–84; he was archdeacon of Winchester at the time of his death. Antony Wood says that Sharrock 'was accounted learned in divinity, in the civil and common law, and very knowing in vegetables, and all pertaining thereunto'. For his botanical and other publications see Bertha Porter in *Dict. Nat. Biography*.

[2] An Oxford, New College MS. of the gloss on the legatine canons (probably New Coll. MS. 214) is cited by the publishers, Appendix I, pp. 14, 15. The publishers reprinted the dedicatory epistles of Jodocus Badius to the *Constitutiones legitime* (Paris, 1504), here dated 13 Sept. 1506, and to the *Provinciale* (Paris, 1506), dated 15 May 1506. The *imprimatur* on the verso of the title of the 1679 edition is dated 23 Mar. 1676/7, and the colophon of the *Provinciale* (p. 356) 11 July 1678.

[3] e.g. B.M. MS. Royal 11 A.xiv, Lambeth MS. 479, Peterborough, Dean and Chapter Libr. MS. 9, and numerous other unglossed texts have the preamble of Arundel's constitutions, 1407 ('Reverendissime sinodo . . . abscindendi') as a fourth chapter to Lib. 1, tit. 2, De constitutionibus.

of the work in various manuscripts. Several of the manuscripts which contain glosses evidently do no more than give précis or excerpts of Lyndwood's gloss, but other glosses may show originality.[1] Can all the commentary in the *textus receptus* be regarded as Lyndwood's, and do any manuscripts contain more? Can any of the manuscripts be identified as the copy from which any of the early printed editions was taken? These are some of the matters which call for further study.

APPENDIX

The following list of manuscripts of the *Provinciale* is only a first rough attempt at a census. Many of the manuscripts are defective, and many have one or more later constitutions appended to the main series, and the sequence of constitutions is not uniform; but these facts are not noted here. Only those copies contain Lyndwood's gloss or some substantial part of it which are so noted here.

I have not myself seen the Cardiff and Edinburgh copies and am grateful to Dr. N. R. Ker and Professor Denys Hay for sending me particulars. I am obliged to the owners and librarians for facilities to consult all the other manuscripts, and especially to Sir Arthur Howard, for lending me the copy which he owns. Dr. R. W. Hunt and Dr. N. R. Ker have kindly provided references to the MSS., marked *, which I overlooked in 1961.

Cambridge (England) Univ. Libr. Ee.6.30.
　　　　　　　　　　　　　,,　　,,　　Ee.6.32, with gloss.
　　　　Corpus Christi Coll. 544.
　　　　Emmanuel Coll. 66 (I.3.14).
　　　　　　　　,,　　　　,,　　107 (I.4.32), excerpts only.
　　　　Fitzwilliam Museum 347.
　　　　　　　　,,　　　　　　,,　　BL16.
　　　　Gonville & Caius Coll. 157 (207) fo. 59 (to Lib. 3 tit. 16
　　　　　　　　　　　　　　　　　　only) with abridged gloss.
　　　　　　　　,,　　　　,,　　　,,　　207 (113) p. 65.
　　　　　　　　,,　　　　,,　　　,,　　222 (237).
　　　　　　　　,,　　　　,,　　　,,　　235 (121) p. 117, abridged.
　　　　　　　　,,　　　　,,　　　,,　　262 (666), with gloss.
　　　　　　　　,,　　　　,,　　　,,　　263 (667), with gloss.

[1] The following list indicates some manuscripts which differ from the *textus receptus* in their glosses; but all the manuscripts have not been thoroughly examined.

*Pembroke Coll. 309, with gloss.
Peterhouse 53, with gloss.
   ,,   54, with gloss.
St. John's Coll. 243.
Trinity Coll. 400 (B.16.38).
   ,,   ,,   401 (B.16.39) fo. 61.
   ,,   ,,   1245 (O.4.14) fo. 148ᵛ, table only.
   ,,   ,,   1356 (O.7.28).
Cambridge (Mass.), Harvard Law School 37 (formerly Dunn) fos. 2 (fo. 1 missing)—167ᵛ.
*Cardiff, 1. 704, 148 (belonged to Justin Plunkett, earl of Fingall, in 1725).
Edinburgh, Univ. Libr. D.b.V.10 (149).
Eton College Libr. 98, with gloss.
Lincoln, Cathedral Chapter Libr. C.5.9 (133).
London, British Museum Harl. 224.
      ,,   ,,   ,,   2352.
      ,,   ,,   ,,   2359.
      ,,   ,,   Royal 9 A.v, with abridged gloss.
      ,,   ,,   ,,   9 A.xiii, with abridged gloss.
      ,,   ,,   ,,   11 A.xiv fo. 93.
      ,,   ,,   ,,   11 C.viii, with gloss.
      ,,   ,,   ,,   11 E.i, with gloss.
Lambeth Palace Libr. 433, with abridged gloss.
      ,,   ,,   ,,   478.
      ,,   ,,   ,,   479.
Lincoln's Inn Libr. 27 (148).
Longleat House (Wiltshire), Marquess of Bath. MS. 35, with gloss.
Oxford, Bodleian Libr. Bodley 18 (Summary catalogue 1861), with abridged gloss.
      ,,   ,,   ,,   65 (S.C.2066).
      ,,   ,,   ,,   248 (S.C.2247), with gloss.
      ,,   ,,   *Lat. th. b.2 (S.C.30588) fo. 28 (bifolium containing parts of Lib. v tit. 14–15)
      ,,   ,,   Lat. th. f.8 (S.C.34476) fo. 51.
      ,,   ,,   Laud misc. 608, with gloss.
      ,,   ,,   Rawlinson A.380.
      ,,   ,,   ,,   C.268.
      ,,   ,,   ,,   C.273.
      ,,   ,,   ,,   C.664.
      ,,   ,,   Tanner 337 fo. 57.
All Souls Coll. 63 fo. 184ᵛ.
Corpus Christi Coll. 71, with gloss.

Magdalen Coll. 143, with gloss.
New Coll. 215 (to Lib. 1 tit. 9 only), with gloss.
Peterborough, Dean and Chapter Libr. 9, with abridged gloss.
Shrewsbury, School Libr. 8.
Steyning (Sussex), Hon. Sir Arthur Howard, Wappingthorn.

Copies were formerly in the libraries of Abraham Sellers and Henry Farmer ([E. Bernard] *Catalogi Librorum Manuscriptorum Angliae et Hiberniae* [Oxford, 1697], tom. 2, nos. 3789 [20] and 9152 [2]). Neither has so far been identified with an existing manuscript. A copy offered for sale by Messrs. Colbeck Radford and Co., Ltd., 8 Bruton Street, New Bond Street, London, in their catalogue, *The Ingatherer*, no. 22 (Feb. 1932), item 5, seems to have been that which formerly belonged to the Dominicans of Woodchester (Gloucestershire): see Hist. MSS. Commission, *Second Report*, pp. 146-7.

9. Some aspects of diocesan legislation in England during the thirteenth century*

A MERE student of ecclesiastical history who tackles a problem of canon law is a bold man, and he must choose his stance with the greatest possible care. But with Monsieur Le Bras the subject of diocesan legislation needs no advocate. This historian of canon law, author of the *Prolégomènes* to the *Histoire du Droit et des Institutions de l'Église en Occident*, is also founder and patron of the 'Commission pour l'Étude des Statuts Synodaux Français'. I shelter under the powerful authority of Gabriel Le Bras, who has told us that 'l'histoire du droit canon inclut tout ce qui concerne la génèse, la détermination et la vie des règles et des institutions ecclésiastiques.'[1] I confine myself to the narrow limits of the English diocese with the more confidence because, as Monsieur Le Bras constantly proclaims with brilliant clarity, 'la plupart des canons conciliaires sont provoqués par des affaires locales.'[2] Statutes often have a history which overflows the boundaries of the province or the diocese of their origin: 'il y a . . . des statuts synodaux dont le destin est œcuménique'.[3] Law, like population, recruits from below.

To define the contents of the diocesan statutes is not an easy task. One may expect to find all manner of topics touching the rights and duties of diocesan officials, and clergy both beneficed and unbeneficed, and their relations with their flocks.

---

* First published in French in *Études d'Histoire du Droit Canonique dédiées à Gabriel Le Bras* (Paris, 1965), i. 41–54.

[1] G. Le Bras, *Prolégomènes* (Histoire du Droit et des Institutions de l'Église en Occident, i (Paris, 1955)), p. 87.   [2] Ibid., p. 61 n. 1, and cf. p. 63.

[3] Ibid., p. 145, and cf. pp. 63, 137 and the remarks of J. Gaudemet, *Institutions ecclésiastiques* (Histoire des Institutions françaises au Moyen Age, ed. F. Lot and R. Fawtier, iii (Paris, 1962)), pp. 317–20.

Above all, the statute-makers have in mind the parson and the parish-priest, their rights and their duties. That is why the statutes provide precious material for the historian, the jurist, and the sociologist. The student of economic history will discover in the mention of a ciborium of *opus lemoviticum* an indication that the enamels of Limoges were beginning to supplant in England the products of the Rhineland.[1] The historian of the religious orders will note the support given to the Friars Minor and Friars Preachers, soon after their arrival in England, by Peter des Roches, bishop of Winchester. The specialist in popular superstitions and sorcery may observe in these statutes traces of the people's veneration for holy wells and springs and stones, and of the invocation of devils in magic circles. The roots go deep into the moral and religious foundations of society. The contents of these statutes are not limited so much by subject-matter (which may range from a warning to parents against rocking cradles to an order to parishioners to pay tithe on hay) as by the need for conformity with the common law of the Church and with provincial canons. Here I am concerned solely with statutes which deal with the education of the clergy and with parochial finance, bearing always in mind the extent to which custom, embodied in local statutes, supplements the common law.

II

The chief importance of English diocesan statutes in the thirteenth century, so it seems to me, lay in the elementary instruction they gave or prescribed for the parochial clergy in matters of theology and law. (I need not labour the point that moral theology and the canon law, at this level as much as at the academic level, grew up together.)[2] The didactic aim so clearly visible in the Paris statutes of Odo de Sully is equally evident in the preamble to the first English diocesan statutes, those of Stephen Langton for Canterbury, 1213 × 1214: 'Necessarium duximus hiis qui ad curam nostram specialiter pertinent formam certam statuendo prescribere quam et in se

---

[1] Synodal statute of Worcester, 1229: *C. & S.* ii. 171. The index of this work will direct the reader to statutes mentioned here without further reference.

[2] Le Bras, op. cit., p. 186.

recte vivendo, si recte fuerint ordinati, et in ecclesia sacramenta divina rite tractando, et etiam erga populum laudabiliter se gerendo debeant observare.'[1] Langton, the Parisian professor of theology, in his capacity of archbishop of Canterbury shared the pastoral interest of the bishop of Paris. Richard Poore, companion of Langton at Paris, was later his suffragan of Salisbury; he it was to whom Robert of Flamborough dedicated his *Liber penitentialis*.[2] Poore ordained that the priests of his diocese should possess his statutes, so that 'ipsas [constitutiones] frequenter habentes pre oculis, in ministeriis et dispensationibus sacramentorum sint instructiores et in fide catholica bene vivendo firmiores.'[3]

Seen as a whole, the statutes of the thirteenth century present the most practical and most conscientious attempt by the ecclesiastical authorities of the time to acquaint a mainly plebeian and ignorant parochial clergy with the rudiments of the Christian faith and the obligations which attached to the cure of souls.[4] Nowhere does one find evidence that the Church had any other plan for their systematic education. The statutes offered in themselves some instruction on the sacraments, their administration, their validity in doubtful circumstances, and so forth. The sacrament of confession and penance is in the foreground; after the Fourth Lateran Council the parson or his deputy had to concern himself more and more with the problems of the confessional. The instruction which the statutes give on the sacraments is short and simple, but neither too short nor too simple for most of the clerks who came to the bishop's synod. Academic books, costly, heavy, and complicated,

---

[1] *C. & S.* ii. 24. For questions of provenance and date see my study, 'The earliest English diocesan statutes', *EHR*, lxxiv (1960), 1–29, pp. 2–18.

[2] P. Michaud-Quantin, 'A propos des premières *Summae confessorum*: théologie et droit canonique', *Recherches de Théologie ancienne et médiévale*, xxvi (1959), 264–306, pp. 276–83; idem, *Sommes de casuistique et manuels de confession au moyen âge, xiie–xvie siècles* (Analecta medievalia Namurcensia 13, Louvain, 1962). See also the critical edition of Robert of Flamborough's *Liber poenitentialis* by J. J. Francis Firth (Studies and Texts, 18: Pontifical Institute of Mediaeval Studies, Toronto, 1971), and above, pp. 143–4.

[3] *C. & S.* ii. 96.

[4] See André Artonne, 'Les statuts synodaux diocésains français', *Rev. de l'Hist. de l'Église de France* xxxvi (1950), 168–81, p. 169: 'Le livre ou statut synodal était le texte auquel le clergé devait constamment se référer et qui suppléait à l'insuffisance de l'enseignement oral.'

were inappropriate. A work such as the *De sacramentis* of Peter Cantor or the *De penitentia* of Thomas of Chobham, however practical in appearance, was far out of reach of the majority of priests with cure, if not downright incomprehensible. Or take another example: the book dedicated by Gerald de Barri (Giraldus Cambrensis), archdeacon of Brecon, to the clergy of his archdeaconry in which he no longer resided, his *Gemma ecclesiastica.* 'I have thought it proper (he says) to instruct you on the subject of difficulties concerning the sacraments, about which you were in the habit of consulting me, in the days when I still lived among you, and on other questions on which knowledge is of use to you and ignorance fraught with danger.'[1] Gerald proceeds to discourse of the administration of the sacraments, teaching by *precepta* (drawn in large part from the *Decretum* and from the works of Peter Cantor) and by *exempla.* The book is lively, anecdotal, not to say scandalous. But Gerald, as always, wrote too much. A work which occupies 360 printed pages in the Rolls Series was perhaps not too long to serve as a bedside book for Pope Innocent III, but it is easy to imagine that this was more than the Welsh country clergy could stomach. Something more succinct was called for.

'Non est leve canonum girare volumina et ignorare medico medicinale officium nimis grave', wrote the Cardinal Otto, papal legate in England in 1237.[2] He therefore required archdeacons and rural deans to instruct the inferior clergy, and examine ordinands and presentees to livings, in their chapters. The response of the English episcopate to this demand is to be found in an abridged form in the statutes of Robert Grosseteste, bishop of Lincoln (about 1239), perhaps the best known during the Middle Ages of all the English statutes. The bishop of Lincoln—at once the most learned and the most zealous of the English prelates of his day—spells out the minimum which should be expected of a parish-priest:[3]

Ut unusquisque pastor animarum et quilibet sacerdos parochialis

[1] *Opera* (RS), ii. 5–6. A. Boutemy indicates the links between Gerald and Peter Cantor in 'Giraud de Barri et Pierre le Chantre', *Rev. du Moyen Age latin*, ii (1946), 45–64.

[2] *C. & S.* ii. 246.

[3] *Roberti Grosseteste . . . epistolae*, ed. H. R. Luard (RS, 1861), p. 154; *C. & S.* i. 268.

sciat decalogum, id est, decem mandata legis mosaice, eademque populo sibi subiecto frequenter predicet et exponat. Sciat quoque que sunt septem criminalia, eademque similiter populo predicet fugienda. Sciat insuper saltem simpliciter septem ecclesiastica sacramenta, et hii qui sunt sacerdotes maxime sciant que exiguntur ad vere confessionis et penitentie sacramentum, formamque baptizandi doceant frequenter laicos in ydiomate communi. Habeat quoque quisque eorum saltem simplicem intellectum fidei, sicut continetur in simbolo tam maiori quam minori, et in tractatu qui dicitur 'Quicunque vult', qui cotidie ad Primam in ecclesia psallitur.

These modest requirements involved teaching the priest how to administer the sacraments, and in particular how to do his duty as a confessor.[1] It was, of course, no new departure. Teaching on the sacraments entered into the law of the Anglo-Norman Church with the legatine canons of Hubert Walter, archbishop of Canterbury, at York in 1195 and his provincial canons of Westminster, 1200.[2] It was prominent in the earliest diocesan statutes, those of Langton and Poore. Before the thirteenth century is out, a dozen dioceses will do the same and re-state the requirements of Robert Grosseteste. In 1281 the Franciscan, John Pecham, archbishop of Canterbury, incorporated in the canons of his provincial council at Lambeth a sketch of Christian doctrine and morals (*incipit*: 'Ignorantia sacerdotum') which followed the same main lines;[3] and Pecham enjoined on the parish-priest that he should expound these topics in the vernacular to the laity, four times a year. So, although the canon carries the rubric 'De informatione simplicium sacerdotum', Pecham resembled Grosseteste in recognizing that the education of the clergy was something not only necessary in itself, but also the means of instructing layfolk.[4]

---

[1] See D. W. Robertson, 'The Manuel des Péchés and an English episcopal decree', *Modern Language Notes*, lx. 7 (Nov. 1945), 441, and 'The cultural tradition of *Handlyng Synne*', *Speculum*, xxii (1947), 162–85.

[2] Wilkins, i. 501, 505; *Chronica mag. Rogeri de Hovedene*, ed. W. Stubbs (RS, 1868–71), iii. 294, iv. 128.

[3] *C. & S.* ii. 900–5.

[4] I cannot, however, subscribe entirely to the opinion of my friend the Revd. Prof. Leonard Boyle, O.P., who supposes that Pecham's canon was formulated purely with the idea of instructing the laity and that it is 'simply a syllabus' which 'presumes rather than imparts knowledge': 'The *Oculus sacerdotis* and some other works of William de Pagula', *Trans. Royal Hist. Soc.*, 5th series v (1955), 81–100,

If the statutes treated religious education as a primary object, it cannot be said that they met all the necessities of the case. But they also gave an impulse to a new sort of writing, which concentrated on the function of the priest as confessor: little treatises which enumerated and commented on the seven mortal sins, and which distinguished between the different conditions of the sinners and the circumstances of their sins.[1] In the third quarter of the thirteenth century a poem on this theme was composed in the Anglo-Norman vernacular, *Le Manuel des Péchés*, available to layfolk as well as clerks.[2] All these writings, like the statutes, were designed to contribute to universal education. It was becoming recognized in this age that the confession of the layman should be prepared for, not only by the questions put to him in the confessional, but by homilies delivered in advance.[3] And a point to notice in this development is the participation of English bishops in the writing of these didactic works. Edmund Rich, archbishop of Canterbury, was the author of a *Speculum ecclesie* which was translated into Anglo-Norman during the thirteenth century.[4] Roger Wessenham (or Weseham) wrote brief *Instituta*.[5] Grosseteste wrote a prolix and daunting manual, *Templum domini*, of which we still possess many more manuscripts than those of his statutes.[6] Other bishops arranged for the systematic distribution of little manuals supplementary to their diocesan statutes, to be preserved and studied under the same sanctions. So,

p. 82, and cf. *Catholic Hist. Rev.*, lii (1966–7), 574. Not all subjects are merely enumerated: they are developed to a certain point; and the motive for this exposition of them is said to be clerical ignorance: 'ne quis a predictis per ignorantiam se excuset, que tamen omnes ministri ecclesie scire tenentur, ea perstringimus summaria brevitate'. The title ('De informatione simplicium sacerdotum') occurs in all manuscripts and shows how the canon was regarded.

[1] See M. W. Bloomfield, *The Seven Deadly Sins* (Michigan, 1952).

[2] E. J. Arnould, *Le Manuel des Péchés* (Paris, 1940). M. Arnould, citing the statute of Grosseteste (above, p. 188), observes that it is 'un chapitre qui pourrait presque servir de table ou introduction à notre *Manuel*' (p. 20).

[3] See Robertson, as cited above, p. 189 n. 1.

[4] *Le Merure de Seinte Eglise by St. Edmund of Pontigny*, ed. Harry Wolcott Robbins (privately printed, Lewisburg, Pennsylvania (1925)).

[5] Published in C. R. Cheney, *English Synodalia of the XIII Century* (Oxford, 2nd ed. 1968), pp. 149–52.

[6] About 70 manuscripts of the *Templum* to about 25 of the statutes; cf. S. H. Thomson, *The Writings of Robert Grosseteste, Bishop of Lincoln* (Cambridge, 1940), pp. 138–40.

relatively early (between 1224 and 1237) a friend and colleague of Grosseteste, Alexander Stavensby, bishop of Coventry and Lichfield, published two little treatises on the seven mortal sins and on penance. Parochial clergy were ordered to copy them with the bishop's statutes.[1] Another friend of Grosseteste, Walter de Cantilupe, bishop of Worcester, who promulgated his statutes in a synod of 1240, wrote: 'Tractatum etiam de confessione fecimus, quem scribi ab omnibus precipimus capellanis et etiam observari in confessionibus audiendis, quia longum esset ipsum in presenti synodo publicare.'[2] After Stavensby and Cantilupe came Peter Quinel, bishop of Exeter, who published in 1287 with his statutes a *Summula* which is a purely didactic work. Quinel (†1291) recalls his great contemporary the 'Speculator', William Durand, bishop of Mende (†1296).[3] The inscription on his tomb in the church of Santa Maria sopra Minerva in Rome runs: 'instruxit clerum scriptis monuitque statutis'; and, sure enough, in modern times a work of his has come to light divided in two parts respectively entitled *Instructiones* and *Constitutiones*.[4] Quinel's *Statuta* and *Summula* offer an exact parallel. With him we approach the end of a long series of English diocesan statutes. The great age of synodal statute-making had come to an end; but the statutes of the thirteenth century continued to be copied and re-read.[5]

---

[1] *C. & S.* ii. 214–26.

[2] Ibid. ii. 305. Prof. Boyle thinks that this is probably the treatise 'Omnis etas', found in MS. Bodley 828 fo. 215ᵛ and elsewhere: see *Catholic Hist. Rev.*, lii (1966–7), 575.

[3] The two works extend to nearly a hundred pages, *C. & S.* ii. 982–1077.

[4] *Instructions et Constitutions de Guillaume Durand le Spéculateur*, ed. Jos. Berthelé and M. Valmary (Archives du département de l'Hérault, *Docts. et Inventaires complémentaires*, tome v fasc. 1), Montpellier, 1905: extrait des *Mémoires* de l'Acad. des Sciences et Lettres de Montpellier, Section des Lettres, 2ᵉ série, tome iii.

[5] In 1361 Simon Islip, archbishop of Canterbury, ordered the clergy of his diocese to copy a manual on the seven deadly sins and the ten commandments, and in 1351 John Thoresby, archbishop of York, brought out a new edition of the canon of Pecham 'De informatione simplicium sacerdotum'. See W. A. Pantin, *The English Church in the Fourteenth Century* (Cambridge, 1955), p. 212, and L. Boyle, 'The "Summa Summarum" and some other English works of canon law', *Proc. of the 2nd International Congress of Medieval Canon Law, Boston College 12–16 August 1963*, ed. S. Kuttner and J. J. Ryan (Monumenta Iuris Canonici, Series C: Subsidia, vol. i, Città del Vaticano, 1965), pp. 415–56.

III

Statutes which envisage the elementary education of the clergy and laity provide the student of history and canon law with the sort of testimony which is hard to come by elsewhere. Here I call attention to a few remarkable points concerning the doctrine of the sacraments and their administration. To begin, it should be noted how, throughout these statutes, the idea of *seven* sacraments is being impressed upon the lower clergy, almost as though it were an article of faith.[1] Also, it should be noted how much publicity is given to current doctrine on the iteration of sacraments.

As regards the sacrament of confirmation, the common law of the Church did not specify the precise age suitable for confirmands. So it is instructive to observe in the statutes the variations of practice in England. Whereas Stephen Langton seems in his first statutes to require the confirmation of infants within a year of birth, he comes round later to the rule enunciated by his friend Richard Poore at Salisbury, that children should be confirmed before their sixth year (that is, 'quinque annos ad plus'). This maximum remains the prescribed age at Salisbury. But in 1228 Poore becomes bishop of Durham, and in revising his statutes for Durham he raises the limit from five to seven years.[2] In the diocese of Worcester, Cantilupe penalizes parents who do not bring their children to the bishop for confirmation within two years of their birth. On the other hand, the bishop of Bath and Wells, about 1258, prescribes confirmation within three years of birth, and this rule is transmitted with the other statutes of Wells to the dioceses of Winchester, York, and Carlisle; Peter Quinel renews the prescription at Exeter in 1287. All these statutes allowed confirmation at an earlier age than was generally permitted. Gautier de Bruges,

[1] É. Dhanis, 'Quelques anciennes formules septénaires des sacrements', *Rev. d'Hist. ecclés.*, xxvi (1930), 574–608, 916–50, xxvii (1931), 1–26; D. W. Robertson, 'Frequency of preaching in xiii[th] century England', *Speculum*, xxiv (1949), 376–88, p. 379.

[2] The manuscripts of the Durham statutes date only from the fourteenth century, but the variant 'septem' is confirmed by the statutes for the peculiars of Durham in the diocese of York, which exist in a thirteenth-century text. The *Speculum ecclesiae* of Edmund Rich (who was treasurer of Salisbury in the time of Bishop Richard Poore) corresponds to the statute of Salisbury.

bishop of Poitiers (1280–1305) disapproved of the confirmation of *infantes*: 'potius convenit dari [confirmatio] ipsis iam iuvenibus, quando concupiscentia incipit eos temptare, ut roborati gratia data in confirmatione illam possit vincere.'[1] Even in England, in the fourteenth century, William of Paull (Pagula), in citing the statute of Salisbury, commented: 'sed secundum iura canonica illi qui debent confirmari debent esse perfecte etatis, et ieiuni ad confirmationem venire debent . . . di. v s. et ieiuni [*Decretum*, de cons. 5. 6].'[2] Evidently the penalties on parents for negligence remained a matter for the discretion of local prelates. It is noticeable that the statutes of an important group of dioceses have nothing to say on the matter of appropriate age.[3]

The celebration of the eucharist demanded very careful supervision by the ecclesiastical authorities if profanation of the Host was to be avoided. This could result from stupidity or negligence. Faulty celebration could even be productive of heresy. Consequently, the provisions of the statutes under this head are sufficiently detailed to provide much of interest to liturgiologists. The statutes also constantly recall the decree of the Fourth Lateran Council which required communion by all the faithful at least once a year. But despite the movement to withhold the chalice from the laity—a move for which theological reasons of a sort had already been stated in the twelfth century—the first indication that the chalice was as a rule withheld from layfolk in England occurs in the provincial canons of Lambeth, 1281. There Archbishop John Pecham ordered priests to instruct their flock at the time of communion:

Instruant sub panis specie simul eis dari corpus et sanguinem domini, immo Christum integrum vivum et verum qui totus est sub specie sacramenti. Doceant etiam eosdem illud quod ipsis eisdem temporibus in calice propinatur sacramentum non esse, sed vinum purum eis hauriendum traditum ut facilius sacramentum glutiant quod ceperunt. Solis enim celebrantibus sanguinem sub specie

---

[1] *Instructiones*, c. 9, ed. A. de Poorter, 'Un traité de théologie inédit de Gautier de Bruges', *Mélanges de la Soc. d'Émulation de Bruges*, v (1911), 28.
[2] Oculus sacerdotis, Dextera pars: Cambridge, Univ. Libr. MS. Gg. 1. 13 fos. 62ᵛ–63ʳ.
[3] Statutes of Lincoln, Norwich, Ely, Coventry, London.

vini consecrati sumere in huiusmodi minoribus ecclesiis est concessum.[1]

This doctrine was in direct contradiction to that found in the influential Salisbury statutes of Richard Poore (1217×1219), who had ordered priests:

Debetis instruere laicos quotiens communicant quod de veritate corporis et sanguinis nullo modo dubitent. Nam hoc accipiunt proculdubio sub panis specie quod pro nobis pependit in cruce, hoc accipiunt in calice quod effusum est de Christi latere; hoc bibunt, ut dicit Augustinus, credentes quod prius fuderunt sevientes.[2]

These statutes of Poore were re-issued by him in the diocese of Durham, and were widely diffused elsewhere. If one can conclude from Pecham's canon of Lambeth that by 1281 Poore's words had ceased to correspond to English teaching in general, one is still not justified in supposing that the practice of communion in two kinds (or the construction put upon the use of the chalice) disappeared abruptly and throughout the land; for Bishop Peter Quinel of Exeter borrowed the words of Richard Poore six years after the Council of Lambeth.[3]

Statutes about the sacrament of confession and penance are too numerous to summarize. I confine myself to calling attention to two abnormal rules. Robert Bingham, bishop of Salisbury ordered confessors (1238×1244): 'quod, licet verbo aut signo prodere non debeant peccatorem, quoniam quedam hereses in partibus istis de novo dicuntur pululare, si sacerdos aliquem hereticum inveniat hoc nobis non tardet revelare; fidem enim illis non credimus observandam qui ab unitate ecclesie recedentes iura fidei catholice violare non formidant'. This statute conforms to the doctrine of Raymond of Peñaforte,[4] with which Robert Bingham was probably acquainted, but it is unparalleled in English statutes. The second rule comes from a later age. In January 1349, at the height of the crisis in English society caused by the Black Death, the ministry in

---

[1] *C. & S.* ii. 895. On communion in two kinds see James J. Megivern, *Concomitance and Communion: a study in Eucharistic Doctrine and Practice* (Studia Friburgensia, N.S. 33. Fribourg, 1963), pp. 46–50.

[2] *C. & S.* ii. 77–8.   [3] Ibid. 991.

[4] Ibid. 371; R. de Peñaforte, Summa de penitentia, 3, 34, 60 (Rome edition of 1603, p. 490). I owe this reference to the kindness of the Revd. F. E. P. S. Langton.

England was in grave danger. Ralph of Shrewsbury, bishop of Bath and Wells, sent out a mandate to his archdeacons,[1] in which he advised confession to laymen—and even to women—in case of emergency and in the absence of a priest. Theologians of the thirteenth century had indeed thought that confession to laymen had its uses in certain circumstances, and canonists (including Hostiensis, Durandus, Guido de Baisio) shared this opinion.[2] But, to my knowledge, no English bishop of the thirteenth century took this possibility into account in composing statutes on confession. And when the bishop of Bath and Wells issued his mandate in 1349 the theological soundness of his advice was in process of being questioned and rejected. Duns Scotus, according to Père Teetaert, was 'le premier théologien qui se soit opposé, non plus seulement au caractère sacremental ou obligatoire de la confession aux laïques, mais même à la légitimité de cette pratique'.[3]

Among the many statutes about marriage I shall call attention to one single category. Some statutes aimed at suppressing the concubinage of layfolk by making marriage the penalty of a relapse. The offender, after a first or second conviction, had to swear in the following terms: 'Promitto tibi quod si te de cetero carnaliter cognovero, te tanquam in uxorem meam legitimam, nisi aliquid canonicum obsistat, consentio.' And a woman swore in the same sense to a man.[4] Bishops of eight English dioceses promulgated statutes of this sort. Several of them give the formula of the conditional contract; three order the contract to be put in writing. We know that the oath was actually exacted and the contract fulfilled in fourteenth-century England, and the practice already obtained in France, in the diocese of Rouen, as early as 1245. But a glossator of the statutes of Exeter (1287) commented on the practice adversely: 'Hec constitutio est contra iura et naturalem equitatem, quia de iure libera debent esse matrimonia et sponsalia, ut notatur *Extra*, quod me. cau. c. abbas [*Extra*, 1, 40, 2] per b', C. de sponsali. 1. si [*Codex Iustiniani*, 5, 1, 4].'[5]

[1] Wilkins, ii. 745–6.

[2] Amédée Teetaert, *La Confession aux Laïques dans l'Église latine* (Louvain, 1926), pp. 434–9.

[3] Ibid., p. 431.

[4] *C. & S.* ii. 385–6.   [5] Ibid. ii. 999 n. 4.

IV

The didactic element and rules for the administration of the sacraments are far from constituting the entire subject-matter of these statutes. To appreciate how much the structure of the Church depended on law-making by individual bishops for their own dioceses one has only to look at questions of diocesan and parochial finance. The statutes throw light on the economic aspect of the cult and the parochial clergy's dependence for a large part of their income on the laity's annual contributions, both obligatory and voluntary. The Corpus Iuris Canonici stated the general principles, but did not settle the details. Yet the resources at the disposal of the hierarchy were bound to dictate the pattern of its integration in medieval society. If the Church were deprived of its possessions and its revenues, it would lose with them the opportunity to exercise much of its influence over layfolk. The types of resources at the disposal of the clergy, and the extent of them, varied greatly. Every region had its own customs, its own economic needs and possibilities. Diocesan statutes enable us to see how bishops applied decree 32 of the Fourth Lateran Council on the *congruens portio* of the perpetual vicar. Another task fell to the bishops: that of fixing the minimum stipend for those many undistinguished and inconspicuous clerks who were neither parsons nor vicars—the *presbiteri stipendiarii*, *capellani*, and *clerici*, who become a little less obscure by reason of their appearance in the statutes. Stipends of vicars and chaplains varied according to time and place, a fact which underlines the need to establish the provenance of statutes which have often been misrepresented in the manuscripts and misplaced by modern scholars. In the diocese of Winchester in 1224 parish priests were supposed to receive at least fifty or sixty shillings; but at Worcester and at Exeter, about 1230, the minimum was as low as forty shillings a year. About 1247 the bishop of Winchester fixed stipends of five marks (i.e. 66s. 8d.) or sixty shillings. At this period five marks was also the minimum at Chichester and York; but as late as 1287 in the West Country, the bishop of Exeter required only a minimum of sixty shillings.

Tithe constituted the chief source of income for the majority of beneficed clergy and, at the same time, provided occasion for almost interminable disputes, sometimes between rival claimants, sometimes between those who claimed and those who owed tithe. The Corpus Iuris Canonici deals at length with problems arising between rival claimants; the diocesan statutes give more abundant information about the levying of tithe, the method of assessment, rebates allowed, the time of collection, the resistance which collectors encountered. The history of tithe, it is true, cannot be written solely from the statutes, but the statutes provide essential evidence. A full history must take into account decretal letters, judicial proceedings and judgements, and every kind of documentary and literary source. Like a circumspect and prudent judge, the historian 'non semper ad unam speciem probationis applicet mentem suam'.[1] If the student of tithe takes a broad view he will see how the demands of the Church increased from the twelfth to the fourteenth century, how tithe customary in one region came to be exacted in others, how the laity put up opposition to these developments.[2] For example, tithe of hay was exacted here and there in the twelfth century 'by laudable custom'. It found no mention in the earliest English diocesan statutes. In 1226 it was the subject of a special concession by King Henry III. Thereafter hay figures in the statutes. In the middle part of the thirteenth century English prelates do their best to settle the custom and law on tithe by strict definition. Down to the fourteenth century the statutes become more and more precise, and they include a number of *spuria* and *dubia* which circulate with the pretended authority of provincial canons, under the name of some archbishop or another.[3]

The offerings made by layfolk when they received the sacraments everywhere created difficulties, which were partly legal, partly theological. Even if one could, according to the canon law, describe these offerings as established customs, and

---

[1] The phrase is used by Pope Innocent III (Migne, ccxiv. 1028), with a reminiscence of the *Digest*.

[2] Norma Adams, 'The judicial conflict over tithes', *EHR*, lii (1937), 1–22.

[3] *C. & S.* ii. 161; C. R. Cheney, 'So-called statutes of Archbishops John Pecham and Robert Winchelsey', *JEH*, xii (1961), 14–37, pp. 27–13, and above, pp. 133–5.

consequently as payments to be required under pain of ecclesiastical censure, a suspicion of simony remained if the sacrament or
sacramental were withheld for lack of payment. Decree 66 of
the Fourth Lateran Council on *laudabiles consuetudines* posed the
problem without solving it. Each bishop had to do his best to
enforce these practices to the profit of the clergy so far as
doctrine permitted. Bishop Richard Poore ordered: 'pro inter-
ragio corpus sepeliri non differatur, set post sepulturam si
quid datum fuerit in elemosinam recipiatur'. On the one hand,
Robert Grosseteste was disturbed by the linking of parishioners'
offerings with their Easter Communion;[1] on the other hand,
several bishops pronounced excommunication on any who
should combine in a conspiracy to withhold the oblations due
for burials, weddings, and the churching of women.[2] According to many statutes the parson could (and should) use excommunication to enforce payment of the oblations which every
parishioner ought to pay on three or four specified feast-days.

The mortuary was one of these customs which varied from
place to place. Henry de Bracton, who was royal judge, archdeacon of Barnstaple, and chancellor of Exeter, in his classic
treatise *De legibus et consuetudinibus Anglie* observes: 'Quibusdam locis habet ecclesia melius averium de consuetudine, vel
secundum, vel tertium melius, in quibusdam nihil; et ideo
consideranda est consuetudo loci.'[3] Diocesan statutes enlarge
on the subject. We learn from them the doctrine that mortuaries
are due from the defunct 'pro decimis suis maioribus seu minoribus indiscrete vel ignoranter detentis seu minus plene solutis'.[4]
Often the statutes order that priests use the weapon of excom-

---

[1] *C. & S.* ii. 205, 271. See a statute of York (1241–55): 'ne, una manu porrigendo eucharistiam altera recipiendo pecuniam, nostre redemptionis mysterium
sit venale' (ibid. ii. 489). Archbishop Robert Winchelsey, after his metropolitan
visitation of Bristol in 1301, condemned fixed charges for baptisms (*JEH*, xii.
22). This was not a matter of concern only to English prelates. One sees the same
problem in Poland in the fifteenth century; the synod of Poznan, *c.* 1420, condemned the sale of sacraments 'sed post sepulturam et alia sacramenta, si quid de
consuetudine laudabili fuit [fuerit] exigendum, exigatis iudicis officio' (Jakub
Sawicki, *Concilia Poloniae*, vii (Poznan, 1952), 159).

[2] *C. & S.* ii. 629 n. 4.

[3] Lib. ii c. 26 (RS, i. 478). See also the royal writ *Circumspecte agatis*: 'si rector
petat mortuarium in partibus ubi mortuaria dari consueverunt' (*C. & S.* ii. 975).

[4] *C. & S.* ii. 416, 717; but sometimes parishioners made separate legacies to
their churches 'pro decimis oblitis' (ibid. ii. 1050 n. 4).

munication to secure their right to a mortuary. As an indication of the importance of mortuaries one may note how, merely by the agency of copyists in the fourteenth and fifteenth centuries, synodal statutes of Salisbury on this subject assume the character of provincial canons, ascribed to Langton, Winchelsey, Islip, or Langham. Thus disguised they circulated throughout England until the end of the Middle Ages and beyond, and so contributed to transform what had been a local custom into a general rule of law.[1]

On yet another financial matter, these statutes tell us something about the maintenance of the church-fabric, and the supply of liturgical books and vestments and altar-furniture. A statute of Salisbury speaks of a fraternity of the fabric. A statute of Exeter orders that the unsuitable garments of over-dressed priests shall be sold for the benefit of the cathedral church.[2] Bishops set out in their statutes the obligations of the laity towards their parish churches in such matters. The custom by which the responsibility for repairing the nave of the church and enclosing the churchyard fell on the parishioners became, little by little, a law for the whole of England. As with the customs relating to mortuaries, these rules became engrained on the authority of so-called provincial canons with a very dubious history. And simultaneously, by much the same process, the laity were saddled with a larger part of the costs of church services.[3]

V

These aspects of diocesan legislation bring out the great importance attached to *consuetudo*. Sometimes the rules and practices recorded in the statutes are peculiar to a single diocese; sometimes they are copied by one diocese from another; sometimes they are modified in transit. Statutes of Norwich even show respect for the custom of the parish: the

---

[1] *EHR*, l (1935), 399, 411. *JEH*, xii (1961), 31; cf. E. Gibson, *Codex Iuris Ecclesiastici Anglicani* (1713), pp. 743–7.

[2] *C. & S.* ii. 91 note j, 230.

[3] *JEH*, xii (1961), 18–19, 22, 25–7; *C. & S.* ii. 513. For a brief view of the state of things in French parishes, see Paul Adam, *La Vie paroissiale en France au XIVe Siècle* (1964), esp. pp. 80–6.

priest ought not to receive money for the sacraments 'ultra debitam consuetudinem parochie sue et consuetam'.[1] The obligations of rector and vicar respectively in repairing the chancels of their churches are to be resolved 'secundum diversas consuetudines et approbatas'.[2]

The legal historian must treat these statutes seriously, for they throw light on the custom of the dioceses in which they originated, the needs of the Church in particular places, the programme of an individual bishop. It is unnecessary to insist that they depended in part on the common law of the Church, as it was to be found in the *Decretum* and *Extra* and in provincial legislation. The diocesan bishop often appealed to these authorities and those who framed English diocesan statutes knew the glossators and theologians of Italy and France. Nevertheless, in many respects these statutes get nearer to the roots of ecclesiastical organization than do the more general laws and academic writings. They are more faithful witnesses of the problems which confronted the bishop of an English diocese and of the instruction which was dispensed to the inferior clergy.

Despite a certain amount of centralization in the Catholic Church in the Middle Ages, regional variety is seen in many persistent peculiarities. Archbishop John Pecham observed in 1281 that the custom of the Church of England was distinct from all others;[3] but (as we have seen already) the Church of England itself had its own varieties of custom. Diocesan statutes do not only allude to the well-known liturgical 'Use' of Salisbury or of York, but also to the 'Uses' of Chichester, Canterbury, London, and Wells. Bishops exert themselves in an attempt to induce the laity to observe feast-days in one fashion throughout their diocese; there is no question of achieving a uniform observance in the province of Canterbury as a whole until 1362.[4] In the matter of publishing banns of marriage the custom of Salisbury in the thirteenth century

---

[1] *C. & S.* ii. 360.

[2] Ibid. ii. 1388 and n. 2.

[3] 'istius consuetudini regionis, que in multis ab omnibus aliis est distincta'. Ibid. ii. 893.

[4] See C. R. Cheney, 'Rules for the observance of feast-days in medieval England', *BIHR*, xxxiv (1961), 117–47.

differed from that prevailing in the neighbouring diocese of Wells, as we learn from the synodal statutes.[1] Both are more explicit than decree 51 of the Fourth Lateran Council, in which the pope said that 'specialem quorumdam locorum consuetudinem ad alia generaliter prorogando statuimus'; and neither the Salisbury nor the Wells custom corresponded to the later assertion of Lyndwood, the fifteenth-century canonist. As for the publication of ecclesiastical censures, here there is equal variation. Thomas of Chobham, subdean of Salisbury Cathedral during the episcopate of Richard Poore and author of a well-known *Summa*, writes: 'secundum diversas regiones sunt diversi canones et diversas institutiones latae sententiae . . . unde oportet quod quilibet sacerdos sciat constitutiones synodales factas in episcopatu suo.'[2]

Custom is made; it does not germinate spontaneously. While sometimes it may derive from century-old observances, sooner or later a moment of time arrives when the need to formulate a rule becomes imperative. Textual study of the statutes helps to establish the chronology of a custom. Once it has been set down in writing it will be transported to other parts. This is something which can be discerned by textual comparison. Chronology, provenance, interdependence: they are all parts of a single problem.[3] Its solution should help to understand better the canon law of the Middle Ages.

In conclusion, one should step back from this material in order to see the subject in perspective. The legal historian can never confine himself to documents of a single sort, and certainly not to legislation alone. The study of these statutes must rest on a solid basis of other source-material. There is evidence at hand of the application of the law in the shape of litigious proceedings, compositions, episcopal mandates, royal writs, acts of pastoral visitations, churchwardens' accounts. Those who have patience to probe into all this will find that it is scrappy but copious. For medieval England has bequeathed to us an incomparable body of Public Records and a fine series

---

[1] Salisbury: 'per intervallum quindecim dierum' (*C. & S.* ii. 375); York: 'cum debitis adminus octo dierum interstitiis' (ibid. 597). The *trina denuntiatio* is already found in the canons of Westminster (1200), c. 11 (Wilkins, i. 507).

[2] As cited by Boyle, *Trans. Royal Hist. Soc.*, 5th series v (1955), pp. 93–4.

[3] See above, pp. 138–57.

of bishops' registers; what is less well known is the archival legacy of the episcopal and archidiaconal courts, in the shape of ordinances, act-books, cause-papers, and formularies. For the most part they are scattered among libraries and local Record Offices up and down the country. Despite enormous losses, these documents offer a field for inquiry where a number of young English and American scholars are already hard at work, searching, winnowing, and evaluating the fragments that remain : *messis quidem multa.*

10. The numbering of the Lateran Councils of 1179 and 1215[*]

IN the description which Father Teetaert gave of the *Liber Poenitentialis* of Peter of Poitiers, canon of St. Victor, and the discussion which he devoted to it in the *Festschrift Grabmann* in 1935, he proposed as the time of its composition the years between 1210 and 1215.[1] The main object of the present note is to show that Father Teetaert misunderstood the chronological data which he brought forward, and that the *Liber* must be assigned, at least in its final form, to a later date. But since the evidence concerns the numeration of General Councils, it may prove to have a wider interest in critical inquiries.

Father Teetaert arrived at a *terminus a quo* for the treatise of Peter of Poitiers by remarking that Peter cited Prepositinus at several points. Now, according to Paul Lacombe, the *Summa* of Prepositinus was composed between 1206 and 1210, and Father Teetaert concluded from this 'que notre traité pénitentiel fut rédigé après 1210'.[2] Strictly speaking, the date of the *Liber* could be earlier than this, for the citations of Prepositinus are not explicitly taken from his *Summa*; however, we need not linger over this consideration, since other positive proof is available to show that the treatise was composed at a still later date.

Pope Innocent III is cited in several places in the treatise, and

---

* A revised version of a note printed in French in *Recherches de Théologie ancienne et médiévale*, ix (1937), 401–4 under the title 'La date de composition du "Liber Poenitentialis" attribué à Pierre de Poitiers'. In revising, I have corrected a few errors which crept into the French translation of the original note and have added a little more evidence.

[1] A. Teetaert, 'Le "Liber Poenitentialis" de Pierre de Poitiers', in *Aus der Geisteswelt des Mittelalters: Studien und Texte Martin Grabmann ... gewidmet* (Beiträge zur Gesch. der Philos. und Theol. des Mittelalters, Supplementband, iii, 1935), i. 310–31.

[2] Loc. cit., p. 325.

Father Teetaert commented on them, without going so far as to identify the references precisely.[1] But he found no trace of the important canon 21, *Omnis utriusque sexus*, of the Fourth Lateran Council. Hence he concluded: 'Le *Liber Poenitentialis* fut donc certainement composé avant 1215, date du IVe concile de Latran.'[2] Some might think this an over-confident argument from silence. In fact, it does not stand up to close examination. The treatise contains several references to the 'Second Lateran Council' (tit. 33 bis, 42). In no case does the reference apply clearly and unambiguously to the Second Lateran Council held by Pope Innocent II in 1139. To render tit. 42 intelligible, Father Teetaert had to correct a text which reads 'Innocent III' by reading 'Innocent II'.[3] At tit. 33, where his text reads 'in secundo concilio lateranensi' and 'in eodem concilio', he could only make sense of the citations by relating them to the Third Lateran Council of 1179.[4] This treatment assumed either confusion by the author or corruption by the scribe of the *Liber*. But the need for emendation of these passages is illusory. Misunderstanding of them has arisen from the change which has taken place in later times in the usual numbering of the councils held at the Lateran in the twelfth and thirteenth centuries.

The council nowadays described as the Second Lateran (1139)—the tenth ecumenical council in the Roman reckoning —did not leave much of a mark on the twelfth-century law books. Its acts were probably not very widely diffused. According to Orderic Vitalis much business was transacted there but scanty records remained, and although its canons were published in all countries, they were not treated seriously by princes and people.[5] Orderic's statement is borne out by the rarity of

[1] The reference in tit. 6 (p. 321) may relate to the decretal of 19 Apr. 1201 (Pott. 1323) and rhe reference in tit. 52 certainly indicates the decretal of 10 Dec. 1203 (Pott. 2038). Both of them were included in *Compilatio III*, published in 1210.

[2] Loc. cit., pp. 328–9; more exactly, composed before the end of Nov. 1215.

[3] Loc. cit., p. 324 n. 80. The same correction to tit. 46 (ibid. n. 83) is no improvement: the canon of the council of 1139 does not fit the citation.

[4] 'Cette prescription toutefois ne se trouve pas parmi les canons du IIe concile de Latran, mais dans le canon 3 du IIIe concile de Latran' (loc. cit., p. 323 n. 73, cf. n. 75).

[5] Ord. Vitalis, *Ecclesiasticae Historiae Libri XIII*, lib. ii *ad fin.*, lib. xiii c. 39.

surviving texts of the canons. In England only one has been found.[1] They were regarded in their day as important, and found their way into the *Decretum* of Gratian, though seldom ascribed to a council and never to a *Lateran* council. Dist. 63 c. 35 has a canon 'in generali synodo Innocentii papae Romae habita'; C. 23 q. 8 c. 32 is ascribed to 'Innocentius secundus in universali concilio'. Canon 29 found its way into *Compilatio I* (5, 19, 1) as of 'Innocentius II' and thence into *Extra* (5, 15, 1) as of 'Innocentius III', without reference to any council. For the generation of lawyers and theologians after the Third Lateran Council celebrated by Alexander III in 1179, this was *the* Lateran Council *par excellence*. They had no occasion to refer by name to Lateran I and II of which the canons were relatively neglected, eclipsed by the more substantial legislation of Alexander and submerged, so to speak, by the spate of decretals of the second half of the twelfth century.[2] When in 1215 Innocent III assembled his even larger general council at the Lateran, his reference to the council of 1179 took the simple form: 'in Lateranensi concilio noscitur fuisse prohibitum . . .' (c. 61, *Extra*, 3, 5, 31). This agrees with the custom of local lawgivers during the intervening years, at councils of Rouen (1189) and Westminster (1200).[3]

After 1215 the canonists and others had to distinguish Innocent III's council from Alexander III's. In *Compilatio IV*, confined as it was to Innocentian decrees and decretals, no ambiguity could arise: after 1, 1, 1 ('Innoc. Papa III in concilio generali constit. I') references to the canons of 1215 usually take the form 'Idem in concilio Lateranensi constit. . . .'. But in *Extra*, which also included the canons of 1179, manuscripts commonly contrast 'Alexander III in concilio Lateranensi' with 'Innocentius III in concilio generali'. In the fourteenth century Guido de Baisio and John Andreae, the canonists, treated the Third Lateran as a General Council; but later on the

---

[1] Oxford, Bodleian MS. Lat. misc. d. 74 fo. 97ᵛ. This was unknown to Z. N. Brooke, *The English Church and the Papacy*, p. 104.

[2] For a broad view of the background and consequences of the legislation of the Second Lateran Council see Raymonde Foreville, *Latran I, II, III et Latran IV* (Histoire des Conciles Oecuméniques, ed. G. Dumeige, vi), 1965.

[3] J. F. Pommeraye, *Sanctae Rotomagensis Ecclesiae Concilia . . .* (Rouen, 1667), p. 173 and Wilkins, i. 505–7.

contrast which had appeared in the rubrics of *Extra* between the Third and the Fourth Lateran was emphasized by a refusal to treat the council of 1179 as 'general' or ecumenical.[1] With this view may be compared the comment of a modern historian of the Lateran Councils on the surpassing importance of the council of 1215; Prof. Raymonde Foreville writes: 'le IVe concile du Latran est le seul des conciles médiévaux susceptible d'être confronté à la fois au concile de Nicée et au concile de Trente.'[2]

Returning to the usage of the thirteenth century, we find that synodal statutes for the diocese of Salisbury as early as 1217×1219 read (c. 107) 'in concilio Lateranensi primo dinoscitur esse statutum et nuper in generali concilio evidentius fuit expressum'.[3] Elsewhere the custom rapidly grew of citing the council of 1179 as Lateran I and that of 1215 as 'Lateranense concilium sub Innocentio papa' or, more often, as 'secundum Lateranense concilium'. The Chapter of the Black Monks of the province of York, refers in 1221 to Lateran I, meaning the council of 1179, while, at about the same time, the Chapter of the province of Canterbury refers to Innocent III's council as Lateran II. Likewise the English Augustinian Chapter quotes the canon *In singulis regnis* (Lateran IV, c. 12) as uttered 'in concilio Lateranensi secundo'.[4] The bishop of Winchester (? 1224) orders 'Lateranensis concilii secundi statuta in episcopatu nostro ab omnibus observentur', meaning the council of 1215.[5] An official of Bishop Hugh de Wells of Lincoln speaks of the bishop's journey to Rome in 1215: 'cum iter arriperet ad concilium Lateranense secundum',[6] and in 1218 and 1221 the same usage is found in correspondence of the English royal

---

[1] This was implied in the councils of Constance and Basel. It was also maintained by the canonist, cardinal Domenico Jacobazzi, in 1512. See R. Baümer, 'Die Zahl der allgemeinen Konzilien in der Sicht der Theologen des 15 und 16 Jahrhunderts', *Annuarium Historiae Conciliorum*, i (1969), 288–313, esp. pp. 291–3.

[2] Foreville, op. cit., p. 158.

[3] *C. & S.* ii. 94.

[4] *Docts. illustrating the Activities of the General and Provincial Chapters of the English Black Monks*, ed. W. A. Pantin (Camden 3rd Series xlv, Royal Hist. Soc., 1931), i. 233 n. 21, 9, 17, 20. *Chapters of the Augustinian Canons*, ed. H. E. Salter (CYS and Oxford Hist. Soc., 1922), p. 2.

[5] *C. & S.* ii. 126, c. 1.

[6] *Rotuli Hugonis de Welles* (CYS, 1909, and Linc. Rec. Soc.), i. 30.

chancery.[1] It turns up again in a business record of the Cistercians between 1246 and 1255,[2] and in a later Benedictine chronicle.[3] All these descriptions of the councils of 1179 and 1215 as Lateran I and II come from English sources; but it is highly probable that many continental parallels could be adduced.[4]

If the citations of 'Lateran II' in the *Liber Poenitentialis* of Peter of Poitiers are scrutinized with this evidence in mind, it will be found that they, too, refer to what we call the Fourth Lateran Council of 1215. Those two passages of tit. 33 which Father Teetaert regarded as derivatives from canons of the Third Lateran (1179) in fact find much closer parallels in canons 26 and 39 of the council of 1215. On the same reckoning, tit. 42 becomes comprehensible without any awkward and purely conjectural emendation of the text. The rescript of Pope Innocent III which is cited in this title is probably the letter addressed to the archbishops and bishops of France, 17 April 1210, which deals with the admission of simoniacs into monasteries.[5] The declaratory canon 'in secundo concilio lateranensi' is canon 64 of the Fourth Lateran, 1215.[6] So it is unnecessary to substitute here 'Innocent II' for what is written: 'Innocent III'. Father Teetaert wrote: 'Je n'ai pu découvrir aucun renseignement précis au sujet du rescrit, ni identifier Guillaume, archidiacre de Paris, qui déposa ce rescrit à Saint-Victor, à moins qu'il ne s'agisse de Guillaume de Champeaux, qui fut archidiacre de Paris, fonda l'abbaye de Saint-Victor en 1113, fut évêque de Châlons-sur-Marne et mourut le 18 janvier 1121.'[7] But the evidence given above shows that the archdeacon cannot have been William de

[1] *Patent Rolls 1216–25* (HMSO), pp. 144, 302, 320.
[2] *Chartulary of the Cist. Abbey of St. Mary of Sallay in Craven*, ed. Joseph McNulty (Yorks. Archaeol. Soc., Record Series, vol. 87, 1933), i. 94.
[3] *Chronicon Angliae Petriburgense*, ed. J. A. Giles (Scriptores monastici, 1845), p. 119.
[4] The council of 1179 is designated Lateran I in synodal constitutions of Noyon, *c*. 1280 (*Actes de la province ecclés. de Reims*, ed. Th. Gousset (1842–4), ii. 417; cf. Hefele–Leclercq, *Histoire des Conciles*, VI i. 265.
[5] Pott. 3976, Migne, ccxvii. 198.
[6] Father Teetaert did not identify any particular canon of the council of 1139. Canons 1 and 2 treat of simony, but not of this particular sort of simony.
[7] Loc. cit., p. 324 n. 80.

Champeaux. A person of the name of William held an archdeaconry in the church of Paris in December 1212,[1] and distinguished himself in the Albigensian Crusade.

None of the passages which draw upon Lateran IV come from canon 21, *Omnis utriusque sexus* (*Extra*, 5, 38, 12), which was of such great importance in the history of confession. It is not surprising that the absence of a citation should have led Father Teetaert astray. But two remarks may be made about this. First, tit. 6 says: 'Nam sicut docet Innocentius III, non solum considerande sunt quantitates peccatorum sed et circumstantie peccatorum et peccantium'.[2] This may refer to canon 21, of which the important words are: 'diligenter inquirens et peccatoris circumstantias et peccati'. In the second place, important though canon 21 was, its principal legislative part would be more in place among the decisions of a provincial council or diocesan synod[3] than in a manual for priests. Canon 21 doubtless became at once a commonplace of the law; 'hoc salutare statutum', it runs, 'frequenter in ecclesiis publicetur, ne quisquam ignorantiae caecitate velamen excusationis assumat'. The author of a manual might therefore suppose that his readers would be cognizant of the canon. Be that as it may, the *Liber Poenitentialis* appears clearly to have been composed after the Lateran Council of 1215.

Considered in a broader context, the evidence shows how the thirteenth century regarded the twelfth-century Roman councils. For canonists and administrators the memorable Roman council was that gathered at the Lateran in 1179 by Alexander III. Seven decrees of his council at Tours, 1163, merited inclusion in *Extra*; but no pre-Alexandrine council ranked with this. Even if papal presidency distinguished some earlier councils, nothing marked out among them the two which were held at Rome in 1123 and 1139.

---

[1] Douët d'Arcq, *Collection de Sceaux*, vol. ii, no. 7412. This is perhaps the archdeacon William who was dead by 1236 (*Cartulaire de l'église Notre-Dame de Paris*, ed. B. Guérard (Collection des Documents Inédits, 1850), i. 410, ii. 517).

[2] Loc. cit., p. 321. Perhaps there is here a reminiscence of Pott. 1323 (*Comp. III*, 5, 20, 1); cf. above, p. 204 n. 1.

[3] As for instance in statutes of Salisbury, Worcester, and Exeter (*C. & S.* ii. 72, 173, 236).

11. The Making of the Dunstable Annals, A.D. 33 to 1242*

THE Annals of Dunstable, first published by Thomas Hearne in 1733 and re-published by H. R. Luard in volume III of the *Annales Monastici* (Rolls Series) in 1866, hardly rank as a neglected source for thirteenth-century history, though they may have been underrated. They extend from A.D. 33 to 1297. While the material for the years before 1200 is wholly derivative, the annals of the next ninety-eight years, which fill 78 out of 85 folios in the single complete medieval manuscript, have never been associated with any other written work and have the air of an original production. Internal evidence makes it clear that the annals were compiled in the Austin priory of Dunstable in Bedfordshire. They are much concerned with the priory's domestic affairs, its relations with the townsfolk and neighbouring landlords, and its patronage of parish churches. Luard indicated the worth of the annals clearly enough.[1] Reinhold Pauli valued them for information on continental affairs, and edited extracts.[2] That the annals were compiled in Dunstable priory has been recognized since the time of Humphrey Wanley and Thomas Hearne. It has also been repeatedly stated that the annals to A.D. 1201 were derived in the main from the writings of Ralph de Diceto, dean of St. Paul's, and that Richard de Morins, prior of Dunstable, compiled the work down to the time of his death in 1242.[3] These findings would be the better for a little more precision and some modification. The present object is to examine the

---

* First published in *Essays in Medieval History presented to Bertie Wilkinson*, ed. T. A. Sandquist and M. R. Powicke (Toronto, 1969).

[1] *Ann. Mon.*, iii. pp. xxxii–iv.

[2] *Monumenta Germaniae Historica, Scriptores*, xxvii (1885), 505–13.

[3] Thus, most recently, F. M. Powicke, *The Thirteenth Century* (2nd ed., Oxford, 1962), p. 733.

origin of the compilation and the way in which the annals were put together in the time of Prior Richard.

THE MANUSCRIPTS

To begin with, a few words about the state of the text. The whole is found in a thirteenth-century manuscript, B.M. MS. Cotton Tiberius A.x, fos. 5^r–89^v (*Tib.*). On the following folios to fo. 115^r are notes and documents, legal and historical, which record events of the fourteenth century and a proclamation of the year 1459.[1] This manuscript was damaged, but the text not seriously harmed, in the Cottonian fire of 1731. A close codicological study of it is precluded by the remounting of the leaves and by the contraction, distortion, and discoloration caused by fire and water; but at least one can see that the early portion was written by hands of the early part of the thirteenth century and that the later entries could have been written not very long after the events they record. Luard and Pauli saw a clear distinction of handwriting in the middle of the annal for 1210 on fo. 12^{r}b.[2] They took this to be the first change of hand, and Luard remarked that the second hand broke off in the middle of a sentence at the foot of fo. 14^{v}a, *s.a.* 1215, after which (according to him) 'the original hand goes on' (p. 45 n. 3). But Luard's analysis of the hands was inadequate: he noted no other change of the main hand of the annals between 1215 and the ending in 1297. No full palaeographical analysis will be attempted here, for reasons to be explained; but some features of the manuscript must be noted which bear upon the compilation of the annals in the first half of the thirteenth century. In the first place, it is not certain that the variations which are seen in the folios preceding Luard's first distinction on fo. 12^{r}b can all be explained by a mere change of pen or ink without change of scribe. On the very first leaf (fo. 5^{r}a) a new start was made at A.D. 96 (and this corresponds to a new start at this point in the Harleian manuscript (*Harl.*) discussed below). Up to the year 96 the scribe of *Tib.* uses the tironian *et* with a stroke

---

[1] Luard printed some parts in his Appendix, *Ann. Mon.*, iii. 409–20.

[2] *Ann. Mon.*, iii. 33, to which references are made hereafter by page number only.

through it; for the rest of fo. 5ʳ and fo. 5ᵛ the stroke is missing (as it is in *Harl.*). From A.D. 96 punctuation is limited to a single point, and the *i* is never dotted. Instead of introducing the year by *Anno* the word is abridged to *a.* On fos. 6ᵛ–7ᵛ, by contrast, the year is expressed as *an.* (from A.D. 636 to 1095).[1]

Coming to A.D. 1210, the change in the style of writing on fo. 12ʳb which Luard discerned is clearly visible. But it is at least possible that this hand was superseded by another on fo. 13ʳb (*s.a.* 1213); and if, as Luard supposed, the scribe of fos. 13ʳb–14ᵛa was in fact the scribe who took up his pen first at fo. 12ʳb, the contrast between fo. 14ᵛa and fo. 14ᵛb (where Luard saw 'the original hand' reappear) becomes less significant: this could be the work of the same scribe, whose adoption of a larger script produces a superficially different impression. Be that as it may, the hand of fo. 14ᵛb continues at least to fo. 17ᵛb (*s.a.* 1220), and thereafter several scribes take their turns recurrently at writing the annals.[2] The poor state of the manuscript does not permit collation by quires nor show how the ruling was carried out. The writing is disposed throughout on two columns to the page, varying from 37 to 49 lines in the column. A new and more careful ruling, apparently prepared leaf by leaf, allowing forty lines to the column, began on fo. 13ʳ (*s.a.* 1212).[3]

Before the Cottonian fire Humphrey Wanley had made, with his customary accuracy, a complete transcript of *Tib.* which is now in B.M. MS. Harl. 4886, and it was this that Hearne printed in his edition of 1733, quoting in his introduction Wanley's discerning remarks about the annals. Luard used both the Cottonian manuscript and Wanley's transcript in preparing his edition. He observed of his predecessor: 'Hearne made little attempt at editing his author or investigating his

---

[1] The remaining fragments of fos. 6 and 7 have been reversed in mounting, so that the text proceeds: 6ᵛ, 6ʳ, 7ᵛ, 7ʳ.

[2] Another physical feature which deserves notice, though it probably has no bearing on the subject of this paper, is the rubrication of *A* in *Anno*, which occurs only for the years 1213 (fo. 13ᵛb), 1213 *bis* (fo. 14ʳa), 1214 (fo. 14ʳb), 1215 (fo. 14ᵛa), 1216 (fo. 16ʳa). No space had been left for the rubric in the first two places.

[3] The ruling continues to allow forty lines a page until fo. 31ʳ, except for fos. 22ᵛ–24ʳ, which have forty-one lines; thereafter the number of lines constantly varies.

authorities, confining himself to printing the text. His notes do not show much antiquarian or historical knowledge' (p. x). The criticism came ill from one who himself made egregious blunders and overlooked highly significant facts.

One other manuscript contains a small part of the annals. In 1714 Wanley acquired a thirteenth-century cartulary of Dunstable Priory, which is now B.M. MS. Harl. 1885.[1] In it he found the verso of one leaf (fo. 41^v)[2] wholly filled by the annals for the years A.D. 33–552, beginning with precisely the same preamble as occurs in *Tib.* The recto of the leaf contained the usual material of a cartulary—private deeds of Edlesborough, Chalton, and Hudnall—in an early thirteenth-century charter hand. The annals, in a different small neat hand of the same period, begin at the extreme top of the verso page, above the original ruling, and are arranged in two columns. Changes in colour of ink suggest new starts at A.D. 33, 96, ? 277, 369, and 420; but the only change of hand appears to be after the preamble, at A.D. 33. The hand of the preamble may be that which makes some references to the civil law and Gratian on fo. 77^r of the cartulary. Wanley's study of the manuscripts led him to conclude that the cartulary was started at the instance of Richard de Morins, prior of Dunstable from 1202 to 1242: 'This is the Man who . . . began the same partly with his own Hand, and partly by the Hands of Others as Occasion Offered. After the Entries of many Matters . . . he began his Annals with his Own Hand; but then, perchance, considering that they would, in time come to be the Foundation of the Annals of the House, he kept on this Book for Chartulary, and began his Annals again, in the same Words, and with the same (that is his own Hand) in another Book, namely that Cottonian MS. above-mentioned. . . .'[3]

---

[1] Extracts were printed by Hearne in *Chronicon sive Annales Prioratus de Dunstaple, una cum excerptis e Chartulario ejusdem Prioratus* (2 vols., Oxford, 1733), ii, pp. 676–713, and a calendar of the whole by G. H. Fowler in *A Digest of the Charters preserved in the Cartulary of the Priory of Dunstable* (*Bedfordshire Historical Record Society, Publications*, x, 1926). Fowler failed to recognize the annals and describes them (p. 119) as 'a Calendar of Saints and Popes, from the Crucifixion a.d. 33 to a.d. 552'.

[2] At that time fo. 40^v, formerly p. 94 and not, as Wanley says, fo. 93^v.

[3] Quoted Hearne, *Chronicon*, i, p. lxxix. Luard accepted the view that the hand of the annals in *Harl.* was 'not improbably the compiler's own' (p. ix).

Leaving on one side for the moment the question whether author and scribe can be treated as identical, we cannot doubt that the bulk of the annals in MS. Harl. 1885, fo. 41ᵛ was written by one hand, and that the hand closely resembles one of the first hands of *Tib.* Comparison of the two texts suggests not only a close connection between them, but (as Wanley supposed) the priority of *Harl.* The close connection appears *s.a.* 50, misplaced in both manuscripts before the entry for A.D. 45, and *s.a.* 282, where both *Harl.* and *Tib.* mark the words 'Albanus beatus' for transposition. The priority of *Harl.* is shown by mistakes in *Tib.* where *Harl.* is correct. Thus, *s.a.* 50: *Harl.* secundo, *Tib.* secundus; *s.a.* 85: *Harl.* Limovicis, *Tib.* Limonicis; *s.a.* 493: *Harl.* cxv, *Tib.* xcv. The last words of the entry for A.D. 493: 'Concilio . . . purgavit' are correctly inserted in *Harl.* but have strayed to the entry for A.D. 467 in *Tib.* Therefore, either *Tib.* was copied from *Harl.* or another text of the annals lies behind both these manuscripts. One curious feature strikes the reader. *Harl.* ends *s.a.* 552 at the bottom of the second column of a well-filled page. *Tib.* has smaller leaves. It reaches A.D. 552 at the bottom of the first column of its second page (fo. 5ᵛa); it then leaves the second column blank, resuming on the next leaf with an entry *s.a.* 584. Wanley may be right in his surmise that the author (or the scribe) decided after completing the first page of *Harl.* that it would be best for him to separate the annals from the cartulary; but we cannot determine whether or no the intention was to devote fo. 5ᵛb of *Tib.* to the events of the next thirty-two years (a generous allowance) and, if so, why the gap was not filled.[1] The explanation may be that *Tib.*, fo. 6 was intended originally as a continuation to the copy begun in *Harl.*, although written on a smaller leaf; and that the scribe, having decided to separate the annals from the cartulary, re-copied the contents of *Harl.* to make a new beginning.

[1] An examination of text C of Diceto (see below) shows only two annals marked for extraction in this period: 562 'Iustiniani temporibus Vigilius . . .' and 565 'David qui et . . .'. The latter is attached by a 'sub quo' to the entry in the Dunstable annals (both *Harl.* and *Tib.*) for A.D. 552 'Pelagius papa'.

THE ORIGIN OF THE ANNALS

I turn to the questions of origin and authorship, which are inevitably interwined. Some of the internal evidence is so clear that it could hardly be overlooked by anyone who picked up the printed text. It is plain for all to see in the first sentence which reads: 'Ab Adam usque ad Nativitatem Christi fluxerunt anni secundum Hebreos tria milia dccccxlviii, secundum Septuaginta Interpretes v milia cxcvi; et exinde usque ad octavum annum nostrum mccx.' The author, that is, began his work A.D. 1210 and was then in the eighth year of the tenure of some office. This leads to the annal for the year 1202 for which year the only entry runs: 'Ricardus canonicus Meretone, adhuc diaconus, fit prior de Dunstaple; et Sabbato quatuor temporum [21 September] ordinatus, die S. Michaelis [29 September] primam missam celebravit.' The first sentence of the annals, therefore, was framed by that Master Richard de Morins who became prior of Dunstable in 1202 and whose death is recorded in the annals *s.a.* 1242.

This opening sentence (ultimately derived through Diceto from Eusebius) is followed by an annalistic sequence beginning: 'Anno xxxiii. Christus crucifixus est octavo kalendas Aprilis'. The dependence of these annals on Ralph de Diceto's *Abbreviationes chronicorum* (to 1147) and *Ymagines historiarum* (from 1148 to 1201) was asserted by T. Duffus Hardy, who declared that 'the chronicles of Florence of Worcester and Martinus Polonus can also be traced.'[1] This statement followed Luard, who had also referred to 'some source which I have not been able to trace' (pp. xiv–xv). It did not occur to Luard and Hardy that Martinus Polonus flourished a generation after Richard de Morins, and they produced nothing from Florence of Worcester that is not to be found in Diceto's *Abbreviationes*. Nor is it necessary to look further than a text of Diceto for Luard's untraced source. To the end of the twelfth century the additions to Diceto are extremely few and unimportant. The Dunstable annalist may be presumed to be responsible for a few reflexions of his own and a few facts: for instance, *s.a.* 1135 'Hinc oritur werra'; under the same year he adds to a list

---

[1] *Catalogue of Materials of British History* (RS) iii. 252.

of monasteries founded in Henry I's reign 'et prioratum de Dunstaple'; *s.a.* 1185 'terre motus' is described as 'apud Lincolniam' instead of 'circa partes aquilonares'; *s.a.* 1198 'Obiit Hugo Coventrensis episcopus'; *s.a.* 1199 'dictus de S. Marie Ecclesia'. With the year 1200 the compiler abandoned Diceto, whose main texts stop before this year.[1]

The failure of previous editors and commentators to identify precisely the source for the years 33–1199 arose from their reliance on the wrong text of Diceto's works. It should be remembered that Stubbs did not produce his edition of Diceto until 1876. The text used by Luard was Twysden's edition,[2] supplemented for the matter before A.D. 589 by B.M. MS. Cotton Cleopatra E.III (Stubbs's *B*). This was Twysden's main text. It is, as Stubbs pointed out, a revised recension of the original text of Lambeth MS. 8 (Stubbs's *A*), from St. Paul's Cathedral. But *A* had been later corrected and its corrections had been mostly incorporated in B.M. MS. Royal 13 E.VI (Stubbs's *C*), where some peculiar passages were added in the text and margins. Twysden made use of *C* (and of another text, *D*), but conflated in such a way as to obscure the differences between his texts. Comparison of them points unmistakably to the source used at Dunstable. The compiler used *C*; and he borrowed it, in the year 1209 or 1210, from the library of St. Albans Abbey, where it had probably been written.

C is a large and handsome manuscript, illuminated in gold and colour, written throughout on two columns in good bold bookhands, about 1200. A fine pen indicated in the margin where corrections were needed in the text, and the corrections were neatly executed. On fo. i^r is the St. Albans library press-mark: 'A 6 gradus 2 p'. A comparison of this *C* text of Diceto's works with the extracts which are in the Dunstable annals shows some verbatim copying, a little condensation, and occasional misunderstanding of the original. Passages occur

---

[1] *Radulfi de Diceto Decani Lundoniensis Opera Historica*, ed. W. Stubbs (2 vols., RS) i, pp. lxxxviii–xcvi; cf. D. E. Greenway, 'The succession to Ralph de Diceto, dean of St. Paul's', *BIHR*, xxxix (1966), 86–95.

[2] *Historiae Anglicanae Scriptores X*, ed. Roger Twysden (1652), cols. 429–710. After giving a small part of the introductory matter of the *Abbreviationes* (ed. Stubbs, i. 18–24, 34), Twysden omits everything before the annal for A.D. 589.

in the Dunstable annals which are not in *B* but are in *C*. One
small but clear pointer occurs *s.a.* 1183, where the Dunstable
annals read: 'moritur Henricus rex iunior anno vicesimo
octavo etatis sue.' These words are taken over from a rubric
in *C* (fo. 98ᵛ), except that 'iunior' replaces 'regis Henrici
filius'; they are not found in MSS. *A* and *B* of Diceto. Again,
the entry in the Dunstable annals *s.a.* 1195: 'Obit Guarinus
abbas sancti Albani' is derived from a passage added to
Diceto by the St. Albans scribe in the bottom margin of *C*
(fo. 125ᵛb, ed. Stubbs, ii. 124 n. 4). Text *C* of Diceto ends with
the year 1199, and Dunstable transcribed with some abridgement the last three entries for that year.

That the original Dunstable annalist went to work with
text *C* of Diceto before him is proved beyond doubt by inspection of MS. *C*. In its careful ruling, two parallel vertical lines
on the left hand of each column mark the space commonly
reserved for the rubricated initials. At intervals, from A.D.
386 in the *Abbreviationes* to the end of the *Ymagines* in 1199,
certain entries have been marked lightly between the parallel
lines by a diagonal stroke made with a reddish-brown pencil.
When these marks are compared with the Dunstable annals
a very close (though not perfect) correspondence appears
between the strokes and the extracts of the annals. Very few of
the passages marked in the Diceto MS. have been wholly
omitted. In some cases the abridgement or conflation is
particularly significant. Thus, Diceto has entries under the
years 857, 859, 860, 862, 864, 868, 872. The only ones with
pencil strokes against them are 857, 868, 872. In the Dunstable
annals the items so marked are gathered up to make one entry
under the year 857: 'Nicholaus papa. Item Adrianus papa
[868] sub quo Adeldredus fit Cantuariensis archiepiscopus
[872].' Occasionally a marginal 'Nota', in the same reddish-
brown pencil, supplements or replaces the diagonal stroke in
C; in nearly all cases this points to an entry in the Dunstable
annals.[1] It looks very much as if Prior Richard, after announcing himself in the preamble, extracted and edited the annals
that interested him as far as A.D. 369, and then marked later

---

[1] The earliest 'Nota' occurs *s.a.* 265 (fo. 12ʳ), concerning the Council of
Antioch: this precedes the series of diagonal strokes.

entries in Diceto with his pencil so that somebody else could carry on the work on the pattern he had set. The extracts were scanty, so that they occupy only eleven printed pages (small type) compared with the 314 pages (large type) of Diceto's book. Annals rather than a history were contemplated.

It was stated categorically above that Richard de Morins borrowed *C* from St. Albans in 1209 or in 1210. Certainty is possible because the St. Albans scribe of Diceto, terminating with King John's accession the copy of his exemplar from St. Paul's, had left half a column blank on fo. 136ʳb and was left with three blank pages in his last quire of parchment.[1] They were ruled for writing like the preceding leaves and invited new entries to keep the chronicle up to date. But there was no attempt to produce a big and ambitious work on the lines of Diceto's *Ymagines*. The original scribe of *C* left ten lines for additions for 1199. Thereafter the marginal dates allow fourteen lines for 1200, sixteen lines for 1201, twelve for 1202, sixteen for 1203, and so on, irregularly spaced to 1215. The spaces are only partly filled, and that by various hands which do not appear in orderly succession. Some of these brief annals seem to have been written soon after the events they record (e.g. an entry *s.a.* 1211), but at least one entry—that for 1202—has been so badly misplaced that it must have been added several years later: it is in a hand which predominates in and after 1211 and was probably written at the same time as the annals of 1211–15.[2]

Liebermann printed these annals of St. Albans in 1879.[3] Elsewhere he observed that, 'slender as they are and much concerned with domestic matters, they are the first beginnings of real history by monks of St. Albans.'[4] He also pointed out

---

[1] The collation of the book is: [sig. 1¹] = fo. i; sigg. 1–xvi⁸ = fos. 1–127; [sig. xvii¹⁰] = fos. 128–37. The signature marks are in roman numerals at the foot of the last verso of each quire; there is no signature for the front flyleaf or for the last quire. An unnumbered blank leaf follows fo. 52, in quire vii.

[2] It sets the Easter crowning of King John in Canterbury in the year 1202, giving the date of Easter (correctly for 1202) as 14 April. But the event belongs to 1201 when Easter Day was 25 March.

[3] *Ungedruckte anglo-normannische Geschichtsquellen*, ed. Felix Liebermann (Strassburg, 1879), pp. 166–72.

[4] 'Sane tenues sunt annales, plerumque in rebus domesticis versantes, sed vera historiae apud Albanenses prima initia', *MGH* xxviii (1888), 7.

that Roger Wendover, naturally enough, had made use of these
annals along with the preceding text of Diceto. (Wendover
copied the erroneous annal of 1202 about the Easter crowning
of King John.) Moreover, Matthew Paris made independent
use of the annal for 1212: he took more of Diceto's *Ymagines*
than Wendover had extracted, and he embellished the Diceto
text with marginal additions in his own hand.[1] But neither
Liebermann nor anyone else, to my knowledge, remarked that
the Dunstable annalist, like the St. Albans historians, laid these
annals under contribution. When text *C* of Diceto came to
Dunstable it must already have contained some of the entries
for the years 1200 to 1209.

Under the year 1200 the sole entry from St. Albans, recording
the death of Bishop Hugh of Lincoln, appears in the Dunstable
annals in the same form. Again, under the year 1201 the sole
annal from St. Albans is copied, almost completely; and this is
the more remarkable because it is a piece of domestic news of
St. Albans: 'Facta est [*om.* finalis] concordia in curia [*om.*
domini] regis [*om.* Iohannis] inter ecclesiam Sancti [*for* Beati]
Albani et Robertum filium Walteri [*om.* et heredes eius] super
nemore de Northhawe [*for* la Norhawe].' The St. Albans annal
of 1202 (already noted as a later addition) is not paralleled in
the Dunstable annals; but after this twelve items in the St.
Albans annals are matched, ending with the consecration of
Otto as emperor at Rome on 4 October 1209. Within this
period the only items omitted are three which were only of
interest to St. Albans and the record of the election and consecration of Stephen Langton at Viterbo on 17 June 1207,
which is noted in the Dunstable annals in different terms. There
can, then, be no doubt that this manuscript, Royal 13 E.vi,
came into the hands of the Dunstable annalist after the entry
had been made concerning the coronation of Otto. This entry
may have been made as early as November 1209, for already
on 12 November, at Mountsorel in Leicestershire, King John
had rewarded the messenger who bore him the news of his

---

[1] *Matt. Parisiensis Historia Anglorum*, ed. F. Madden (RS), i. p. x, note; *Catalogue of Royal MSS. in the British Museum*, ed. G. F. Warner and J. P. Gilson (1921),
ii. 113; Richard Vaughan, 'The handwriting of Matthew Paris', *Trans. Cambridge Bibliog. Soc.*, v (1953), 391.

nephew's triumph.[1] On the other hand, whereas the St. Albans annals next record, with the date 20 December 1209, the consecration of Hugh de Wells as bishop of Lincoln by Archbishop Stephen Langton at Melun, Hugh's promotion appears in a briefer form and a different context in the Dunstable annals. It may be guessed, then, that the news of the consecration of their diocesan had not reached the monks of St. Albans when the manuscript was lent to Dunstable. The end of 1209 or the early months of 1210 are indicated as the time of borrowing. This agrees perfectly with the preamble to the Dunstable annals which announced 1210 to be 'our eighth year'—the eighth year of Richard de Morins's priorate.

It is one thing to determine the origin of the Dunstable annals in the year 1210; it is quite another thing to discover how the work was continued after the manuscript of Diceto had been returned to St. Albans. It is one thing to feel justified in the inference that Prior Richard was personally responsible for its inception; it is another thing to be satisfied that he was the author of it from the point where it ceased to depend on Diceto. Although it has been generally assumed that Richard de Morins composed it from the beginning to his death in 1242, this assumption needs testing. Again, the relationship of author to scribe cries out for consideration. Does Tiberius A.x present us with the annals as they were first written down, so that the changes of handwriting show stages of composition and changes of authorship? Or is it the work of a series of copyists, told to make a fair copy of a more disorderly original? If this is a fair copy, may it not conceal under its uniformity additions made by others to the author's original draft? One may not be able to settle all these matters with certainty, but the questions must be asked. I shall proceed to some particular observations on the annals from 1200 to 1242 in the hope that they will throw light on the problem and help to illustrate the way in which such works as this evolved.

---

[1] *Rotuli de Liberate ac de Misis et Praestitis*, ed. T. D. Hardy (Record Com., 1844) p. 138.

The mere external appearance of *Tib.* is enough to raise doubt whether this can be the original manuscript of the compilation. It is altogether too tidy. Several hands have been at work; but from beginning to end there is no sign of those second thoughts or retouchings which an author could hardly resist. Spelling mistakes are very rare; where they occur, they are uncorrected.[1] Very occasionally, two words are marked for transposition. In the entry for A.D. 493, already noted, an extract from Diceto is correctly placed in *Harl.* and wrongly placed in *Tib.* The change of script which Luard noted as a return to the original hand of fo. 14ᵛb of *Tib.* occurs in the middle of a sentence: it cannot indicate a change of authorship. At later points in the manuscript where new starts occur there appears to be an alternation of hands: if each were to represent a change of authorship the course of composition would seem most erratic. But if this is a fair copy it follows that changes of pen and ink and hand provide no proof of stages of production of the annals. Even if a palaeographer suggests approximate dates for the hands he will only be providing the dates before which certain parts of the annals were composed. To verify the view that *Tib.* is a fair copy we must look at the contents of the annals as well as at their physical appearance. If it is a fair copy it is only from the contents that we can form any idea of the process of composition.

AUTHORSHIP OF THE ANNALS

Comparison with the St. Albans annals has already established that the Dunstable extracts to the year 1209 were made in 1210 or very soon afterwards, for additions to the St. Albans annals were made soon afterwards, when the book had been sent home. The Dunstable scribe of the lost exemplar which lay behind *Tib.* may have imitated the St. Albans scribe in leaving space for additions under each year from 1200 to 1209. He

---

[1] On fo. 9ʳb (p. 20, *s.a.* 1171) 'mandato ee' has been neatly corrected to read 'mandato ecclesie', by the original hand, which adds 'eccᵉ' in the margin and expunges 'ee' on the next line. This looks like the work of a copyist who had originally misread the abbreviation for 'ecclesie' as that for 'esse'.

made numerous short additions, amounting to nearly five pages of Luard's printed text. Within each year they show no chronological order, and two entries (deliberately, it seems) overrun the ends of the years 1208 and 1209 in which they begin. If we reject the idea that *Tib.* is the autograph of the compiler we must reckon with the possibility that its exemplar was a composite work, compiled by several hands; unco-ordinated, unedited, marginal additions may have been grafted on to the original after it was first written down in 1210 or 1211. But the Dunstable annals of these years might well be material already assembled by Prior Richard with some such work in view when he borrowed the St. Albans Diceto. There is nothing in them which presupposes a knowledge of events later than 1210. Almost all the events, moreover, lie well within the range of Prior Richard's experience and to some extent reflect his special interests.

Master Richard de Morins was a man of repute as a canonist. A graduate of Bologna, he was probably still a secular clerk, perhaps engaged in teaching and writing, until the year 1200.[1] Then he became an Austin canon at Merton Priory and in 1202 became prior of Dunstable. The annals of these years record his promotion, ordination as priest, and first celebration (above, p. 214). They contain many details connected with Dunstable Priory. The royal taxation of 1207 and 1210 is noted with special reference to what Dunstable paid. They tell of the prior's mission to Rome for the king in 1203, and of his activity as a delegate of the papal legate in 1206. They show an interest in ecclesiastical councils which Richard may have attended in 1200 and 1206. They record (as an event of January 1210) the hanging of two clerks at Oxford which caused the schools to disband. Under 1208 they note the otherwise unchronicled fact that Master Honorius, archdeacon of Richmond, was

---

[1] J. C. Russell, *Dictionary of Writers of Thirteenth Century England* (1936), pp. 111–3; Stephan Kuttner, in *Dictionnaire de droit canonique*, ed. R. Naz (1960), vii. 676–81. As Master Richard de Mores (the name given by Matthew Paris to the prior of Dunstable) he witnesses an act of Hubert Walter, archbishop of Canterbury, probably to be dated 1200 or 1201, without indication that he is a regular (*Acta S. Langton*, ed. Kathleen Major (CYS), p. 50). This appearance in a witness-list is not enough to prove that Master Richard was a 'familiaris' of the archbishop, as claimed by Charles E. Lewis in *Traditio*, xxii (1966), 469–71.

imprisoned at Gloucester. It is not fanciful to suppose that the prior was interested in the fate of this man, another distinguished canonist with whom he was certainly well acquainted.[1] It is unlikely that any ordinary canon of Dunstable would have thought the news noteworthy, even if it came his way.

But although the prior's mind may be behind the annals of these years, it would be unwise to attribute all to him. In the first place, it is difficult to believe that a man so well versed in public affairs would be guilty of two inaccuracies which occur. King John's second marriage (1200) is assigned to 1201. Under 1209 'Otto, son of the duke of Saxony' is said to have visited England before his coronation as emperor (pp. 31–2). Either there is confusion here with the visit of Otto's elder brother Henry in spring 1209, or the entry results from a faulty transcription of an annal for 1207, when Otto himself came to England. Neither mistake could very well be one made by the prior of Dunstable in 1210.[2] In the second place, there are slight but unmistakable signs that the compilation has received additions from written sources besides Royal 13 E.vi. Entries for 1200 and 1201 (pp. 27–8) resemble passages in the *D* text of Diceto (or his continuator) under the year 1200,[3] and a list of episcopal promotions under the year 1209 (p. 31) offers a more correct version of a list which occurs in the annals of Tewkesbury.[4]

---

[1] The Dunstable annalist is the only chronicler to report the death of Master John of Tynemouth (*s.a.* 1221), who belonged to the same circle of canonists.

[2] Other mistakes occur under the year 1208: the bishops of Salisbury and Rochester actually went to Scotland in November 1209, and Walter, archbishop of Rouen, died in November 1207. The abbot of Ramsey resigned, and the abbot of Chertsey died, in 1206.   [3] Diceto, i, pp. xci–xcii and ii. 169–70.

[4] *Ann. Mon.*, i. 59; cf. ibid. iv. 397–8 (Worcester annals) and B.M. MS. Cotton Faustina B. 1, fo. 24ʳ (Winchcomb annals) which omit the words 'cancellarius regis in Coventrensem et magister Nicholaus de Aquila' and so erroneously make Walter de Gray bishop-elect of Chichester (Luard tried to correct by emending to Chester). The common source would seem to be that which Liebermann believed to lie behind so many south-country annals: see *Ungedruckte anglo-norm. Gesch.*, pp. 173–82; Moses Tyson, 'The annals of Southwark and Merton', *Surrey Archaeological Collections*, xxxvi (1925), 24–57, and N. Denholm-Young, 'The Winchester-Hyde Chronicle', *EHR*, xlix (1934), 85–93, reprinted in his *Collected Papers on Medieval Subjects* (Oxford, 1946), pp. 86–95. Another trace of the common source is possibly the record in Dunstable, *s.a.* 1219: 'Obiit Hugo Herfordensis episcopus, cui successit Hugo Foliot' (p. 55), also in Winton-Waverley annals (*Ungedruckte anglo-norm. Gesch.*, p. 188).

In the decade after 1210 the Dunstable annals show few if any features which could be construed as signs of the prior's authorship, although from time to time they record his personal activities. He investigates the churches' losses during the Interdict (p. 39), he attends the Fourth Lateran Council and spends a year in the theological schools of Paris on the way home (p. 44). Much later, in his old age, he acts as papal judge delegate in 1239, in an important lawsuit over metropolitan rights of visitation (p. 151). The fact that these records generally refer to 'prior noster' hardly affects the question of authorship. Humphrey Wanley, who regarded him as the author, wrote: 'I may believe that he might often dictate the Matter, even when he himself is mentioned in the Third Person, as we see that Moses often writeth of himself in that manner.'[1] The personal element is exemplified in the record of the apparition (*visio*) to 'our prior' on the night of St. Martin of two Jews who foretold to him the coming of Antichrist (p. 33). But even if the prior was instrumental in recording these facts, the main responsibility for the compilation might rest in other hands. The compiler, to be sure, displayed keen interest in legal matters concerning his priory, but such an interest does not necessarily denote the professional canonist, and it is equally a feature of the annals before and after Prior Richard's death. Any intelligent obedientiary of the house, acquainted with its temporal affairs, could chronicle these events, for which the priory's cartulary preserved complementary documents. Pauli, who thought that *Tib.* was the original authors' manuscript, saw no reason to think that Prior Richard composed the annals beyond the point where the hand of *Tib.* changes under the year 1210.

METHODS OF COMPOSITION

Granted that the annals before 1209 were for the most part written down by 1210 or 1211, what was the method of composition thereafter? Luard thought 'that the greater portion of the chronicle was written from year to year as the events occurred or were reported' (pp. xxxi–ii). A thirteenth-century

---

[1] Hearne, *Chronicon*, i, p. lxxix.

pattern for such a procedure is provided by the compiler of annals contained in MS. Cotton Vesp. E. iv, fo. 153^r, called by Liebermann 'Winton-Waverley'.[1] The annalist begins by saying that he has assembled various chronicles and annals from neglected sources. He continues: 'It will be your business to see that there is always a sheet attached to the book, on which may be noted in pencil deaths of illustrious men and anything in the state of the kingdom which is worth remembering, whenever the news comes to hand. But at the end of the year let a man appointed to the task—not just anyone who so wishes —write out briefly and succinctly, in the body of the book, what he thinks truest and best to be passed down to the notice of posterity. And then the old leaf can be removed and a new one put in.' This sort of pattern may have been in the mind of Richard de Morins when he inaugurated an historical work in his priory; but, if so, it was not maintained in the decade after 1210.

At several points events have clearly been recorded at least three or four years after they occurred. Thus the prophecy of Peter of Pontefract, earlier than May 1213, is noted with a comment that could only have been written after King John's death in October 1216 (p. 34). With the imprisonment of Stephen Ridel in the summer of 1212 is also recorded his death several years later (p. 34). A lawsuit undertaken by the priory in July 1213 is said to have been interrupted by the outbreak of war: this must have been written later than May 1215, perhaps much later (p. 38). Delay is suggested when the fate of the pseudo-Emperor Baldwin is reported *s.a.* 1225 and the annalist observes: 'Populares tamen *usque hodie* credunt ipsum verum comitem fuisse Baldewinum . . . unde multa miracula in locis sue passionis postmodum acciderunt' (p. 95).[2] Now, it is theoretically possible that every one of these few examples of 'hindsight' is the result of a later addition to a contemporary text, and that their origin as marginalia is obscured because in *Tib.*, instead of the original manuscript, we have only a fair

---

[1] Liebermann, *Ungedruckte*, pp. 173–202. The preamble is not printed here, but is printed by Luard in his edition of the annals of Worcester, *Ann. Mon.*, iv. 355.

[2] Cf. *s.a.* 1235: '. . . ita quod *nondum habemus* in ea nisi veterem pensionem' (p. 141).

copy which has smoothed out the anachronisms and irregularities. True though this is, we must take into account two other features of the annals which, when added up, make a systematic contemporary and unified composition unbelievable. These features are, first, inaccurate chronology in the decade 1210–20 and, secondly, duplication in the reporting of events both before and after 1220.

Pauli stated that 'the author who first succeeded Prior Richard in the reign of King John made the mistake of ascribing everything not to its own year but to the preceding one.'[1] Had this been the only error, we might have blamed it on the copyist of *Tib.* But in fact Pauli's own extracts show that the chronological confusion in this period was much more serious. Strangely enough, it was disregarded by Luard.[2] The author's disease was apparently infectious: not even the appearance of Magna Carta in 1214 moved Luard to dissent, and he was capable himself of speaking of the Fourth Lateran Council of 1214 (p. xi) and of the campaign between John and Lewis in 1215 (p. xvi).

If we look at the annal for 1210 an interesting fact emerges. The first entries (pp. 32–3) are all correctly assigned to this year—the year in which Prior Richard inaugurated the work. But as soon as a new hand appears in *Tib.* errors of dating appear. At first sight this might seem to support Pauli's view that this is the original manuscript and that the new hand is that of a less accurate annalist who took over the work from Prior Richard in 1210. But reasons have been given for supposing that *Tib.* is a copy, not the original. The fact that the quality of the annals changes with the change of hand in this copy can be understood on the supposition that the original annals first stopped at this point, hung fire for several years, and were only resumed by a less careful compiler (perhaps even in a different book) several years after our existing fair copy of the annals to 1210 had been made. It has already been noted that the annals for 1210–20 were written up at least three or

---

[1] 'Notandum vero . . . auctorem, qui primus post Ricardum priorem Iohanne regnante annales continuavit, ita errasse, ut omnia non suo, sed precedenti singula anno ascriberet', *MGH*, xxvii. 504.

[2] He refers to 'errors and instances of confusion' only in relation to the doublets he cites (p. xxxi); see below, p. 226.

four years after the events. The gap may have been longer, for the compiler seems to be chronologically all at sea. The prophecy of Peter of Pontefract (earlier than May 1213) is placed under the year 1210. Under this year, too, come the peace with Scotland (1212), the death of Roger de Lacy (1211), and events of strictly local interest which would be well known at Dunstable: the death of Robert de Braybrook (1211) and a lawsuit over Pulloxhill church (1212). Almost all the events *s.a.* 1211 belong to 1213. But then many of the chief events of 1213 are recorded *s.a.* 1212. Here occur the details of King John's reconciliation with the church, the damages paid by John to the clergy, and the preaching of the crusade. A few of the entries under this year relate to the first months of 1214. The confusion continues in the following years. A complete analysis is unnecessary, but it is desirable to insist that the misplacement is not consistent. The first entry *s.a.* 1213 is the appointment of Master Alexander Nequam as abbot of Cirencester, and this did take place in July 1213; but the battle of Bouvines (July 1214) appears under the same year. *S.a.* 1214 events of that year are combined with the account of the baronial revolt and Magna Carta. *S.a.* 1215 the Fourth Lateran Council is correctly dated but the campaign of Prince Louis in England in 1216 and 1217 is also included. So it continues. Only in and after 1220 does the chronology at last become fairly reliable.[1]

Another feature of the disorderly annals of 1210–19 is duplication. Luard noted entries which are (more or less) doublets, and commented thus: 'There are not unfrequently traces of different authorities being employed, and thus many facts are repeated in different language, and occasionally with different dates,—a rumour of an event having reached the priory before it really took place, and being at once inserted in the chronicle' (pp. xxx–xxxi). The examples which Luard proceeds to give (and some others) do not bear out his suggestion of anticipatory rumour and contemporary record. They do, none the less, show that the compiler (or compilers) of the annals in their present form had indeed access to several authorities, and had copied them slavishly, without regard to

---

[1] Later examples of misdating occur *s.a.* 1238 (events of 1236 and 1239, p. 148) and *s.a.* 1241 (an event of 1240, p. 156).

their redundancy or mutual incompatibility. The compiler shows his carelessness very early, for the first entry in *Tib.* written by the new hand *s.a.* 1210 reads: 'Eodem anno rex Otto fit imperator per Innocentium papam' (p. 33). This event had already been correctly noted *s.a.* 1209, with its precise date (4 October), from the St. Albans annals. The election of a new abbot of Westminster appears both wrongly under 1213 (with a wrong initial) and rightly under 1214. These are the only doublets before the year 1220; whereas there are at least fifteen examples between 1220 and 1242. This again points to a different method of composition.

Doublets appear commonly in medieval annals, and must be taken as symptoms of the practice of conflation. For instance, the annals of Worcester, contained as a single series in the fifteenth-century manuscript from which Luard printed them, show reliance in part on 'Winton-Waverley', in part on other sources. The compiler—or conflater—did not avoid the occasional doublet.[1] In the Winchcomb annals in B.M. MS. Cotton Faustina B.1 an intermediate stage can be visually observed. Here the scribe first abridged a series of Tewkesbury annals (which lay behind those printed by Luard). He set the entry for each year as an island in a little sea of blank parchment. Then he added new islets of text, spread all round the original entry: sometimes there are as many as six for one year. Their sources, Worcester annals and others, overlapped with the original source, so that (for instance) *s.a.* 1202 there are three accounts of the capture of Prince Arthur at Mirebeau.[2] Duplication of this sort was incidental to the normal habit of supplementing annals copied from one book by reference to another. It was most likely to arise when the annalist had access to several books of pre-digested annals; and this may well have been the position of the Dunstable compiler, filling out his local information with news of public characters and affairs, for the years 1220–42. But for the period 1210–19, when doublets are few and the chronology is confused, when the information is

---

[1] *Ann. Mon.*, iv, pp. xxxix–xl. Cf. the doublet in the Waverley annals for the Third Lateran Council of 1179 (*Ann. Mon.*, ii. 214) and the two eulogies of Abbot Walter in the Tewkesbury annals, *s.a.* 1202 and 1205 (ibid. i. 56–8).

[2] Fo. 23ʳ. For an edition and critical study of the Winchcomb annals, 1182–1232, see the unpublished M.A. thesis (Manchester, 1949) of Mr. Eric John.

copious and excellent though the dating of it is wrong, a different method of composition is more likely. In the light of the observations made above one may envisage the following process.

Prior Richard de Morins had borrowed the St. Albans Diceto in 1210 to lay foundations for annals of his own time. He had begun the work of extraction himself but soon handed over the task to one of his canons. For the years 1200–10, when Diceto failed him, he could trust to his own experiences and memory for some information. That the scribe who wrote in 1210 was relying largely on personal reminiscences is implied by the comparative scarcity of precise dates in the earlier years, the greater precision as he approached 1210. The annals were brought up to date by the time Diceto's book had to be returned to St. Albans; though a few of the items for those years found in *Tib.* were probably added later. For the future the prior— if he took an interest in the sequel—may have proposed the method which the Winton-Waverley annalist wished to be observed. Pencilled notes of important events were to be jotted down as they were reported, and these were to be digested and edited annually. But his advice was a counsel of perfection: the Dunstable annals show what might actually happen. When we look at the annals for 1210–19 in *Tib.*—with their abundance of good material, evidence of later writing, and gross mistakes of dating—it is easy to imagine a background of rough jottings on odd scraps of parchment, allowed to accumulate in chaos and only edited when it was much too late. It may have been only about 1220 that something was done to bring order out of chaos, and then the work was not done intelligently. It is hardly credible that the existing muddle could have arisen if Prior Richard himself had supervised the compilation. But it is unlikely that the delay was longer. For from about 1220 onwards the standard of record-keeping was much higher and another and better compiler was at work. He made no attempt to revise the preceding annals; but for the future he introduced much better order. The range of information is now very wide, extending often to continental affairs; the entries are on an ampler scale than before; and documents concerning Dunstable Priory are sometimes quoted in full.

Whereas the entries under the years 1200–9 occupy four and a half of Luard's printed pages and those under the years 1210–19 occupy twenty-four, the annals for 1220–9 fill sixty-eight pages, and those for 1230–41 nearly thirty-four. Perhaps Prior Richard, having observed the failure of the annalist to do his job properly between 1210 and 1219, lent a hand or kept an eye on the work during the rest of his priorate. He may have contributed items of his own. His academic interests had been revived by a year at Paris, and he may have had contacts there. This would explain the obituary on Philip Augustus, 'pater populi et mater scolarium', and several entries about the university of Paris and the English scholars there (pp. 81, 97–8, 116, 125).[1] It is a plausible conjecture, but nothing more. The character and scale of the annals do not abruptly change when Richard de Morins dies in 1242. One detail, nevertheless, points to a change of direction in the year after his death. The annal for 1243 begins: 'Anno incipiente a festo Annunciationis dominice' (p. 161, cf. p. 167). This marks an innovation, for although the practice of calculating the year of grace from 25 March was already very common in the English church, some chroniclers still preferred to reckon from Christmas to Christmas.[2] Diceto had used the Christmas dating;[3] and there are a few indications in the Dunstable annals, *s.a.* 1203, 1206, and 1221 which come near to proving—what is suggested by other entries—that the compilers used the same system.

Since much of this paper has been devoted to the short-comings of the annals of Dunstable, it may be as well to conclude by endorsing Luard's high estimate of their historical value (p. xxxii). As they advance through the thirteenth century they give an incomparable view of the ordinary secular proceedings of an English monastery,[4] and at the same time preserve the texts of records and make interesting comments on

[1] No other English chronicler speaks of Philip Augustus in these terms (few do more than record his death), and none mentions the troubles of the university of Paris during the twenties.

[2] Cf. Mr. Denholm-Young's comment on a change of practice in this matter in the Winchester-Hyde chronicle in 1261, *EHR*, xlix. 88–9.

[3] Diceto, ii. 124.

[4] The cartulary, calendared by G. H. Fowler, adds important documentation at many points.

public events, amplifying our information from other quarters. The prior of Dunstable, after all, was a man of some consequence,[1] and the priory, about thirteen miles north-west of St. Albans on the Watling Street,[2] was well placed to get news of political and ecclesiastical happenings. Even in the period 1210–19, when the dating is utterly untrustworthy, the annals have a contemporary quality: that is, the drafts on which they depend were probably written soon after the event. Consequently a judicious reader, making all allowances for the limitations of chronicle material, must take their evidence seriously. They give a local view of the working of the papal interdict on England. They record some of the measures taken by the suspicious king in the crisis of 1212 (the imprisonment of Stephen Ridel is not otherwise recorded). They describe the king's levy of free men in 1213 'sub nomine culvertagii' (p. 35), and by using that rare word go some way to support the genuine quality of the royal writ found in Roger Wendover's *Flores*. For the civil war of 1215–17 and the activities of Prince Louis in England they provide useful information.

[1] Miss J. E. Sayers lists no less than 43 cases between 1207 and 1242 in which Richard acted as papal judge delegate (*Papal Judges Delegate in the Province of Canterbury, 1198–1254* (Oxford, 1971), pp. 296–301).

[2] It is the next place to St. Albans marked on the maps of Matthew Paris, monk of St. Albans. See *Four Maps of Great Britain* designed by Matthew Paris about A.D. 1250 (British Museum, 1928), plates A, C, and D.

12. The 'Paper Constitution' preserved by Matthew Paris*

HISTORIANS of the thirteenth century have long been puzzled by the document which Matthew Paris inserted in his *Chronica maiora* after his account of King Henry III's dispute with the barons and clergy in November 1244.[1] The rubric which introduces the document reads: *Haec providebant magnates rege consentiente inviolabiliter deinceps observari.* Then follows a series of startling, radical provisions for the control of executive and judicature. These were certainly not put into effect in 1244 or at any other time in Henry III's reign, and historians, hard put to relate the document to the known circumstances of 1244, have felt uncomfortable about accepting it at its face-value. In 1943 Mr. Denholm-Young offered a bold and attractive solution of the problem, buttressed with elaborate arguments.[2] He points out that in 1238 there was a political crisis of the first order, when provisions were made and sealed which have not survived (loc. cit., p. 408), whereas there is no recorded crisis in 1244 to explain the existing document (p. 405). He joins the known document to the known crisis of 1238 and contends that there was no comparable crisis in 1244. Hesitatingly, Sir Maurice Powicke described the document under the date 1238, without being sure that it belongs to that year.[3]

* First published in *EHR*, lxv (1950), 213–21. Professor R. F. Treharne very kindly read and criticized a first draft of this paper. I am also deeply obliged to Mr. Denholm-Young for reading it before publication. He permitted me to say that, while he was impressed by the contention as to 'sancto viro', he considered the other points to be far more controversial.

[1] *Chron. maiora* (RS), iv. 362 ff. The document begins on p. 366.

[2] *EHR*, lviii (1943), 403–23, reprinted in the author's *Collected Papers on Mediaeval Subjects* (1946), pp. 130–53. See also the same writer's *Richard of Cornwall* (1947), p. 36.

[3] *Henry III and the Lord Edward* (1947), i. pp. vi, 291, 300 n.; 'The composition of the "Chronica Maiora" of Matthew Paris', *Proc. British Academy*, xxix (1944), 16 n. 2; *The Thirteenth Century 1216–1307* (Oxford Hist. of England, 1953), pp. 77, 79. Cf. G. O. Sayles, *Medieval Foundations of England* (1948), p. 421: 'In 1244 (a case has been made for 1238) a more ambitious scheme was adumbrated.'

On the other hand, Professor Bertie Wilkinson defended Matthew Paris's date: 1244.[1] The matter is open, and deserves further examination.

Mr. Denholm-Young uses so skilfully his intimate knowledge of the sources for the political history of the period that his arguments are not to be lightly assailed. There seem, nevertheless, to be certain features in the Paper Constitution, as Stubbs calls it, which compel reconsideration. We may begin by summarizing Mr. Denholm-Young's main arguments for the earlier date; then some criticisms will be offered.

I

(i) The *Chronica maiora* of Matthew Paris is exceptionally valuable for the many official letters, memoranda, and laws which its author inserts in his narrative, besides those included in the *Liber additamentorum*. But in the process of incorporation inaccuracies occurred. Mr. Denholm-Young points to several documents which are demonstrably set under the wrong year. One such error, he argues, would explain a misdating of the Paper Constitution by six years. 'At first sight it may seem more difficult for a scribe to err by six years than by a round number like ten, but it is an error which could be due to one stroke— xxix for xxii Henry III' (p. 404). Thus, to quote Sir Maurice Powicke, he has 'shaken an important document loose from a date which has caused historical scholars much embarrassment'.[2]

(ii) Mr. Denholm-Young is first led to expect this chronological error by his view of the events of the year 1244. Matthew Paris does not tell us 'that the magnates "provided" anything, still less that provisions were made with the king's consent. . . . Such a scheme could hardly be drawn up and agreed to by the king unless the barons were for the moment in a position to enforce their demands' (p. 402). The king was stronger in 1244 than he had been for some time past and 'there was no point at which such a plan could have been seriously considered' (p. 406). 'Further, possible opposition had been anticipated by the king's action in appointing four English-

---

[1] *The Const. Hist. of England 1216–1399, with select documents*, i (1948), 118–22.
[2] *Proc. Brit. Academy*, xxix. 16 n. 2.

born councillors, "which greatly conciliated the magnates". [*Hist. angl.* ii. 481.] Finally, the committee [of magnates in November 1244] was set up to make provision for an aid to the king, but the plan makes no such provision' (p. 407).

(iii) Thirdly, Mr. Denholm-Young suggests certain positive reasons in favour of transferring the Paper Constitution to 1238. Matthew Paris reports, under 1242, that in February 1238 four baronial commissioners were appointed to guard and superintend the expenditure of the thirtieth granted to the king.[1] The four *libertatum conservatores* of the Paper Constitution may well have developed out of these. Also, 'we have three precise links between this document and the only baronial provision mentioned by Matthew Paris before 1258. These are the heading of the document, the mention of a special tax which has already been granted (which will fit no other year), and the topical allusion to the attack on Neville in 1236. Finally, we have the fact that Matthew knew of the provisions of 1238 and might be expected to have obtained a draft of them from the person most concerned [i.e. Richard of Cornwall]' (p. 420).

II

Before we examine these views on the occasion of the Paper Constitution a remark about the form and nature of the document is called for. Its title, *Haec providebant magnates rege consentiente inviolabiliter deinceps observari*, is followed by some fifty-five lines of text which Mr. Denholm-Young describes as 'formal memoranda' (p. 404), or 'draft provisions' (p. 405). Such a description, joined to such a title recalls the document headed *Ista sunt capitula quae barones petunt et dominus rex concedit*, to which King John's seal was attached at Runnymede in 1215. But if we read the text of the Paper Constitution we soon realize that it could not have been brought to the king for sealing in this form. It is not merely a draft, but a rough draft and an unfinished one. After a few carefully phrased provisions come the words: 'Memorandum quoque de sententia ferenda in contradictores. Item de obligatione sacramenti in

---

[1] Mat. Paris, *Chron. maiora*, iv. 186.

invicem. Item de itinere iustitiariorum.' These are mere headings or agenda. More provisions, fully framed, follow and then the jottings: 'Duo iustitiarii in banco. Duo barones in scaccario. Unus ad minus iustitiarius Iudaeorum.' This is followed by provisions for the election of certain persons, possibly the judges just named,[1] and for the removal of suspect and unnecessary persons from the king's side.

It is not enough to say, with Mr. Denholm-Young, that this 'is only a draft and has no doubt been paraphrased in places' (p. 409).[2] We have here no more than a sketch, of which the various parts are in different stages of completeness. Its form provides strong evidence of authenticity, but disproves the applicability of the title to the text. As Dr. Wilkinson says, 'the title may only have indicated what was proposed, not what happened'.[3] Mr. Denholm-Young is not logical in stating dogmatically that 'the contents are obviously in accordance with the heading' (p. 407). In considering the chronological problem, we need only look for a time when provisions were drafted with a view to the king's consent. We may go further and say that nothing proves this document to represent the considered policy of the assembly of magnates. It is not even probable that it records provisions agreed upon by the committee of twelve. More probably it represents what one individual or group contributed to the committee's discussions. The identity of the individual or group remains a matter for pure conjecture. In recent years light has been thrown on the

---

[1] It has generally been assumed that this passage refers to the judges, but in a rough draft it might be a displaced alternative version concerning the election of justiciar and chancellor.

[2] In his later work on *Richard of Cornwall*, p. 36, he justly describes the document as 'the incomplete, staccato, and sometimes fragmentary memoranda'.

[3] Op. cit., p. 120. He continues: 'It was careless to keep it in the document as inserted in the chronicle, but not so careless as to insert the document six years out of its proper place.' But it is also possible that the title was invented by Matthew Paris or his scribe. I have, in the text above, accepted the view generally held by modern historians that the title should be translated, 'These things the magnates provided with the king's consent to be henceforth inviolably observed.' But it might be differently construed: 'to be observed subject to the king's consent'. William Prynne read it thus: 'The Bishops and Nobles, before their departure, agreed on these Propositions to be presented and assented unto by the King, before they would grant him any Ayde.' (*The Second Tome of an Exact Chronological Vindication, etc.* (1665), p. 610.) Professor R. F. Treharne kindly told me that he always assumed that the title should be read in this sense.

diffusion of documents related to, but not identical with, the final version of Magna Carta, 1215. In particular, Prof. J. C. Holt has pointed out that Matthew Paris's predecessor, the St. Albans chronicler Roger Wendover, had access to an intermediate draft of that charter.[1] Here, as elsewhere, we clearly must reckon with the circulation of many unauthorized and fragmentary records of political debates. This has to be borne in mind in any appraisal of the record which Matthew Paris has preserved *s.a.* 1244.

III

(i) Matthew Paris is accused of placing the documents which he uses under wrong dates. Mr. Denholm-Young cites first of all the writ of watch and ward of 1242, misdated in the *Liber additamentorum* by ten years.[2] As for this, it need only be said that the chronicler has not attempted to relate this document to the sequence of events and, if Sir Maurice Powicke is right, the faults of the *Liber* are not necessarily to be attributed to Matthew Paris or to the scribe of the *Chronica maiora* in C.C.C.C.MS. 16.[3] Mr. Denholm-Young's other examples of Matthew Paris's anachronisms are (*a*) an undated letter of Honorius III to Henry III which the chronicler inserts in Wendover's narrative *s.a.* 1218 and which Potthast preferred, for no apparent reason, to put under 1216;[4] (*b*) 'three letters of 1232 and one of 1233 are given under 1237' (p. 404 n. 3). These are the correspondence of the Patriarch of Constantinople and Pope Gregory IX about reunion.[5] The episode to which they relate had not been mentioned by Wendover; rather than interpolate them awkwardly in Wendover's narrative, Matthew chose to introduce them in 1237 as a preliminary to his account of the pope's project of a crusade against John Vatatzes in that

---

[1] 'The St. Albans Chroniclers and Magna Carta', *Trans. Royal Hist. Soc.*, 5th Series, xiv (1964), 67–88. Cf. C. R. Cheney, in *BJRL*, l (1967–8), 282 and V. H. Galbraith, 'A draft of *Magna Carta* (1215)', *Proc. Brit. Academy*, liii (1967), 345–60.

[2] Loc. cit., p. 404. Cf. *EHR*, lvii (1942), 469; lviii (1943), 128.

[3] *Proc. Brit. Academy*, xxix. 9–12.

[4] *Chron. maiora*, iii. 34 and Pott. 5406. It is only known from Matthew Paris.

[5] *Chron. maiora*, iii. 448–69.

year. The displacement had a logical reason and Matthew very properly retained the correct pontifical year in the dating of the pope's first letter. I can add at least one better example of displacement to this short list,[1] but when these facts are considered in relation to the vast quantity of documents correctly placed by the chronicler, they do not permit us to convict him or his copyist of habitual chronological inexactitude. Even if we cannot go so far as to say with Dr. Wilkinson that 'perhaps the strongest argument for the date 1244 for the Paper Constitution is the fact that the writer of the revised copy of the *Chronica maiora* placed it under that date, in the midst of the proceedings of the parliament of 1244',[2] the onus of proof lies heavily on those who wish to detach the document from its position in the chronicle.

(ii) In favour of the date 1244 there are two points of internal evidence on which Sir Maurice Powicke put his finger without, perhaps, recognizing their full importance: 'the reference to the archbishop as though he were no longer alive and the demand for the election of a chancellor as though no chancellor existed'.[3] Let us examine these in turn.

(*a*) The Paper Constitution speaks of the sentence of excommunication declared (in January 1237) 'a sancto viro Ædmundo'. Edmund, archbishop of Canterbury, died in 1240 and was canonized in 1246. It is unbelievable that he should have been referred to in these terms during his lifetime, even in the rough draft of an official document. Mr. Denholm-Young recognizes this and goes further:

In formal memoranda [he writes] this phrase strikes a false note, and in any case would be equally incorrect at any time before 1246. But the use of some such phrase is intelligible—indeed we get 'Beatus Edmundus' and 'Sanctus Edmundus' a few pages earlier— in a text written after 1257. But the 'viro' is a solecism and cannot

---

[1] Innocent III's letter to Richard I, 29 May 1198, is put *s.a.* 1207 with a fanciful introduction and an address to King John (ibid. ii. 512). Matthew may have misplaced the barons' letter to the pope *s.a.* 1239 (cf. ibid. iii. 610). R. Vaughan, *Matthew Paris* (Cambridge, 1958), p. 136, says: 'it is only very occasionally that an event or document is inserted under the wrong year. In the dating of events within the year, however, the *Chronica maiora* is often unreliable.'

[2] Op. cit., p. 121.

[3] *Henry III and the Lord Edward*, i. 291 n 2.

have been present in draft provisions of any date. I therefore suspect
a purely scribal error (pp. 404–5).

Since he believes the document to belong to Edmund's lifetime, he presumably supposes that, in the process of copying,
'sancto viro Ædmundo' was substituted (by one or two stages)
for 'domino archiepiscopo Cantuariensi Ædmundo', or some
such phrase. Surely this is highly improbable? If Matthew
Paris or his scribe were making a gratuitous change of this
sort, why did he not write 'beato *or* sancto Ædmundo', as he
did at an earlier stage in the narrative?[1] To eliminate the word
'viro' as a solecism is to ignore a crucial piece of evidence. For
Edmund could be called 'sanctus vir Ædmundus' precisely in
those years when he was neither alive nor yet a canonized
saint. He was a holy man whose claims to canonization were
being pressed between 1241 and 1246. 'Sanctus vir' was
a phrase employed in official letters written to and from the
commissioners for canonization.[2] It was therefore proper to
the draft of an official record prepared in 1244.

(*b*) Mr. Denholm-Young maintains that 'the plan does not
say that the two offices [of justiciar and chancellor] were vacant'
(p. 419). He does not remark that the document refers twice to
the election of these officers. First, 'justitiarius et cancellarius
ab omnibus eligantur'. Then, following other rules about the
chancellor, 'nullus substituatur justitiarius vel cancellarius nisi
per sollempnem omnium convocationem et assensum'. Unless
these sentences are to be regarded as two different ways of
saying the same thing, they mean that a justiciar and chancellor
were then to be elected, who were not subsequently to be
replaced except by the agreement of the general body. The
double arrangement makes it extremely difficult to accept Mr.
Denholm-Young's contention that 'the plan simply states the

---

[1] *Chron. maiora*, iv. 102, 330, 336: here he was talking of the process of canonization. When he speaks of the oath which Edmund swore on the king's behalf
(iv. 363) he calls him 'archiepiscopus Cantuariensis Ædmundus' and the narrative
regularly gives him this title in his lifetime.

[2] Martène and Durand, *Thesaurus novus anecdotorum* (1717), iii. 1841, 1902. The
same title, *sanctus vir*, is bestowed on Gilbert of Sempringham by those who wrote
to the pope in support of his canonization in 1200 and 1201 (R. Foreville, *Le
livre de S. Gilbert de Sempringham* (1943), pp. 10, 17, 18, 27, 29).

theory, as in 1258, that the justiciar and the chancellor are to be responsible to the baronage' (p. 419). He supports this interpretation by saying, 'We do not assume that half the judicature was vacant because the appointment of five judges is next mentioned'. But if we relate the sentence about appointments ('Hac vice per communem fiant electionem . . .') to the judges previously enumerated, we may surely understand by 'hac vice' that immediate appointments of new judges were intended. The most natural inference is that there was neither justiciar nor chancellor when the Paper Constitution was drafted.

Now this was the state of affairs, as the magnates saw it, in November 1244. The history of the justiciarship after the removal of Hubert de Burgh is, indeed, obscure. Hubert was succeeded by Stephen de Segrave until 1234, but thereafter no one judge wielded comparable power. William Raleigh was the chief of the justices *coram rege* between 1234 and 1239, but he did not fill the place of his predecessors. Other justices appear during the next twenty years whose wages are higher than their fellows'; but none of these was a principal minister of state, so far as we can tell, and when the barons in 1258 asked for a justiciar they had in mind someone more exalted than the chief justices of the past decades. We may say, therefore, that, whether or no the magnates would have recognized William Raleigh's claim to the title of justiciar in 1238, in their eyes no justiciar existed in 1244.[1] The question of the chancellorship in the years 1238 to 1258 is hardly less obscure,[2] but certain facts are clear. We know that until 1 February 1244, when Ralph de Nevill died, there was a chancellor whom all recognized as such. After this, the chancery was reformed, the title of

---

[1] The foregoing depends on Moses Tyson's unpublished work 'The early history of the *Placita coram rege*' (Manchester, Ph.D., 1927), especially pp. 121–6, 135, 197. On p. 198 Tyson says, 'In 1244 . . . the barons . . . were thinking of a justiciar who was a much more powerful person than the chief of the justices with the king. The chief justice was very important, but he clearly differed from the justiciar the barons had in mind as much as in 1258 Hugh Bigod with his noble origin and his 1000 marks a year salary differed from Roger of Thurkelby, the leading justice of the Bench, with his 100 marks a year.' Cf. R. F. Treharne, *The Baronial Plan of Reform* (Manchester, 1932), p. 21.

[2] Cf. L. B. Dibben, 'The chancellors and keepers of the seal under Henry III', *EHR*, xxvii (1912), 39–51; T. F. Tout, *Chapters in Admin. History* (Manchester, 1920), i. 284–9; B. Wilkinson, *The Chancery under Edward III* (Manchester 1930), pp. 194–8; R. F. Treharne, op. cit., pp. 22–3; F. M. Powicke, op. cit. i. 270 n. 2.

chancellor was seldom used, either officially or unofficially, and the first of those keepers of the seal who may possibly have enjoyed the title was Silvester of Everdon, who received the seal on 14 November 1244.[1] We can hardly doubt that the magnates, when they asked in that same month for a properly elected chancellor, considered that the post was vacant.

This leads us to compare the Paper Constitution with Matthew Paris's narrative of the events of 1244–5. In contrast to Mr. Denholm-Young, Dr. Wilkinson sees no serious discordance.[2] Matthew does not, to be sure, suggest that the king agreed to any provisions in this year (or in any year between 1238 and 1258), but this is explained by the palpable discrepancy between the title of the plan and the plan as it stands (above, p. 233). It is the draft of rejected provisions, made in the committee of twelve described in Matthew's narrative.[3] The committee which Matthew describes was formed to present a draft proposal to the assembled magnates, lay and ecclesiastical, respecting the terms on which an aid should be granted to the king. But Matthew Paris was mainly interested, as we are, in the *quid pro quo*; and his account of the provisions, like the Paper Constitution, does not directly concern the aid. Matthew implies that the magnates' provisions (which he calls a *petitio*)[4] complained of the failure to observe the charter of liberties which had been sworn to in the past, and of the malversation of aids previously granted, and of writs often issued contrary to justice. The magnates petitioned for the election of a justiciar and chancellor. In these particulars the narrative resembles the accompanying document, though the Paper Constitution contains other features of great constitutional importance. Mr. Denholm-Young objects that the Paper Constitution provides for the control of an aid already granted (p. 407); but this seems to put too rigorous an interpretation on the phrase 'pecunia ab universis specialiter concessa, et ad commodum domini regis et regni, expendatur secundum quod melius viderint expedire'.

---

[1] *Close Rolls, 1242–47*, p. 266. Cf. Dibben, loc. cit., p. 44; Wilkinson, *Chancery*, p. 194 n. 4.

[2] *Constit. Hist.*, pp. 120–1.

[3] *Chron. maiora*, iv. 362–3.

[4] Cf. the 'capitula quae barones petunt' of 1215 and the 'petitiones baronum' of 1258.

An aid was, after all, to be the consideration for the king's acceptance of provisions, and in the event he got an aid.[1]

Matthew Paris's *Historia Anglorum* has been cited to support the view that Henry III, by appointing four new English councillors earlier in 1244, had 'greatly conciliated the magnates' and anticipated possible opposition. We cannot take this very seriously in the light of Matthew's account of the crisis of November 1244. The magnates, he says, then agreed to a postponement of the question until next February; 'quod si mera voluntate rex interim tales conciliarios eligeret, et taliter iura regni tractaret, quod magnates contenti essent, ad terminum illum super auxilio faciendo responsuri providerent'.[2] Everything points to a state of considerable excitement and discontent in the assembly of magnates at Westminster in November 1244. They may not have been sufficiently united to agree upon provisions for a radical reform, and the king was not so weak as to accept such provisions; but these considerations are not enough to displace the Paper Constitution from its place in Matthew Paris's narrative.

(iii) The chief positive arguments for 1238 have been mentioned above (pp. 232–3). Regarding the view that four commissioners already appointed to deal with an aid had their competence extended until they became *libertatum conservatores*, this is not borne out either by Matthew Paris's narrative of 1238, or by the terms of the Paper Constitution. The latter suggests that the *conservatores* are a newly devised group which, incidentally, was intended to include the justiciar and chancellor. The other links with 1238 which Mr. Denholm-Young enumerates are not very strong. There were indeed provisions made in 1238 after an aid had been granted, provisions to which the king gave his assent. It would seem natural for Matthew Paris to have a copy (and not merely the copy of a rough draft). Matthew's narrative, however, does not suggest that he knew the details of the futile concordat of 1238. The political crisis was evidently sharp, but our knowledge of it is scanty. It is all very well to connect the Paper Constitution with the weakness of the king and the momentary solidarity of the opposition and try to fit the document to these circumstances. But in our

---

[1] *Chron. maiora*, iv. 372–4.   [2] Ibid. iv. 363.

present state of ignorance about these years, we must argue rather on the strict basis of what the documents say than on the broader ground of which political crisis or stage in constitutional growth they seem to suit best. Some such document might have been produced during the crisis of 1238, but the Paper Constitution is not it. Apart from the other arguments which have been raised for leaving it in 1244, two peremptory reasons have been given for excluding 1238. When the Paper Constitution was drafted, the archbishop of Canterbury was dead and there was no justiciar or chancellor. Archbishop Edmund lived until 16 November 1240, Ralph de Nevill the chancellor until 1 February 1244. The *terminus a quo* is thus February 1244, and the title of Edmund suggests a *terminus ante quem* early in 1247. No occasion for the Paper Constitution can, on present evidence, be preferred to the assembly of November 1244.

13. Gervase, Abbot of Prémontré: A Medieval Letter-Writer*

T HE career and writings of Gervase, abbot of Prémontré, have passed unnoticed in modern times by historians who might have found them instructive. Yet he was a fairly important figure in ecclesiastical affairs during the first decades of the thirteenth century. English by birth, he joined the Order of Prémontré as a canon of the abbey of St. Just, in the diocese of Beauvais, before the end of the twelfth century. In course of time he became abbot of this house, then abbot of Thenailles, in the diocese of Laon, and in February 1209 or 1210 abbot of Prémontré itself and president of the whole Order. After he had occupied this position for eleven years, he was provided by Pope Honorius III to the bishopric of Sées, in Normandy. He died in possession of this see in 1228, and was buried in a Premonstratensian abbey in the diocese.

A few bibliographers and monastic historians have described this man in the course of the last three hundred years or so: most of them call him Gervase of Chichester or, by obvious corruption, Gervase of Chester.[1] But while there is no doubt about his christian name and while his nationality is fairly certain,[2] there is no shred of evidence of a cognomen such as

---

* A lecture delivered in the John Rylands Library on the 11 Jan. 1950. First published in the *Bulletin* of the Library, xxxiii (1951–2), 25–56.

[1] He is described as of Chichester in *Hist. litt. de la France*, xviii. 41–50 (by Daunou); *Gallia christiana nova*, xi (1874), 693—but not in *Gallia christiana*, xi (1759), 693; T. Wright, *Biographia britannica literaria*, ii (1846), 448; C. U. J. Chevalier, *Répertoire des sources . . . bio-bibliog.* (1905), i. 1765; A. Molinier, *Sources de l'hist. de France*, iii (1903), no. 2222; *Lexicon für Theol. und Kirche*, ed. M. Buchberger (Freiburg, 1932), iv. 448.

L. Goovaerts, *Ecrivains, artistes et savants de l'ordre de Prémontré* (1899–1902), i. 305, describes him as of the diocese of Lincoln or of Chichester; so also A. Zák, 'Episcopatus Ord. Praem.', *Analecta praemonstratensia*, iv (1928), 303.

Jacques Le Long, *Bibliotheca sacra* (1723), ii. 743, describes him as 'Gervasius, Anglus, Cestriensis'.

[2] The chronicle of St. Evroul describes him as English; so also the epitaph

Chichester. According to an eighteenth-century historian of the Premonstratensians, C. L. Hugo, Gervase came of a noble family of Lincoln, or Lincolnshire.[1] The name of Chichester has arisen from the confusion of two separate persons, and the result has been to foist on to the Premonstratensian Gervase not only the name but also the writings of another man.

For there was a Gervase of Chichester known to the literary historian. Not much is known about him, to be sure, but a substantial basis lies beneath the elegant and fanciful account given by Pits and the rest of the tribe of bibliographers. The facts are these. One Master Gervase of Chichester appears as a clerk of Thomas Becket, when Thomas was King Henry II's chancellor, about 1158–60.[2] He is briefly described by Herbert of Bosham, Becket's biographer, as a young man among the *eruditi Sancti Thome*.[3] A mutilated manuscript in the British Museum contains works of his written, so he says, late in life.[4] They consist of a commentary on the prophet Malachi concerning the instruction of the priesthood, and portions of homilies on St. Thomas Becket. Our next informant is the expert on books whom Henry VIII employed, John Leland, who devotes a rather flowery notice to Gervase of Chichester and mentions the commentary and the homilies, having seen them (perhaps in this very manuscript) at Gloucester Abbey. He says that he has seen elsewhere (if his memory is accurate) a commentary by Gervase on the Psalms.[5] On this foundation John Bale wrote a biography of Gervase for his *Scriptorum*

recorded on his tomb in the abbey of Silly (Ord. Vitalis, *Hist. eccl.*, ed. A. Prévost, v (1855), 165 and *Gallia christiana*, xi. 693). J. Le Paige, *Bibliotheca praemonstratensis ordinis* (Paris, 1633), p. 925, states that Gervase composed the epitaph.

[1] 'origine Lincolniensis, sanguine clarus' (C. L. Hugo, *Sacrae antiquitatis monumenta historica, dogmatica, diplomatica* (Etival, 1725), i. praefatio). Hugo cites at a later point in his account of Gervase 'Vita Gervas. MSS. Viconien.'. I have found no other mention of this work; Vicoigne was a Prem. abbey whose manuscripts chiefly passed to the neighbouring town of Valenciennes. It is noticeable that Hugo does not repeat the reference to 'Lincolniensis' in referring to Gervase in his later work, *Sacri et canonici ord. praem. annales* (Nancy, 1734–6). On Hugo, who was abbot of Etival (d. 1730), see *Analecta praem.*, i. 174–86, 261–85.

[2] *Rec. des actes de Henri II*, ed. L. Delisle and E. Berger (1909–27), i. 199, 323; cf. *Chron. Stephen, Henry II and Richard I* (RS), iv. 197, 345, 346, 356–7.

[3] *Materials for hist. of Th. Becket* (RS), iii. 527.

[4] Royal MS. 3 B. x.

[5] J. Leland, *Commentarii de scriptoribus britannicis* (Oxford, 1709), ch. 187.

illustrium catalogus,[1] and this was later embellished by Pits.[2] Bale credited Gervase definitely with the commentary on the Psalms about which Leland was doubtful, although he cited no authority other than Leland. He added to the book-list *alia plura*, presumably on the assumption that if a man wrote so much as was recorded, he probably wrote some more besides. Pits went further and added a fresh work: on the institution of the priesthood; but this is merely making two works out of the commentary on Malachi. The lengthening of the book-list becomes relevant to the present subject when we find both the name and the books transferred by some eighteenth- and nineteenth-century scholars, in their less scholarly moments, from Thomas Becket's clerk to the thirteenth-century abbot of Prémontré.

The first stage in the confusion may have been reached in the seventeenth century. For in 1633 Jean Le Paige, describing Abbot Gervase in his *Bibliotheca praemonstratensis ordinis*, says that he wrote 'epistolas ad diversos, homilias aliquot ut erat ecclesiastes egregius. Item et breves Commentarios in Psalmos et Minores Prophetas.' While we have no trace of so many writings by Gervase,[3] he doubtless preached sermons,[4] and he may very well have composed some short commentaries. But Le Paige's list is strongly reminiscent of Bale: and the catalogue by Bale of 'Homelias aliquot' and 'In Malachiam commentarios . . . In Psalmos Davidis' must surely raise the question: had Le Paige any independent authority for fathering such writings on Abbot Gervase? The answer seems to me doubtful. In any case, almost all who have mentioned the abbot thereafter have copied Le Paige. Le Long went further in 1723 by conflating what he found in Le Paige and in Leland.[5]

---

[1] *Script. ill. maioris Brytanniæ catalogus* (Basel, 1557–9), ii. 206.

[2] J. Pits, *Relationum historicarum de rebus anglicis*, i (Paris, 1619), 224.

[3] Hugo, *Annales*, i. 18–19, says that he had looked everywhere for these works but in vain. Similarly, Lienhart Georgius (*Spiritus literarius norbertinus* (Augsburg, 1771), ii. 237–8): 'qui an adhuc extent, an temporum iniuria perierint definire nolim'. The *Lexicon für Theol. und Kirche* (*ut sup.*) says of these works: 'nur hand-schriftl.'. All references seem to lead back to Le Paige.

[4] Cf. ep. 38 in Hugo's *Monumenta*. Following references to the printed letters are to this edition.

[5] The confusion is undeniably evident in Le Long's work (*ut sup.*). He cites Le Paige as authority for Gervase's authorship of commentaries on the Psalms,

II

The one certain literary production of Gervase, the abbot of Prémontré, is his letters. In the twelfth and thirteenth centuries (not for the first or last time) the epistolary art was practised by high ecclesiastics very extensively. The letter to a friend was the form commonly chosen for a light essay, a sermon, a factual account of a battle, or a philosophical treatise, or a display of literary fireworks about nothing in particular. The technique of letter-writing developed on definite lines laid down in contemporary works on *dictamen,* and even the business correspondence of prelates obeyed its rules. The letters of Abbot Gervase which survive are of this last sort. They contain good doctrine, no doubt; but most of them were not written primarily for edification. They occasionally include passing comments on personal matters, such as the abbot's state of health; but there is nothing in them that is intimate or tender. Every one of the letters, even though it obeys the fashion of filling out plain statements with rhetorical tropes, dealt with some practical problem which necessarily engaged the energies of Gervase as the father-abbot of a great monastic Order, concerned to control and defend dependencies which ranged from Börglum in Jutland to Brindisi in Apulia, and from Ireland to the Holy Land.

The letters interest the historian today mainly for the light which they throw on the Premonstratensians in the thirteenth century, and on the political and ecclesiastical history of the time. They may have survived, however, for another reason. When Gervase was still abbot of Prémontré, in 1218, a canon of the house whom he employed as secretary or amanuensis made a collection, including perhaps a hundred of Gervase's letters. This collection received additions which belong to the abbot's last two years of office and which, with letters found elsewhere, bring the total to 118. The collected letters are not

Isaiah, and minor prophets and refers to Leland for the commentary on Malachi. Daunou (loc. cit., p. 43) attributes to the abbot the commentary on Malachi, but adds uneasily: 'Il se pourrait que ce livre fût d'un autre personnage du même nom, d'un Gervais de Chester, contemporain et ami de Thomas Bekket.' Wright pointed out the error, though he retained the name of Gervase of Chichester (op. cit. ii. 448, cf. 217). Stubbs exposed the confusion thoroughly in *Hist. Works of Gervase of Canterbury,* i (RS, 1879), xxxiii–xxxvi, cf. pp. ii. xlvii–l.

in chronological order and often lack evidence of date, but those written by Gervase all belong to the time of his abbatiate at Prémontré (1209–20), and most of them to the years 1216–19. We are so often presented with medieval collections of letters without knowing how or why they were formed, that the letter with which Gervase's secretary prefaced his collection is of special interest. The disciple seems to regard his master's letters as a monument rather to literary skill than to pastoral and administrative activity. This is how he writes:[1]

To his worthy and worthy-to-be-loved friend and former comrade, Simon, canon of St. Mary of St. Eloi-Fontaine,[2] brother Hugh, least of the brethren of Prémontré, sends his greeting, his prayers (for the little they are worth), and his love.

When formerly you and I, as youths, passed on from the pagan tales of the secular schools to study a superior philosophy and took the habit of religion in different monasteries, it happened that after my probation was over and I had made profession and vowed stability in the monastery and become a canon, I was often summoned by my most revered and dear father Dom Gervase, who begot me through the Gospel, to write down in his presence the letters which he composed (*dictabat*); for, as you know, I was accustomed to the practice of penmanship (*scribendi usum*) from childhood. I relished these letters, albeit incapable of discriminating between them, and I had heard from several people that many commended my abbot for his style of speech and composition (*dictandi*). For these reasons I have put together some letters composed (*dictatas*) by him and written by me, and some others which were before my time and which I lately found thrown aside; so that just as he was the pious teacher and kindly instructor of my youth, so I, if God grant it, might be his humble and diligent imitator both in way of life and in art of writing (*dictandi scientia*).

But since I should not deem complete any pleasure of mine which you did not share, I have decided to send you the collection I have made, together with a *Summa de stylo romani dictaminis* produced, so it is said, by Pope Gregory VIII of holy memory, and another *Summa*, entitled Master Transmundus' *De arte dictandi*—books which my abbot got for me; so that, tasting, you may approve, if you relish what has been already tasted and approved by my

---

[1] Hugo, *Monumenta*, i. l. On the texts of the collected letters see Appendix I below.

[2] Arrouasian abbey of regular canons, canton of Chauny, arrond. of Laon.

hungry self. Admittedly, you may, with the satiety which comes from the discrimination of an unusual intelligence, regard as Abellanian nuts what I, in my hunger, account as precious delicacies. You must know, however, that I have thought fit to slip into this little book some letters sent to my abbot, not so much because their style was elegant as because their senders were important. Therefore I beg you, out of a feeling of intimate friendship and at the risk of forfeiting it, treat carefully this collection which several people have already seen (who, having read it in part, wish to read it through and perhaps transcribe it); keep it properly and return it soon; lest, if it fell out otherwise, David might be obliged to care no more for Jonathan, or—to address you according to the fables of the pagans—Theseus might abjure Pirithous, Pilades ignore Orestes, Tydeus forget Polynices.[1] Farewell, excellent brother, and may these works I send you so work on the mind of the reader that they will be found to have brought profit to his soul, since, when you are engrossed in them, you will forget the world you have forsaken.

Dated at Prémontré in the year of grace 1218, not long after the feast of St. John the Baptist.

The interest of this letter needs no underlining, showing as it does something of the abbot's way of working, the distinction between *dictare* and *scribere*,[2] the compilation and circulation of an epistolary collection, to say nothing of the literary style of the secretary himself.[3] The treatises on *dictamen* which Abbot Gervase had procured for Canon Hugh were two fairly recent and very famous works on the subject, which represented the teaching dominant in Rome and the French schools. Transmundus was a papal notary who flourished in the 1180s, while Gregory VIII (Albert de Morra), for nine years before he

---

[1] 'Thideus nesciat Pollicidem': so Caillieu's text. Hugo's text reads 'Thisbe nesciat Pyramum', which is less satisfactory. The reference is probably to Statius, Thebais, 9, 35 seqq.

[2] Cf. IV Lateran Council ch. 18: 'Nec quisquam clericus literas dictet aut scribat pro vindicta sanguinis destinandas.'

[3] Points of comparison with this letter may be seen in the first of the collected letters of Herbert Losinga, bishop of Norwich (†1119), addressed to his secretary (*Epp. H. de Losinga*, ed. R. Anstruther (Caxton Soc., 1846), p. 1), and in the prefatory letter by Peter of Poitiers to the collected letters of the abbot of Cluny (*Letters of Peter the Venerable*, ed. Giles Constable (Harvard, 1967) i. 1–3). For some features of medieval epistolary collections see ibid. ii. 1–44 and comments by R. W. Southern in *Medieval Humanism* (Oxford, 1970), pp. 86–8, 110–20.

became pope in 1187, was chancellor to his three immediate predecessors. There was perhaps an additional reason why his work should be studied at Prémontré, for he is thought to have been himself a Premonstratensian canon.[1]

Abbot Gervase had certainly taken the lessons of these authors to heart. He handles words with great skill and says what he wants to say fluently and forcefully. His literary style is a trifle less portentous than that of his secretary—F. Petit calls him 'un styliste délicat'[2]—but it is similar in character and obeys the rules of the gregorian *cursus*. His diction is characteristic of his age and circumstances in the free borrowing of biblical expressions; he seldom refers explicitly to other literary sources.[3]

III

The subject which dominates the correspondence is the government of the Premonstratensian Order. The Order was founded by St. Norbert, nearly ninety years before Gervase became fourteenth abbot of the parent-house. It was an Order of regular canons, who lived a monastic life, possessing their property in common, but who were prepared to undertake the ministry of parishes and were much concerned with missions. Like most of the monastic reforms of the early Middle Ages, it had started in France, but its outward spread was rapid. Norbert himself carried it to the frontiers of Germany and the Slav lands, and others planted Premonstratensian houses in all the regions newly organized in the Latin Church of the twelfth and thirteenth centuries—in Sweden, Scotland, Ireland, Spain, Hungary, Greece, and Palestine. The constitution of the Order provided that abbots should attend annual General Chapters at Prémontré and be subject to visitation by representatives of the abbot of Prémontré. The second half of the twelfth century had been the period of greatest expansion. Gervase had

---

[1] See F. Petit, *La spiritualité des Prémontrés aux 12ᵉ et 13ᵉ siècles* (Études de théol. et d'hist. de la spiritualité, ed. E. Gilson and A. Combes, tome x, Paris, 1947), pp. 81–2.

[2] Ibid., p. 279.

[3] He twice quotes Horace's epistles: 1. 2. 40 (ut ait Philosophus) in ep. 13 and 1. 18. 84 (verbum illud Ethnicum sed et ethicum) in ep. 107.

probably joined the Order himself when it was at the height of its popularity in England. Of thirty English abbeys of Premonstratensian canons which existed when he ceased to be abbot, fifteen had been founded within the past forty years. But in the first decade of the thirteenth century (between 1203 and 1209) Prémontré had been ruled by corrupt and inefficient abbots, who had lowered the prestige of the Order.[1]

It fell to Abbot Gervase to remedy this. He had to restore discipline within and to persuade Pope Innocent III that the Order was an instrument for good in the Church, which deserved papal protection. In a strong letter which Gervase wrote to the Pope in 1213[2] he begs him urgently and humbly 'to revert to all your original kindness towards the Order of Prémontré and to go on as you began'. He reminds Innocent that at the beginning of his pontificate he had granted many of Gervase's requests for the good of the Order. 'I know', he says, 'that they would have been more beneficial if the disputes of certain people who sought their private profit had not turned away your favour both from them and from the rest of the Order. Let not your Apostolic Piety be angry for ever with all on account of the sins of a few, as seems to have been the case for some time past.' The pope has turned a deaf ear to his propositions made for the common good. Can it be because the abbot had communicated them by humble messengers, when more dignified envoys were not available?[3] He continues:

[1] Hugo, *Monumenta*, i. praefatio.

[2] Ep. 13. This was written after Gervase heard the pope's summons to a General Council read at Reims. The papal letter is dated in the register 19 Apr. 1213. According to the register (Migne, ccxvi. 826) a copy of this summons was sent to the abbot and convent of Prémontré, but this copy may have only reached Gervase after he heard the copy sent to the archbishop of Reims.

[3] See Innocent III's statement of the correct practice in a letter to Otto, emperor elect, Migne, ccxvi. 1160, and cf. P. Herde, *Beiträge zum päpstlichen Kanzlei- und Urkundenwesen im 13. Jht.* (2nd edn. Kallmunz, 1967), pp. 77–8. Archbishop Robert Winchelsey apologized in 1297 to Boniface VIII for not sending 'ambassatores celebriores ad presens' (*Reg. R. Winchelsey*, ed. R. Graham (CYS), i. 531); and Clement V complained that a messenger of the king of France was of humble station and travelled on foot: 'Magnificentie igitur regie hoc duximus intimandum ut diligenter advertat quod secundum statum negotii pro quo mittere ad nos contigerit studeat deinceps nuntios ipsi negotio congruos destinare' (quoted, Berger, *Les Registres d'Innocent IV*, i (1884), xl–xli). On the rank of envoys see also P. Chaplais in *The Study of Medieval Records: Essays in honour of Kathleen Major* (Oxford, 1971), pp. 33–4, 40–2.

'I humbly prostrate myself at the feet of your Holiness, and thank you most devoutly that, as my returning messengers tell me, you always inquire with fatherly affection what I am doing and what fruits reward my labour. But to this I reply to you plainly that had I not hoped for some relief from your Holiness, I should long ago have cast from my shoulders the burden which is laid upon me. I work hard, hardly to any purpose; nor can I succeed unless your Piety gives ample help to me and my colleagues. For I firmly believe that if your favour towards the Order of Prémontré had lasted until now as it began and if those who ruled the Order meanwhile had responded to the favour you extended to them and had worked in it with proper humility and devotion, there would not be a religious Order today to which clergy and laity would more devoutly flock.'

Gervase's remonstrances took effect. When the abbot attended the Fourth Lateran Council in 1215, he received favours for himself and his Order.[1] Moreover, Innocent III commissioned him to plant Premonstratensian canons in the monastery of St. Quirico, Antrodoco, in the diocese of Rieti, from which some evil-living Benedictine monks, who had murdered their abbot, were expelled.[2] This settlement caused Gervase a lot of worry in the next few years, as we learn from his letters to the abbot whom he had installed under a mistaken view of his capacity, and to the cardinal-priest Leo, on whom he relied to supervise a house so far removed from the mother-house at Prémontré. He has to warn the abbot[3] against incautiously harbouring fire in his bosom: 'you will be harbouring it', he writes, 'if you receive into your monastery monks of the Abruzzi who wish to make profession in our Order; for they are Lombards, and cunning beyond measure and practised of old in the flatteries of the deceitful.' To the cardinal he complains[4] that he had taken pains to choose an abbot who was religious-minded and lettered, and he is convinced that he had found such a man; 'but now', he says, 'I am still more firmly convinced that he is such a simpleton that he is like a sprig of vine stuck in the earth which retains its greenness without

---

[1] *Mon. Germ. Hist. SS.* xxvi. 457 (Anonymi Laudunensis canonici).
[2] Epp. 26–32.   [3] Ep. 28.   [4] Ep. 30.

spreading its shoots out wide or lengthening its roots in depth, certain to die without giving fruits or sets; for he is said to be no good, as regards spiritual edification, at choosing brethren or as regards temporal advantage, at constructing buildings, nor is he successful in promoting the business of his Order in the Roman Curia.'

Questions of discipline naturally called for most correspondence when they cropped up in distant provinces. Then the abbot of Prémontré could not visit in person and sometimes had to look outside the Order for a deputy. He writes to the bishop of Thebes[1] to ask him to supervise the Premonstratensians in his diocese (of whom the old historians of the Order have no other trace). He appoints the abbot of Milevsko to visit the monasteries of eastern Europe, saying: 'We have sent visitors and correctors not once but many times, concerning whom it fell out (if we are rightly informed) that either they neglected their charge or they were not admitted with proper respect by those to whom they were sent.' He expresses alarm at rumours about the prevalence of private property among the Premonstratensians of Poland, Bohemia, and Hungary, and quotes the Rule of St. Augustine on the subject.[2]

The distant monasteries often caused anxiety of a different sort to the head of the Order. Twice on his travels the abbot had to subvent a wretched canon of Börglum who was reduced to terrible straits by poverty and robbers during his journey to and from Rome on conventual business.[3] On another occasion, Abbot Gervase sent Isaac, an Irish canon of Tuam, to the abbot of Vicoigne.[4] Isaac had appeared at Prémontré to learn French and to see how the mother-house maintained the discipline and rigour of the Rule, 'which', writes Gervase, 'he perhaps does not see in his own church, for the canons there are few and the people are barbarous'. Gervase approves his intention but would have approved it still more had he come properly clothed. Last year, in the depth of winter, three other brethren of the same house had come ill-clad to Prémontré, and this year there were seven other guests who needed clothing. So

---

[1] Ep. 88. See Backmund, i. 402–3 for the abbey of Hermokastron.
[2] Ep. 119. Milevsko was founded 1187, near Tabor, in the diocese of Prague.
[3] Ep. 108.   [4] Ep. 73.

the abbot of Vicoigne is asked to take his share of the burdens which fall on Prémontré and admit Isaac. He must console him, as one who has not been brought up in the strictness of the cloister and the rigour of the Rule.

Besides this letter about the Irish and another[1] addressed to Whitehern in Galloway (where the cathedral church was manned by Premonstratensians), a dozen of these letters are addressed to England. It is therefore remarkable that no English historian has (to my knowledge) made use of the collection.[2] One of these letters, to Hubert de Burgh, congratulating him on his appointment as justiciar, shows that the abbot contemplated the union of the abbeys of St. Radegund, Bradsole, and West Langdon, on account of poverty:[3] this union never took effect. Another letter permits the reception of the widowed mother of the abbot of Alnwick 'in the house of Ghines'.[4] It is significant of the vague nature of the attachments which often bound nunneries to particular religious Orders that Abbot Gervase says: 'this house of Ghines is entirely unknown to me'. Modern historians are hardly in a better case. For though the place may be identified with Guyzance, on the Coquet, the evidence for the existence of a nunnery there is scanty in the extreme.[5] A third letter to England appoints the abbot of Begham as visitor of St. Radegond's. Others arrange for the admission of a canon to Alnwick, and for the punishment of two forgers, who were canons of Egglestone and St. Agatha's, Easby.[6]

Letters 40 and 41 are addressed to the cardinal Guala Bicchieri, during his legation in England (1216–18) to safeguard the exemption of the English Premonstratensians from the Crusading tax of a twentieth and to plead for the less culpable

---

[1] Ep. 92.

[2] T. D. Hardy noticed them in his *Cat. of Materials for Brit. History* (RS, 1862–71), iii. 48, but Gross did not. The most startling neglect of them is in *Collectanea anglo-praemonstratensia* (Camden 3rd series, vi, x, xii, 1904–6), ed. F. A. Gasquet. Mr. H. M. Colvin uses them in *The White Canons in England* (Oxford, 1951).

[3] Ep. 77.   [4] Ep. 69, cf. 70.

[5] See Colvin, *White Canons*, pp. 332–4 and C. T. Clay, *Early Yorkshire Charters*, xii (Yorks. Archaeol. Soc. Record Series, Extra Series vol. x, 1965), 13–15. The priory's existence was unknown to the editors of *Mon. Ang.* and *Coll. anglopraem*.   [6] Epp. 80, 128, 125.

among those English canons of the Order who had supported
the rebels against King John and had thus incurred sentence of
excommunication. But letter 41 is also of interest for an obscure
comment on the political situation in England. There has been
a threefold peace-proposal, said to have emanated from the
Apostolic See, which—had any part of it been put into effect—
would have disgraced the whole Church and the legate.[1] This
letter was probably written in summer 1216;[2] but it is difficult
not to associate this *triplex forma* with the 'triplex forma pacis,
quarum quelibet honesta et rationabilis erat et a viris dominum
timentibus merito acceptanda', to which the bishop of Winchester and his colleagues had referred in their letter of
5 September 1215 to Archbishop Stephen and his suffragans.[3]
The earlier reference has been taken to point to the settlement
at Runnymede,[4] but the phrase does not necessarily imply that
the peace-terms had taken effect and the context suggests that
the opposition of the magnates to them preceded their first
diffidation and the capture of London. Moreover, the pope is
said to have provided this *forma* in the presence of and with the
consent of the magnates' messengers. These facts, together with
Gervase's statement, point to some rejected (and lost) proposals
for peace made to the magnates' messengers at Rome in March,
1215, about the time when John obtained papal letters to
Langton and his suffragans and to the magnates and barons of
England.[5]

Of all the letters to England, no. 13 is of most general
interest. It is addressed to Archbishop Stephen Langton and
from internal evidence may be dated July–August, 1215, before

[1] 'Triplex forma pacis quae (ut dicitur) a sede apostolica emanavit, quarum
quaelibet (si fuisset ad effectum perducta) in totius ecclesiae et vestram nihilo-
minus ignominiam redundasset. . . .'

[2] Cf. references to Gervase's illness here and in epp. 2 and 33. Certainly not
before Guala went to England in May, 1216.

[3] Edited by F. M. Powicke, *EHR*, xliv (1929), 92.

[4] Ibid., p. 87 and H. G. Richardson, *BJRL*, xxix (1945), 192.

[5] *Foedera* (Rec. Commission), i. i. 127. In reaching this conclusion I have been
helped by Miss Stella Whileblood's discussion of the letter of 1215 in her unpublished thesis, 'Anglo-papal relations 1213–1216' (Manchester M.A., 1947).
Sidney Painter independently criticized the accepted view in his *Reign of King
John* (Baltimore, 1949), pp. 345–6. See also C. R. Cheney in *BJRL*, xxxviii
(1955–6), 316–17. J. C. Holt, *Magna Carta* (Cambridge, 1965), pp. 293–5, discusses further the problem of the *triplex forma*.

news had reached Prémontré of the renewal of civil war after Magna Carta and of the condemnation of that document by the pope. It has been overlooked by the historians of the period. Since it shows how the political disturbances of England might appear to an Englishman abroad in 1215 and also illustrates well the abbot's literary style, it shall be quoted in full:

Gervasius Stephano episcopo Cantuariensi.[1]

Sine sollicitudine nescit esse dilectio, nec permittit charitas quiescere cor amantis, donec de dilecti statu aliquid certi cognoverit, unde debeat vel in adversis compati vel in prosperis collaetari. Solebant sane sciscitanti mihi valde laeta de vobis ab intermeantibus responderi quod illa videlicet dilectionis aurora, quae post longam irarum caliginem illucescens dudum erga vos serenavit cor regis, iam in perfectum diem profecerit, adeo ut non auderet quis casum ponere quo, qui videbatur fervor, deberet in vesperam declinare. Laetatus sum satis hinc non immerito, quod inde fuit nacta oportunitas unde data facultas ut in multitudine populorum quae vestrae sollicitudini est commissa verbi dei semina spargerentur, et lucra fierent animarum. Sed dum sustinui pacem, ut multiplicaretur in dies, dum quaesivi desiderio mentis bona, ut scilicet laetis laetiora succederent, ecce quidam auribus meis nuper in alleluia paschalium gaudiorum triste aliquid infuderunt, videlicet quod suscitata dissensio inter regem et principes pacem regni turbasset, et iratis invicem qui regere videbantur in discrimen tribulationis et angustiae qui regi debuerant offendissent. His igitur auditis incommodis non potui, fateor, non sollicitari pro vobis, attendens nimirum quia paterne curaretis tumultuantes filios mitigare, hinc plebium pusillanimitatem erigere, quae prae timore consolationem vix rapiunt, hinc effraenos principum motus reprimere, qui prae feritate consilium non admittunt. Non enim potui de vobis praesumere, quod sine mentis perturbatione possetis videre mala gentis vestrae, nec sine animi cruciatu maiorum discordias, minorum formidines, et quod amplius est, intermissa animarum negotia sustinere. Sed postquam iratus fuerit, recordabitur misericordiae suae deus, et rebus per gratiam suam et laborem vestrum compositis, excocto iam semine lachrymarum, fructum vos faciet colligere gaudiorum, curretque ut coepit velociter sermo eius per quem in coelestes recubitus gregatim animae inferentur. Sane cum, sicut didici, desiderata

[1] The protocol is both abridged and corrupted. Other letters in the collection show the usual formulae of title and address. Gervase would undoubtedly have put Stephen's name before his own.

pax inchoata sit, congratulor non immerito non modicum ipsi paci, quae licet nondum consummata sit pro voto, quia tamen, ut ait Philosophus, dimidium habet facti, qui coepit, ipsam pacem inchoatam non censui sine congratulatione debita relinquendam, plenam concipiens ex dei benignitate fiduciam quod qui coepit in vobis ipse perficiet, firmabit, solidabitque, et pacem desideratam iamdiu concludet exitu glorioso. Sane quia culpa est, sicut scitis, persequi culpam totam, necesse est propter malitiam dierum praesentium et frigescentem in pluribus et fere in omnibus charitatem ut cum moderamine exerceatur severitas et aliquid habeat admixtum mansuetudinis rigor ecclesiasticae pietatis, ne peccator cogatur contemnere cum venerit in profundum, et qui delinitus potuit invitari ad veniam, exacerbatus provocetur ad culpam. Prorsus cum iam regis ferocitas in parte non modica mitigetur, per quod digne potest praesumi de eo quod sanctae ecclesiae sit satisfacturus ad plenum, si tamen tractetur non aspere, sanctae paternitati vestrae consulo quatenus in causa ecclesiae pro qua vos dominus murum opposuit contra eum, in quantum permiserit iustitia et honestas mansuetudinem exeratis, quae si fuisset, ut credimus, exerta iampridem ecclesia pro qua statis non inferiorem fuisset gloriam consecuta. Valete.

Besides being a fine specimen of Gervase's skill in the *ars dictandi*, this letter shows a more detached attitude to the troubles in England than we can expect to get from the opposing parties. And although the abbot of Prémontré may have been less well informed of the true facts than were people on the spot, he was an Englishman by birth, his connections with England were close, and he knew some of the parties concerned.

Amid the flowers of rhetoric in this letter we first discern a reference to the settlement between Church and State reached by King John and Pandulf in May, 1213. This was the dawn of the king's favour. Daylight increased with the welcome to Langton in July, 1213, the lifting of the Interdict in July, 1214, and various royal acts in favour of the Church which were done in the winter of 1214–15. And then, at Easter 1215, had come news of the dispute between king and magnates which was gradually coming to a head since January. The ensuing peace of which Abbot Gervase has heard and which impels him to write must be the settlement at Runnymede. King John announced that he had made peace with his barons on 19th June, and Stephen Langton with other bishops ratified that peace. The exhortation to Langton to exercise moderation has more than a touch of criticism about the conduct of the Church's case against John in the past. Maybe it was not good advice that Gervase gave, but it was characteristic of him and we cannot dismiss it as manifestly unreasonable. With it we may compare a remark by Gervase in a letter written in the summer of 1216 to Simon, archbishop of Tyre, legate in France. This shows that Gervase had no sympathy with the clergy who supported the baronial party when Prince Louis came on the English scene at their invitation. He says: 'I am deeply grieved that when England was on the verge of peace, it was prevented by just four clerics: would that they had never learnt their letters.'[1]

The proportion of this correspondence which stands outside the normal business of the Order is not large, but is considerable. The most important letters in the category are certainly those which concern Crusades. The relief of the Holy Land was a cause which lay very near the heart of Innocent III, and one in which the Premonstratensians distinguished themselves by their preaching.[2] These letters include several to and from the king and patriarch of Jerusalem,[3] others about the collection of money from Crusaders for commuted vows,[4] and two letters[5] of outstanding interest from Gervase to Innocent III (in June 1216) and Honorius III, which probably state more forcibly than any other contemporary document some defects in the organization of the Crusade. It was the one great common endeavour of Latin Christendom in this age, but Gervase warned the pope not to let the French and Germans travel upon it together (for they never agree in any great enterprise), not to allow the funds to be embezzled, not to let the privileges of the nobles be a scandal to the poorer pilgrims, and so on.

---

[1] Ep. 34. Simon Langton, Gervase of Hubbridge, Elias of Dereham, and Robert of St. Germain had been concerned with bringing Prince Louis to England (C. Petit-Dutaillis, *Étude sur . . . Louis VIII* (1894), p. 161).

[2] See H. Roscher, *Papst Innocenz III und der Kreuzzüge* (Göttingen, 1969); M. Maccarrone, *Studi su Innocenzo III* (Padua, 1972), pp. 86–163; F. Petit, *La spiritualité*, ch. v: 'L'esprit de la croisade'.

[3] Epp. 36–8, 84, 115.   [4] Epp. 33–5, cf. 2.

[5] Epp. 2, 4 (translated in *Hist. litt. de la France*, xviii. 45–50). Ep. 4 is reprinted in *Rec. des hist. de la France*, xix. 618–20.

Other letters, relating to the Albigensian Crusade, include the letter[1] which Alice de Montfort and her sons wrote to Gervase to announce the death of Simon de Montfort before Toulouse on 28 June 1219: an event which led Gervase to observe in his reply that 'precious in the sight of the Lord is the death of his saints', while it drew bitterly ironical verses from a poet of Languedoc: 'If by killing men, . . . by consenting to murders, . . . by starting conflagrations, . . . by seizing lands, by advancing the proud, by kindling evil and extinguishing good, by killing women and children, one can gain Jesus Christ in this world, he may well wear a crown and shine in Heaven.'[2] Abbot Gervase had already sent one of his canons on a preaching tour to stimulate the faithful to attack as early as February 1213.[3] He now promised further support.

IV

It is tempting to continue with quotation and analysis. But we may conclude by remarking, first, how many important trivialities are embedded in these letters; secondly, how much emerges from them about Gervase himself.

Some throw light on the ways by which news was transmitted in the thirteenth century,[4] and the use of merchants as postmen (especially when hirelings of the excommunicate Emperor Otto lay in wait for clerks bearing letters from the Curia);[5] others demonstrate the danger of getting papal letters drafted in the wrong form,[6] and the tiresome ambiguity of some papal mandates.[7] We see, too, the haste to execute a papal mandate when the pope was ill (lest he should die and the mandate be invalid).[8] We learn that it was difficult to hire large

[1] Ep. 97. The reply is ep. 98.

[2] *Chanson de la croisade albigeoise*, ed. Paul Meyer, i. 351.

[3] Ep. 43.

[4] Epp. 37, 41, 72, 88.

[5] Epp. 108, 120. See 'Chronicon Emonis' for a Premonstratensian's experience in 1212 (Hugo, *Monumenta*, i. 437).

[6] Epp. 15, 108. In the second of these letters MS. Rawl. C. 533 (ep. xxxix) supplies a necessary emendation to Hugo's text: 'excepto quod in eis de ecclesia vestra nulla mencio facta fuit quod esset cathedralis.'

[7] Epp. 2, 8; cf. above, p. 36.

[8] Ep. 8. Cf. *Extra*, 1, 29, 19; also Migne, ccii. 1538–9 and *Extra*, 5, 32, 2.

carts in springtime in Picardy,[1] and that lodgings were dear in Rome at the time of the Fourth Lateran Council.[2]

As for Gervase himself, his letters contain no reminiscences, no intimate revelations of his feelings. They are not letters of kinds to show all sides of his character; but something of the man is revealed by the friends with whom he corresponds and by his reaction to the situations which the letters describe. Pope Innocent III had been friendly towards him long before he reached the headship of his Order, and when the pope was dead, Gervase recalled[3] that 'in his lifetime he loved me and greatly honoured me'. It is even possible that they knew each other in the schools of Paris before Gervase took the cowl, and that Gervase, as a canon and proctor of his Order, had appeared at the Curia before Innocent in 1198. At Paris, too, he might have formed the friendship which emerges from these letters with Master Philip the Chancellor,[4] with Master Stephen Langton, and with one Master Peter of Northampton, a regent master in canon law.[5] Gervase was evidently on fairly familiar terms with Peregrinus, archbishop of Brindisi, and several of the cardinalate at Rome. When he writes to Hubert de Burgh, he wishes to be remembered 'to my venerable friend your chaplain, Luke,' of future fame as archbishop of Dublin, a man influential in Church and State. The chancellor of Wells Cathedral is another English correspondent to whom the abbot writes familiarly.[6]

These indications suggest that Gervase was a man who moved freely among ecclesiastical statesmen and scholars. His

---

[1] Ep. 112.   [2] Ep. 108.   [3] Ep. 114.

[4] Epp. 10, 87. He wrote to Honorius III on Philip's behalf and at his request, when the latter was summoned to Rome to answer charges against him in 1219 (cf. Pott. 6173). For Philip see J. B. Schneyer, in *Beiträge zur Gesch. der Philosophie und Theologie*, xxxix. 4 (1962) and N. Wicki in *Lexicon für Theologie und Kirche*, viii (1963), 452–3, 450 for the distinction between him and Philip de Grève.

[5] Ep. 57. The name is *Norhant* in Hugo's edition, *Northampton* in Rawl. MS C. 533 fo. 53ᵛ. Gervase writes a testimonial to the *scolasticus* of Reims for Peter, whom he describes as 'dilectus et familiaris noster' and who wishes to 'regere in facultate sua' at Reims. This may be the Master Peter of Northampton who appears later in Lincoln records (*Rotuli Hugonis de Welles* (CYS ii. 271) and *C. & S.* ii. 274 n. 2).

[6] Ep. 72. The initial *L.*, which appears in the printed editions and the Rawl. MS., does not agree with the name of any known chancellor.

English origin may account for the high proportion of Englishmen among those just named. He was not by any means the
only Englishman to be found on the continent in the habit of
a Premonstratensian. Bartholomew, a canon of Prémontré, was
a relative of the abbot, employed by him in Italian affairs.[1]
A sub-prior of Prémontré in his time apparently hailed from
Northumberland.[2] Soon after his time, William, abbot of Dale,
became head of the Order. There may have been an earlier
English Premonstratensian of some distinction, named Richard,
who went to Germany about 1180.[3] The anonymous chronicler
of Laon, who stopped his annals at 1219, is thought to have
been a Premonstratensian and an Englishman.[4] But it is
significant that the Anonymous did not think the English
origin of Abbot Gervase worthy of comment, although he
found space to praise him. Nor did the English connection
disqualify Gervase in 1220 from being appointed to rule the
bishopric of Sées, recently transferred from the Angevin empire to the kingdom of France. Like Stephen Langton and
other Englishmen of his day, Gervase had been content to
live for many years under the rule of Philip Augustus, while
that king was at war with the king of England; and whatever
his sentimental attachment to England, political nationalism
was not among the obligations of his office.

The letter to Stephen Langton shows that Gervase was disposed to live on good terms with the lay power, despite the
disputes over jurisdiction which were always disturbing relations between Church and State in one part of Europe or
another. He was evidently on good terms with William des
Roches, seneschal of Anjou,[5] and with Simon de Montfort the
elder;[6] and in conducting the affairs of his Order in Bohemia
he steered a careful course in the midst of the battle over
clerical privilege which was raging between King Ottokar II

---

[1] Epp. 29–30.   [2] Ep. 70.

[3] Colvin, *White Canons*, p. 324. Cf. N. Backmund, *Monasticon praemonstratense*,
ii (1952), 19.

[4] Cf. G. Waitz, *Mon. Germ. Hist., SS.*, xxvi. 442.

[5] Ep. 95: 'cum a longis retro temporibus constet nobis quod sis vir bonus,
faciens iustitiam et promovens aequitatem . . .'

[6] Ep. 98: 'quem, dum viveret, tenerrime dileximus, sed et ipse, secundum
quod credimus, tenerrime nos dilexit. . . . Quem, dilectus ab ipso specialiter,
a tenera sua iuventute dilexi.'

and Bishop Andrew of Prague. His letters to the king and the marquis of Moravia are diplomatic expressions of neutrality.[1] This reflects the traditions of the Premonstratensian Order, which seems to have leaned heavily on the lay power. In Germany the canons distinguished themselves in the service of the Empire.[2] In England some of the principal patrons of the Order were the great civil servants of the Angevin kings, Ranulf de Glanvill and his nephews, Hubert and Theobald Walter, William Brewer, Geoffrey FitzPeter, and Robert Turnham.[3] On 23 December 1208, when Gervase was on the point of succeeding to the headship of Prémontré, the Order obtained from the pope a significant privilege: its members were not bound to cite, admonish, or excommunicate magnates and nobles within whose lands the property of the Order lay.[4]

Just as his efforts to please the laity did not preclude plain speaking upon occasion, so in his relations with the popes he combined the most profound reverence for papal authority with firmness and frankness in the statement of his recommendations and complaints. He won the respect of both Innocent III and Honorius III. The Anonymous of Laon notes as a sign of the favour he enjoyed at the Curia in 1215 that 'neither the pope nor any of the cardinals would receive any gift from him';[5] it was, if true, a singular compliment. In the words of Gervase, 'all churches come out from the womb of the sacred Roman Church, just as all rivers come out from the sea and return again to it';[6] and 'when we are bitten by the fiery serpents of the world's malice', the Apostolic See is the brazen serpent on which we gaze in order to be healed.[7] 'The Lord Pope', so Gervase reminds two Bohemian abbots, 'is the head of the universal Church.'[8] 'Rebellion is as the sin of witch-

---

[1] Epp. 99–101. e.g. ep. 100 (to the marquis): 'Si dicti rex et episcopus sint discordes, nos in neutrius favorem interponimus partes nostras, sed oramus pariter pro utroque, ut pax Christi exultet in cordibus eorundem.'

[2] 'in imperii obsequiis'—the words are of the Austin canon Rahewin, quoted J. de Ghellinck, *L'essor de la litt. latine au xiie siècle* (Brussels, 1946), i. 201.

[3] Cf. Stubbs, in *Chronica R. de Hovedene* (RS), iv p. lxiii n. 1 and Cheney, *From Becket to Langton*, p. 38.

[4] Le Paige, op. cit., p. 649 (Pott. 3582).

[5] Loc. cit., p. 457.

[6] Ep. 20. Cf. Eccles. 1: 7.

[7] Ep. 45. Cf. Num. 21: 6–9.

[8] Ep. 72.

craft.'¹ But these sentiments do not prevent the abbot from speaking bluntly to the pope. When the pope issues mandates in ignorance of the facts of a case, this is what Gervase writes:²

When the atmosphere of Apostolic calm is disturbed by the fraud and malice of petitioners, so that thunderous mandates descend from the eminence of the Roman See, I should be troubled and stricken with grievous terror, did I not know that even this same Vicar of Christ, who holds the position of Peter's oarsman, can in such matters be deceived like a mortal man; his temper must, I am sure, become tranquil, when the cloud of falsehood is dispelled by the sun of justice, so that the ray of truth shines forth.

This is a prelude to the exposure of his adversaries and the thinly-veiled assertion that the pope does not know what he is about. His protests recall the better-known complaints of Robert Grosseteste to the Curia. There is the same mixture of candour, argumentation, and submissiveness.

He was a vigorous defender of his Order. That not only emerges from the letters³ which record particular attacks upon its exemption; it is visible in his exhortation to abbots to avoid occasions for disciplinary action by the pope,⁴ and in his faintly slighting references to monastic Orders deemed stricter than his own. Let an apostate Premonstratensian abbot be forced either to obey the regulations of his own Order or to betake himself 'to other religious, more excellent than the Premonstratensians, whom he may choose to obey'.⁵ Within the Order itself, he believed in exercising strict authority over all the daughter-houses, and set store by the formalities of obedience. Among the collected letters is one from the sub-prior of Prémontré to the abbot of Alnwick;⁶ the writer ends with a piece of advice: 'Take care about one small matter. When you write to the abbot of Prémontré, do not leave out the word "obedience" in your preliminary greeting. Say *salutem et devotam obedientiae voluntatem*; otherwise your letters may get a rough reception.'

---

¹ Ep. 63. Cf. 1 Kings 15 : 23. This was a commonly quoted text: e.g. Gregory, *Moralia*, lib. 35, 13, contained in Gratian's *Decretum*, C.8, q.1, c. 10.
² Ep. 16, cf. 17–19.
³ Epp. 5–6, 15, 20–5, 44–8.   ⁴ Ep. 78.
⁵ Ep. 11, cf. 314 and 125.   ⁶ Ep. 70.

This insistence on the etiquette of letter-writing does not indicate a martinet. The abbot's discrimination in awarding and recommending punishment[1] bespeaks a man who was not merely a competent organizer and administrator but also a pastor of experience and sensitiveness. He recognized that his office demanded a great variety of qualities and he had no use for abbots who were decrepit or unfit to administer property or control a community.[2] When he wrote[3] to the prior and convent of Clarholz, instructing them to elect a new abbot, he told them what sort of man to choose:

Such a person as shall not be too simple in the conduct of external business, since St. Gregory says[4] that those are to be appointed to the rule of churches in these days who not only think of the cure of souls but also are provident and prudent in the management of worldly affairs, and who know how to turn from Mary's contemplation to the carefulness of Martha.[5]

This was, indeed, no more than a commonplace. The idea is prominent in Gregory's *Pastoral rule*, and in the time of Abbot Gervase we find it expressed (for instance) in the customs of English Austin canons.[6] Nevertheless, it shows the type of life which Abbot Gervase tried to live, his energies divided between things spiritual and temporal. He does not figure prominently among the spiritual authors of Prémontré; and yet, when a modern writer on the subject goes out of his way to drag Gervase into their midst, the good abbot does not seem to be in uncongenial company. These letters of his are not notable sermons, like some of St. Bernard's or of Gervase's contemporary the Cistercian Abbot Adam of Perseigne; but in them we discern the balanced person whom the Anonymous

[1] Epp. 41, 67–68, 110, and below, Appendix II, no. lxvi.
[2] Epp. 83, 111 (? both concerned with the abbot of Vicoigne), and above, p. 250.
[3] Ep. 106.
[4] The sentiment is expressed in the *Regula pastoralis*, pars. ii. 7, but a closer parallel is in Gregory's letters, lib. 8, ep. 40, contained in *Decretum*, D. 39 c. 1.
[5] Luke 10: 38–41. Cf. below, p. 273 n. 2, and Innocent III's letter in Migne, ccxvi. 25–6.
[6] *Observances in use at . . . Barnwell*, ed. J. W. Clark (1897), p. 43: 'The Prelate ought to be specially careful to attend to spiritual things in such a way that he be not dull in temporal things; and to be careful about temporal things in such a way that he neglect not spiritual things.'

of Laon described on his elevation to Prémontré. He called Gervase *vir modestus, religiosus, et discretus.*

APPENDIX I

THE TEXTS OF THE LETTERS OF ABBOT GERVASE

The first printing of a letter of the abbot seems to be by Aubert Le Mire, in *Ordinis praemonstratensis chronicon* (Cologne, 1613), p. 162. This is the letter addressed to the patriarch of Jerusalem, numbered by Hugo ep. 38. Le Mire does not clearly state his source; and as he is obviously ill informed about Abbot Gervase, it is unlikely that his text came directly from an extensive collection of the letters. It shows, however, few variants (mostly they are obvious corruptions) from Hugo's edition. In 1633 Le Paige (*Bibl. praem. ord.*, p. 305), noted that Gervase 'scripsit epistolas ad diversos'. In 1663 Fr. Norbert Caillieu published at Valenciennes a collection containing seventy letters, with the prefatory letter of Canon Hugh, which is translated above, from a manuscript then in the Premonstratensian abbey of Vicoigne.[1] I have been unable to trace the manuscript. In 1725 the Premonstratensian abbot C. L. Hugo published at Étival his *Sacrae antiquitatis monumenta historica, dogmatica, diplomatica*;[2] this contains 137 letters, with the prefatory letter. Hugo found this collection in a manuscript of the abbey of Steinfeld, in Westphalia; I have been unable to trace this.[3] Another

---

[1] The only copy I have traced is in the Bibliothèque Nationale. The title-page reads: *Epistolae reverendissimi in Christo patris ac domini D. Gervasii Praemonstratensis abbatis, postea Sagiensis episcopi, ex veteri celeberrimae Viconiensis monasterii Bibliothecae manu-scripto editae, opera R. P. F. Norberti Caillieu, facultatis Parisiensis doctoris theologi, nec-non archimonasterii Praemonstratensis prioris.* 'Gloria eorum non derelinquetur.' Eccli. 44 [printer's device] *Valencenis, Typis Ioannis Boucher, sub nomine Iesu, 1663.* The book is licensed by an abbot of the Order, 8 November 1662, and by a censor at Valenciennes, 22 December, 1662. In addition to the letters, which occupy pp. 1–104, there are eight letters by the editor concerning Jean Launoy's attack on the privileges of the Order, and seventeen *pièces justificatives* (pp. 105–61). Three unnumbered pages follow with a list of the Gervase letters. *Hist. litt. France*, xviii. 44 states that Caillieu's edition was published at Mons in 1662. I have found no confirmation of this.

[2] Imprint: 'Stivagii, J. M. Heller.' It is also found with the title: *Accessiones novae ad historiam ecclesiasticam et civilem*, and the imprint: 'Francofurti ad Moenum apud Franciscum Varrentrapp 1744.'

[3] After the canons fled from Steinfeld during the French Revolutionary wars, books from the library were badly treated and many doubtless destroyed: see F. X. Boos, 'Fragment eines Necrologiums der Abtei Steinfeld aus dem xiii. Jh.', in *Eüfalia*, iii (Trier, 1829), 43–50. I am indebted to the late Walther Holtzmann for the above reference and for notice of nine former MSS. of Steinfeld in

collection exists in a manuscript of the latter part of the thirteenth century, of English origin, now MS. Rawlinson C.533 in the Bodleian Library. On fos. 27ᵛ–116ʳ are copied 101 letters, numbered and rubricated, with the original title: 'Incipit quedam pars registri G. abbatis Premonstr.'¹ In addition to these collections, Hugo has given us a letter of Gervase to Pope Celestine III on behalf of the warlike Philip de Dreux, bishop of Beauvais, who had been imprisoned by Richard I,² and a letter of Gervase to Innocent III on behalf of Master Emo, canon of Werum in Frisia, on his way to the Curia in 1211.³

The contents of the three collections—Caillieu's, Hugo's, and the Rawlinson MS.—show differences of some interest.

1. The seventy letters in Caillieu's edition correspond to epp. 1–2, 4, 33–43, 14–29, 44–83 of Hugo's collection, in that order. These include nothing demonstrably later than the date of Canon Hugh's preface to the collection, i.e. end of June, 1218. Letter I was probably written in 1209.

2. Hugo's 137 letters include all those found in Caillieu's collection, with additions of various dates both before and after 1218. Of these, 108 are written in Gervase's name, four in the name of the General Chapter of Prémontré, and twenty-five by twenty-one other correspondents (mostly addressing Gervase). They include letters of Abbot Gervase which belong to 1219 and possibly 1220, and still later letters of his successor Conrad and of Pope Gregory IX. We infer that Caillieu's collection represents the compilation of Canon Hugh (in original or copy) and that Hugo's is a second recension made after 1227.

3. MS. Rawl. C. 533 seems to be limited to letters written between 1214 and 1219. It is not prefaced by the letter of Canon Hugh; while it contains eighty-nine of the letters found in Hugo's edition

modern German collections. Two others survive in B.M. MSS. Add. 21109, 24682. Cf. Norbert Backmund, *Monasticon praemonstratense*, i (Straubing, 1949), 193. Dr. Rose Graham called my attention to stained glass from Steinfeld in the Victoria and Albert Museum.

¹ For the full contents of the MS. see W. D. Macray's catalogue. The letters are numbered vii–civ, with unnumbered letters xii *bis*, xxii *bis*, xxxvii *bis*. A folio missing between fos. 112–13 contained the latter part of the hundredth letter (ep. 99 in Hugo's numeration).

² *Monumenta*, sig.a verso, from 'Vita Gervas., MSS. Viconien.'.

³ Ibid. 436–437 (in the *Chronicon Emonis*). A valuable letter of the men of Hythe to Gervase is printed in *Mon. Ang.*, vii. 942a. I do not note existing routine official *acta* of Gervase preserved elsewhere (e.g., Hugo, *Annales*, II. ii. p. cxc) nor do I note the papal letters addressed to him as head of the Order or as bishop of Sées.

(of which fifteen are not the abbot's),[1] and all of Caillieu's collection save the first letter, it also has twelve others (of which six are not the abbot's), which are not found in either of the printed editions.

It seems, then, that collections 1 and 2 are closely related, while 3 stands apart. But all three are sufficiently similar to suggest that a single official or semi-official collection was the ultimate source of all. The title of the Rawlinson collection (*quedam pars registri*) points to the regular registration at Prémontré of some at least of the abbot's official correspondence. In the early thirteenth century, indeed, something of the sort had become the order of the day in many secular and ecclesiastical chanceries, even if systematic and classified registers belong for the most part to a later generation. Mr. Pantin has shown how English monastic letter-books of the later Middle Ages combined the objects of legal record and of formulary and might include, into the bargain, letters of purely personal or historic interest.[2] In the Bodleian MS. Ashmole 1519 we have such a register prepared for Bishop Richard Redman, Premonstratensian abbot of Shap (*c.* 1459–1505).[3] But if a register of official correspondence, including letters received as well as letters set out, was kept at Prémontré in Abbot Gervase's time, it does not follow that the letters copied into the Rawlinson manuscript represent a complete section of this register or even follow the sequence of letters in the original. For they can have been only of formal or historic interest at the time of copying. In other words, the compiler of Rawlinson C.533 or its archetype had much the same interests as had Canon Hugh, whose letter precedes the Caillieu and Hugo collections. Neither compiler was concerned to make a complete copy of the material at his disposal, and so their selections differ. Neither compiler was interested in maintaining chronological order, and so the sequence of letters differs.[4]

Finally may be noted another collection which has not been traced, which appears in the catalogue of books of St. Radegund's Abbey, near Dover, written about 1300. Here, significantly enough among the books *De Gramatica*, occurs 'liber epistolarum Gervasii

---

[1] It omits Hugo's epp. 1, 5–13, 30–2, 84, 87–94, 105–7, 115–37. The sequence of letters common to the two collections varies greatly.

[2] 'English monastic letter-books', in *Hist. Essays in honour of James Tait* (Manchester, 1933), pp. 201–22, especially pp. 204, 206, 209.

[3] Used by Gasquet for *Collect. anglo-praem.* (see i., pp. xiv–xix). See also H. M. Colvin in *JEH* viii (1957), 96–7. The formulary-element is evident in the extracts it contains from letters of Peter of Blois (i. 205–7, cf. 252–63).

[4] There is, of course, no reason to suppose that strict chronological order was maintained in the official register (cf. Pantin, loc. cit., p. 210).

abbatis praemonstratensis duplex cum aliis inscriptis in duobus voluminibus'[1].

A similar register from the end of the thirteenth century probably lies behind the collection in Soissons, Bibl. municipale MS. 8, described by C. V. Langlois in *Notices et Extraits des MSS. de la Bibliothèque Nationale* . . ., xxxiv 1ᵉ partie (1891), 305–22: 'Le formulaire qui occupe les 64 premiers folios a été compilé à Prémontré par un anonyme qui disposait de la correspondance de l'abbé Guillaume de Louvignies [1287–1304] et de ses prédécesseurs immédiats, très probablement pendant le pontificat de cet abbé.' It is followed by the *Summa dictaminis* of Master Ralph of Vendôme. Mr. Colvin kindly called my attention to Langlois's account of this volume.

APPENDIX II

The following letters,[2] of which six are Gervase's, occur in the *Pars registri G. abbatis* in MS. Rawlinson C. 533 and are not in the collections printed by Caillieu and Hugo (cf. Appendix I, above). They are printed here with the numbers and titles which appear in the manuscript.

[fo. 56ʳ] xxxv. *Obligacio pro nuncio.*

Universis Christi fidelibus etc. Ad sedem apostolicam nuncium et canonicum sacerdotem latorem presencium pro certis negociis dirigentes, per hoc scriptum certam caucionem prestamus quod si idem noster nuncius necessarium habens mutuo accipere pecuniam pro commissis sibi negociis promovendis debitum usque ad centum marcas argenti vel infra contraxerit cum aliquo creditore, nos ipsi vel ipsius certo nuncio ad representacionem scripti presentis satisfacere curabimus competenter, in eo termino atque loco qui de nostri nuncii et ipsius creditoris[3] assensu fuerint constituti.

[fo. 83ᵛ] lxvi. *Exauditur supplicacio pro recepcione monialium.*

Reverendo in Christo patri et domino dei gracia venerabili Tullanensi electo[4] G. dei paciencia Premonstrati dictus abbas salutem et tam devotum quam debitum reverencie fa-[fo. 84ʳ]mulatum. Generositas sanguinis exquirit a vobis quod degeneres mores

---

[1] *EHR*, liii (1938), 92.

[2] I am obliged to Professor Otto Skutsch, for reading these letters and for making several suggestions which I have adopted.

[3] MS. *credidoris.*

[4] Gerard de Vaudemont, elect of Toul, 1218, died in 1219.

persequi debeatis, et excellencia nichilominus dignitatis exposcit
ut sic diligatis personas quod sciatis culpas nec fovere nec diligere
in personis. Nuper sane recepimus literas vestras deprecatorias pro
sororibus ecclesie de Chebrel,[1] que cum propter inobedienciam
manifestam excommunicate sint ab abbate suo, immo per abbatem
a nobis, ad vos habere confidunt recursum, sperantes quod in hac
novitate vestra debeatis omnium misereri et de facili suggestiones
illarum admittere que primo adcedunt ad vos gratia supplicandi.
Verum si exposita esset vobis infamia qua laborant et cognita ad
plenum dissolutio diutina earundem, aut non rogaretis pro illis, aut
non esset vobis molestum si preces pro eisdem porrecte non
haberent effectum. Verumtamen cum noticiam vestri habuerimus
ab antiquo, nolentes primicias precum vestrarum omnino repellere,
de multa misericordia et quodammodo contra honestatem nostram
ad preces vestras permittimus ut ille que obedientes mandatis ordinis
exierunt et morate sunt aliquandiu in domibus alienis in locum pristi-
num [fo. 84ᵛ] revertantur. Ille vero que usque modo in sua contumacia
perstiterunt, modis omnibus exeuntes, extra claustrum suum moram
faciant usque ad proximum capitulum generale, tunc quidem sub
condicione huiusmodi reversure quod conversacione honesta dis-
solucioncm redimant retroactam, et in novitate spiritus ambulantes[2]
in famam convertant infamiam[3] qua laborant, sciture[4] proculdubio
quod si ex resumpta conversacione priori cicatrix infamie recrudes-
cat, nullius a nobis intervencio optinebit quin partes morbidas que
fomentum non senciunt, ut dignum fuerit, abscidamus.

[fo. 87ᵛ] lxxi. *Accusatus iniuste exposcit ut reconcilietur.*

Reverendo domino et patri G. dei providencia Premonstrati
abbati venerabili frater J.[5] sue sanctitatis servus se totum in fide et
lenitate[6] ad pedes. Si loquor ad dominum meum cum sim pulvis et
cinis, canis mortuus, pulex unus, arrogancie non ascribat. Nam
quasi loquendi veniam impetrat ac meretur quod immerito sum
affectus quod absque [fo. 88ʳ] offensa offensus est michi pater in
quo sperabam, tanquam erraverim corde et posuerim os in celum,
extendens manum ad archam et in Christum deum verbum mittens.

---

[1] Chebret (dep. of Aisne) in the diocese of Toul.
[2] Cf. Rom. 6 : 4 and 7 : 6.
[3] MS. *infamiam convertant in famam.*   [4] MS. *scituri.*
[5] The following letter shows that this was a canon of the Prem. abbey of
Val-Secret (dep. of Aisne), in the diocese of Soissons.
[6] Cf. Ecclesiasticus 45 : 4. This is the first of twenty-four obvious correspon-
dences with the Vulgate which have been noticed in this letter. The rest will not
be noted here.

Domine, qui omnia nosti, qui scrutaris renes et corda, si super-
exaltatum est cor meum et elati sunt oculi mei contra dominum et
amicum, si grandia sum locutus vel solo verbo modice deroga-
cionis montem tetigi utpote unde sperabam auxilium michi suo
tempore proventurum, fiam sicut ablactatus super matrem suam vel
sicut fenum tectorum de quo non implebit manum suam qui metet
et qui manipulos colliget sinum suum.[1] Saltem antequam turbaretur
dominus meus et a corde suo evomeret servum suum, descendere
primitus debuisset et videre utrum verbum quod ad ipsum cum
massis palatarum suarum Siba detulerat verum esset, et tunc demum
vel persequeretur suo domino detrahentem vel odio delatorem[2]
haberet qui ponebat michi scandalum et meis cupiebat carnibus
saturari. Neque enim esset adeo detestabile factum eius si inter
fratres vel pares discordiam seminaret, cum omnis similitudo amica
sit sibi et paria cito conveni-[fo. 88ᵛ] ant. Set cum domino servum,[3]
magistro discipulum, et subiectum exosum fecerit potestati, quatenus
peccaverit satis patet, cum minor non possit repellere vim maioris
cum efferbuerit ira eius. O, si michi desuper datum esset ut sermones
illi quibus iram merui saltem in plumbi lamina scripti essent, ex
eorum inspeccione dominus meus proculdubio quievisset nec
tanquam mortuum a corde oblivioni traderet servum suum qui
ab ipsa puericia ipsum verbo, opere, et veritate dilexi. Quem enim
videns, omnia diligencius commendavi, quem super capud meum
libercius promovissem dum adhuc preesset ecclesie Sancti Iusti,[4]
vel quem maiori dilexerim caritate tu nosti. Unde qui inperas ventis
et mari et obediunt tibi, redde michi graciam salutarem, ne si
recesserit a me dominus et amicus operiat confusio faciem meam,
et pene penitus deficiam cum de dampno meo gavisus fuerit inimicus.
Memoretur igitur bonus pater quo desiderio, quo ardore, sue
quondam caritatis visceribus sim insertus,[5] nec eum peniteat admi-
[fo. 89ʳ]sisse in suam amiciciam oleastrum,[6] qui quosdam olive
ramos trunco nobili fictis vel pocius falsis ramusculis adherentes in
fructu amicicie vellem precedere, si meis vel ope vel operibus
indigeret. Testor itaque deum et sanctos angelos eius quod in illo
verbo michi imposito et opposito non peccavi, et tamen in amaritudine moratur oculus meus et cor meum conturbatum est intra me

---

[1] Ps. 128: 6-7 reads: Fiant sicut fenum tectorum, quod priusquam evellatur
exaruit: De quo non implevit manum suam qui metit, et sinum suum qui manipulos colligit.

[2] MS. *dolatorem*.   [3] MS. *dominum servo*.

[4] Gervase was abbot of St. Just (dioc. Beauvais) from 1195 to 1199.

[5] MS. *ingertus*.

[6] MS. *oleastram*. Cf. Romans 11: 17, etc.

quaqua plaga[1] doloris. Cicatrix iam et tempore et racione debuisset obduci illorum et relacione abbatum per quos super hoc apud excellenciam vestram credo me habundancius excusatum.[2] Neque enim cum de mandato vestro fecissent scrutinium patres illi, in tota multitudine vel unicus est inventus qui michi testimonium non redderet meam innocenciam proclamanti, cui eciam accusatoris calumpnia non pateret. Super quo eciam venerabilis in Christo patris abbatis Vallis Christiane[3] literas apologeticas impetravi, ut si michi non creditis in re mea, eius saltem credatis apicibus fidedignis. Unum dico et non perfunctorie set fideliter et audacter, quod in toto ordine non est homo quem vobis preferam in amore; quapropter eius [fo. 89ᵛ] michi memoria est amara qui elongare a me amicum et proximum attemptavit, pro quo si volueritis resistam ei in facie coram vobis ac de falsi suggestione convincam. Nam cum nemo propheta acceptus sit in patria sua, non esset michi difficile, precipue cum plures me advocent nobiles et potentes, mutare locum et habitum, ut, iuxta poetam,[4] qui[5] color est albus, cesset contrarius albo. Set cum in vobis fixerim ancoram spei mee, indecens esset ut ibi fluctuaret et periclitaretur conteri, ubi eam pro quietis et pacis dulcedine collocavi. Sedebo itaque solus et repletus amaritudine donec aspiret dies et inclinentur umbre, donec voce vel literis certioratus fuero de vestra michi amicitia restituta, qua cum sim citra merita spoliatus, restitucionem eius piis non omittam precibus postulare.

lxxii. *Excusatur frater innocens.*[6]

Reverendo patri ac domino G. dei providencia abbati Premonstrati frater R. eiusdem permissione Vallis Christiane dictus abbas salutem et obedienciam debitam ac devotam. Memorari posse vestram credimus sanctitatem venerabili in Christo fratri L. abbati Carthouor'[7] ac nobis per vestras quondam literas precepisse quatinus, ad ecclesiam Vallis [fo. 90ʳ] Secrete[8] personaliter accedentes, de quadam commocione facta contra abbatem loci et quibusdam

---

[1] MS. *plage*. Possibly the original had *quaque plaga*.
[2] Cf. no. lxxii, below.
[3] Val-Chrétien (dep. of Aisne), in the diocese of Soissons.
[4] Ovid, *Metam*. ii. 541 reads: Cui color albus erat, nunc est contrarius albo.
[5] MS *qui*, which appears also as a variant in some Ovidian MSS. This pretended quotation is not easy to construe, though the meaning is clear that the writer contemplates removing from the Order of White Canons to the Order of Black Monks.
[6] This is obviously the letter referred to in no. lxxi, above.
[7] Chartreuve (dep. of Aisne), in the diocese of Soissons.
[8] Val-Secret.

contumeliis quibus idem abbas sicut dicebatur afflictus fuerat et affectus diligenter inquirere veritatem et eam vobis sub sigillis nostris clausam transmittere curaremus. Vestrum igitur exsequentes mandatum ad ecclesiam venimus supradictam, et scrutantes diligencius de premissis, pacata omnia invenimus et placata. Set ne vestri videremur suppressores mandati, communi commemoracione exulcerati, fecimus factum illud, in virtute obediencie et sub periculo animarum omnibus inperantes quatinus nos instruerent de eodem, precipue autem de quodam verbo quod abbas non ex certa scientia set firma quadam opinione inponebat fratri Johanni, videlicet quod absque vestra gracia ipsum promoverat in abbatem sollicite perscrutantes et aliquandiu laborantes, maxime propter instanciam et inportunitatem eiusdem J. qui purgare innocentiam suam per omnium testimonia nitebatur, dolens et conquerens vehementer quod apud beatitudinem vestram falso fuerat accusatus, pro certo didicimus quod non protulerat verbum illud nec [fo. 90ᵛ] quicquam aliud quo vestra intumescere sanctitas debuisset, qui etiam erubescebat et confundebatur nimium perturbatus eo quod nec opinari quidem tale quid voluistis de eo qui ab ipsa puericia vos dilexit. Nolentes ergo quod opinio alicuius prevaleat vel preiudicet veritati, ad peticionem eiusdem ipsum literulis nostris duximus excusandum, ne fumus mendacii vestrorum[1] obfuscet circa amicos aciem oculorum.

lxxiii. *Pax reformatur inter abbatem et quosdam nobiles.*

G. dei paciencia Premonstrati dictus abbas venerabili in Christo fratri N. abbati Belle Vallis[2] salutem et scinceram in domino caritatem. Nostis sane ut credimus quamdiu et quantum viri nobiles castellanus moromensis[3] et sororius eius laboraverunt ut quedam filia ipsius reciperetur apud Cresciacum[4] in sororem, racione cuiusdam obligacionis qua de recipiendis mulieribus successive que directe de castellanis moromensibus nascerentur asserunt ecclesiam Belle Vallis sibi esse astrictam. Quia igitur idem R. intencionem suam probavit per testes, volentes paci petentium in presenti et vestre indempnitati[5] in posterum provi-[fo. 91ʳ]dere, concessimus eis ut filia memorati R. quam ab eo volumus vobis exprimi nomina-

---

[1] MS. repeats here *circa amicos.*

[2] Belval-Bois-des-Dames (dep. of Ardennes), in the diocese of Reims. Abbot Nicholas was in office in 1209 (Hugo, *Annales*, i. 258).

[3] Probably Mouron (dep. of Ardennes), S.E. of Vouziers.

[4] Crécy, near Grand-Pré (dep. of Ardennes). Cf. Hugo, *Annales*, i. 561 and Backmund, *Monasticon*, i. 25.

[5] MS. *idemptitati.*

tim ab instanti Nativitate Sancti Johannis Baptiste in annum recipiatur Cresciaci in conversam. Volumus autem ut supradicti nobiles
caveant vobis super obligacione predicta quod causa vel occasione
ipsius non debeat ecclesia vestra aliquo tempore in posterum
molestari.[1]

[fo. 91ᵛ] lxxv. *Conquestio de abbate dampnoso et quod advocata permittat
quod alius abbas preficiatur.*

Illustri matrone in Christo karissime M. domine Sablolii senes-
calle andegavensi[2] G. etc. Meminimus nos olim scripsisse vobis et
cum affectione multimoda vos rogasse ut pauperem ecclesiam de
Bosco Ranulphi[3] quam recolende memorie R. de Sablolio pater
vester fundavit vestro foveretis auxilio et illis precipue qui in ea
extirparent vicia et virtutes insererent prestaretis solacium et
iuvamen, ita ut ex ipso solacio adhoc [fo. 92ʳ] eis prestito, et ecclesie
provectus ordinis et vobis proveniret incrementum salutis. Verum
cum nuper significatum sit nobis quod ipsius ecclesie ordinacioni
et provectui resistatis, in eo maxime quod pastorem illum reprobum
et delicatum fovetis qui in ea abbatis et nomine gaudens et locum
occupans bona pauperis ecclesie exinanire non desinit, per hoc
quod senciens se religiosorum graciam amisisse ob captandum
favorem secularium non erubescit cum illis in exquisitis epulis con-
vivari, miramur plurimum quod in manifesta dilapidacione bonorum ecclesie que ex patrimonio vestro fundata est reticetis et cum
tot clamantibus non clamatis, ut confusi actus eius in discussionem
veniant licet sero. Tolerari tamen posset utcunque quod ignominiam
eius silencio verecundo contegitis, set quia adicitis ut laudetis
peccatorem et benedicatis iniquum insuper et ne deiciatur resistitis,
hoc est precipue super quo et de vobis miramur et ecclesie condo-
lemus. Verumptamen cum status ipsius ecclesie per insufficienciam

[1] In 1225 it was found that the number of nuns at Crécy had increased, but
not the endowments, and it was ordered that no more nuns be admitted (Hugo,
Annales, i. 563).

[2] Margaret, daughter of Robert IV, lord of Sablé, in Anjou, married William
des Roches, seneschal of Anjou about 1190 (G. Dubois, in *Bibl. de l'École des
Chartes*, xxx (1869), 381). The following letter in the Rawlinson MS. is addressed
to her husband on the same matter, and uses some of the same phraseology as
this letter. The letter to William is in Hugo's collection, ep. 95.

[3] Bois-Renou, either identical with or transferred to Le-Perray-Neuf (Perre-
dium, arr. La Flèche, dep. of Sarthe) in the diocese of Angers. According to
Hugo, the abbot of whom complaint is here made is Stephen, and the date 1216
(*Monumenta*, i. 84 notes, *Annales*, ii. 546). By 1218 there was an abbot to whom
Gervase entrusted the supervision of a most unusual form of abbatial election
by lot at L'Étoile (dep. of Vendôme) in the diocese of Chartres (ep. 76). The
lady Margaret was buried at Le-Perray-Neuf in 1235.

eius multimodam et vicinis in opprobrium et nobis datus sit in lamentum, cum eciam dissolucio eius tanta sit ut illustris viri W. mariti [fo. 92ᵛ] vestri discrecionem et modestiam superarit, ita ut idem maritus vester ei exprobrando obiecerit quoddam verbum quod dignum memoria nullatenus esse debet, nobilitatem vestram affectuose rogamus quatinus sustineatis benigne immo et interponatis sollicitius partes vestras, si tamen opus fuerit, ut amoto eo quem publica convincit infamia instituatur abbas alius ibi qui et in spiritualibus dilapsa resuscitet et resuscitata multiplicet et in temporalibus dispersa congreget et congregata conservet. Nuncios autem nostros quibus ordinacionem loci vice nostra committimus vestre caritati attencius commendamus.

[fo. 99ᵛ] lxxxv. *Admonicio super spoliacione restituenda.*

A. sancti Petri et R. sancti Vedasti decanus Suession'¹ dilecto in Christo presbitero de Septem Vallibus salutem in omnium salvatore. Auctoritate domini pape qua fungimur in hac parte vobis firmiter iniungendo mandamus quatinus Colardum, parochianum vestrum, diligencius ammonentes ad hoc inducere satagatis ut cum ipse quibusdam terris, vineis, arboribus ecclesiam Premonstrati [fo. 100ʳ] spoliaverit, prout ex confessione ipsius in iure facta didicimus manifeste, in possessionem omnium rerum ablatarum mittat ecclesiam memoratam et de fructibus medio tempore perceptis satisfacere non omittat. Quod si ad ammonicionem vestram id facere recusarit, singulis diebus dominicis et festivis, accensis candelis, excommunicetis eundem necnon et omnes illos qui eum in contumacia sua fovere aut ei sive in molendino sive in furno sive in negociacione aut alio quocunque modo presumpserint communicare. Hoc igitur mandatum nostrum, immo apostolicum, taliter impleatis ne ecclesia sepedicta pro defectu iusticie ad nostram audienciam recurrere compellatur et nos a vobis et culpam requiramus et penam.

[fo. 105ʳ] lxxxxii. *Regraciacio oracionum concessarum.*

Reverendo in Christo patri G. abbati premonstratensi et abbatum eiusdem ordinis generali conventui Engelbertus dei permissione sancte coloniensis ecclesie archiepiscopus² salutem et intime dilectionis constanciam. Gracie vestre literas per abbatem de Kenestede³

¹ The deans of the churches of Saint-Pierre-du-Parvis and Saint-Vaast, Soissons.

² Engelbert I, archbishop of Cologne, 29 Feb. 1216–7 Nov. 1225.

³ Gottschalk I (1216–26), abbot of the Prem. house of Knechtsteden (Kr. Neuss), in the diocese of Cologne. (Hugo, *Annales,* ii. 5 and Backmund, *Monasticon,* i. 177).

dilectum nostrum nobis transmissas ea qua decuit recepimus benignitate, et inspecto earundem tenore, quod participacionem [fo. 105ᵛ]
oracionum et omnium spiritualium beneficiorum que in ordine
vestro decetero fient nobis concedere dignati estis, ad graciarum
vobis assurgimus uberimas acciones, quod pro tanta gracia a sancti-
tate vestra nobis concessa, cordi nostro non modica iocunditas est
infusa, cum id supra meritorum nostrorum exigenciam nobis
duxeritis concedendum. Indubitatam igitur de fraternitate vestra
gerentes fiduciam, vobis devotissime supplicamus ut quod circa
personam nostram liberaliter fecistis, de vestra solita clemencia
dignemini innovare, securi de nobis quod vigili cura et studio
diligenti super hiis intendere curabimus que comodum vestrum
pariunt et honorem.

lxxxxiii. *Innovacio oracionum conceditur.*

[R]everentissimo in Christo patri et domino E.¹ dei providencia
sancte coloniensis ecclesie venerabili archiepiscopo frater G. dei
patiencia Premonstrati dictus abbas et abbatum eiusdem ordinis
capitulum generale salutem et cum oracionibus scincere devocionis
obsequium. Dignacionis vestre litteras grato recipientes affectu,
evidenter satis comprehendimus in eisdem et eum quem erga
ordinem nostrum geritis paterne scinceritatis affectum et proprie
cautelam salu-[fo. 106ʳ]tis. Unde istud laudabile in vobis exhiberi
videmus quod in prelatis nostri temporis passim minime reperitur,
quod in rerum videlicet culmine constituti, quod pontificali dignitate vigentes, inter mundi turbines et negociorum perplexa volumina non obliviscimini status vestri, ut de Marthe sollicitudine
interdum fiat reditus ad Mariam et inter Lye lippitudines² interioris
sollicitet iocunditatis amplexus pulcritudo Rachelis, sitque ipsa
sponsa variis hinc inde sumptis nominibus, ex meritis accionum
nigra pariter et formosa.³ Sane oraciones quas innovari petistis
libenter et fideliter innovantes, ut in conspectu domini aromatum
fumus ascendat, et perpetue caritatis incensum vigeat iugiter in altari,
concedimus vobis plenam omnium oracionum et spiritualium beneficiorum tocius nostri ordinis participacionem ad mortem pariter et
ad vitam, et preter hec cum generali capitulo sub testimonio presencium vester fuerit obitus nunciatus, tantum fiet pro vobis quantum
pro uno ex nostris, in missis, oracionibus, et in psalmis. Quia
denique spirituali quadam proximitate utpote frater ordinis astrictior

---

¹ MS. *G.*, but Engelbert is obviously intended.
² Cf. Gregory, Moralia, vii. 37 and Hom. Ezech. ii. 2.
³ MS. *pariter* follows *et formosa*, marked for transposition; cf. Cant. 1 : 4.

solito nobis estis, vestre dilectissime fraternitati [fo. 106ᵛ] supplicamus humiliter et attente quatinus intuitu dei et proprie honestatis
ecclesiam claholtensem[1] protegere et defensare velitis, ut sub alis
vestre proteccionis in eius obsequio cui servire regnare est et
devota permaneat et secura consistat. Specialiter autem cuiusdam
Frederici[2] qui in eadem ecclesia fuit, in qua sibi multum nocuit et
aliis parum profuit, necnon et consanguineorum eius reprimatis
insultus, ne vir religiosus qui ipsi ecclesie modo preest per im-
portunitatem ipsorum, si locum habuerint malignandi, inpedi-
mentum accipiat quominus proficere possit in spiritualibus et in
temporalibus reformandis. Dat' Premonstrati anno gracie m° cc°
xviii in crastino beati Dionisii [10th Oct., 1218].

[fo. 107ᵛ] lxxxxv. *Oraciones ordinis conceduntur episcopo linguonensi.*[3]

[R]everendo in Christo patri et domino G. dei gracia quondam
lynguonensi episcopo[4] frater G. dictus abbas Premonstrati et abbatum eiusdem ordinis capitulum generale salutem et cum oracionibus scinceram ad obsequia voluntatem. Receptis literis paternitatis
vestre in quibus nostre ordinis petistis vobis oraciones concedi, ex
humili earum peticione quadam sumus erga paternitatem vestram
speciali affectione commoti. Attendentes igitur et humilem peti-
tionem necnon et vestram devocionem erga ordinis nostri ecclesias
pariter et personas, plenam omnium oracionum et spiritualium
beneficiorum tocius ordinis nostri participacionem ad vitam concedimus et ad mortem. Specialiter autem inobitu vestro, cum nostro
capitulo generali sub presencium testimonio fuerit nunciatus, tantum fiet pro vobis quantum pro uno ex nostris in missis, oracionibus,
et in psalmis. [fo. 108ʳ] Rogamus autem quatinus, recentis huius ac
spiritualis fraternitatis intuitu, devocio quam erga ordinem nostrum

---

[1] Clarholz (Kr. Wiedenbrück), in the diocese of Osnabrück.
[2] Other letters about Frederick and his predecessor are in Hugo's collection,
epp. 11, 94, 104–7. Ep. 94 is addressed to Archbishop Engelbert, and is
dated [1218] by R. Knipping, *Die Regesten der Erzbischöfe von Köln*, iii (1909),
42 n. 222. Knipping does not record the letters printed above. For the wicked
Frederick of Clarholz 1188–1216, see J. P. Schneider, 'Propst Friedrich von
Clarholz' in *Westfäl. Ztsch.* (1884), 107–28, and *Anal. praem.*, v. 333–6, vi. 281–
332. Ep. 122 was written by Gervase to Engelbert on another matter.
[3] Besides this and the preceding letters, there are several in Hugo's collection
requesting or granting confraternity with Prémontré: ep. 51 (to Queen Inge-
borg), 52 (from the bishop of Bamberg), 53–4 (from and to the bishop of Laon),
90 (to the bishop of Winchester), 91 (to the archbishop of Sens). Another *forma*
for a letter of this sort, employing some of the same phrases, is printed by Le
Paige, *Bibliotheca*, i. 323–4.
[4] Guillaume de Joinville, bishop of Langres 1209–18, translated to Reims early
in 1219.

hactenus habuistis in posterum non tepescat set cotidianum sumat ex divino munere incrementum.

[fo. 114ᵛ] Centesimum iii. *Ne convocacio aut festa fiant in primis missis celebrandis.*

Frater fratri salutem et scinceram in domino caritatem. Veniens pridie Premonstratum R. celerarius de Radulphi Vadis[1] rogavit me ex parte vestra ut cum ipse et frater G. venirent Cussiacum,[2] ego cum illis veniens vestre prime misse satagerem interesse. Ego itaque ad ammonicionem eius proposueram ut venirem, set cum idem R. post prandium evocans me in partem moneret me semel et iterum ut venirem munitus pittancia bona pariter et honesta, concidit vultus meus et aversum est cor meum a proposito veniendi. Porro si ex sensu suo hoc dixerit, indulgeatur ei, quia novi eum esse et in verbis facilem et in loquendo minime circumspectum. Set si processit ex vestro mandato vel consilio verbum illud, scire vos volo quia non proposui pre gaudio presbiteratus vestri facere neomenias vel eciam scenophegias veteris testamenti,[3] in quibus secundum nominis interpretacionem solebant veteres in umbraculis [fo. 115ʳ] epulari. Scenos enim umbra, fagin comedere, dicitur, sicut forsitan ipsi nostis. Consulo igitur vobis et mando ex debito fraternitatis affectu, quatinus, cooperante dei gracia caveatis ne primicie divini ministerii quod geritis appetitu inanis glorie vicientur, set ad hoc precipue dirigatur intencio ut sacerdocium vestrum illi proveniat ad honorem qui ex dignacione sua pocius quam ex meritis vestris in usum huius ministerii vos assumpsit. Exturbetur a mente vestra omnis appetitus preminencie temporalis, ut in ea humilitas solita perseveret, ne dum exterior homo vester causa presbiteratus extollitur, interior detrimentum ex inani gloria paciatur. Plura siquidem de ordine presbiteratus ad exhortacionem vestram in modum tractatuli scriptitarem nisi fraternitatis affeccio quam in vobis sencio tepidam, immo nullam, a scribendi proposito me averteret, vim tamen michi faciens si aliquando exoccupatus fuero, extorquebo forsitan a meipso ut in hac parte exequar quod propono, cum tamen in vobis resuscitatum comperero fraternitatis affectum. Ceterum quidam nescio quis Henricus de Florefia qui ut intellexi Cussiaci moram [fo. 115ᵛ] facit, misit michi nuper ridmum

---

[1] Presumably the house said by Hugo to have been founded from Cuissy, and described by him (*Annales*, i. 114) as *Rodulphi Vadum*, or Roüez, near to Genlis. This was presumably Rouy, a few kilometres S.E. of Villequier-Aumont, or Genlis (arr. Laon, dep. of Aisne), in the diocese of Laon.

[2] Prem. abbey of Cuissy (dep. of Aisne), in the diocese of Laon.

[3] Cf. 2 Chr. 2 : 4 and 1 Macc. 10 : 21.

quendam adulatorium, cui libenter si multiplices mee occupaciones permitterent responderemus, eo quod videbatur michi rithmus ille multis vigiliis et studio comparatus. Illum autem H. peto ex parte mea velud specialem amicum attencius salutari. Valete in domino et super consequenda humilitate intima pro me et pro vobis apud dominum laborate.

ciiii. *Abbas petit ut episcopus auxilietur canonico suo in agendis.*

Tusculanensi[1] episcopo. Cum semper crediderim ex quo in noticiam vestram veni quod personam meam licet immeritam dilexeritis et ipsa dileccionis veritas erga me et multociens et multipliciter apparuerit in effectu, curavi hactenus et semper deo dante curabo ut erga vos iugiter in graciarum accione persistam et ad vestre obsequia sanctitatis devotam habeam voluntatem, paratus per omnia devocionem ipsam exerere per effectum cum modicitati mee vel posse dabitur vel oportunitas offeretur. Unde fit ut cum necessitate aliqua ad apostolicam sedem recurrens serenitati vestre me oportet pro [fo. 116^r] petendo consilio supplicare, ipsa promptitudo obsequii quam in me sencio supplicandi dat ausum, et benignitas quam in vobis ex premissis conicio[2] inpetrandi pollicetur effectum. Sane licet vobis in iterata peticione possim forsitan onerosus videri, attendens tamen quod is ex cuius dileccionis veritate presumitur ex peticionis frequencia non lassatur, serenitati vestre omni qua possum devocione, attencione supplico et affectu, quatinus latores presencium N. et N. habeatis in domino[3] commendatos et eisdem in procurandis negociis que illorum sollicitudini sunt commissa, et illo precipue super quo alias scripsi vobis etiam pro quo[4] sum constitutus in arcto, eo quod michi nondum ab apostolica[5] dignacione responsum est super illo, consilii vestri velitis patrocinium inpertiri. Porro ut pro dicto negocio supplicarem secundo compulit me quidem et necessitas qua coarctor et confidencia qua presumo.

---

[1] MS. *Tusculanessi*. Nicholas, cardinal-bishop of Tusculum, to whom Gervase wrote a similar letter in Hugo's collection, ep. 61.
[2] MS. *cōnicio*.
[3] MS. adds *collaudatos*, expunged.
[4] MS. has *alias . . . quo* as a marginal addition by the original hand.
[5] MS. adds *sede*, expunged.

14. A Letter of Pope Innocent III and the Lateran Decree on Cistercian Tithe-paying*

IT has long been recognized that the decrees of the Fourth Lateran Council of 1215, which marked so important an advance in papal lawmaking for the Church Universal, were not the product of a sudden impulse which moved the Fathers of the Council to think out novel doctrines, new remedies for abuses, new administrative devices. All, or almost all, represent a careful digest, presumably prepared in the Curia before the Council opened, of rules which had been stated locally but not universally, or adumbrated but not defined or, if defined, not enforced. Some were theological tenets long debated in the Schools, others were practices hallowed by local enactment or usage. As a whole the decrees mark the culmination of a period of speculation and experiment in matters of doctrine and Church government which can be traced uninterrupted from at least the pontificate of Alexander III; on several matters they indeed only reiterate Alexander's decrees in the Third Lateran Council. The famous decree of the Fourth Lateran, *In singulis regnis* (c. 12), which inaugurated a system of provincial chapters for the Black Monks and the Black Canons, great innovation as it was, was avowedly based upon Cistercian experience; moreover, it had been foreshadowed in the papal correspondence of the earlier years of Innocent III.[1]

Another decree which concerned the monasteries was c. 55: this too had its antecedents.[2] It required the Cistercians to pay

---

* First published in *Cîteaux: Commentarii Cistercienses*, 1962, fasc. 2, pp. 146–51. The letter has been printed in French translation from this text by R. Foreville, *Latran, I, II, III et Latran IV* (1965), pp. 332–3.

[1] See on this subject M. Maccarrone, *Studi su Innocenzo III* (Italia Sacra, vol. 17: Padua, 1972), pp. 226–62, and works cited there.

[2] C. J. Hefele, *Hist. des Conciles*, ed. H. Leclercq, V. ii (1913) 1376–7 and *Extra*, 3. 30. 34.

tithe on lands which they acquired in future to those churches
which had received the tithe in the past, even if the monks
cultivated the land by their own hands or at their own cost;
or else they were to compound for the tithe. The rule was extended to other Orders possessed of similar privileges. The
rule was made, it was said, to encourage prelates to protect the
monks more effectively against ill-doers and to observe their
privileges more perfectly. It was an important decree which,
though it did not preclude later arguments and appeals about
its interpretation, was manifestly an attempt to end the wrangling over tithe-privileges which had disturbed the Church and
given the Cistercians a bad name in many quarters for many
years. A quarter of a century earlier the General Chapter of
Cîteaux had forbidden (except in certain cases) the acquisition
of more land by purchase, the object being 'to moderate greed
and to remove the taint of constantly acquiring with which we
are charged'.[1] In this context the Lateran decree has been commented upon by modern historians of the Order.[2]

But the preamble to the decree deserves special notice:
'Nuper abbates Cisterciensis ordinis in generali capitulo con-
gregati ad commonitionem nostram provide statuerunt ne de
caetero fratres ipsius ordinis emant possessiones de quibus
decimae debentur ecclesiis, nisi forte pro monasteriis noviter
fundandis. Et si tales possessiones eis fuerint pia fidelium
devotione collatae aut emptae pro monasteriis de novo fundandis
committantur aliis excolendae, a quibus ecclesiis decimae per-
solvantur.' The statute of the General Chapter to which the
pope referred survives: in the edition of Fr. J.-M. Canivez it is
c. 54 of the year 1214, and it reappears but slightly modified
in 1215 as c. 65.[3] Although it resembles the preamble of the

---

[1] *Statuta Capit. Gen. Ord. Cisterciensis*, ed. J. M. Canivez, i (Louvain, 1933),
117: 1190 c. 1.

[2] E. Hoffmann, 'Die Entwicklung der Wirtschaftsprinzipien im Cister-
zienserorden während des 12. und 13. Jahrhunderts', *Hist. Jahrbuch*, xxxi (1910),
716–18, 722; D. Knowles, *Monastic Order in England*, pp. 351–6; J. B. Mahn,
L'Ordre Cistercien et son Gouvernement des Origines au milieu du xiiie Siècle (1945),
pp. 106–15; Joseph Turk, 'Cisterciensium patrum instituta', *Cistercienser-Chronik*,
lii (1940), 101–7, 118–23, 132–41.

[3] *Statuta*, ed. Canivez, i. 427–8, 448. Whether the statute of 1215 represents an
official reissue or some confusion in the textual tradition does not affect the
present discussion.

Lateran decree closely enough to be identifiable, there are differences between the two documents. The statute forbids the purchase or acquisition of lands, vineyards, ovens, or mills, unless they are given in pure alms and solemn gift; and if they are given they shall not be cultivated by the monks' hands or at their expense, but sold to others or committed to others for cultivation. Nothing is said about tithe; nothing is said of an exception in favour of newly founded houses. The disparity may possibly explain why, in the General Chapter of 1216, it was proposed to reconsider or re-draft (*retractare*) the statute.[1] But it is more significant, for our present purpose, to note the pope's statement in the Lateran decree that the Chapter of Cîteaux acted on his admonition.[2]

Hitherto, no such general admonition seems to have been known to modern historians. True, one letter that has some bearing on the case has been known from its inclusion in the papal register. On 20 June 1213 Innocent III had written to the Cistercians and Hospitallers of the diocese of Pécs (Fünfkirchen), in Hungary, complaining that according to their diocesan they were buying vineyards and selling the produce, which was in excess of their own needs. Their privileges meant that churches which had previously received tithe from these vineyards were now deprived of it. The pope admonished them to desist from such practices, which caused scandal; otherwise the General Council (already summoned to meet in November 1215) would have to curtail or revoke their privileges. The pope ended his letter with his familiar threat that they who abuse a privilege deserve to lose it.[3] But there is no suggestion here that the General Chapter of the Order of Cîteaux was being invited to provide a remedy.

---

[1] Ibid. i. 449 (1216 c. 2): 'Sententia de non acquirendo retractatur'. This was noted by H. D'Arbois de Jubainville, *Étude sur l'État intérieur des Abbayes Cisterciennes* (1858), p. 279, who regarded it as a repealing of the statute ('on la raya l'année suivante', cf. p. 294). This meaning is not excluded, but recurrent orders 'de retractandis deffinitionibus', committed to the abbot of Cîteaux and others, suggests that revision, not rescission, was intended (*Statuta*, 1214 c. 31, 1215 c. 15, 1216 c. 52, 1217 c. 54).

[2] As noted by Hoffmann, loc. cit., p. 722 and L. J. Lekai, *Les Moines Blancs* (1957), p. 265.

[3] Migne, ccxvi. 886–7. Cf. for example, Migne, ccxiv. 426, ccxv. 755, 788, 874. For the origin see Friedberg's note to *Decretum*, C. 11 q. 3 c. 63.

It may be that such an invitation appears in the letter printed below. This is the second of two letters of Innocent III which were entered by two early thirteenth-century hands on the last leaf of a copy of Rabanus Maurus super Libros Regum, well written *circa* 1200, bearing an inscription (? xiii century) on fo. 1ʳ: 'Liber Sancte Marie de Kyrkestede'.[1] The first of the letters, to the prior and convent of Durham (29 April 1206), is a well-known defence of the right of monks to move *ad arctiorem ordinem*;[2] but the one which concerns us has no address and, so far as ascertained, is not known in any other copy. Perhaps it was addressed to the Cistercian abbots of England or of some other region, but the solemnity of its comprehensive indictment and the reference in the Lateran decree to an admonition of this sort at least make it possible that the pope was addressing the abbot of Cîteaux and all the abbots of the Order assembled in the General Chapter. Since its contents are uncomplimentary to the Order it would not be surprising if few copies were made. Its publication may reveal whether other copies survive in other parts of Europe.

This letter, like the letter of 20 June 1213 to the Hungarian monks and Hospitallers, threatens action in the General Council.[3] But it is now not only the Cistercians' use of their tithe-privilege that calls for condemnation. The pope claims to be selecting from a great variety of common complaints in accusing the Order of departing from its early statutes. Besides reducing parish churches to ruin by depriving them of tithe, the Cistercians are said to be acquisitive of more possessions and to buy and rent more land when they already have enough to maintain themselves, so that they may farm for profit. They are accused of forms of trade which are reprehended even in laymen and seculars. They are accused of receiving parish churches with the cure of souls; and of accepting generally the burial of wealthy and influential persons in their churches.

If, as is surmised, the letter came before the General Chapter, it explains unwonted activity recorded in the Chapter of

---

[1] Cambridge University Library MS. Ff. 4. 1. Kirkstead was a Cistercian abbey in Lincolnshire, founded 1139. Few books of its library survive: see *Medieval Libraries of Great Britain*, ed. N. R. Ker, 2nd edn. (Royal Hist. Soc., 1964), p. 107.

[2] Pott. 2763; Migne, ccxv. 874; *Extra*, 3, 31, 18.

[3] This time, action by the pope in the council, not by the council.

September 1214.[1] Nothing like the same number of general enactments had been established during the opening years of the thirteenth century. Not only was there the statute c. 54, already cited. Statute c. 55 ordered that on all Cistercian estates (*locis*) where there had been churches with cemeteries, of which traces remained, altars were to be set up if the churches were standing; if the churches were ruinous, new chapels were to be built, and mass might be said there twice a week.[2] This is a pretty clear admission that the Cistercian method of exploiting the land had led to expropriations and the decay of villages, a process closely connected with the complaints about loss of tithe. Statute c. 57: 'let no one receive parish churches',[3] responded to one of the pope's complaints. Statute c. 58 renewed an older statute which forbade partnerships with seculars in tillage and stock-rearing; its declaration: 'nec liceat alicui terras alienas excolere vel conducere ad excolendum' recalled the pope's accusation that 'culturas . . . alienas conducitis ut de vestris lucrari laboribus valeatis'. On the matter of prohibited trading, there was already a twenty-year-old statute which forbade purchase of goods for resale and usurious practices.[4] This was not renewed; but it is recalled by an order made in this Chapter concerning English *conversi* who were said to buy wool in order to sell it more dearly: the abbots of Fountains and Whitland were commissioned to look into the report and punish by order of the Chapter.[5] Only one article in the pope's complaints found no echo in the recorded Chapter acts; nothing is said about the burial of seculars in Cistercian churches.[6]

Taken together, the pope's letter of 19 July 1214, the Chapter acts of September 1214, and the Lateran decree provide powerful confirmation of the substantial truth of

[1] The General Chapter had decided in 1210 that the Chapter should meet annually on 13 Sept. (*Statuta* , i. 369 c. 2).
[2] Next year it was glossed: 'Sententia de reaedificandis capellis intelligitur de illis tantum quae sunt infra grangias' (ibid. i. 436: 1215 c. 8).
[3] Cf. the repetition, 1215 c. 63 (ibid. i. 448).
[4] Ibid. i. 171: 1194 c. 3.
[5] Ibid. i. 426: 1214 c. 45 (cited by D'Arbois de Jubainville, op. cit., p. 322).
[6] Nor in the following years are any individuals recorded as brought to book for infringement of the rule. In 1217 a statute (c. 3) permitted seculars to be buried in Cistercian cemeteries if their priests gave leave (*Statuta*, i. 465).

contemporaries' charges against the Cistercians. Towards the end of the twelfth century, so Dom David Knowles has said, they 'have a reputation, in certain circles at least, for avarice and sharp practice in extending or improving their property at the expense of others'; and he observes that 'the chapter of Cîteaux implicitly acknowledged its justice by taking steps to escape the odium'.[1] Nor can this reputation be ascribed simply to the irresponsible ill nature of a few critics and satirical writers, of whom Gerald of Wales, Walter Map, and Nigel Wireker are outstanding examples.[2] Their extravagant abuse was a symptom, but not the cause, of widespread concern which reached the pope himself and the heads of the Order. Exposed though the pope was to the workings of misrepresentation and slander, Innocent III was too acute to believe every unsupported scandal poured out by Gerald of Wales. It is impossible, and indeed unnecessary, to believe that he had no better information. When we consider the particular charges which Gerald brings against the Cistercian Order as a whole, it is remarkable to find what confirmation comes from more sober sources. If Walter Map complained that the Cistercians made solitude where once were inhabited places, this was no more than is implied in the Chapter's statute for the rebuilding of chapels and replacement of altars; and it is clearly set out in the records of particular abbeys. In certain parts of Europe the Cistercians, not content with assarting, were disturbing the existing peasant population.[3] If Gerald of Wales accused the monks of importunity in

---

[1] *Monastic Order in England*, p. 352.

[2] On their opinions see Knowles, op. cit., ch. 39 'The critics of the monks' and C. V. Graves, 'The economic activities of the Cistercians in medieval England', *Analecta Sacri Ordinis Cisterciensis*, xiii (1957), ch. 4 'Contemporary social criticism'.

[3] See R. A. Donkin, 'Settlement and depopulation on Cistercian estates during the twelfth and thirteenth centuries, especially in Yorkshire', *BIHR*, xxxiii (1960), 141–65, and R. V. Lennard in *The Agricultural History Review*, xii (1964), 86–8. In *Nottingham Medieval Studies*, i (1957), 75–89, M. W. Barley examines the effect of the policy of the twelfth-century monks of Rufford on rural settlement. German examples are cited by J. Batany on p. 12 of 'Les moines blancs dans les "états du monde", xiiie–xive siècles', *Cîteaux: Commentarii Cistercienses*, xv (1964), 5–25, in which he reviews complaints by French moralists and satirists about Cistercian land-grabbing. Colin Platt's description of 'a programme of resettlement rather than depopulation' (*The Monastic Grange in Med. England* (1969), pp. 92–3) does not present the whole picture.

seeking to buy their neighbours' land, this was no more than the pope says in the letter printed here, though Gerald salted his story with much improbable detail.[1] Similarly with the common charge that the Cistercians acquired parish churches contrary to their statutes. Pope Alexander III had complained about it,[2] and so does Innocent III; the Chapter by implication admits the charge, and the records of abbeys confirm it.[3]

Cambridge, University Libr. MS. Ff. 4. 1 fo. 130va.

Innocentius etc. Illius testimonium invocamus qui testis est in celo fidelis quod ordinem vestrum corde puro, conscientia bona, et fide non ficta diligimus, sicut opera protestantur que certum testimonium[a] perhibent veritati, sperantes vestris suffragiis adiuvari apud iustum iudicem et piissimum patrem qui iustorum meritis consuevit indigentium necessitatibus suffragari. Quapropter vestrum in domino commodum zelantes et honorem, querimonias contra ordinem vestrum multas et magnas ad nos sepe delatas quantum decuit et oportuit hactenus dissimulare curavimus. Set adeo invalescunt quod eas amodo sine vestro et nostro periculo non possumus obaudire. Ut enim de multis aliquas exprimamus, super decimis quas de laboribus vestris non redditis tantus contra vos clamor ascendit quod propter hoc multe parrochiales ecclesie perhibentur desolate. In tantum etiam adquirendis possessionibus inhiatis quod propter instantias et molestias [fo. 131vb] importunas quas vicinis vestris frequenter ingeritis eas vobis donare vel vendere compelluntur. Preterea cum ad opus vestrum sufficientes culturas in vestris possessionibus habeatis, alienas conducitis ut de vestris lucrari laboribus valeatis. Talium etiam negociationum commercia exercetis que in laicis et secularibus hominibus reprobantur. Ecclesias quoque parrochiales recipitis que curam habent animarum adnexam, et ad sepulturam passim recipitis divites et potentes contra primaria ordinis vestri statuta, que in hiis et in aliis ita relaxastis ut nisi quantocius in statum debitum reformentur, ordinis vestri excidium in proximo timeatur, cum a multis subtracta sit[b] ei reverentia consueta. Quocirca devotionem vestram rogandam duximus

[a] testimonium *added in margin.*
[b] fit.

[1] *Opera* (RS), iv. 225–31.
[2] Migne, cc. 1004–5.
[3] D'Arbois de Jubainville, op. cit., p. 295; Knowles, pp. 354–5, 656–7; Mahn, p. 18; Graves, pp. 9–11. Discussions of this evidence have not always distinguished clearly between patronage and appropriation.

et monendam quatinus super hiis et aliis que puritatem vestri ordinis denigrant illud protinus per vos ipsos studeatis consilium adhibere quod non oporteat nos in generali concilio apponere manus nostras, tales personas ad idem concilium dirigentes qui secundum scientiam habeant zelum dei, de gratie nostre favore[c] securi, quia deferre vobis intendimus quantum cum nostra possumus honestate. Vos denique, filii abbates, etc.[d] Dat' Witerb', xiiii kal. Augusti pontificatus nostri anno xviio. [Viterbo, 19 July 1214.]

[c] favore *interlined, and also added in same ink in margin.*

[d] *This may be extended according to common form*: super vobis ipsis et credito vobis grege taliter vigilare curetis exstirpando vitia et plantando virtutes, ut in novissimo districti examinis die coram tremendo iudice, qui reddet unicuique secundum opera sua, dignam possitis reddere rationem. (Cf. Migne, ccxvi. 883, ccxvii. 221).

15. Harrold Priory:
A Twelfth-Century Dispute*

THE cartulary of Harrold Priory in British Museum MS. Lansdowne 391 contains on fo. 11ᵛ the brief abstract of documents concerning the church of Stevington (Beds.), a neighbouring parish church which this Austin nunnery held by the grant of Baldwin of Ardres in the twelfth century and which was appropriated to the priory by Bishop Hugh de Wells of Lincoln in or before 1227.[1] The abstract was printed in translation by the late Dr. G. H. Fowler in *Beds. Hist. Rec. Soc.* xvii. 35–6. At that time the text of the documents abstracted was unknown. The originals or copies had been among the muniments of Harrold Priory concerning Stevington when the cartulary was compiled in the fifteenth century,[2] and the compiler noted of one of them (no. 2): 'a copy of this charter is in the fair psalter' (*copia istius carte est in pulcro psalterio*). This must be the copy which has now come to light, in a series of no less than nineteen documents concerning Stevington church, copied in the early part of the thirteenth century into a handsome psalter belonging to the nuns of Harrold.

Dr. N. R. Ker, when examining the psalter in the summer of 1950, discovered these documents and kindly brought them to the notice of the Bedfordshire Historical Record Society. The psalter is now in the library of the Baptist College at Bristol (Z. c. 23), to which it was bequeathed in 1784 by Andrew Gifford;[3] and the documents are here published by the kind permission of the College authorities. Dr. Ker points out that the psalter belonged earlier to Sir James Ware, in whose

* First published in *Bedfordshire Historical Record Society Publications*, vol. xxxii (1952), 1–26.

[1] For the constitution and history of the priory, which originally included canons as well as nuns, see G. H. Fowler, *Beds. Hist. Rec. Soc.*, xvii. 7–14.

[2] Dr. Fowler describes the traces of classification in the priory's records, ibid., pp. 5–6.   [3] See *D.N.B.*

catalogue (Dublin, 1648) it is listed as 'Theol. ms. 3 : Psalmi Davidis sive Psalterium. Adjiciuntur chartae quaedam domus monialium de Harewold in Com. Bedfordiae, in 4o [i.e. quarto] membran.' He adds that the psalter is of the twelfth century, and is preceded by a Christ Church, Canterbury, calendar, in which an obit in a late twelfth-century hand shows that the book was at one time in Kent and came to Harrold second-hand. At the end of the psalter are various prayers. A sixteenth-century owner, John Sunnyng, 'vicarius de Luswe (?)' wrote his name on the last page of the text. Two preliminary leaves contain an original inserted document, a grant of confraternity by Simon Tunstede, provincial of the Friars Minor, to the rector of the church of Northill, 1363 : this is a generation earlier than any original Franciscan letter of confraternity noted by Prebendary Clark-Maxwell,[1] and was granted at Bristol on 15 August, in a hitherto unrecorded provincial chapter. At the foot of the document is copied a letter of Emma, the prioress, and the convent of Harrold, presenting John Fretter to the vicarage of Harrold (27 March 1415). The documents which are printed below occupy the lower part of the last page of the book's text, together with the whole of the following two leaves.[2]

Apart from the incidental value of correcting a bad error in the abstract given in the cartulary, where the compiler has mistaken Pope Celestine III (1191–8) for Pope Celestine IV (1241) and so confused the whole chronology, the nineteen full texts provide such a quantity of detail about a lengthy lawsuit as is altogether exceptional in this period. The documents are evidently far from providing a complete record of litigation which went on intermittently for sixteen years; but they

---

[1] *Archæologia*, lxxv, lxxix.

[2] Six lines at the foot of the last page are in a fifteenth-century hand and concern Milton Ernest:

[Mi]delton'. Carta data priorisse et conventui de Harewold' in villa de Midelton' in comitatu Bedef'. In primis de domino Stephano filio Galfridi de Lega militis x acr' et iii rod' prati. Item tota terra manerii in villa de Midelton'. Item duo messuagia in eadem villa que quidem messuagia Stephanus le Gynnour et Stephanus Piscator quondam tenuerunt. Item communis pastura dicte ville dictis monialibus.

Cf. *Beds. Hist. Rec. Soc.*, xvii. 105–7.

contain enough of interest to justify publication *in extenso*. They throw light on the problems which small religious houses, and the nuns of Harrold in particular, might encounter over their church-patronage; they provide good samples of procedural documents of the Church courts; and they show how disputes which involved ecclesiastical patronage might, despite the Constitutions of Clarendon, come up repeatedly for settlement before ecclesiastical judges, provided that the case could be treated as one concerning disputed incumbency and that the words 'patronage' and 'advowson' were avoided.[1] The rest of the present Introduction will not enlarge on the value of the documents from the point of view either of the local historian or of the legal historian. All that is attempted is to elucidate the actual sequence of events from the documents before us and from a few relevant entries in the public records.

Between the years 1136 and 1146 Baldwin, lord of Ardres, gave property to Harrold for his soul and the souls of his father Arnulf and his mother and his brother Arnulf. It included the church of Stevington with all its appendages (*appendicia*). The grant was made in the presence of Gervase, first abbot of Arrouaise, to whose congregation Harrold then belonged. The priory became independent of Arrouaise in 1188.[2] Baldwin's charter is no. 1 in our series.[3] Ardres is a place in the modern département of the Pas-de-Calais, which in the eleventh and twelfth centuries was the centre of a powerful lordship, nominally part of the county of Guines. But the lords of Ardres were disposed to be independent, and the neighbouring counts of Boulogne were anxious to extend their influence. It is therefore of interest to find Baldwin of Ardres described here as knight and tenant of Eustace, count of Boulogne, who confirmed his grant [no. 2].[4] The nuns also obtained, as was canonically proper, an episcopal confirmation

---

[1] See J. W. Gray, 'The Ius praesentandi in England from the Constitutions of Clarendon to Bracton', *EHR*, lxvii (1952), 481–509; C. R. Cheney, *From Becket to Langton* (Manchester, 1956), pp. 108–17; J. E. Sayers, *Papal Judges Delegate in the Province of Canterbury 1198–1254* (Oxford, 1971), 183–95.

[2] L. Milis, *L'Ordre des Chanoines Réguliers d'Arrouaise* (Bruges, 1969), i. 291, 297.

[3] References to 'no. 1', etc., hereafter refer to the documents printed below.

[4] The tenancy was presumably in respect of lands held by Baldwin of the honor of Boulogne, in England. Stevington was part of the honor.

from Alexander, bishop of Lincoln (d. 1148). In the first half of the twelfth century the gift by a layman of 'a church and its appendages' might include a good deal more than the advowson of the church, and the gift was usually accompanied by some reservation of the rights of the existing incumbent or by a statement of the recompense he would receive for resignation. In this case, the charter provided that the nuns of Harrold were only to obtain their church after the death of 'G. the priest'. For all we can tell, 'G' may have died soon afterwards, but he may have lived on for forty years: examples of equal longevity are not unknown among parsons, and a long tenure of the church by this priest would help to explain the trouble which arose in the next generation.

Nothing more is heard of Stevington church until 1192. In the interval since Baldwin of Ardres' gift, the priest had died, the donor had died, and the land which Baldwin held in Stevington had descended through his brother Arnulf's daughter, Christiana of Ardres (d. 1177) to her husband Baldwin II, count of Guines (d. 1205).[1] We are not told precisely the background of the litigation which now began, but it can safely be inferred from the documents. When G. the priest had died, the nuns had failed to establish their rights in the church, as they should have done, by presenting a clerk to the diocesan bishop for institution. It is observable from no. 3 that the nuns claimed the church *de iure*; they did not claim to have had possession. The count of Guines, on the other hand, had treated the advowson of the church as an appurtenance of his manor of Stevington instead of a separate incorporeal possession of the nuns—a 'gross' (as the Edwardian lawyers came to call it).[2] He had acted as patron and presented to the living his own clerkly son, Baldwin. Not improbably, the young Baldwin was instituted by the bishop of Lincoln or

---

[1] For the pedigree see the Chronicle of Lambert of Ardres (below, no. 1, note) and further A. Duchesne, *Histoire généalogique des maisons de Guines, d'Ardres, de Gand, et de Coucy*. . . . (Paris, 1631). Count Baldwin II had thirty-three children (Duchesne, ii. 134).

A late twelfth-century list of fees of the honor of Boulogne (*Book of Fees*, i. 236, cf. 240) gives to the count of Guines three knight's fees in 'Stivinton' et Parva Wahull' in Bedeford' '.

[2] F. Pollock and F. W. Maitland, *Hist. of Eng. Law*, 2nd ed., ii. 136–7.

his *locum tenens*, who might well act in ignorance of the alienation of the church from the manor provided for by charter some forty or fifty years earlier.

Of Baldwin the clerk not much is known beyond the facts recorded in these documents. The chronicle written in honour of the family by the contemporary *curé* of Ardres, Lambert, tells us that Baldwin was a canon of the cathedral church of Térouanne, *procurator et persona* of the church of St. Peter of Nielles-sous-la-Montoire, and likewise *provisor et persona* of churches in England at Stevington, Stisted, Malling, and 'Baigtonia'.[1] He died in or shortly before 1229.[2]

Baldwin apparently encountered opposition from the nuns of Harrold when he took possession of the church of Stevington. They appealed to the pope against him, but he persisted none the less in what they termed his illegal occupancy of the church. Therefore, in 1192, the nuns sought from Pope Celestine III a commission to three judges-delegate: Payen, abbot of Wardon (O. Cist.), Walter, prior of Chicksands (O. Semp.), and Robert of Hardres, archdeacon of Huntingdon. On 4 April the pope issued his mandate: the delegates were to force Baldwin or any agent of his holding the church either to restore it to Harrold Priory or to do what seemed to them to be just, in their presence [no. 3]. When the delegates took action is uncertain. It appears from their letter to the diocesan, St. Hugh of Lincoln, in 1198–9, that Baldwin had been strong enough to impede the process for six years and had obtained a royal writ of prohibition to stop action on the case in a court christian [no. 4]. But the nuns and their appointed judges persisted. The nuns procured another letter from Pope Celestine dated 15 April 1196 [no. 7]—this time a 'letter of grace'— which confirmed to them the churches of St. Peter of Harrold and of Stevington, with their possessions, which were confirmed to the monastery by the donors' charters. Since the papal letter included the precautionary formula common to

---

[1] *Lamberti chronicon*, p. 161, cf. 430. No connection of Baldwin with 'Baigtonia' (unidentified) or with Stisted has been traced, but in March 1206 the vacancy of Stisted (said to be in the king's gift *sede vacante* Canterbury) coincided with the vacancy of East Malling 'que fuit Baldewini de Ginnes et vacat' (*Rotuli litterarum patentium*, ed. T. D. Hardy, p. 60*a*, cf. 59*b* and below, no. 12).

[2] Duchesne, op. cit. ii. 278. His eldest son survived him.

such confirmations, 'according as you possess them justly and without dispute', it could not settle a lawsuit which was *sub judice*; but it shows the effort of the nuns to accumulate muniments.

The delegates, for their part, were not idle. At what time between 1192 and 1198 the events occurred which are recorded in the delegates' letters patent [no. 3], we cannot say. Probably Baldwin's obstruction caused delay at various stages in the process. Since he had not immediately submitted in the face of the nuns' claim, the due process of canon law (*iuris ordo*) was set in motion. The nuns would produce their *libellus*; this would be met by Baldwin's contradiction and the *litis contestatio*. Both parties then adduced witnesses, whose attestations were put in writing and 'published' at Bedford [no. 10]. Debate on this material followed on appointed days, at fixed intervals, twice at St. Neots and later, in a three-days' session, at Bedford [no. 10, cf. 3 and 4]. At one of the sessions at St. Neots the nuns produced witnesses to prove that they had possessed a confirmation-charter of Bishop Alexander concerning the church of Stevington, and had lost it [no. 8 cf. 10]. At none of these sessions did Baldwin appear personally, and his place was taken by his duly appointed proctor, Master Roger of Luton [no. 6].[1] The attestations and documents which were produced completely satisfied the judges, who took the advice of skilled lawyers [no. 4], and fixed a day for giving sentence at Bedford [no. 8]. The pope's mandate had provided, as usual in such cases, for any two of the delegates to act if necessary without the third.[2] In the event, the archdeacon of Huntingdon, having attended some sittings of the court in person or by deputy (*per interpositam*) [no. 3], could not be present at the final session and sent his apologies for absence in writing [no. 5].

The delegates, in transmitting their record of the case to the diocesan late in 1198 or early in 1199, called upon him in the usual fashion to execute the sentence [no. 4]. There is no

---

[1] Baldwin's letter of proxy shows that he was also, or expected to be, defendant in a suit with the abbot 'de Parco'. This is identified by Milis, *L'Ordre des Chanoines Réguliers d'Arrouaise*, p. 293 n. 4 as Notley, *alias* Crendon Park.

[2] *Extra*, 1, 29, 6.

direct evidence that St. Hugh put Harrold Priory in possession of the church; still, we may infer that he did so from the fact that the nuns subsequently claimed to have had possession, whereas they previously claimed the church *de jure*.[1] But at this stage matters become hard to disentangle, and what follows can only claim to be a plausible interpretation and elaboration of the incomplete evidence contained in nos. 8–11. The nuns, having obtained possession of the church, must have been ejected by Baldwin of Guines and his accomplices almost immediately, and not later than the first months of 1199. (It may be remarked, parenthetically, that the bishop of Lincoln was at this time abroad, and had been overseas since August 1198.) The nuns therefore appealed again to the pope and for the protection (*tuitio*) of the archbishop of Canterbury, adopting a procedure of which little is recorded at this early date, by which an appellant might obtain immediate protection of person and property and, if justified by a summary enquiry conducted by the archbishop, have his support in prosecuting an appeal to Rome. The appellants on this occasion presumably strengthened their appeal with letters nos. 8 and 10, addressed to the archbishop's officials[2] at the instance of the nuns. In no. 10 the original judges gave their résumé of the case. Abbot Payen of Wardon, the first of the judges, had meanwhile retired from the headship of his house and had some difficulty in laying hands on the documents in the case; however, he and the prior of Chicksands forwarded such as they could find. At the instance of the nuns, Master Warin de Hubaldeston also provided the archbishop's officials with his testimony about the lost charter of Bishop Alexander. The reason for surmising that a 'tuitorial appeal' such as is described above was the procedure adopted by the nuns lies partly in this evidence of an approach to the archbishop's court, and still more in the contents of nos. 9 and 11.

From no. 9 we learn that the archbishop had issued to the dean of Lincoln, Master Roger de Rolveston, a mandate which

---

[1] Possibly, however, their claim to possession depended only on their violent attempt to secure it, which is mentioned in no. 11.

[2] Archbishop Hubert Walter was abroad Sept. 1198–Jan. 1199 and Mar.–May 1199.

the dean had transmitted to Lawrence, archdeacon of Bedford. The archdeacon, on this mandate, enquired in his archdeaconry, 'whether the church of Stevington had been reasonably adjudged to the nuns of Harrold by sentence of judges-delegate of the lord pope'. He learnt that sentence had indeed been given in their favour and they had for some time (*aliquo tempore*) possessed the church; but Baldwin of Guines and his accomplices then unjustly occupied it. The archdeacon ordered restitution of the church, but the intruders would not withdraw. Acting on the mandate of the archbishop and the dean, the archdeacon thereupon excommunicated them for 'this manifest and notorious intrusion'. Nevertheless they were persisting in their temerity at the time of the archdeacon's report.

This report must have been written before the end of May 1199. Whether no. 11 represents parallel or later action we cannot tell;[1] but the officials, it appears, issued a commission, to make inquiry and hear witnesses in the case, to the heads of three local religious houses: G., the prior of St. Neots, Alexander, the prior of Canons Ashby, and the prior of Huntingdon. These three commissioners were so inundated with depositions that they were occupied for three days, each separately examining witnesses. The surviving letter of the prior of St. Neots [no. 11] probably accompanied their full report of the case to the officials, to explain one point in it: a comment at the end of the testimony of Simon Blund might mistakenly be supposed to be part of his testimony, whereas it was a comment of the examiner, who puts on record that 'almost all the witnesses coming from Northill and Southill and Harrold swore that they had been in the company of those whom the nuns had assembled to drive out Baldwin of Guines from their church of Stevington which he had occupied.' The documents tantalizingly make no further reference to the nuns' attempt to recover the church by main force, and we can do no more than conjecture that this episode took place about 1199.

All the action described in letters 8–11 may well have

---

[1] In no. 9 the archdeacon of Bedford implies that the latest action in the case was that of the original judges-delegate. He could hardly have ignored the proceedings indicated in nos. 8, 10, and 11, had they happened earlier.

occurred during the year 1199. It was all to no purpose. In the first months of 1200 Baldwin offered the king the price of a gentle falcon for a writ of prohibition.[1] The writ is probably to be explained by an extraneous document[2] which shows that between May 1199 and February 1205 the nuns had again appealed to Rome and obtained as judges Archbishop Hubert of Canterbury, Master Simon of Sywell, and Master John of Tynemouth. We learn of this interlude from the letter of excuse of G. prioress of Harrold and the convent, appointing 'R. de Brak'' as their proctor before these judges, in the case between Harrold and B., clerk, over the church of Stevington. But there is no evidence that the judges took action. Baldwin, one must remember, was the son of an influential magnate with territorial interests on both sides of the Channel, whose support was of moment to the king of England in the midst of his war with the king of France.

In 1206 Harrold Priory still had not possession of Stevington church. The sees of Lincoln and of Canterbury were both vacant, and the nuns appealed to a papal legate who arrived in England towards the end of May. Not much is known of the legation of John of Ferentino, cardinal deacon of S. Maria in Via Lata[3] and no. 13 is one of his rare surviving *acta*, hitherto unknown. This gives a brief narrative of the litigation before him. The proceedings reached the point where the proctors of both parties appeared in court to debate the evidence of witnesses. The nuns' proctor is not named; Baldwin's was one Master A. of Edinburgh (*de Castro Puellarum*) [no. 12]. At this stage, after hearing some of his opponents' arguments, Master A. withdrew without leave and would not put in an appearance again. Baldwin wrote to the legate asking that, since he had no proctor in England, the legate would appoint a day when he might appear to conduct his own defence, and appealing, lest any other procedure be adopted, to the apostolic see. Many

---

[1] *Rotuli de oblatis et de finibus*, ed. T. D. Hardy, p. 52: 'Baldewinus filius comitis de Ginges dat domino regi i falconem gentilem pro quodam brevi de placito prohibendo de advocatione ecclesie de Stiventon' versus moniales de Erewell'.' This writ cannot be the one referred to in no. 4. The record incidentally shows that the advowson as well as the incumbency was in question.

[2] *Letters of Innocent III*, ed. C. R. and M. G. Cheney, no. 606.

[3] C. R. Cheney in *EHR*, xlvi (1931), 443–52 and lxxvi (1961), 654–60.

people regarded this as a 'frustratory appeal'—an appeal to frustrate justice—since Baldwin had in fact appointed a proctor for the case and furnished him with a letter of proxy [no. 12]. But since the legate was about to leave England, he thought best to refer the matter to the pope. He had the depositions of witnesses placed under seal at St. Augustine's Abbey, Canterbury, until they could be shown to the judges to whom the pope would delegate the hearing. Cardinal John left England in October or November 1206.

It is of some interest to find that the nuns were still dispossessed of their church in the summer of 1206, for they had already, earlier in the year, acquired another title-deed in the shape of a royal charter, granted on 5 April, which confirmed to them 'the church of Stevington with all its appendages which they hold by the gift of Baldwin of Ardres as the charter of the same Baldwin which they have thereon reasonably witnesses' [no. 19]. It is still more interesting to find that on the same day another royal charter was given, confirming to the nuns of Malling (Kent) the church of East Malling by gift of Archbishop Hubert; for this church was also claimed by Baldwin of Guines.[1] This points to a common policy determined upon by these religious houses against a common enemy.

Next year the dispute was carried a stage further. On 6 April 1207 the pope, acting on the plaint of the nuns, appointed fresh judges-delegate, Master Alard of Burnham, dean of St. Paul's, Master John of Kent, chancellor of London, and Richard of Ely, the archdeacon of Colchester [no. 15]. It was their business to examine the evidence taken by the cardinal-legate and deposited by him at Canterbury, and to terminate the case. The judges delegate, having obtained the former attestations from the abbot of St. Augustine's [no. 14], cited Baldwin de Guines to appear in person or by proctor before them. Because he failed to come or send in response to a peremptory citation, they adjudged the possession of the church of Stevington to the nuns *causa rei servande* [no. 15]. This canonistic procedure, based on a comparable procedure in Roman civil law, was designed to prevent a contumacious

[1] Cf. note to no. 12.

litigant from interfering with, or abstracting, the property in dispute.[1] The abbot of Lavendon, on the instructions of the judges, went personally to Stevington and gave the nuns custody of the church, probably on 26 August 1207 [no. 16]. But this was only an interim judgement which left the way clear to Baldwin to reopen the case within a twelvemonth. The nuns therefore entered an appeal for true possession and proprietorship in the presence of the abbot, when he installed them. Still Baldwin made no move; and after the lapse of a year the judges-delegate awarded the nuns true possession, reserving the right of Baldwin to contest the proprietorship of the church. The nuns promptly appealed in the presence of the judges for the apostolic tuition of their right. The judges then instructed Master Alexander of Elstow, archdeacon of Bedford, to see that the nuns have the possession which had been adjudged to them undisturbed [no. 17]. This victory for Harrold Priory cannot have been earlier than August 1208 (and may have been considerably later). By this time all England lay under interdict. The election of a new bishop of Lincoln was delayed until April 1209, and when Hugh of Wells, the bishop-elect, went abroad for consecration in November 1209 he stayed overseas in exile until King John made his peace with the Church in 1213. It is unlikely that the letter of the judges-delegate reporting the case to the bishop [no. 18] was written before his return to England in July 1213: it must have been written before John of Kent ceased to be chancellor of St. Paul's, early in 1214.

The story may be completed from the episcopal register of Hugh of Wells. This contains a record that Bishop Hugh II (i.e. Hugh of Wells) allocated an annual pension of sixteen marks to the nuns of Harrold in the church of Stevington in the sixth year of his pontificate (i.e. 20 December 1214–19 December 1215).[2] Since Bishop Hugh went to Rome for the Fourth Lateran Council in the autumn of 1215, this action must be dated in the months of political unrest which led up to,

---

[1] R. W. Lee, *Elements of Roman Law* (1944), p. 442, and cf. *Extra*, 2, 6, 3 and 2, 15: 'De eo qui mittitur in possessionem causa rei servande.' See also Sayers, *Papal Judges Delegate*, pp. 75–8, 153–4, and for an earlier English example of the procedure *Chron. abbatiae de Bello*, ed. J. S. Brewer (1846), p. 115 (1154×1159).

[2] *Rotuli Hugonis de Welles*, ed. F. N. Davis (CYS and Lincoln Rec. Soc.) iii. 93.

and followed, Magna Carta. The record shows how the bishop interpreted the grant of the church to the nuns. It was not a grant specifically *in proprios usus*, and the judgement in favour of Harrold had not meant that the nuns stepped into the position of rector. But the bishop, by requiring the rector to pay the nuns a pension, allowed them more than the mere advantage of the advowson. Twelve years later, in 1227, the register shows that the further step of appropriation had been taken. The bishop then instituted a priest as vicar of Stevington on the presentation of prioress and convent, and made an assignment, or ordination, of revenues for his support.[1]

From the point of view of ecclesiastical authority, the matter was now closed; and ten years later the nuns safeguarded themselves against a claim on the advowson in the lay court by making a fine with Robert of Guines (brother of Baldwin III, count of Guines), who had succeeded to the lordship of Stevington. By a final concord, dated in May 1237, and by a separate charter to the nuns, Robert renounced all right and claim on the church of Stevington for himself and his heirs, and in return 'the prioress received Robert and his heirs into all benefits and orisons which in future should be made in her church of Harrold, for ever.'[2]

To conclude this Introduction, we may indicate a few points of incidental interest in these documents. Since charters of King Stephen's son Eustace are quite excessively scarce,[3] no. 2 is a useful indication of the diplomatic of his *acta* and shows in his company his influential relative, Faramus of Boulogne, as well as his mother, King Stephen's queen. Others of the documents provide names and dates of office-holders: no. 10 shows that Payen, abbot of Wardon, did not die in office but retired in 1198 or 1199. An oddity in dating occurs

[1] *Rotuli Hugonis de Welles*, iii. 15. The reference to *rotulus institutionum anni xiiii* (i. 187) is presumably wrong; the correct year is *xviii*. The surviving document is not the appropriation-deed itself, which was abstracted in the Harrold cartulary (*Beds. Hist. Rec. Soc.*, xvii. 36).

[2] *Beds. Hist. Rec. Soc.*, vi. 107 and xvii. 37–8.

[3] Other acts of Count Eustace are in *Mon. Ang.*, vi. 153; *Sussex Rec. Soc. Publications*, xxxviii. 109, 161; *Regesta Regum Anglo-Normannorum*, iii. ed. H. A. Cronne and R. H. C. Davis (Oxford, 1968), nos. 222, 229a, 239e, 551, 847. For the charters and style of Eustace's brother and successor, William, see Charles Clay, *Early Yorks. charters*, viii (1949), 47–51.

in no. 16, where the birth of Henry III is used to fix a date five weeks before that event.[1]

TEXT

Hec sunt transcripta cartarum de Harewold'[2] *super ecclesia de Stiventon' et*[3] *processu cause.*

1. Universis sancte matris ecclesie filiis tam presentibus quam futuris B. de Arde salutem. Universis notum fieri volo me dedisse in puram et perpetuam elemosinam sanctimonialibus de Harewold' pro anima patris mei Ernulfi senioris fratrisque mei Ernulfi[4] iunioris et[5] matris mee et mea sexies xx acras terre et xx acras nemoris, scilicet xxx acras terre in exitu de Walerod' de dominio meo, xxx acras terre iuxta viam qua itur Pudintun' de Walrod' ad Westerodes, pro xxx acris, decem acras inter minorem Wahull' et aquam de dominio in locis proximioribus terre de Harewold', decem acras de dominio meo inter Wahill' et Walerod', decem acras trans viam de Walerod' inter viam et nemores[6] et quantum habetur nemoris inter viam qua itur Asmewaud' ad angulum de Westcroftes usque ad viam de Walerod' pro xxx acris, tres acras prati de dominio meo in propinquiori loco ponti de Harewold', totam decimam segetum dominii mei minoris Wahull'. Concessi etiam eis ecclesiam de Stiventon' cum omnibus appendiciis suis post decessum G. sacerdotis. Volo igitur ut supradicte sanctimoniales et earum procuratores hanc meam elemosinam quam manu mea optuli super altare ecclesie de Harewold' pacifice, honorifice, et libere, ab omni exactione seculari teneant de me et de heredibus meis tempore perpetuo. Hiis testibus Gervasio abbate de Arowaicarda,[7] Willelmo filio Roberti canonici, Dalvino fratre eius,

---

[1] Mr. J. W. Gray kindly read this in typescript and made valuable suggestions. In transcribing the text I have copied without comment the inconsistent spelling of the manuscript, but have not retained its punctuation and capitals. The letters are not numbered in the manuscript.

[2] in com. Bedford *added in a xvii cent.* (?) *hand.*

[3] cum *added in a later hand, above the line.*

[4] fratrisque mei Ernulfi *obscured by traces of writing on the recto, seen through the parchment, and therefore repeated in left-hand margin.*

[5] et *interlined.*

[6] nemoris.

[7] *Sic, for some form of* Arowasia.

Stephano de Leya, Hugone filio eius, Michaele de Wahell',
Edrico preposito de Stiventon', Almero preposito minoris
Wahell'.

1136–46. G. H. Fowler suggested 1136–8, the supposed date of foundation of
Harrold Priory (*Beds. Hist. Rec. Soc.*, xvii. 12). The latest possible date is fixed
by the departure of Baldwin of Ardres for Jerusalem in 1146. For the pedigree of
the house of Ardres see *Lamberti chronicon ghisnense et ardense*, ed. D. C. Godefroy
Menilglaise (Paris, 1855), facing p. xxx.

Gervase, abbot of Arrouaise, was recipient of another gift for the nuns of
Harrold, 1138–47 (*Beds. Hist. Rec. Soc.*, xvii. 19). For Stephen de Leya and his son
see ibid., pedigree 5.

Pudintun: Podington.
Wahill', etc.: Odell.
Walerod': cf. similar forms elsewhere (Walecroft, *Beds. Hist. Rec. Soc.*, xiii.
119; Walecote, xxii. 100).
Asmewaud: perhaps a local name derived from wold; cf. the form Harewaud
(*E.P.N.S. Beds and Hunts.*, p. 32). The land in question appears to be on the
Harrold–Odell border, not far from the modern Wold Farm.

2. Comes Eustachius filius regis Angl' universis sancte matris
ecclesie filiis tam francis quam anglicis salutem. Sciatis quod
ego concedo et confirmo elemosinam et donationem illam quam
B. de Arda meus miles et meus tenens fecit sanctimonialibus
de Harewold', scilicet de parva Wahill' que est de feodo meo
sexies xx acras terre et xx acras nemoris iuxta Lingswod', et
totam decimam dominii eiusdem parve Wahill', et ecclesiam
de Stiventon' post decessum G. presbiteri. Hanc igitur elemosinam illis concedo et sigilli mei patrocinio confirmo pro
salute mea et regis et regine matris mee et pro animabus
omnium antecessorum meorum. Hiis testibus Matilide regina,
Faramo, Rogero de Felines, Rogero de Chahu, Ricardo abbate,
Manesero cantore de Bolonia.

Christmas 1146?–May 1152. The terminal points are determined by the creation of Eustace as count (*Gesta Stephani, Chron. Stephen*, etc. (RS), iii. 132), and
by the death of his mother Matilda (May, 1152). Eustace, count of Boulogne, was
the eldest son of King Stephen, and died August 1153.

For Faramus of Boulogne see J. H. Round, in *The Genealogist*, n.s. xii (1896),
145–51. Manasser the precentor of Boulogne witnesses with Faramus (as *Manasse
cantore*) a grant by Eustace's successor, William, to Furness Abbey (ibid., p. 148).
Roger de Felines (or Fiennes) was probably the brother of Eustace II, whose son
married the daughter and heiress of Faramus (ibid. and *Lamberti chronicon*, facing
p. xxx). Roger de Chahu witnesses another act of Count Eustace as *Rogerus de
Caio* (*Mon. Ang.*, vi. 153). Baldwin de Chayho and his brother Robert witness
an act of Count Eustace in the Lewes cartulary (*Sussex Rec. Soc. Publ.*, xxxviii.
161).

Processus cause priorisse et monialium[1] *de Harewold' per priores iudices super ecclesia de Stiventon'.*

3. Universis sancte matris ecclesie filiis tam presentibus quam futuris P. abbas de Wardon' et prior de Chikessaunt salutem in domino. Literas domini pape in hec verba suscepimus: Celestinus episcopus servus[2] servorum dei dilectis filiis P. abbati de Wardon', R. archidiacono de Huntendon' et priori de Chikessaunt salutem et apostolicam benedictionem. Sicut dilectarum in Christo filiarum nostrarum monialium de Harewold' transmissa nobis conquestio patefecit, B. clericus ecclesiam de Stiventon' ad eas de iure spectantem post appellationem ad sedem apostolicam[3] interpositam illicite occupavit et detinere contendit. Ut igitur eisdem monialibus auctoritate apostolica in sua iusticia consulatur, discrecioni vestre per apostolica scripta mandamus quatinus memoratum clericum vel quemcumque illius inveneritis ecclesie detentorem ut ipsam sine difficultate restituat vel quod iustum fuerit in vestra presencia exequatur per censuram canonicam appellatione remota compellatis. Quod si omnes hiis exequendis interesse nequiveritis duo vestrum ea nichilominus exequantur. Data Laterani ii non. Aprilis pontificatus nostri anno primo. Harum auctoritate partibus coram nobis consistentibus litem contestantibus, tandemque testes ad assercionem suam fundandam producendo et alia que cause commoditas exspectabat[4] agendo prosequentibus, tandem attestationes fecimus publicari[5] solempniter. Disputatione autem pluribus diebus ad hoc per varia intervalla datis super attestationibus sufficienter celebrata, cum de iure monialium nobis luce clarius constaret meritis cause exigentibus predictam ecclesiam supradictis monialibus sententialiter adiudicavimus, collega nostro R. archidiacono de Huntendon' tempore diffinitive sentencie sui inpotentiam[6] protestante, et absentiam suam per literas simpliciter excusante, in anterioribus vero cause agende articulis in propria persona vel per interpositam mandatum summi pontificis nobiscum exequente. Cuius

[1] monialium ? *written over* monialiarum.
[2] servus *interlined.*   [3] appostolican.
[4] exspectebat.
[5] publicari fecimus *marked for transposition.*
[6] inpotententiam.

rei seriem ne in recidivam dubietatem possit devenire, presenti pagina perpetue memorie commendandam et sigillorum nostrorum appositione censuimus communiendam.

1192–1198. The extreme dates are fixed by the mandate of Pope Celestine III (4 April 1192) and the death of this pope (8 January 1198); probably no. 3 was written at the same time as no. 4.

Abbot Payen of Wardon (O.Cist., Beds.) was abbot 1186 and resigned in 1198 or early in 1199 (Abbot Warin had succeeded him by Whitsun 1199). For his seal see F. M. Stenton, *Facs. of early charters* (Northants. Rec. Soc., iv), pl. xxvii. The prior of Chicksands (O.Semp., Beds.) may have been Walter (cf. 'W.', no. 4) who was prior in Nov. 1203 (*Feet of fines*, ed. J. Hunter, i. 55). Robert of Hardres was archdeacon of Huntingdon 1191–1207.

B. *clericus*: Baldwin, son of Baldwin II, count of Guines; see Introduction and no. 5 below.

4. *Litere ipsorum iudicum per quas ipse moniales fuerunt misse in possessionem ecclesie de Stiventon' sub hac forma.*

Reverentissimo domino et patri H. dei gratia Lincoln' episcopo P. dictus abbas de Wardon' et W. prior de Chikessaunt salutem et debitam cum reverentia obedientiam. Paternitati vestre significamus quod cum causa que vertebatur inter moniales de Harewold' et B. clericum de Ginnes super ecclesia de Stiventon' nobis pariter et archidiacono de Huntendun' iam sex annis et eo amplius elapsis de mandato summi pontificis esset commissa, tum per potentiam B. de Ginnes cum propter regiam prohibitionem moniales a iusticia consequenda sunt impedite et nos oportuit subsistere. Verum tandem a prefatis monialibus requisiti, ne argueremur inobedientia et ut debitam summo pontifici cui omnes tenemur astricti exhiberemus reverentiam, partes convocavimus et post legitimas sicut in iure cautum est productiones attestationes publicavimus, et post attestationes publicatas diem ad dicendum in testes et dicta testium partibus prefiximus, et postea alium, et postea tercium ne premature pronunciaremus. Tandem vero archidiaconus[1] inpotenciam suam literatorie excusante, cum satis de iure monialium instructi essemus et nobis quam plenissime tum per testes omni excepcione maiores tum per autentica instrumenta moniales in ecclesia de Stiventon' ius habere constaret, communicato consilio virorum prudentum et discretorum ac iurisperitorum, iuris ordine per omnia observato, prefatis monialibus

[1] archid' *deleted and repeated*.

de Harewold' memoratam ecclesiam de Stiventon' sententialiter[1] adiudicavimus. Unde vestre sanctitati significamus ut sententiam a nobis latam executioni demandare velit vestra discretio. Valeat in domino vestra paternitas.

1198–May 1199 is indicated by the judges' reference to the mandate issued above six years ago (cf. no. 3) and by the retirement of Abbot Payen of Wardon early in 1199.

Hugh (St.), bishop of Lincoln 1186–1200.

5. Litere R. archidiaconi de Huntindon' in quibus excusat se non posse interesse ventilationi cause.

P. abbati de Wardon' et W. priori de Chikessaunt R. archidiaconus Huntendon' salutem. Pluribus prepeditus negociis ventilationi cause que vertitur inter moniales de Harewold' et B. filium comitis de Ginnes super ecclesia de Stiventon' vobis et michi a summo pontifice pariter commisse, interesse non possum. Quare vobis mando quatinus, me non exspectato, quod vestrum est libere exequamini. Valete.

1192–May 1199, probably in the latter part of the period (cf. notes to nos. 3 and 4)

6. Litere B. de Ginnes per quas constituit procuratorem magistrum Rogerum de Luton' contra plures.

Universis sancte matris ecclesie filiis Baldewinus persona de Stiventon' salutem. Noverit universitas vestra quod magistrum Rogerum de Lueton' in omnibus causis meis tam delegatis[2] a summo pontifice quam aliis procuratorem meum ac defensorem meum constituo, sive vertantur inter abbatem de Parco et me sive inter moniales de Harewold' et me, vel inter me et alios, ratum habiturus quicquid in illis causis meis vel aliis gesserit. Iudicatum quoque solvi pro eo promitto et si transegerit, transactionem ratam et gratam habebo.

1192–May 1199 (see notes to no. 3).

Master Roger of Luton appears as witness to documents concerning other Bedfordshire religious houses in this period (*Beds. Hist. Rec. Soc.*, vi. 11; x. 34 and *Cartulary of Old Wardon*, ed. G. H. Fowler (Manchester, 1931), pp. 44, 109). He appears in the king's court in 1200 as attorney for another landowner from northern France, William, advocate of Béthune, who was friendly with the count of Guines (*Curia Regis rolls*, i. 174, 230).

The abbot *de Parco* was probably Robert, abbot of Notley, 'de Parco Thame' (Arrouaisian), Bucks.

----

[1] sententialiter *interlined.*   [2] tam delegatis *repeated and deleted.*

7. *Litere Celestini iii in quibus confirmat monialibus de Harewold'*
ecclesiam de Stiventon' cum omnibus possessionibus.

Celestinus episcopus servus[1] servorum dei dilectis in Christo
filiabus priorisse ac monialibus cenobii de Harewold' salutem
et apostolicam benedictionem. Iustis petentium desideriis[2] dignum est nos facilem prebere consensum, et vota que a rationis
tramite non discordant effectu prosequente complere. Eapropter, dilecte in domino filie, vestris iustis postulationibus grato
concurrentes assensu, monasterium vestrum cum omnibus que
in presenciarum rationabiliter possidetis vel in futuro deo
propicio poteritis adhipisci sub beati Petri et nostra protectione
suscipimus. Specialiter autem ecclesias sancti Petri de Harewold' et de Stiventon' cum possessionibus, que per donatorum
scripta eidem sunt cenobio confirmate, sicut eas iuste et sine
controversia possidetis, vobis et per vos ipsi cenobio auctoritate apostolica et presentis scripti patrocinio communimus,
statuentes ut nulli omnino hominum liceat hanc paginam nostre
protectionis et confirmationis infringere vel ei ausu temerario
contraire. Siquis vero hoc atemptare presumpserit, indigna-
cionem omnipotentis dei et beatorum Petri et Pauli apostolorum
eius se noverit incursurum. Dat' Laterani xvii kal. Maii
pontificatus nostri anno sexto.

15 April 1196. The dating clause shows that the pope is Celestine III, and not
Celestine IV, as inferred from a copy without this clause in the Harrold cartulary
(*Beds. Hist. Rec. Soc.*, xvii. 53–4).

8. *Litere magistri Warini de Hubaldeston' in quibus testificatur quod*
moniales habuerunt cartam Alexandri episcopi.

Venerabilibus viris officialibus domini Cantuar' Warinus de
Hubaldeston' salutem. Ad instantiam monialium de Harewold'
requisitus ut super hiis que me presente acta sunt testimonium
perhiberem veritati, discretioni vestre significo quod cum causa
verteretur inter B. filium comitis de Ginnes et moniales de
Harewold' super ecclesia de Stiventon' coram abbate de Wardon',
priore de Chikessaunte, et[3] archidiacono de Huntindon' auctoritate domini pape, post publicationem attestationum dies prefixus

---

[1] servus *omitted.*
[2] iustum *added and expunged.*
[3] et *interlined.*

fuit apud Sanctum Neotum disputationi faciende. Ad illum vero diem presens fui et me presente coram abbate de Wardon' et priore de Chikessaund, archidiacono Huntendon' excusante inpotentiam suam, super attestationibus satis fuit disputatum et ut michi videbatur satis fuit per testes sufficienter probatum quod super eadem ecclesia confirmationem Alexandri episcopi habuerunt et eam ammiserunt. Ne autem iudices premature sententiarent, diem alium sententie proferende apud Bedeford prefixerunt. Hiis agendis apud Sanctum Neotum interfui et quod hoc verum sit in veritate que deus est vobis testificor. Valete.

Late 1198–May 1199? see Introduction. Master Warin de Hubaldeston' probably took his name from Hibaldstow, Lincs., and was the Master Guarinus de Hibaldestowe who gave a 'Liber Aristotelis' to Lincoln Cathedral Library soon after 1200 (R. M. Woolley, *Cat. of the MSS. of Lincoln Cath. Chapter Library* (Cambridge, 1927), p. viii). A *magister* of this name was a tenant of Peterborough Abbey, and had a wife Margaret and a son Ralph (Peterborough, D. & C. Library, MS. 5 fo. 97ᵛ). He may be identical with Master Garinus, official of the archdeacon of Bedford, 1193×1198 (C. R. Cheney, *English Bishops' Chanceries* (Manchester, 1950), p. 145 n. 6) and/or the Master Warinus, vicar of St. Mary's, Bedford, 1200 (*Curia Regis Rolls*, i. 298). See also *Beds. Hist. Rec. Soc.*, x. 44, 98–9.

9. Litere Laurentii archidiaconi Bedeford' in quibus testificatur moniales possedisse ecclesiam de Stiventon' et quod excommunicaverat B. propter intrusionem.

Venerabili domino et amico karissimo magistro R. decano Lincoln' suus L. archidiaconus Bedeford' salutem in vero salutari. Post suscepcionem literarum domini Cant' michi denuo transmissarum, diligenti facta inquisitione per archidiaconatum Bedeford' utrum ecclesia de Stiventon' sententia iudicum a domino papa delegatorum monialibus de Harewold' rationabiliter esset adiudicata, assercione multorum michi constitit predictam ecclesiam sententialiter fuisse monialibus adiudicatam et ipsas eam aliquo tempore possedisse; quam cum B. de Ginnes et complices sui iniuste occupassent et detinerent contra iusticiam occupatam ipsum, ut decuit, commonui ut monialibus predictam ecclesiam restitueret et a¹ tam enormi² temeritate desisteret. Quem cum salubres monitus meos contempnere et

---

¹ a *interlined.*
² anormi, a *expunged.*

manifestum et notorium intrusorem viderem, sicut ex mandato domini Cant' et vestro suscepi, ipsum B. et complices suos ob manifestam et notoriam intrusionem sententia excommunicationis innodavi et ab omnibus quasi excommunicatos caucius evitari precepi. Ipsi vero nichilominus ab incepta temeritate non[1] desistunt.

> Late 1198–May 1199. Later than no. 4, and earlier than Whitsun 1199 when Lawrence, archdeacon of Bedford, had been succeeded as archdeacon by one Richard (*Cartulary of Old Wardon*, p. 109). Lawrence had been one of those nominated for the see of York in 1186. *Gesta Henrici*, i. 352. Cf. C. T. Clay, *York Minster Fasti*, i (1958), 89, 91. He bequeathed C.U.L. MS. Kk. 4.21 to St. Mary's Huntingdon.
>
> The dean of Lincoln was Master Roger de Rolveston (1195–1223), the archbishop of Canterbury Hubert Walter (1193–1205).

10. *Litere iudicum delegatorum in quibus testificantur quod constitit eis moniales habuisse confirmationem Alexandri episcopi.*

Venerabilibus dominis et in Christo dilectis domini Cantuar' officialibus P. quondam[2] dictus abbas de Wardon' et prior de Chikessaunt salutem et canonicam cum reverentia obedientiam. Ad iustam monialium de Harewold' requisitionem super processu cause que inter illas et B. de Ginnes super ecclesia de Stiventon' coram nobis vertebatur, que pro certo recolimus excellencie vestre intimare curavimus. Publicatis siquidem suo die apud Bedefort utriusque partis attestationibus,[3] ad inquirendum de vita testium ad instituendam[4] disputationem alium diem apud Sanctum Neotum prefiximus. Quo convenientes disputationem partium supradictarum testium diligenter audivimus. Alium quoque diem post intervallum legitimum in eodem loco prefixum in prosecutione institute disputationis solempniter exegimus. Et quia veritas sepius exagitata magis splendescit in lucem, tercium diem sub competenti dilatione apud Bedefort constituentes et ad ipsum convenientes, rationes hinc inde continuatis ad hoc duobus diebus cum omni diligentia audiendo cognovimus et tandem causam secundum modulum discrecionis nobis a deo date simul cum consilio virorum discretorum et honestorum assidencium per sententiam terminavimus, ad hos omnes dies B. quidem licet[5] vocato non comparente sed

---

[1] non *omitted.*   [2] quondam *interlined.*
[3] attestationibus *altered from* attestationes.
[4] instituendam *altered from* instituandam.   [5] licet *interlined*

magistro R. de Luiton' vices suas cum omni visu exequente. Quoniam autem quidam nituntur asserere super carta Alexandri episcopi a monialibus habita nullam per testes probacionem coram nobis fuisse exhibitam, attestationes coram nobis super hoc legitime deo teste confectas, que nobis in scriniis nostris querentibus ad presens occurrunt, sub sigillis nostris clausas cum ipso tenore suo vobis transmittimus. Fuerunt et testes super amissione instrumentorum monialium sub iureiurando testificantes, quorum dicta licet diligenter quesierimus non habemus. Que licet ad fidem vobis faciendam sufficerent, ex habundanti tamen et ne quid desiderate instructionis deesse videretur, priorissam de Harewold' iurantem inspeximus quod non dolo fecit[1] quo minus appareret eadem carta sed productio eius inpossibilis erat ammisimus.[2] Ego autem P. quondam dictus abbas, quia iam claustralis sum et sigillum non habeo, sigillum abbatis nostri quod ad hoc michi commodavit apposui. Valeat in Christo sanctitas vestra.

Late 1198–May 1199? see Introduction.

11. *Litere prioris de Sancto Neoto in quibus testificatur quod moniales adunaverant quamplures ad expellendum B. de Ginnes de ecclesia sua de Stiventon' quam violenter occupaverat.*

G. dei gratia Roffensi episcopo et aliis domini Cant' officiali-bus G. dictus prior de Sancto Neoto salutem et debitam reverentiam cum salute. Cum inquisitio super causa que verte-batur inter moniales de Harewold' et B. de Ginnes prioribus de Essebi et de Huntendon' et michi auctoritate vestra facienda fuisset commissa, nos cum omni diligentia[3] sicut decuit manda-tum vestrum exequentes, testes admisimus et pre multitudine testium per intervalla trium dierum continuo productorum oportuit nos ad invicem separari ad tot testes examinandos. Ego vero testes monialium examinavi, ad quarum instanciam vobis significare curavi quod clausula illa que sequitur testi-monium Simonis Blundi dictum est examinantis[4] et non solius S. testificantis, quia in veritate que deus est recolo quod fere omnes testes provenientes de Nortgivel' et de Sutgivel' et de

---

[1] quod non dolo fecit *expunged and repeated.*   [2] *sic, for* admisimus.
[3] dililentia.   [4] dictum est examinantis *interlined.*

Harewold'[1] iuraverunt se fuisse in comitatu eorum quos moniales de Harewold' adunaverant ad B. de Ginnes expellendum de ecclesia sua de Stiventon' quam occupaverat. Valete.

Late 1198–July 1205, probably 1198–9. See Introduction.

Gilbert Glanvill, bishop of Rochester (1185–1214). Alexander, prior of *Essebi* (Canons Ashby), O.S.A., Northants., was a well-known religious writer (see J. C. Russell, *Dict. of writers of xiii cent. England* (1936), pp. 12–13 and R. W. Hunt, *Trans. Roy. Hist. Soc.*, 4th series, xix (1936), 28–9). The prior of St. Neots (O.S.B., Hunts., a cell of Bec) was probably Geoffrey, occurs 1199–1204 (*Heads of Religious Houses*, ed. D. Knowles, C. N. L. Brooke, and V. London (Cambridge, 1972) p. 108). The prior of Huntingdon (O.S.A.) may have been William, mentioned 1199–Nov. 1202 (ibid., p. 166).

Nortgivel, Sutgivel: Northill, Southill (Beds.).

12. *Litere B. de Ginnes in quibus constituit procuratorem ad totam causam.*

Venerabili in domino patri J. dei gratia Sancte Marie in Via Lata diacono cardinali apostolice sedis legato B. de Ginnes temporalem et eternam[2] in domino salutem. In causa que vertitur inter moniales de[3] Malling' et W. de Wrotham ex una parte et me ex alia parte super spoliatione ecclesie de Estmalling' variis prepeditus negociis interesse non possum. Ideo in hac causa magistrum A. de Castro Puellarum procuratorem meum constituo, ratum habiturus quicquid ab eo in hac causa in presentia vestra mediante iusticia actum fuerit.[4] Eundem etiam A. in causa que vertitur inter moniales de Harewold' ex una parte et me ex alia parte super ecclesia de Stiventon' procuratorem constituo, promittens pro eo iudicatum solvi. Idem partibus significo.

May–Oct. 1206. Dated by the legation of John of Ferentino, cardinal deacon of S. Maria in Via Lata (see *EHR*, xlvi (1931), 443–52).

On 6 March 1206 the king presented William of Wrotham, archdeacon of Taunton (on whom see *EHR*, xl (1925), 570–9) to the church of East Malling 'que fuit Baldewini de Ginnes et vacat,' on the grounds that it was in the gift of the archbishopric of Canterbury, now vacant in the king's hand (*Rotuli litt. patentium*, ed. T. D. Hardy, p. 60a). But a month later (5 April) the king recognized by charter to the nuns of Malling that Archbishop Hubert had appropriated the church of East Malling to their use (*Rotuli chartarum*, ed. T. D. Hardy, p. 164b); on the same day he confirmed the church of Stevington to the nuns of Harrold (no. 19).

[1] et de Harewold' *interlined.*
[2] et eternam *interlined.*
[3] Harewold' *added and expunged.*
[4] fuit.

13. *Processus cause inter moniales de Harewold' et B. de Ginnes coram Johanne Sancte Marie¹ in Via Lata diacono cardinali tunc apostolice sedis legato.*

Johannes dei gratia Sancte Marie in Via Lata diaconus cardinalis apostolice sedis legatus universis Christi fidelibus ad quos presens scriptum pervenerit in vero salutari salutem. Ad vestram volumus notitiam pervenire quod cum moniales de Harewold' ecclesia de Stiventon' per Baldewinum de Ginnes se assererent contra iusticiam spoliatas et ipsum se in eam per violentiam intrusisse ac super hoc lis coram nobis fuisset contestata et testes hinc inde producti, tandem attestationibus de assensu parcium puplicatis, ad disputandum super attestationibus partibus statuimus certum diem ad quem, licet utriusque partis accesserit procurator, is tamen quem B. procuratorem statuerat quibusdam ab adversa parte propositis, a nobis illicenciatus abcessit nec postmodum voluit comparere. Interim vero idem per suas nobis literas supplicavit quod cum procuratorem in Anglia non haberet certum diem prefigeremus eidem ne indefensus forsan contrariam sententiam reportaret et ne aliter in causa procederemus eadem, ad sedem apostolicam appellavit. Licet autem quampluribus appellatio eius frustratoria videretur, ex eo presertim quod coram nobis ad totam causam certum procuratorem constituerat et literas procuratorias ei duxerat concedendas, quia tamen iam conceperamus propositum transfretandi, domino nostro summo pontifici per nostras duximus literas intimanda ut auctoritate apostolica suppleretur quod supplendum fuerit in hac causa. Attestationes etiam que fuerunt super eodem² facto recepte apud monasterium Sancti Augustini Cantuar' deponi fecimus, nostri sigilli munimine roboratas, illis iudicibus exhibendas quibus causa super hoc fuerit a summo pontifice delegata.

October 1206. Cf. no. 12 note.

14. *Litere abbatis Sancti Augustini in quibus testificatur quod recipit in deposito attestationes monialium de Harewold' et B. de Ginnes sub sigillo legati, et quod misit ipsas attestationes iudicibus delegatis sub sigillo ipsius legati sicut eas recepit.*

¹ Sancte Marie *omitted*.   ² negocio *added and expunged*.

Viris venerabilibus et in Christo dilectis A. decano, J.
cancelario Sancti Pauli London' et R. archidiacono Colecestr'
R. dei gratia abbas Sancti Augustini Cantuar' et eiusdem loci
humilis conventus salutem in quo est salus omnium. Noverit
vestra discretio nos de voluntate domini J. Sancte Marie[1] in
Via Lata diaconi cardinalis tunc apostolice sedis legati attestationes monialium de Harewold' et B. de Ginnes in iudicio
coram ipso legato super ecclesia de Stiventon' receptas sub
sigillo ipsius legati in nostra presentia signatas in deposito
admississe, illis iudicibus exhibendas quibus dominus papa
ipsam causam duxerit committendam. Et quia tam ex inspec-
tione literarum domini pape[2] quam ex mandati vestri tenore
nobis constat quod dominus papa vestre discretioni eandem
causam duxit committere terminandam, de fide ac fidelitate
Stephani de Haversam clerici confisi, vobis per eundem
Stephenum ipsas attestationes sic sigillo antedicti[3] cardinalis
signatas prout eas recepimus salvo transmittimus. Et in huius
rei testimonium sigillum ecclesie nostre huic scripto aposuimus.
Valete.

May–Aug. 1207. See Introduction and nos. 15 and 16.

The abbot of St. Augustine's, Canterbury, is Roger of Lurdingden (1175–
1213), the dean of St. Paul's Master Alard of Burnham (1201–16), the chancellor
Master John of Kent (1204–14), and the archdeacon of Colchester Richard of
Ely (1192–1214). Stephen of Haversham, the abbot's clerk, is untraced.

15. *Litere A. decani Lond' et coniudicum suorum quarum auctoritate
moniales de Harewold' misse fuerunt in possessionem ecclesie de
Stiventon' per abbatem de Lavendon'.*

A. decanus Sancti Pauli London' et R. archidiaconus
Colecestr' viro venerabili dei gratia abbati de Wardinton' vel
Lavenden'[4] salutem in domino. Literas domini pape in hec
verba suscepimus: Innocencius episcopus servus servorum dei
dilectis filiis . . . decano . . . cancelario Sancti Pauli London' et
archidiacono Colecestr' London' diocesis salutem et apostolicam benedictionem. Significarunt nobis priorissa et moniales
de Harewold' quod cum inter ipsas ex una parte et B. de Ginnes
Cantuar' diocesis ex altera parte super ecclesia de Stiventon'
in qua dictum B. proponebant fuisse violenter intrusum coram

[1] Sancte Marie *omitted.*   [2] pape *interlined.*
[3] legati *added and expunged.*   [4] vel Lavenden' *interlined.*

dilecto filio J. Sancte Marie in Via Lata diacono cardinali tunc apostolice sedis legato questio verteretur, receptis testibus et etiam publicatis procurator eiusdem B. causam ipsam[1] reliquid penitus indefensam, propter quod memoratus B. per literas suas ad sedem apostolicam appellavit, et licet altera pars proponeret quod non esset appellationi huiusmodi defferendum, cardinalis tamen quia iam ad reditum festinabat, in causa ipsa ulterius non processit. Quo circa discretioni vestre per apostolica scripta mandamus quatinus receptis attestationibus iam dicti legati sigillo signatis causam eandem mediante iusticia sublato appellationis obstaculo terminetis, facientes quod decreveritis per censuram ecclesiasticam firmiter observari, nullis literis veritati et iusticie preiudicantibus a sede apostolica impetratis. Quod si non omnes hiis exequendis potueritis interesse duo vestrum ea nichilominus exequantur. Dat' Laterani viii idus Aprilis pontificatus nostri anno decimo. Huius igitur auctoritate[2] mandati dictum B. de Ginnes edicto peremptorio legitime vocari fecimus ut coram nobis vel per se vel per sufficientem responsalem compareret ipsis monialibus secundum formam mandati apostolici sibi sufficienter editi responsurus et iuri pariturus. Et quia die sibi competenter edicto peremptorio statuto non comparuit nec pro se aliquem responsalem mittere curavit, propter ipsius manifestam contumatiam iuris ordine observato sepedictis monialibus possessionem ecclesie de Stiventon' causa rei servande adiudicavimus, magistro J. de Cantia ecclesie nostre cancellario collega nostro se ad diem illum per literas suas sufficienter excusante. Nos igitur auctoritate domini pape qua fungimur in hac parte vobis mandamus quatinus ipsas moniales vel earum procuratorem in possessionem ecclesie de Stiventon' causa rei servande mittere non postponatis. Si quos autem resistentes inveneritis, ipsos per censuram ecclesiasticam percellatis.

May–Aug. 1207. Pope Innocent III's mandate of 6 April 1207 cannot have been received before May, and the abbot of Lavendon took action at latest in August (see no. 16).

Wardinton' vel Lavenden': Lavendon Abbey (O. Prem.) Bucks. Wardinton is not the present Wardington, Oxon., but Warrington, Bucks., which adjoins Lavendon (cf. *Mon. Ang.*, vii. 888). Mr. H. M. Colvin kindly informs me that the abbot's name, W. (cf. no. 16), is found in no other dated record.

---

[1] ipsan.   [2] auctoritate igitur *marked for transposition.*

16. *Litere ipsius abbatis de Lavenden' vel de Wardenton' in quibus significat iudicibus quod misit ipsas moniales de mandato eorum in possessionem ecclesie de Stiventon' causa rei servande.*

Viris venerabilibus et in Christo dilectis A. decano, J. cancellario Sancti Pauli London' et R. archidiacono Colecestr' W. dictus abbas de Lavenden' salutem in domino. Noveritis nos[1] literas vestras in hec verba suscepisse: A. decanus, J. cancelarius Sancti Pauli London', et R. archidiaconus Colecestr' dilecto sibi in Christo W. dei gratia abbati de Lavenden' salutem in domino. Literas domini pape in hec verba suscepimus: Innocensius episcopus, *etc. sicut superius continetur in literis iudicum usque ad finem, scilicet usque* percellatis. Ego siquidem, vobis et mandato vestro libenti animo parens ac devoto, ad ecclesiam sepedictam in propria persona accessi, ipsasque priorissam et moniales nullo resistente vel contradicente in possessionem ipsius ecclesie iuxta formam mandati vestri misi, et cum in plena essent possessione et pacifica pro iure suo et possessione me presente sedem apostolicam appellaverunt. Facta autem fuit hec missio proxima die mercurii ante festum beati Johannis Babtiste proximum antequam Henricus filius domini regis Johannis natus esset apud Winton' ab Ysabel regina. Et in huius rei testimonium huic scripto sigillum meum apposui. Valete.

October 1207? Not earlier, since the king's son Henry was born 1 October 1207. The feast of St. John the Baptist was probably the Decollation, and the date of the admission of the nuns 26 August.

17. *Litere ipsorum iudicum in quibus mandant archidiacono Bedeford' quod adiudicaverunt monialibus veram possessionem ecclesie de Stiventon', et quod faciat eas ipsam ecclesiam pacifice possidere, nec permittat eas ab aliquo super hoc vexari.*

A. decanus, J. cancellarius Sancti Pauli London' et R. archidiaconus Colecestr' dilecto sibi in Christo magistro A.[2] archidiacono Bedeford' salutem in domino. Cum causa que vertitur inter priorissam et moniales de Harewold' super ecclesia de Stiventon' ex una parte et B. de Ginnes ex altera nobis a domino papa esset commissa fine canonico terminanda, ob manifestam et multiplicem ipsius B. contumatiam posses-

---

[1] nos *interlined.*   [2] A. *interlined.*

sionem ecclesie de Stiventon' causa rei servande ipsis monialibus adiudicavimus et ipsas in possessionem ecclesie causa rei
servande per venerabilem virum abbatem de Lavenden' induci
fecimus. Et quia nobis postmodum sufficienter constitit quod
annus elapsus est infra quem dictus B. se iudicio sisti offerre
non curavit, veram[1] possessionem ipsis monialibus adiudicavimus, sepedicto B. reservata questione proprietatis. Postquem
sententiam a nobis latam procurator ipsarum monialium ad
hoc coram nobis constitutus ad iuris sui tuitionem sedem
apostolicam apellavit. Ideoque vobis auctoritate domini pape
qua fungimur mandamus quatinus ipsas priorissam et moniales
dictam ecclesiam pacifice possidere[2] faciatis nec eas ab aliquo
super possessione sua a nobis adiudicata vexari permittatis, quin
ipsum perturbatorem per censuram ecclesiasticam percellatis.

After Aug. 1208. Cf. no. 16: a year has elapsed since the possession was
awarded *causa rei servande*.

The archdeacon of Bedford is Master Alexander of Elstow.

18. *Litere eorundem iudicum in quibus mandant domino Lincoln'*[3]
sicut superius mandaverunt archidiacono Bedeford'.

Reverendo domino et patri in Christo karissimo H. dei
gratia[4] Lincolniensi episcopo A. decanus Sancti Pauli Lond' et
R. archidiaconus Colecestr' salutem et tam devotam quam
debitam in omnibus reverentiam. Literas domini pape in hec
verba suscepimus: Innocencius episcopus servus[5] servorum dei
etc. sicut superius continetur in literis iudicum usque Vestre igitur.
Vestre igitur volumus innotare[6] paternitati quod nos huius[7]
auctoritate mandati dictum B. de Ginnes edicto peremptorio
legitime vocari fecimus ut coram nobis vel per se vel per
sufficientem responsalem compareret ipsis monialibus secundum formam mandati apostolici sibi sufficienter editi responsurus super memorata ecclesia et iuri pariturus. Et quia die sibi
competenter edicto peremptorio statuto non comparuit nec
pro se aliquem responsalem mittere curavit, propter ipsius

---

[1] veram *interlined, over* ipsam *expunged.*
[2] permittatis *added and expunged.*
[3] Lincoln' *interlined.*   [4] gratia *interlined.*
[5] servus *omitted.*   [6] innocere.
[7] huius *interlined.*

manifestum contumatiam iuris ordine observato sepedictis monialibus possessionem ecclesie de Stiventon' causa rei servande adiudicavimus, magistro J. de Kancia collega nostro se ad diem illum per literas suas sufficienter excusante, et ipsas in possessionem causa rei servande per venerabilem virum abbatem de Lavenden' induci fecimus. Et quia postmodum nobis sufficienter constitit quod annus elapsus[1] est infra quam dictus B. se iudicio sisti offerre non curavit, veram possessionem ipsis monialibus adiudicavimus, sepedicto B. reservata questione proprietatis. Et post ipsam sententiam nostram a nobis latam procurator ipsarum monialium ad hoc coram nobis constitutus pro iure suo et possessione sedem apostolicam appellavit et ad sue appellationis tuitionem ad dominum Cantuar' vocem appellationis remisit. Ideoque auctoritate domini pape qua fungimur vestre discretioni significando mandamus[2] quatinus ipsas priorissam et moniales dictam ecclesiam pacifice possidere faciatis, nec eas ab aliquo super possessione sibi a nobis adiudicata vexari permittatis, quin ipsum perturbatorem per censuram ecclesiasticam percellatis. Bene ac feliciter valeat sanctitas vestra in domino.

July 1213–April 1214 (see above, p. 295). The bishop of Lincoln is Hugh of Wells (1209 35).

19. Johannes dei gratia rex Anglie dominus Hybernie, dux Normannie et Aquitannie, comes Andegavie, archiepiscopis, episcopis, abbatibus, comitibus, baronibus, iusticiariis, vicecomitibus, prepositis, et omnibus bailliis et fidelibus suis salutem. Sciatis nos intuitu dei et pro salute nostra et pro animabus antecessorum et heredum nostrorum concessisse et hac carta nostra confirmasse monialibus de Harewod'[3] ecclesiam de Stiventon'[4] cum omnibus appendiciis suis quam habent de donatione Baldewini de Ard'[5] sicut carta eiusdem Baldewini quam inde habent[6] testatur. Quare volumus et firmiter precipimus quod predicte moniales habeant et teneant predictam ecclesiam de Stiventon'[7] cum omnibus pertinenciis

---

[1] elepsus.
[2] *preceded by* manda- *at the end of the preceding line.*
[3] Harwd' *Charter roll.*   [4] Stivinton *Charter roll.*
[5] Arda *Charter roll.*   [6] *add* rationabiliter *Charter roll.*
[7] Stivinton *Charter roll.*

et libertatibus suis bene et in pace et libere et quiete, integre et honorifice, sicut predictum est. Teste domino J. Norwic' episcopo et Cantuar' electo, domino P. Winton' episcopo, G. filio Petri comite Essexie, R. comite Cestrie, W. comite Sar', Petro de Stok'. Dat' per manum Hugonis de Well' archidiaconi Well' apud Rumenel, v° die Aprilis anno regni nostri septimo.

5 April 1206. The official enrolment of this charter is printed in *Rotuli chartarum*, ed. T. D. Hardy, p. 164*b*, the formal passages being abridged. A much less complete version is printed from a lost Cottonian manuscript in *Mon. Ang.*, vi, 331*a*.

16. The Downfall of the Templars and a Letter in their Defence*

IN the years between 1307 and 1314 the downfall of the Templars shocked Western Christendom profoundly, and it has excited interest and passion among historians and moralists ever since. In the course of centuries more information has come to light than was available at the time to any but the principal actors. One can now make a cool, reasonable assessment of the damage done to various reputations by this dismal affair, thanks to the records of interrogations and confessions found in various quarters, to the appeal of the accused sent to the Curia in 1310 and preserved in Paris and Rome and, finally, to the Aragonese ambassadorial dispatches discovered and published by Finke. Yet this cannot, if historians are permitted to entertain any generous sentiment, preclude a feeling of compassion for the victims, disgust at the behaviour of the chief engineers of their ruin, despair at the mixture of blindness, impotence, and indifference displayed by official leaders of the Church.[1]

In 1307, through the direct action and the influence of Philip IV of France, the Templars were all imprisoned, and the world at large was told that the whole Order lay under heavy suspicion

---

* First published in *Medieval Miscellany presented to Eugène Vinaver*, ed. F. Whitehead, A. H. Diverres, and F. E. Sutcliffe (Manchester, 1965).

[1] This is not the place to recapitulate the whole history of the affair. Half a century ago it received serious and balanced treatment from Mgr. Mollat, Finke, Lizerand, and Dom Henri Leclercq (in his translation of Hefele's *Histoire des Conciles*, VI. i, 1914), but it still remains a hunting-ground for the fanciful and sensational writer. A good account is in G. Mollat, *Les Papes d'Avignon* (9th ed., 1949), pp. 367–89, with a bibliography, pp. 562–5. A comprehensive *Bibliographie de l'Ordre des Templiers* (1927), was compiled by M. Dessubré. Heinrich Finke's *Papsttum und Untergang des Templerordens*, Vorreformationsgeschichtliche Forschungen, v. (Münster, 1907) contains invaluable texts in the second volume. Georges Lizerand re-edited many previously published documents in *Le Dossier de l'Affaire des Templiers*, Classiques de l'Histoire de France au Moyen Âge (1923); references will be given below to this convenient edition (cited as *Dossier*) in preference to those of Dupuy, Raynouard, Michelet, and others.

of being renegades and heretics, guilty of nameless vices. Confessions by apostates from the Order and delation on hearsay by outsiders were followed by confessions extracted under torture in France from the Grand Master, Jacques de Molai, and many other Templars. The evidence such as it was, seemed damning. But then came retractations and stubborn denials. When in May 1310 fifty-four Templars were burned at Paris and nine more at Senlis, having been condemned by a provincial council as relapsed heretics and handed over to the secular arm, one and all declared their innocence with their dying breath. When the same fate overtook the Grand Master on 19 March 1314, he likewise professed his orthodoxy at the stake. This shook public opinion. A learned theologian of Paris, Master Jean de Pouilli, might find sophistry to satisfy himself that this obstinacy was only further proof of guilt,[1] but not all the doctors of Paris were of his mind. Pierre de La Palu, having himself witnessed in 1310 the examination of some Templars, gave indeterminate testimony which seems to be favourable to the Order rather than the reverse.[2] A Dominican inquisitor of probity and experience, Bernard Gui, seems to have been baffled by the contradictory evidence.[3] Another Parisian theologian, the Cistercian Jacques de Thérines, abbot of Chaalis, reviewed in 1311 the reasons for and against believing in the truth of the accusations against the Order. He still had an open and a troubled mind: 'Si vera sunt quae dicuntur', 'si talia non haberent veritatem', 'si vera sunt universaliter quoad omnes' indicate his perplexity, and he concludes with the prayer that the Lord may reveal the truth of the matter before the closure of the General Council at which the fate of the Order was being decided.[4] Beyond the cautious expression

---

[1] See the article on him by Noël Valois in *Histoire Littéraire de la France*, xxxiv (1914), 229.   [2] *Dossier*, pp. 192–4.

[3] E. Baluze, *Vitae Paparum Avenionensium*, ed. G. Mollat (1914–22), i. 68; and in *Recueil des Historiens des Gaules et de la France* (hereafter *RHF*), xxi. 719.

[4] For Jacques see Valois in 'Deux nouveaux Témoignages sur le Procès des Templiers', Académie des Sciences et Belles Lettres, *Comptes Rendus* des séances de l'année 1910, pp. 229–41, and in *Hist. Litt. de la France*, xxxiv. 179–219. He shows that the common spelling 'Thermes' for 'Thérines' is mistaken. As a monk of Chaalis, Jacques was one of the fourteen Parisian masters who replied in an unfavourable sense to Philip IV's enquiry about his jurisdiction over the Templars and their property (below, p. 319). His discussion of the Templars

of doubt no high ecclesiastic who valued his reputation in 1312 could afford to go. And the same caution must have infected lesser men. Such was the violence of the action against the French Templars that a man would think twice before coming to their defence. As F. J.-M. Raynouard observed, when he edited some of the documents in 1813, 'rarement des proscrits trouvent des apologistes'.[1] The author of the chronicle attributed to Geffroy de Paris was, according to its latest editor, 'visiblement pas dupe des . . . accusations officielles portées contre les Templiers'.[2] It is observable how cautious are his expressions:

> 3418   Je ne sai a tort ou a droit
> Furent li Templiers, sanz doutance,
> Touz pris par le royaume de France;

and he compares their arrest at dawn on a Friday with Our Lord's passion. Other phrases point the same way: 'Se voirs estoit qu'en disoit d'elz' (3426), 's'il est voir' (3430 and 3450), 'si fu la verité trouvee' (3574).

> 3476   Car il s'estoient trop meffet,
> Si comme assez de genz le dïent;
> Mes je ne sai se il mesdïent.
> Mes l'en doit tenir chose a voire,
> Ce qu'apostoile a voulu fere
> Et du monde le grant conseil,
> Por ce de ce taire me veil.
> 3549   Et molt de foiz, selon l'escrit,

occurs in his 'Contra impugnatores exemptionum', written at the time of the Council of Vienne, printed by Bertrand Tissier, *Bibliotheca Patrum Cisterciensium* (1660–9), iv. 298–9, whence reprinted by Ewald Müller, *Das Konzil von Vienne, 1311–1312* (Vorreformationsgesch. Forschungen, xii. (Münster, 1934)), pp. 691–2. Müller was apparently unacquainted with the work of Valois, who translates this passage (*Comptes Rendus*, pp. 239–40, *Hist. Litt. de la France*, xxxiv. 198–9).

[1] F. J.-M. Raynouard, *Monuments historiques, relatifs à la Condamnation des Chevaliers du Temple et à l'Abolition de leur Ordre* (1813), p. 8.

[2] Armel Diverres, *La Chronique métrique attribué à Geffroy de Paris* (1956), p. 13 n. 2. Dr. Diverres considers it possible, without stressing the possibility, that a second author composed the latter part (see p. 15 n. 3). If so, both were at one in their reservations about the Templars' trial: cf. ll. 5757–70 with the passages quoted here. Raynouard was the first to call attention to the significance of these passages (op. cit., p. 30).

Celz que le prelast maleïst,
Que justement Dieux les assost,
Car Diex tout voit et si set tout.
Et mains, ou monde condempnez,
Sont lassus ou ciel coronnez.
3557 Mes ça aval, en ceste Yglise,
Nous couvient trestouz la devise
Tenir du pape et l'ordenance.
Et celui qui en fet doutance
Fet une espece d'heresie.

There lay the main reason for silence. Gabriel Le Bras well said: 'Comme toute société religieuse, l'Église chrétienne a besoin d'orthodoxie, de rites et de pratique. Elle déteste plus que les païens les hérétiques, tout autant les schismatiques et elle exècre les critiques et les opposants: elle s'efforce de prévenir, découvrir, punir tous ceux qui sapent ou paraissent saper son *credo.*'[1] To be associated with heretics was dangerous, and the common man in Paris was reminded of the fact by other burnings in 1310 besides the holocaust of Templars.

Compassion and bewilderment there evidently was. Giovanni Boccaccio's father was in Paris on business in 1314 and saw the burning of Jacques de Molai: he testified that 'in compassionem sui miseros eciam provocavit'.[2] The Latin continuator of Guillaume de Nangis bears this out. Many of the populace, he says, were amazed and greatly perplexed at the sight of the Templars' constancy at the stake. This passage in the chronicle was transformed in the *Grandes chroniques* to suit the official view, but the new version is even more telling: 'Mais yceus, tant eussent à souffrir de doleur, onques en leur destruction ne vouldrent aucune chose recognoistre; pour laquelle chose leurs âmes, si comme il estimoient, en porent avoir perpetuel

---

[1] G. Le Bras, *Histoire du Droit et des Institutions de l'Église en Occident: Prolégomènes* (1955), p. 27.

[2] *Ioannis Bocatii . . . De Casibus Virorum Illustrium, lib.* ix, c. 21 (Augsburg 1544), p. 262: 'Et sic qui pridie suo fulgore regis tam maximi invidiam irritare potuit, ut aiebat Bocatius genitor meus, qui tunc forte Parrhisius negociator honesto cum labore rem curabat augere domesticam, et se his testabatur interfuisse rebus, ictu fortunae atrocissimo factus civis [*sic*], in compassionem sui miseros etiam provocavit.' The printed edition of 1520 (facsimile ed. by Louis B. Hall (Gainesville, Florida 1962)), fo. cxi^r and Cambridge, University Libr. MS. Ll. 2.8, fo. 124^r supply the necessary emendation of 'civis' to 'cinis'.

dampnement, car il mistrent le menu peuple en très grant erreur.'[1]

Doubts about the guilt of the Templars, we may suppose, were more often whispered than written. Certainly most of the surviving chroniclers, even those who express sharp criticism of Philip IV's unworthy motives and avarice, tend to recount with relish the horrid details of the accusations and leave readers to assume that they represent the truth.[2] Royal propaganda and papal authority had their effect, and until now little positive contemporary defence of the Templars has attracted notice beyond the appeal presented to the papal commissioners by a group of members of the Order on 7 April 1310: 'un beau mémoire', comments M. Lizerand, 'qui est à la fois le plus pressant réquisitoire contre les procédés des agents du roi et une défense qui vaut celle des érudits modernes'.[3]

The text printed below seems to merit publication precisely because it presents not mere doubts or tepid sympathy with the Templars in their sufferings, but a reasoned defence of the Order combined with savage partisanship. It is a piece of outspoken propaganda. Who wrote it and on what occasion remain uncertain. The author—no wonder—is an anonymous *dictator presencium*, and there is a wide field for conjecture, which will not be fully explored here. He writes as a Frenchman. He is so well informed of the rule and customs of the Order that he might be a Templar himself; but, if so, he contrives to write as though he were only a disinterested friend. He hates the Mendicants, and his reference to 'quidam monachus vel verius demoniacus' suggests that he was probably a secular clerk. His respect for the king, whom he represents as misguided, may simply indicate discretion or may be thought to

---

[1] The Latin continuator, as edited by H. Géraud (Soc. Hist. France), i (1843), 378 and in *RHF*, xx. 601; the *Grandes Chroniques*, as edited by J. Viard (Soc. Hist. France), viii (1934), 272–3, and in *RHF*, xx. 685.

[2] See the chronicle of Jean de S. Victor (*RHF*, xxi. 649–50) and the anonymous chronicle to 1308 (ibid. xxi. 137); also Gervais du Bus, in book 1 of *Le Roman de Fauvel*, which was completed in 1310, ed. A. Långfors, Soc. Anciens Textes Français (1914–9), ll. 930–1028. *Purgatorio*, xx. 91–3 condemns Philip IV's action but throws no light on Dante's opinion of the Templars.

[3] *Dossier*, pp. ix, 176–88, 214*–214****. Lizerand slightly abridges the text as printed by P. Dupuy and J. Michelet, but introduces emendations to B.N. MS. latin 11796 from Vatican Archives, MS. AA Arm. D. caps. ix.

point to someone in the king's service. It would be unwise to jump to conclusions. The complaint purports to be addressed to the doctors and scholars of Paris; but this may be no more than a literary device. If it was really a letter, it was probably an open letter.

As for the time of its composition, this seems to be fixed in the first months of 1308 by the statement that the Templars have been suffering indescribable pains for the space of three months since their arrest: they were arrested throughout France on Friday 13 October 1307. By the time that this *Lamentacio* was written confessions had been extracted by torture, and many of the prisoners had already died under their harsh treatment; some were known to be still holding out against the inquisitorial methods of William of Paris, O.P., the king's confessor. This may be compared with the deposition of the Templar, Ponsard de Gizy, on 27 November 1309, that it was after three months of torturing that he had made the confession he now retracted.[1] But from other sources it seems that early in 1308, after the first months of terror and demoralization, the Templars were taking heart from the knowledge of Clement V's disagreement with Philip of France and that they hoped for justice from a papal commission. It was then (in February) that the pope suspended the activity of the inquisitors in France. At about the same time Jacques de Molai displayed his lacerated body to the pope's representatives[2] and retracted his confession. In March Philip IV sought justification of his treatment of the Templars from the theologians of the university of Paris and in reply received an unwelcome denial of his rights.[3] The month of February, then, might well seem a good moment to the writer of the *Lamentacio* to enlist the sympathy of the doctors and scholars and expose to them the horror of the situation. His closing sentence ('concilium tale proferat')

---

[1] *Dossier*, p. 156.

[2] Or so it was reported in an anonymous despatch found in the Aragonese archives: '"Veus, senyors, quens na fet dir ço quals an volgut." E va mostrar los brasos, que totç los ach trencatç e descarnatç, que parech, que atans (?) fos escapatç, que noy ac romas mas los ossos el nervis, que tota la carn e la peil ne fo levada del esquena e del ventre e de les cuxes . . . E con los cadernals viren la gran error e la gran malvestat, ploraren fort agrament, que non podian res dir.' Finke, *Papsttum und Untergang*, ii. 117, cf. ibid. i. 168–9 and *Dossier*, p. 119 n. 3.

[3] *Dossier*, pp. 56–70.

indeed suggests that it may have been addressed to the university in the knowledge that the king was consulting it, and it may have influenced the masters' reply.

One objection which might be advanced to so early a date must be faced. Some passages in the *Lamentacio* rather closely resemble the dossier of exculpatory depositions, made between November 1309 and April 1310 which was sent to the Curia by the papal commissioners. The *Lamentacio* says that thirty-six prisoners had died in the Paris house: so does the deposition of Ponsard de Gizy already cited; are we to suppose that no other deaths were known to have occurred between February 1308 and November 1309? Again, the phraseology of this and a few other passages in the *Lamentacio* closely resembles that of the appeal by a group of Templars on 7 April 1310;[1] in particular, the description of the brethren's admission to the Order is stated in almost exactly the same words in both documents. But while this might suggest that the author of the *Lamentacio* had seen the dossier prepared in 1310, it is easier to suppose that the connection of the two texts, if real, is the reverse. Much had happened between February 1308 and April 1310. The Grand Master, who retracted at the beginning of 1308, made another confession before two cardinals, at Chinon on 20 August 1308.[2] Moreover, the pope had made efforts in the course of that year to gain control over proceedings in France, and papal enquiries were put in train in many other regions. By his bull, *Regnans in celis*, dated 12 August 1308, the pope had also summoned a General Council to meet at Vienne on 1 October 1310 (subsequently postponed for twelve months). It is wellnigh incredible that these developments should not be mentioned in the *Lamentacio* if it were written as late as 1310. The pope's authority is not so much as mentioned. The better conjectural dating is *c.* February 1308.

One or two passages of the *Lamentacio* preserve opinions or facts which do not appear in the other records of the proceedings: the bitter attack upon the Mendicants, who wish to endow their nunneries with the Templars' wealth, the account of the hundred brethren of the Order said to be languishing in

---

[1] The similarities appear in the notes on the text below.
[2] *Dossier*, pp. 150-1.

Egyptian prisons. But the most impressive feature, visible through all the rancour and rhetoric, is the reasoned condemnation of a procedure which was designed not to elicit the truth but to convict the suspect. The fundamental argument against the guilt of the Order as a whole could scarcely have been better stated than it was stated here and in the appeal of 7 April 1310.[1] Centuries later, le grand Arnauld hardly improved upon them with his ponderous words, when he took up the Templars' cause: 'Il n'y a presque personne qui ne croie maintenant, que les Templiers avoient été faussement accusés de faire faire des impiétés, des idolâtries et des impuretés à tous les Chevaliers qu'ils recevoient dans leur Ordre, quoique ceux qui les ont condamnés l'aient pu faire de bonne foi; parce qu'il y en eut plus de deux cents qui l'avouoient, et à qui on donnoit grace à cause de cet aveu. Mais, parce qu'il y en eut aussi, quoique moins en nombre, qui aimèrent mieux être brûlés, que d'avoir leur pardon, en reconnoissant ce qu'ils disoient être faux, le bon sens a fait juger, que dix hommes qui meurent, pouvant ne pas mourir en avouant les crimes dont on les accuse, sont plus croyables que cent qui les avouent, et qui, par cet aveu, rachetent leur vie.'[2]

The letter printed below is found in Cambridge, Corpus Christi College MS. 450,[3] and I have encountered no other text. Probably others exist, but it is unlikely that a document so ephemeral and so clearly contrary to official policy as this is would survive in many copies. In the Corpus manuscript, which is of English origin, it occurs in an anthology of politico-ecclesiastical records which may reflect the interests of an English clerk

[1] *Dossier*, pp. 176–88, 214**–214***.

[2] Antoine Arnaud, *Apologie pour les Catholiques*, in *Œuvres* (1775–83), xiv. 471–2: the work was called forth by the iniquities of Titus Oates and others in the 'Popish Plot', and the passage quoted was prompted by the execution of Viscount Stafford, 29 Dec. 1680. Elsewhere (in the *Apologie pour les Religieuses de Port Royal*), in arguing about the infallibility of condemnations by a pope or general council, he touches on the undeserved fate of the Templars.

[3] I wish to thank the Master and Fellows of Corpus Christi College for permission to print this text. The manuscript forms part of the bequest to the College by its former Master, Archbishop Matthew Parker (d. 1575), and has characteristic underlinings in red pencil by one of his circle. The title of our text was noted in James Nasmith's catalogue of the manuscripts (1777) and a somewhat fuller description was given by M. R. James in his catalogue (1912). It seems to have attracted no other notice.

in the service of the king or of some prelate in the reign of Edward II.[1] M. R. James made the shrewd suggestion that the book was 'probably the property of a notarial personage' in the diocese of Durham.[2] Whoever the compiler was, his sympathies seem to have lain with the English opposition to papal exactions which was such a marked feature of the last years (and especially the last year, 1307) of Edward I. For he includes, with Pope Boniface VIII's bull, *Clericis laicos*, the pope's conciliatory interpretation and Pope Clement V's revocation, and also that rhetorical piece of anti-papal propaganda which was read publicly in the Parliament of Carlisle in January 1307, the letter of 'Peter son of Cassiodorus, *miles catholicus, pugil Christi devotus*', to the English Church.[3] The *Lamentacio* is printed here with a minimum of emendations; the punctuation and capitalization of the manuscript has not been followed.

Corpus Christi Coll., Cambridge, MS. 450, p. 169.

Lamentacio quedam pro Templariis.

Honorabilibus doctoribus et scolaribus universis Parisius commorantibus salutem.

Miranda non modicum forciusque stupenda humani generis inimica crudelitas, in Gasconie finibus instigante diabolo prodicionaliter adinventa,[4] temporibus istis in Francie regnum noscitur esse conversa, que si diligenter inspicitur ad vere compassionis merorem et amare compunctionis lacrimas fidelium debent corda convertere, dum vivus fons iusticie dicti regni, qui totum orbem suis exemplis et moribus irrigabat, penitus desiccatur; accensa quoque veritatis lucerna, que super corone

---

[1] One group of letters (pp. 127–8) relates to the privileges and exemptions of royal clerks.

Among other things the volume contains the 'Summa notariæ' of Archbishop John Pecham's notary, John of Bologna, and the 'Apocalipsis Goliæ episcopi'. I have returned to a discussion of some of the contents in *BJRL*, lv (1972–3).

[2] M. R. James, *Descriptive Catalogue of the Manuscripts in the Library of Corpus Christi College, Cambridge* (Cambridge 1912), ii. 364.

[3] p. 175. It is known in several manuscripts and was printed by Bale and Fox in the sixteenth, and Goldast and Prynne in the seventeenth century. It is most accessible in *The Chronicle of Walter de Guisborough (Hemingburgh)*, ed. H. Rothwell (Royal Historical Society, Camden 3rd Series, lxxxix, 1957), pp. 371–4.

[4] The first informers were Gascon (Mollat, *Papes d'Avignon*, p. 372). Cf. the letter of King Edward II to Philip le Bel, 30 Oct. 1307 (Rymer, 11. i. 10).

candelabrum residere solebat, non solum ipsum regnum set cuntas gencium illustrans naciones, posita est[a] sub modio ne lucescat;[1] quod satis evidenter apparet ex inordinato et iniquo processu contra Templarios edito, nullam prorsus iusticiam set sevam tirannidem continente, dum subito captivati, repente sine iure vel cause cognicione cum exterminato furore[2] turpiter et inhoneste incarcerati, improperiis, comminacionibus[b] gravissimis, et diversis generibus tormentorum [p. 170] afflicti, mori compulsi vel absurda proferre mendacia que protinus ignorabant, in manibus inimicorum sunt perperam[c] traditi,[3] qui ipsos per eadem tormenta dicere cogerent lectionem fedam, turpissimam, et mendacem, quam nec auris humana concipere posset nec in cor hominis cadere deberet.[d] Verum cum fratres ipsi prefata proferre mendacia tanquam eis prorsus incognita recusarent, ab urgentibus satellitibus tormentis ad mendacia cotidie movebantur[e] ut ea dicentes coram Iacobinis assererent esse vera si vitam servare volebant et copiosam a rege graciam optinere. Set ex ipsis plurimi, eligentes deo servire pocius quam Mammone, veritatem forcius amplectentes, tanquam athlete Christi per eadem tormenta numero .xxxvi. in domo Paris' solummodo, preter alios per diversas partes ipsius regni modo simili flagellatos quorum numerus est infinitus, per palmam martirii migrantes ad dominum regna celestia sunt adepti.[4] De reliquis vero plures divina accincti[f] virtute, a prefatis satellitibus in tormentis extincti, pro mortuis sunt semivivi relicti. Velut bellatores fortissimi semper veritatis sentenciam tenuerunt, dicentes qualiter fratres Templi[5] in religionis

---

[a] *ms.* posite.   [b] *ms.* in propriis communicacionibus.   [c] *ms.* proprie.   [d] *ms.* debere.   [e] *ms.* moriebantur.   [f] *ms.* actincti.

---

[1] Cf. Matt. 5 : 15.

[2] *Exterminato furore*: for a use of this term in 1265 see DuCange, *Glossarium*, *s.v.* exterminato.

[3] Cf. Ierem. 44 : 30, etc.

[4] Cf. the statement of Ponsard de Gizy in November 1309: 'triginta sex de dictis fratribus fuerant mortui Parisius per jainnam et tormenta, et multi alii in aliis locis' (*Dossier*, pp. 154–6), and the appeal of 7 Apr. 1310: 'qui, tamquam Christi martires, in tormentis pro veritate sustinenda cum palma martirii decesserunt' (ibid., p. 180).

[5] The following passage (to 'et hoc') is found in almost identical words in the appeal of 7 Apr. 1310 (*Dossier*, pp. 182–4).

ingressu substancialia quatuor promittentes, videlicet obedienciam, castitatem, paupertatem, et se totis viribus exponere
servicio Terre Sancte, ad honestum pacis osculum sunt recepti;
cruce dominica cum habitu simul assumpta, mores et regulam
ab ecclesia Romana et sanctis patribus eis traditam servare
docentur;[a] et hoc idem passim fratres dicti ordinis referebant,
asserebant, et asserunt proprio iuramento. Set dicti satellites
et etiam fratres Iacobini, iniquitatis tante magistri vel pocius
assessini, a dicta veritate quam concipere non valebant aures
more aspidis obturabant[1] et velut[b] venenosus coluber torque-
bantur, quoniam de malicia iam concepta forum optatum
attingere cupiebant, nam ardens invidia decepit eosdem et seva
cupiditas[2] excecavit. Sperabant enim suas monachas vel con-
versas ex aliena iactura ditari, hoc est de bonis Templi reddere
pinguiores, ut de fructibus possent ab ipsis percipere con-
tinuam porcionem; et ideo cum furore Templarios veridicos[c]
in tormentis tam diu torqueri mandabant donec vel ex penis
huiusmodi morerentur vel veritate subpressa cogerentur men-
tiri se deum negasse, crucem Christi vilipendisse, et alia proferre nequissima que non solum sunt actu set pocius indigna
relatu. Preterea nisi hec dicerent tam ante quam eciam post
tormenta semper in obscuris carceribus tenebantur, solum cum
pane doloris et aqua[d] angustie[3] hiemali tempore urgente frigore
cum suspiriis et merore iacentes absque pannis et stramine
super terram. In obscuro noctis ad maiorem terroris formi-
dinem nunc unus nunc alius de carcere ad carccrem trahebatur
[p. 171]. Et quos in tormentis occiderant occulte sepeliebant
in stabulo vel[e] in orto, timentes ne talis horribilitas et sevicia
ad aures regias pervenirent, cum pro certo narraverant et
narrabant fratres predictos non ex violencia set sponte dicta
facinora confiteri.[4] Qui pro voluntate satellitum et Iacobinorum

---

[a] *ms.* decenter.   [b] velut *interlined in ms.*   [c] *ms. adds* mori.   [d] *ms.*
aque.   [e] stabulo vel; *ms.* stabilurilis: *the emendation is very doubtful and can
hardly be justified on palaeographical grounds.*

---

[1] Cf. Ps. 57: 5.
[2] Cf. the appeal of 7 Apr. 1310: 'zelo cupiditatis et ardore invidie' (*Dossier*,
p. 184).
[3] Cf. III Reg. 22: 27.
[4] On 24 Oct. Jacques de Molai declared on oath that he had not been tortured
and had confessed the truth; others followed suit (*Dossier*, p. 36).

in tormentis devicti mendacia talia proferebant, quando pro
mendaciis debuisent puniri, si vero nollent levabantur in
cameris ubi cunta necessaria leta facie ministrabantur eisdem
ut perseverarent. Nunc comminacionibus, nunc asperis nunc
blandis sermonibus, continue monebantur. Preterea quidam
monachus vel verius demoniacus qualibet hora diei et noctis
per cameras discurrere non cessabat, fratres predictos temp-
tando et monita perdicionis omnibus porrigendo. Et si quem
inveniebat de dictis mendaciis penitentem statim ad prefatas
angustias et penurias remittebat. Et quid amplius loquatur! In
summa dico quod humana lingua non possit exprimere penas,
angustias, miserias, improperia, et dira tormentorum genera
que dicti passi sunt innocentes per spacium trium mensium
a die capcionis eorum, quia die nocteque assidue non cessabant
ploratus[a] et suspiria in carceribus, clamores et stridores den-
cium in tormentis. Quid ergo mirum est si dicebant torquen-
cium voluntatem, cum veritas eos occideret et mendacia eos
a morte liberarent. Certe non humanum set divinum omnino
fuit veritatem posse tueri sicut multi divina virtute miraculose
fecerunt. Set qui tantis concussi terroribus et flagellis mentiti
fuerunt tormentis cessantibus in pura veritate persistunt. De
reliquis autem formidolosis et timidis qui solis terroribus hec
dixerunt, profecto mirandum non est, cum pena unius multorum sit metus.[1]

Attendite, igitur, viri prudentes, et videte dolorem, cum
similis non est dolor.[2] Ha, deus, quid est hoc quod tantus error
et tanta cordium cecitas,[3] tantaque demencia et sensuum
ebetudo, diebus nostris in christicolas apparuerit absque causa.
Vere stupendum est et terrendum. O, bone Iesu, pic pater,

---

[a] *ms.* plorabant.

[1] 'Ut unius poena metus possit esse multorum' (*Codex Iustiniani*, 9, 27, 1).
The whole passage compares with the appeal of 7 Apr. 1310: 'Omnes fratres
generaliter sunt tanto timore et terrore percussi quod non est mirandum quodam
modo de hiis qui menciuntur, sed plus de hiis qui sustinent veritatem, videndo
tribulaciones et angustias quas continue veridici paciuntur et minas et con-
tumelias et alia mala que cotidie sustinent et bona, commoda et delicias ac libertates quas habent falsidici et magna promissa que sibi cotidie fiunt' (*Dossier*,
p. 180, cf. 186).
[2] Cf. Lament.Jer. 1 : 12.
[3] Cf. Eph. 4 : 18.

quali ducitur consilio tantus princeps qui tuo semper nutu regere consuevit et regi. Nonne ipsum privilegio singulari super alios mundi principes decorasti, eo quod in terra non est simile brachium ecclesie et decus nomine christiani. Utquid ergo toleras tam prava consilia sibi dari, cum ipse bonus in se, iustus, misericors, et benignus existat. Evigila ergo et infunde spiritum tui consilii super ipsum, aperi solite iusticie fontis venas antiquas, tolle modium et super ipsius candelabrum repone lucernam, ut inspecta veritate fratres Templi prefatos in statum revocet primitivum et falsos puniat detractores, qui coronam auream honoris et glorie signo sanctitatis expressam et omne regnum sibi subiectum totaliter diffamarunt, inducentes tam grave scandalum et peccatum cui [p. 172] simile ab inicio mundi non legitur esse commissum, quod quidem redundat in opprobrium et contemptum non solum ipsius regni set ecclesie sancte ac tocius fidei christiane. Nam totus mundus refert et videt quod hec est iniquitas manifesta solum a tota cupiditate, que nulla potest tergiversatione celari. Quisnam crederet liber homo[a] quod cuiuscumque status fuerit vel condicionis in detrimentum et mortem anime sue petat religionis ingressum, se subiturus perpetue servituti, hoc est, obediencie regulari. Certe satis fatuus esset et insanus. Absurdumque videretur et est penitus incredibile, vel melius inpossibile tam diffuse religionis per mundum universum fratres nobiles, clericos, burgenses, fuisse talibus criminibus irretitos qui pro salute animarum dedicarunt seipsos obsequio virginis gloriose, crucem perpetuo deferentes ob reverenciam crucifixi et in sue memoriam passionis.[1] Insuper antiquis temporibus et modernis ex levitate cordis plurimi exierunt, qui sic apostatantes[b] et a parentibus et amicis audiebant improperia multa eo quod religionem suam dimiserunt. Cur si tales maculam novissent in ordine tacuissent quin saltem ad excusacionem sui dixissent se nolle inter viros morari talibus sceleribus involutos. Qui postmodum penitentes et precibus lacrimosis cum instancia longa, captata

---

[a] *ms.* "liber homo "crederet, *marked thus for transposition.*
[b] *ms.* apostotantes.

---

[1] Cf. the appeal of 7 April 1310: 'cum cruce quam perpetuo deferunt circa pectus, ob reverenciam Crucifixi pro nobis, in sue memoriam passionis' (*Dossier*, p. 182).

gracia redeundi, per annum et diem comedebant in terra, sextas ferias ieiunantes in pane et aqua, singulis diebus dominicis nudi cum femoralibus tantum ad altare accedentes in missarum solempniis de manu presbiteri disciplinam admittentes, nec habitum poterant nec fratrum recuperare consorcium nisi primo annualem penitentiam sic humiliter et devote perfecissent.[1] Quomodo igitur tales redissent more canis ad vomitum ut in anime periculum et corporis vituperium tantam penitenciam suscepissent. Alii, et qui taliter peccaverant quod secundum statum religionis captare non poterant graciam redeundi, cur non detegebant predicta, nisi quod incredibilia et inaudita mendacia narrare non poterant. Fratres eciam dicti ordinis circa centum, ut credo, sunt adhuc in carceribus Babilonis, qui plus eligunt in eadem mori penuria ut vitam adquirant eternam quam aliquid agere contra fidem; et si se vellent reddere contra fidem, honorarentur a Sarracenis et haberent uxores, equos, et arma, et inter nobiles ponerentur; set malunt in obediencia religionis finire quam pro transitoria vitam perdere sempiternam. Liquide ergo cognoscere potest quisque prudens innocenciam oppressorum iniuste pauperum fratrum Templi quibus hucusque iusticia simul et audiencia denegantur. Et quoniam varie voces ignorancium que non sunt audiende de iure quandoque clamant quod fulminari deberet sentencia contra eos, idcirco vobis dictator presencium studuit premissorum scribere veritatem. Consideret igitur magna vestre circumspeccionis prudencia collecta [p. 173] quid et qualiter sit agendum, sublatoque cuiuslibet timoris,[a] odii, vel amoris obstaculo, solum deum habendo pre oculis, concilium tale proferat super ipsos quod a domino premium et ab hominibus laudes assequi mereatur. Amen.

---

[a] *ms.* cuilibet timore.

[1] Cf. *La Règle du Temple*, ed. H. de Curzon (Soc. Hist. France, 1886), pp. 162, 165 (§§ 262, 270).

17. English Cistercian Libraries: the First Century*

To know what books English Cistercian monks used is to illuminate to a certain extent their way of life and their interpretation of the monastic ideal. This paper is intended to assemble facts bearing upon this subject. The history of the Order of Cîteaux in England begins in 1128 with the foundation of Waverley, in Surrey, a daughter-house of the abbey of L'Aumône, which sent another colony of monks to Tintern in Monmouthshire three years later. In 1132 Rievaulx (a colony of Clairvaux) and Fountains were founded in Yorkshire. Within twenty years the Order numbered fifty establishments of monks in England and Wales and ten nunneries. Most of the later foundations were effected within a century of the first planting at Waverley, that is, during the twelfth and the first third of the thirteenth century. From the point of view of scholastic and literary history this period may fitly be treated as a whole. Later, the recruitment of monks is checked by the competition of the Mendicants, the intellectual crisis of thirteenth-century academic life reaches the Order, the economic situation changes. Although I dispose of insufficient

---

* Based on a paper written in 1953 and published in a slightly abridged and modified French version in *Mélanges Saint Bernard* (XXIVe Congrès de l'Association Bourguignonne des Sociétés Savantes, 1953), Dijon, Association des Amis de Saint Bernard, pp. 375–82. No attempt has been made to incorporate the mass of more recent work on Cistercian scholarship and literary interests, though the paper has been corrected and revised at a few points, and a few references added. I note particularly C. J. Holdsworth, 'John of Ford and English Cistercian writing 1167–1214', *Trans. Royal Hist. Soc.*, 5th series xi (1961), 117–36, and two papers by M. A. Dimier, 'Les premiers cisterciens étaient-ils ennemis des études?' and C. H. Talbot, 'The English Cistercians and the universities', both in *Studia Monastica* (Montferrat), iv (1962), 69–91 and 197–220.

bibliographical means, I want to try to isolate from all the medieval manuscripts which have come down to us those which seem probably to have belonged to Cistercian abbeys in England and Wales around the year 1230, or earlier. This is easier said than done. For the books themselves have been dispersed and the marks of their origin are often eradicated. Catalogues of Cistercian libraries are scarce; and where they exist they are often found to be incomplete or ambiguous in the facts they offer.

The original state of Cistercian libraries is bound to be obscure because of the dispersal as early as the sixteenth century. There was then no transfer in bulk to public institutions, such as happened later on in France, where scholars may now examine hundreds of manuscripts coming from Cîteaux at Dijon or from Clairvaux at Troyes. I have not found as many as forty volumes from any single Cistercian house, and the thirty-six identified manuscripts which form the poor remains of the library of Fountains are split up between sixteen collections in five countries. The evidence is terribly defective. One can only hope for approximate results; but the attempt at an approximation seems worth while. This would not be possible without the tool which Dr. N. R. Ker has provided: *Medieval Libraries of Great Britain*, first published by the Royal Historical Society in 1941, of which a second edition, much enlarged, appeared in 1964. Even so, it must be remembered that the majority of books from English medieval libraries have lost all trace of provenance and that the rate of loss has been most irregular, from house to house.[1] This makes any numerical evaluation dubious.

According to my calculation, there are some 240 manuscripts of which one may say that they were probably written before about 1230, which were, moreover, at some time in an English Cistercian library, and which were not demonstrably acquired later than our *terminus ad quem*. These 240 manuscripts represent

[1] For the dispersal in the sixteenth century see Ker, *Medieval Libraries*, pp. x–xv and *The English Library before 1700*, ed. F. Wormald and C. E. Wright (1958). A scrutiny of C. H. Talbot, 'A list of Cistercian manuscripts in Great Britain', *Traditio*, viii (1952), 402–18, which is concerned with Cistercian authors, not with Cistercian manuscripts, would doubtless yield books of Cistercian provenance although their exact location cannot be discovered.

the sole identifiable relics of forty-five monastic libraries. It is a poor harvest; of many Cistercian libraries not a single book is known to survive. The survivals are supplemented by only three or four catalogues of English Cistercian libraries. In addition, there are brief notes left by John Leland, who made a sort of 'Voyage littéraire' in the interests of his sovereign, Henry VIII, shortly before the dissolution of the monasteries.[1] I shall not labour the need for a cautious approach to such imperfect material, and content myself with giving the result of a preliminary inquiry on the books and the catalogues. My inquiry does not extend to a survey of English Cistercian writers. It is concerned more with readers than with authors, who will be mentioned only in relation to manuscripts from Cistercian libraries.

First, a few words about the writing of the books. Since the Order of Cîteaux did not allow the institution of oblature and recruited only adults, it sometimes happened that a clerk would bring his books with him into the monastery. Thus, Dean Hugh of York brought very valuable books to Fountains in 1134.[2] We also hear of abbots who acquired books for their houses, apparently by purchase, at Meaux and at Louth Park early in the thirteenth century.[3] Gerald of Wales tells how the monks of Strata Florida proposed to hold his books in pawn when he needed ready money to go to Rome; but then, at the last moment, when it was too late for him to raise the money elsewhere, they told him that they found in their *Liber Usuum* that they were permitted to buy books but not to receive them as pledges. So Gerald, protesting, sold them.[4] Not all Cistercian books, then, were written in the cloister. Very few indeed bear the name of a monk-scribe.[5] But many

---

[1] Most of these notes are in his *Collectanea*, as printed by T. Hearne (2nd ed., 1770), vol. iv, but see also J. R. Liddell in *EHR*, liv (1939), 88–95. I have not examined the Franciscan register of books in monastic libraries (late thirteenth-century) and the catalogue of writers attributed to John Boston of Bury (late fourteenth-century); cf. Holdsworth, loc. cit., p. 127.

[2] *Memorials of Fountains Abbey*, i (Surtees Soc., 42, 1863), 53.

[3] *Chron. monasterii de Melsa* (RS, 1866–8), i. 326 and *Chron. abbatie de Parco Lude*, ed. E. Venables (Lincolnshire Record Soc., 1891), p. 13.

[4] *Giraldi Cambrensis Opera* (RS, 1861–91), iv. 154–5, cf. i. 117.

[5] Cambridge, Univ. Libr. MS. Mm. 4. 28, from Biddlesden, has the name of the twelfth-century scribe. Late in the thirteenth century 'Frater Willelmus de

of the finer Cistercian books of this period have the appearance of originating in the house they belonged to. They bear contemporary *ex libris* inscriptions of fine calligraphy which in style resembles that of the texts. Their decoration is generally sober: there are no large miniatures or historiated initials, and gold is very rarely used. But red and green and blue initials alternate with decorative effect; and in a book written at Buildwas in 1176 the red of initials and titles is touched up with silver.[1] Cistercian artists of the first generation were not forbidden to indulge in elaborate figure-ornament, as the bible of Stephen Harding and related manuscripts show;[2] but the movement towards a more austere style had supervened in the Order by the time that its first English settlements had achieved the stability and comfort conducive to the production of grand books. A twelfth-century bestiary from Holme Cultram (B.M. MS. Cotton Nero A. v) is devoid of the illustrations that seem proper to a bestiary. It contains only one line-drawing of a beast, although the exemplar evidently had pictures, for there are frequent spaces with written descriptions: for instance, 'hyena hic pingitur qui cupidum hominem significat'. One of the rare examples of figure-drawing in an English Cistercian book is in B.M. MS. Cotton Cleop. C. xi, written early in the thirteenth century. It contains works of St. Anselm, the Vision of the monk of Eynsham, etc., and has full-page, half-page, and marginal drawings here and there. But there is nothing to show when the book reached Dore Abbey, to which it belonged about the year 1500. Again, a manuscript of the *Ymago Mundi* from Sawley (Corpus Christi College, Cambridge, MS. 66) has illustrations of Fortune's wheel and other subjects; but we cannot be sure that this is Cistercian

Wodecherche, laicus quondam conversus Pontis Roberti' wrote Bodleian MS. Bodley 132 for Robertsbridge.

[1] B.M. MS. Harl. 3038; the scribe writes on the verso of fo. 7: 'Liber Sancte Marie de Bildewas. Scriptus anno ab incarnatione domini millesimo centesimo septuagesimo sexto.' Sir Roger Mynors argues that Balliol MSS. 40, 129, 150 and 'less certainly 39, were ornamented and presumably written at' Buildwas (*Catalogue of MSS. of Balliol Coll., Oxford* (Oxford, 1963), p. 29).

[2] C. Oursel, *La Miniature du xii⁰ Siècle à l'Abbaye de Cîteaux* (Dijon, 1926) and 'Les principes et l'esprit des miniatures primitives de Cîteaux', *Cîteaux in de Nederlanden*, v (1955), 161–72; T. S. R. Boase, *English Art 1100–1216* (Oxford Hist. of English Art, Oxford, 1963), pp. 154–5.

work.[1] The less showy collections of Cistercian provenance, with narratives of local events and *excerpta*, may well have been usually compiled and written in the monasteries which owned them.

Of the 240 or so manuscripts in which we are interested, the abbey of Buildwas in Shropshire (originally Savigniac) accounts for thirty-eight volumes, or nearly one sixth of the total. Six other houses have a hundred between them. That leaves only about a hundred manuscripts shared by thirty-eight other houses.

The books which survive from Buildwas comprise for the most part biblical texts and commentaries and patristic works, particularly Jerome, Augustine, Gregory the Great. Only three volumes contain works of Cistercian writers: Balliol College MS. 150 is a collection of St. Bernard's sermons; St. John's College, Cambridge, MS. 77 contains the *Speculum Caritatis* of Ailred of Rievaulx, Lambeth Palace MS. 488 has Ailred's homilies *De Onere Babilonis*. Buildwas also possessed sermons of Peter Comestor (Trinity Coll. MS. 1337) and commentaries of Peter Cantor (Bodleian MS. Bodley 371). Pembroke College, Cambridge, MS. 154 contains Cyprian's letters, the meditations of St. Anselm, the *De Disciplina Claustrali* of Peter de Celle, and some opuscula of Peter of Blois. The curious book *De Claustro Anime* of the Augustinian Hugh de Fouilloy is represented by a twelfth-century manuscript (Lambeth MS. 107), decorated with coloured drawings 'de duabus rotis'.[2] Other Augustinians are Alexander Nequam on the Canticles (Balliol College MSS. 39, 40) and William of Newburgh (Lambeth MS. 73), who wrote his History at the instance of the abbot of Rievaulx.[3] For the rest, the survivals from Buildwas do not amount to much. Of Latin classics there is nothing but extracts from Seneca's epistles ad Lucilium (Lambeth MS. 457 fos. 193–254). With the exception of William of Newburgh there is no history. If we look for grammar, law, or medicine, we find none

---

[1] Eric G. Millar, *English Illuminated Manuscripts from the Tenth to the Thirteenth Century* (Brussels, 1926), pl. 54.

[2] For an early thirteenth-century manuscript from the abbey of Aulne, Brussels Bibliothèque Royale, II. 1076, cf. C. Caspar and F. Lyna, *Les principaux Manuscrits à Peintures de la Bibl. Royale de Belgique* (Paris, 1937), i. 128–9 and pl. xxviii.

[3] *Chron. of the reigns of Stephen, Henry II, and Richard I* (RS, 1884–9), i. 3.

of the fundamental books: only a few nondescript pieces appended to volumes of Holy Writ or sermons (Trinity College, Cambridge, MSS. 27, 37, 1337).

Dr. Ker has warned us that 'survival has been usually a matter of chance'.[1] Evidently it would be unwise to base upon the Buildwas survivals a conclusion about the contents of its library as a whole, still less about the contents of English Cistercian libraries in general. Counting titles is not enough; and it distorts the picture to enumerate in a statistical table every Bernardine opuscule, every anonymous sermon or model letter added to a volume composed mainly of other works. A rough impression is all that we can hope for, supplementing our general view of the classes of work encountered in the manuscripts with an eye on the catalogues and on the notes left by John Leland.

Everywhere, as at Buildwas, there appears a preponderance of glossed biblical texts and commentaries and of the best-known patristic works.[2] These fine books, generally folios, written in two columns, in hands at once firm and delicate, formed the heart of every Cistercian library. Among the commentators are several twelfth-century authors, including Englishmen. There is Robert, prior of Bridlington, who wrote his commentary on the twelve minor prophets at the request of Gervase, first abbot of Louth Park (St. John's College, Oxford, MS. 46). There are Robert of Melun and Alexander Nequam and, above all, Stephen Langton, a secular master of Paris very sympathetic to the Cistercians. Being consecrated archbishop of Canterbury at Viterbo and excluded from England in 1207, Stephen spent part of his exile during the Interdict on England at Pontigny. Copies of Langton's works, especially of his commentaries, are found in a dozen of the Cistercian libraries; and at the abbey of Stratford Langthorne John Leland noted 'omnia fere opera Stephani'.[3] Grabmann and Miss Smalley have remarked upon the contrast between

---

[1] *Medieval Libraries*, p. xi.

[2] But it must be recognized that they were more likely to survive because of their subject-matter and their attractive format. Remaining books may simply reflect what appealed to those who had the chance of acquiring them in the sixteenth century.

[3] *Collectanea*, iv. 161.

the exegetic methods of Langton and of Peter Lombard. Whereas the Lombard is above all the theologian and the dialectician, Langton is interested in biblical and moral questions. This trait links him with the school of St. Victor; and along with Langton's works those of Hugh of St. Victor were fairly numerous in these Cistercian libraries. Here the White Monks found an exegete and theologian who tried by study to enrich the contemplative life and the hours spent in *lectio divina* and meditation.[1]

It seems certain that the moralistic approach to biblical studies made a strong appeal to the English Cistercians of these days. So Ralph, abbot of Coggeshall, celebrates Peter Cantor 'who at this time was deemed the chief and most outstanding of the doctors of theology'; and he accords him special praise because his 'short and lucid glosses on the Psalter and the Pauline epistles were composed in a religious and moral style rather than with pompous eloquence'. Ralph notes with satisfaction that Peter died in the monastic habit in the Cistercian abbey of Longpont. The same author describes Peter of Poitiers as *doctor egregius in theologia*. These comments are all the more significant because Ralph mentions no other contemporary men of learning in his chronicle.[2] Another English Cistercian abbot of an earlier generation, Gilbert of Hoyland, or Swineshead (†1172), author of forty-eight sermons which Leland saw at Byland and at Kirkstead, condemns the brethren who read with more assiduity than they pray: for 'reading ought to serve our prayer, prepare our mood [for contemplation], not encroach on our time and weaken our character.'[3] *Lectio* was, as Mr. Holdsworth puts it, 'more a process of rumination than reading, directed towards savouring the divine wisdom within a book rather than finding new ideas or novel information'.[4]

[1] See B. Smalley, *The Study of the Bible in the Middle Ages* (2nd ed., Oxford, 1952), pp. 196 sqq. and P. Barzillay Roberts, *Stephanus de Lingua-Tonante: Studie, in the Sermons of Stephen Langton* (Pontifical Inst. of Toronto, Studies and Texts 16, 1968).

[2] Radulphi de Coggeshall, *Chronicon anglicanum* (RS, 1875), pp. 79, 161.

[3] Smalley, *Study of the Bible*, p. 282, quoted from Migne, clxxxiv. 43. Cf. E. Mikkers, 'De vita et operibus Gilberti de Hoylandia', *Cîteaux: Commentarii Cistercienses*, xiv (1963), 33–43, 265–79.

[4] Holdsworth, loc. cit., p. 124.

The works of piety to be found on Cistercian bookshelves—homilies, meditations, hagiography, and narratives of the miraculous—were very numerous. From the Benedictines came the *Meditationes* of St. Anselm, the homilies on the Canticles of his pupil and friend, Gilbert Crispin, abbot of Westminster, the big sprawling commentary on Leviticus of Ralph of Flaix (contained in a huge folio from Kirkstead, B.M. MS. Royal 3 D. ix),[1] the sermons of Odo, abbot of Battle. The theological works of the Augustinian Robert of Cricklade, prior of St. Frideswide's (*c.* 1141–79) were seen by Leland at Rievaulx and Waverley. Turning to Cistercian spiritual writers, apart from St. Bernard—and some of his writings were to be found everywhere—the continental Cistercians are not much in evidence. The sermons of Guerri of Igny were at Dore and at Rievaulx. A copy of Ernaud of Bonnevaux on the five words of Christ comes from Wardon. That is almost all. But England produced in the twelfth century one Cistercian author of the first rank and several writers of homilies who enjoyed a certain reputation in their own time and country. This is not the place to speak of the spiritual and literary gifts of Ailred of Rievaulx, which made his writings, *Speculum Caritatis*, *De Spirituali Amicitia*, *De Anima*, some of the best-known works of his Order. I confine myself to noting that various of his writings are to be found in manuscripts coming from five English Cistercian houses.[2] Among less celebrated authors there survives from Jervaulx Abbey (Lambeth MS. 210) an important collection of works of Baldwin of Ford, later archbishop of Canterbury; Leland saw others at Byland and Revesby.[3] Devotional works addressed to Baldwin by another monk of Ford, named Roger, have not been found in any manuscript which can be assigned to any particular Cistercian library.[4]

---

[1] Cf. B. Smalley, 'Ralph of Flaix on Leviticus', *Recherches de Théologie ancienne et médiévale*, xxxv (1968), 35–52.

[2] Vol. i of his *Opera omnia* (Opera ascetica) ed. by A. Hoste and C. H. Talbot (Corpus Christianorum: Continuatio Mediaevalis, Turnholt, 1971). For bibliography see A. Hoste, *Bibliotheca Aelrediana* (Steenbrugge, 1962) and supplement in *Cîteaux: Commentarii Cistercienses*, xviii (1967), 402–7, with other articles in this volume.

[3] Baudouin de Ford, *Le Sacrement de l'Autel*, ed. with French translation by J. Leclercq, J. Morson, and E. de Solms (Paris, 1963).

[4] Cf. Holdsworth, loc. cit., pp. 125–6. Mary Bateson, in *D.N.B.*, xvii. 106–7,

A successor to Baldwin in the abbacy, John of Ford, left a long series of homilies to his Devonshire abbey, and manuscripts of his works were seen by Leland in two other abbeys in the south of England, Beaulieu and Buckfast.[1]

Leland also saw homilies of Gilbert of Hoyland in the libraries of Byland and Kirkstall, and at Fountains homilies by its second abbot, Richard, and the *Flosculi Moralium* of Abbot William of Buckfast. Another Cistercian author, known only by a Rievaulx manuscript (now Paris, B.N. MS. lat. 15157), has been identified in modern times by Dom André Wilmart: he is Matthew precentor of Rievaulx who, at the beginning of the thirteenth century, composed short pieces in verse and prose on the Incarnation, the Virgin Mary, monastic discipline, the tomb of William de Monte, the Interdict on England, and much besides: a real mixture, in which one detects the spiritual influence of Abbot Ailred together with some literary training. Matthew was, as Dom Wilmart wrote, 'poète, épistolier, sermonnaire, voire exégète et moraliste'—all in the space of ninety-five small leaves.[2]

One of the most interesting types of Cistercian book is the miscellany (for want of a better description). Sometimes a volume of biblical commentary has a few leaves filled with jottings which reveal the tastes and reading habits of the writer.[3] In other cases, the miscellany makes the book. B.M. MS. Cotton Titus D. xxiv from Rufford Abbey is a farrago which defies brief description. Among other things it includes a short chronicle of English history to 1195, a list of Roman emperors, Marbodus De Gemmis, hymns, epitaphs, verses *De Corpore Christi* attributed to Hildebert of Lavardin, and a treatise on the way to prepare colours for writing and illuminating, written in Latin and French. B.M. MS. Royal 8 F.i

referred to two English manuscripts of unknown provenance, Bodleian MS. Bodley 83 and St. John's College, Oxford, MS. 169.

[1] The sermons are now edited by E. Mikkers and H. Costello, in Corpus Christianorum: Continuatio Mediaevalis, vols. xvii, xviii (Turnholt, 1970). For John see Holdsworth, loc. cit.

[2] A. Wilmart, 'Les mélanges de Mathieu préchantre de Rievaulx au début du xiiie siècle', *Revue Bénédictine*, lii (1940), 15–84.

[3] e.g. B.M. MS. Harl. 3038, from Buildwas, written in 1176, a glossed Leviticus with preliminary matter.

from Revesby Abbey was written about 1200: it contains Ailred *De Spirituali Amicitia,* the *Meditationes* of Guigo the Carthusian, Richard of St. Victor's allegories on the Old and New Testaments and his *Benjamin Minor,* and an anthology of moral reflections mainly drawn from classical sources, and Boethius and Isidore, with a few additions by the compiler. A collection given to Fountains by Henry of Knaresborough, written in several early thirteenth-century hands, consists of sermons and theological pieces.[1] *Florilegia* of *sententiae* (according to the use of the word sentence in monastic circles), such as we find in the Revesby book, were much in vogue in Cistercian abbeys. The biographer of Ailred, Walter Daniel, left in his abbey of Rievaulx a whole series of literary works of which his own *Centum sententiae* still exist in John Rylands Library MS. Latin 196.[2]

The Cistercian miscellanies show a marked taste for versification. Couplets or longer pieces, mostly of a devotional nature, fill up odd spaces, margins and flyleaves. The tendency to break into verse (often of a low order, simply supplying a mnemonic jingle) also appears among the Cistercian annalists, perhaps to a more marked degree than in other English chroniclers.[3]

Towards the end of the twelfth century we meet with the dictionary-guides to spiritual topics known as *distinctiones.*[4] They could be serviceable as handbooks to the homilist and the confessor. In the Cistercian libraries, alongside the *Clavis Sancte Scripture* of the pseudo-Melito (an early example of this genre), come the *Distinctiones super psalterium* of Michael of Meaux, archbishop of Sens (†1199) in a manuscript from Dore

[1] See E. G. Millar *Descriptive Cat. of the Western Manuscripts in the Library of Alfred Chester Beatty* (Oxford, 1930), vol. i no. 37. The manuscript is now the property of Mr. H. Vyner of Studley Royal, on permanent loan to the Leeds Public Library, Archives Department.

[2] Holdsworth, loc. cit., p. 132 n. 1 calls attention to another anthology in Bodleian MS. Lyell 8, of which there is a detailed account in the catalogue of the Lyell collection by Miss A. De la Mare (Oxford, 1971).

[3] Margam occasionally, Waverley often, and cf. the Melrose Chronicle. Verse also appears in the *De expugnatione Terrae Sanctae* attributed to Ralph of Coggeshall. For verses in non-Cistercian annals see the annals of Tewkesbury and Winchester (*Ann. Mon.* (RS), i. 64, 113, ii. 68, 70, 71); also Roger de Hoveden's *Chron.* (RS), iv. 83–5.

[4] Smalley, *Study of the Bible,* pp. 246–8; P. Lacombe, *Vie et Œuvres de Prévostin,* pp. 117 sqq.

(Bodleian MS. e Musaeo 82); and the *Numerale* of William de Monte of Lincoln was at Meaux and Rievaulx.[1] Bodleian MS. Rawl. C. 22, from an unidentified Cistercian house, contains among other works 'extracts from patristic and medieval writers, and a section of miscellaneous verses, written towards the middle of the thirteenth century. The latest authors excerpted are Alexander Nequam (†1217), Stephen Langton (†1228), and the author of the *Distinctiones monasticae*.' It appears to be of Cistercian workmanship.[2]

To judge by the remains of the library of Buildwas, it included little in the fields of history, classics, grammar, law, or medicine? Was this normal? Or do accidents of survival from Buildwas present a misleading picture which can be corrected by other evidence? Under the rubrics of law and medicine nothing of importance survives to indicate a lively concern with these subjects. If the *Collectio Canonum* of Anselm of Lucca from Pipewell had reached the abbey in this period it was already so far out of date as to provide no evidence of canonistic studies in the monastery.[3] On the other hand, a late twelfth-century decretal collection of primitive type can probably on internal evidence be safely assigned to Fountains and testifies that even Cistercian monks might find it desirable to assemble recent legal pronouncements of the popes.[4]

Of pagan classics Cicero is only represented by *De Amicitia, De Officiis, De Senectute,* and the *Rhetorica,* and only in four libraries. At Beaulieu Leland saw a Claudian, *De Statu Animae* and at Dunkeswell *Epistolae Symmachi.* Horace, Persius, and Ovid occur together in a collection referred to below. Byland had the work of Palladius *De Agricultura.* But what poverty this is! Grammar shows a few later books to compensate for

---

[1] The Rievaulx manuscript is now Jesus College, Cambridge, MS. 34. Two copies were catalogued (with other works of this author) at Meaux (*Chron. mon. de Melsa,* iii. pp. lxxxv, xc). Cf. R. W. Hunt, in *Trans. Royal Hist. Soc.,* 4th series xix (1936), 21.

[2] See R. W. Hunt, 'Notes on the *Distinctiones monasticae et morales*', in *Liber floridus . . . Paul Lehmann gewidmet* (St. Ottilien, 1950), p. 357, and Holdsworth, loc. cit., p. 130 and n. 7.

[3] Now Corpus Christi College, Cambridge, MS. 269. Cf. Z. N. Brooke, *The English Church and the Papacy* (Cambridge, 1931), p. 241.

[4] Bodleian MS. Laud misc. 527. Cf. C. Duggan, *Twelfth-century Decretal Collections* (1963), pp. 80–1.

the shortage of classical authors. From Buildwas comes a commentary on Martianus Capella (Trinity College, Cambridge, MS. 27). Dore had the *Panormia* of Osbern of Gloucester, Kirkstall had the *Derivationes* of Huguccio. In this connection the most singular mixture is in Trinity College, Cambridge, MS. 609, from Holme Cultram Abbey, on the unquiet Scottish border. It begins with the *Contra Hereticos* of Alain of Montpelier[1] and continues with *Distinctiones Theologice*; then come Horace, *Ars Poetica, Satires,* and *Epistles,* the *Satires* of Persius, the *Remedium Amoris* of Ovid, the *Poetria Nova* of Geoffrey of Vinsauf, the *Distinctiones* of John of Garland, and the *Doctrinale* of Alexander of Villedieu.

The shortage of historical works at Buldwas is not matched elsewhere. The survivals indicate a lively curiosity among English Cistercians, extending beyond the needs of edification. History was in part for profit, largely for recreation. There is an occasional Orosius or Josephus, a Dares Phrygius, an abridged Justinus, but none of the great Roman historians. Nor are the universal histories of the Middle Ages there. On the other hand, English history is well represented by Gildas, Nennius, Bede, and by the twelfth-century writers, William of Malmesbury, Henry of Huntingdon, Roger of Howden. The historical writings of English Cistercians show the same marked tendency to be insular. Some, indeed, purport to be annals of general history, but their compilers emphasize local events, as at Coggeshall, Waverley, and Margam. Others confine themselves to narratives about the origin of a particular house, as at Fountains, Ford, and Kirkstall.[2] A composite volume which forms one of the principal sources for north-country history in the twelfth century, Corpus Christi College, Cambridge, MS. 139, has an early *ex libris* mark of Sawley Abbey, Yorkshire. The evidence of books, in short, confirms the observations of Powicke and Dom David Knowles on the

---

[1] Cistercians took a prominent part in the propaganda against the Albigensians.

[2] For recent studies of these texts and the problems they raise see D. Nicholl, *Thurstan Archbishop of York* (York, 1964), pp. 251–8 and L. G. D. Baker, 'The genesis of English Cistercian chronicles: the foundation history of Fountains Abbey I', *Anal. Cisterciensia,* xxv (1969), 14–41, idem, 'The foundation of Fountains Abbey', *Northern History,* iv. (1969), 29–43, idem, 'The desert in the north', ibid. v (1970), 1–11.

strong sense of history and of regional patriotism among English Cistercians.

Allied to their interest in history was a taste for hagiography. Bernard had made his contribution in the Life of St. Malachy, of which a copy was at Jervaulx (St. John's College, Oxford, MS. 99). Ailred's hagiographical works on St. Edward and St. Ninian appear frequently and emphasize the Celtic and Anglo-Saxon traditions which prevailed in twelfth-century Northumbria. John of Ford wrote the Life of St. Wulfric of Haselbury, Jocelin of Furness the Life of St. Waldef, and Walter Daniel the Life of Ailred. Moreover, Ailred had inspired Reginald, a monk of Durham, to report the miracles of St. Cuthbert and St. Godric and declared it to be 'sacrilege to know and yet conceal the Lord's miracles and the manifestations of divine piety'.[1] So the Lives of saints form an appreciable, if not a bulky, part of surviving Cistercian books. Along with an understandable interest in local saints (for example, the Life of St. Milburga from Croxden in B.M. MS. Add. 34633), there is a wider interest. A Harvard manuscript from Holme Cultram has the Lives of Anselm, Maieul, Odilo, and Odo of Cluny. The Life of St. Alexis appears in a fragment from Byland (B.M. MS. Cotton Faust. B. iv fos. 180–2). And a liking for the Lives of saints carried with it a liking for the miraculous in general. A manuscript from Valle Crucis preserves a unique recension of the *Navigatio S. Brendani*, St. Patrick's Purgatory by the Cistercian Henry of Sawtrey occurs in various texts, and Ralph of Coggeshall may be the author of the Vision of Thurkill. A Dore manuscript at Hereford (MS. P. i. 13) includes 'Miracula que contingunt in domo de Dore'. The taste for history and legend was matched by a thirst for information about the natural world, especially when it was given a moral or theological twist. Cistercians welcomed the *Ymago Mundi* of Honorius Augustodunensis as well as his encyclopaedic *Elucidarium*; the former was seen by Leland at Kirkstead, the latter is contained in manuscripts from Byland and Rievaulx. From Holme Cultram comes a bestiary.[2]

---

[1] Quoted, Walter Daniel, *Life of Ailred*, ed. F. M. Powicke 1950), p. lxxix.

[2] Cf. J. Morson, The English Cistercians and the Bestiary', *BJRL* xxxix (1956), 146–70.

To handle this evidence is a delicate operation. So little has survived of which the provenance can be determined without longer researches. But it is reassuring to find concurrent testimony in other quarters. The avowed opinions of Cistercians on book-learning, the scholarly and literary tastes they display in their own writings, and the few catalogues of books which remain point, on the whole, in the same direction. Here I confine myself to noting some of the features of the catalogues. We have three thirteenth-century catalogues, possibly a little later than the *terminus* I have chosen: for Flaxley a list of seventy-nine volumes,[1] for Rievaulx a list of about 212,[2] and for an unidentified northern house, which I believe *may* be Cistercian, a list of 127.[3] The fourth and largest catalogue comes from the Yorkshire abbey of Meaux and was probably compiled about 1396.[4] Consequently, it provides far less reliable evidence for the books available at Meaux—which was founded in 1150—during the first eighty years of its existence. Catalogues suffer from a serious deficiency as evidence in this sort of enquiry: their descriptions are summary, often ambiguous, even false. Moreover, they normally give no idea of the time at which a book was acquired. In view of this it is relevant to note that Abbot Alexander of Meaux, at the beginning of the thirteenth century, left a reputation as 'librorum maximus perquisitor'.[5] Finally, the catalogues (as so often the surviving books themselves) give no idea of when the books were read. I shall not attempt to give a complete survey, even sketchy, of these lists. We can use them to discover the presence of books which are of a kind we have not yet encountered or which appear from the catalogues to have been more common than we should otherwise suppose.

Each catalogue contains most, if not all, of the works which

---

[1] Ed. H. Omont in *Centralblatt für Bibliothekswesen*, ix (1892), 205–7, and see Ker, *Medieval Libraries*, p. 87.

[2] Ed. M. R. James, *Descr. Catalogue of Manuscripts of Jesus College, Cambridge* (Cambridge, 1895), pp. 44–52 and A. Hoste, *Bibliotheca Aelrediana*, pp. 150–76. There are two lists, but the second seems to be substantially a rearrangement of the first.

[3] Ed. H. Omont, loc. cit., pp. 204–5. Attributed to the Austin priory of Bridlington tentatively in Ker, op. cit., p. 12.

[4] *Chron. mon. de Melsa*, ed. E. A. Bond (RS, 1866–8), iii. pp. lxxxiii–c.

[5] Ibid. i. 326.

are found in surviving books. The unknown library provides a Palladius to match the Byland manuscript; the Rievaulx catalogue lists the sermons of Guerri of Igny, found in a manuscript from Dore. Commentaries on the bible and patristic works preponderate here as well as among the survivals. There are perhaps proportionately more of the great spiritual authors of the eleventh and twelfth centuries—of St. Anselm and Hugh of St. Victor. By contrast to the surviving books, which only include one Peter Lombard from Rievaulx, the Master of the Sentences is well represented in the three catalogues of known provenance. In the matter of history, the evidence of existing manuscripts is confirmed: there are Josephus, Hegesippus, Eusebius, Orosius, and the histories of Troy, and the British and English historians; but only in the late catalogue from Meaux do we find Sallust (two copies) and Suetonius, *Lives of the Caesars*. As regards other pagan classics Rievaulx had in one volume the old logic, 'Ysagoge Porphirii in cathegorias Aristotelis', and 'alii libri dialectici', and 'versarium de libris ethnicorum'; the catalogue of Meaux provides the names of Ovid, Macrobius, Martial, and Valerius.[1] In all four catalogues there are traces of the grammarians, Priscian and Donatus. The catalogues also contain more works on *dictamen*, more formularies, than appear in surviving books. Books of medicine are rare: the *Antidotarium* of Nicholas of Salerno and another book at Rievaulx, John or Matthew Platearius at Meaux, and a 'Phisicus liber anglice' at Flaxley. Rievaulx had an arithmetic book ('Argorismus').

As for law books, at Rievaulx are listed the *Codex* and *excerpta* of *Justinian*, the *Decretum* of Gratian and 'Johannes super decreta'; also two copies of the *Panormia* of Ivo of Chartres and a *Corpus canonum*. Flaxley possessed the *Decretum* of Ivo and 'Epistole decretales'. Meaux possessed (in the fourteenth century) the *Panormia* of Ivo (two), Tancred (two), *Summa Bernardi episcopi super decretalibus*, Goffredus of Trani on the decretals, Rufinus on Gratian, and the *Summa* of Master John of Kent.[2] The catalogue of the unidentified library gives

---

[1] 'Plato *de natura rerum*' at Meaux (ibid. iii. p. xcvii) may be the work of Nequam or some other, but not Plato.

[2] Ibid. iii. pp. lxxxviii, lxxxiv, xciv. For John of Kent see *Traditio*, vii (1949–51), 320.

no canonistic texts; but this may be explained by its title: 'Libri magni armarii'. For in a Cistercian house the law books ought to be kept in a place apart, in accordance with a decree of the General Chapter of Cîteaux of 1188 (c. 7): 'Liber qui dicitur *Corpus Canonum* et *Decreta Gratiani* apud eos qui habuerint secretius custodiantur, ut cum opus fuerit proferantur, in communi armario non resideant, propter varios qui inde possunt provenire errores.'[1] Presumably a rule which applied to Gratian should have been applied to other works of canon law. Cistercian abbots sometimes tried to avoid the onerous tasks of papal judges delegate,[2] and the Order also encouraged them to settle their own cases out of court.[3] These efforts probably made for less professional legal study, without excluding it from all Cistercian cloisters.[4]

The libraries of which we know the catalogues consisted of almost exclusively Latin works, but the Rievaulx catalogue notes briefly two 'Libri de littera anglica', while Flaxley, besides the 'Phisicus liber anglice', had two English books unspecified and the lives of St. Godric and St. Thomas Becket in French ('gallice'). At a later date Meaux possessed homilies in French and the *Manuel de pechiez*.[5]

It is particularly significant that even the insufficient details of the catalogues point to a considerable number of miscellanies of the type already described. At Rievaulx Walter Daniel's *Centum Sententiae* was one out of a dozen analogous works. The cataloguer of Meaux concludes his description of a mixed bag: 'et alia multa valde commoda',[6] and lists other miscellanies and anthologies as 'sententie utilissime', 'excepta de glosis evangelii', 'proverbia de libris poetarum'.

[1] *Statuta capitulorum gen. Ord. Cisterciensis*, ed. J. M. Canivez, i (Louvain, 1933), 108.

[2] C. R. Cheney, *From Becket to Langton*, p. 69 and J. E. Sayers, 'English Cistercian cases and their delegation in the first half of the thirteenth century', *Anal. Sacri Ord. Cisterciensis*, xx (1964), 85–102.

[3] J. E. Sayers, 'The judicial activities of the General Chapters', *Journal of Eccles. Hist.*, xv (1964), 18–32, 168–85 and eadem, *Papal Judges Delegate in the Province of Canterbury 1198–1254* (Oxford, 1971), pp. 213–14.

[4] Columban Bock, 'Les Cisterciens et l'étude du droit', *Anal. Sacri Ord. Cisterciensis*, vii (1951), 3–31.

[5] *Chron. mon. de Melsa*, iii. pp. xcii, xcviii.

[6] Ibid. iii. p. lxxxv.

Books and catalogues together leave the impression that the English Cistercians, in the first hundred years or so, accumulated substantial collections of the 'basic' works necessary for the *lectio divina* which the Rule of St. Benedict and their own customs required. Also, they multiplied *florilegia*. Their collections did not differ from the libraries of other monastic Orders or collegiate churches in containing works which were not to be found in those other libraries. Even so, it cannot be said that the English evidence supports the view of J. S. Beddie that by the thirteenth century Cistercian libraries were indistinguishable from their neighbours', in point of content.[1] The English Cistercians, either unconsciously or more probably deliberately, restricted their libraries to a much narrower range of topics. They did not respond often to the new currents of philosophical thought or the new ways of teaching in the Parisian schools. The revival of taste in the Latin classics, so marked a feature of what is called 'the twelfth-century renaissance', passed them by. Thomas Becket bequeathed a fine library of classical authors to the monks of his cathedral church of Canterbury;[2] it apparently occurred to nobody to make a similar gift to a Cistercian abbey.

The white monks seldom copied or acquired books wholly devoted to profane subjects. The singular appearance in a manuscript from Kingswood of goliardic poetry sandwiched between a commentary on the Apocalypse and the Institutes of Cassiodorus is altogether exceptional. The sentiment of the verses: 'Meum est propositum in taberna mori' was hardly suitable for the edification of ascetics. Yet this uncharacteristic survival may be a salutary reminder that Cistercian life was not lived, even in its first century, at the lofty level represented by the saints and spiritual writers whose works adorned the *armaria*. The more stately and more elevating books may not have been those which were most often read. Moreover, the English Cistercian showed a marked interest in historical narrative and biography, particularly when it bore on his own

[1] *Anniversary Essays in Medieval History by Students of C. H. Haskins* (Boston, 1929), p. 22.
[2] M. R. James, *Ancient Libraries of Canterbury and Dover* (Cambridge, 1903), p. xlii.

neighbourhood, and in that pursuit he occupied himself from time to time with topics remote from the monastic ideal. But when allowance has been made for such considerations as these, it remains true to say that Cistercian libraries did, in the main, present features which conform to the view expressed by Walter Daniel: 'Our master Christ did not teach grammar, rhetoric, dialectic in his school; he taught humility, pity, and righteousness.'[1] These libraries were definitely libraries for monks, and very practical. To understand how the monks chiefly used their libraries it may be well to insist once more on the collections, not very original in content, which survive under the name of *excerpta, sententiae,* and so forth. These collections, and the miscellanies to which they are often joined, may provide valuable clues. The title given to MS. Rawlinson C. 22 was 'Dulce mentis solatium', and that perhaps indicates the way in which the pious Cistercian approached his reading. As Étienne Gilson has said so well; 'Les Cisterciens ne se sont pas fait une conception scolaire de la vie monastique, mais une conception monastique de la vie scolaire.'[2]

---

[1] Cited by Powicke in Walter Daniel, *Life of Ailred,* p. xxxvi n.
[2] *La Théologie mystique de S. Bernard* (1934), p. 82.

18. Church-building in the Middle Ages*

ANY years ago, that great liturgical scholar and antiquary, Edmund Bishop, wrote a delightful essay entitled 'How a cathedral was built in the fourteenth century'.[1] He used the accounts of Milan Cathedral from 1387 onwards to give a vivid picture of the variety of effort and ingenuity of organization which were used to raise funds for this enormous enterprise. There were house-to-house collections and money boxes put on shop counters. All sorts of gifts in kind came in and a jumble sale was held weekly or fortnightly to dispose of them. The craft-gilds of armourers, drapers, and others, mobilized their members to work on the site without payment. Penitents paid money to the fabric-fund as part of the satisfaction for their sins. An unexpected contribution came when old coins were dug up in the foundations, to the value of six pounds thirteen shillings.

Every one of our great medieval churches is the result of similar prolonged and varied efforts. France and England could produce parallels to all the methods of the Milanese.[2] I wish here to consider this matter of raising funds for churches in connection with the uses for which churches were designed and the reason why men responded to appeals. I shall confine myself to the great churches attached to cathedrals and monasteries. Most of my remarks will directly concern English and French churches within the four centuries between 1100 and 1500, but you will readily discern how they apply to other periods and places.

* A lecture delivered in the John Rylands Library on Wednesday, 10 Jan. 1951. First published in the *Bulletin* of the Library, xxiv (1951–2), 20–36.

[1] *Downside Rev.*, July 1893, reprinted in his *Liturgica historica* (1918), pp. 411–21.
[2] Cf. C. Enlart, *Manuel d'archéologie française*, i (Architecture religieuse), 3rd edn., i (1927), 85–9; Otto von Simson, *The Gothic cathedral* (1956), 170–2; Robert Branner, 'Historical aspects of the reconstruction of Reims Cathedral 1210–1241', *Speculum*, xxxvi (1961), 23–67.

How and why were the churches built? The questions, though separate, are related. I am concerned, not with the technique of building or the history of the masonic craft in the Middle Ages, but with certain ways in which money was found for advancing these great projects and with the shape the churches took. Each part of my subject is covered by an ample and learned literature. Yet there is, maybe, justification for trying to deal—imperfectly and at the risk of confusion—with several questions in one, and to treat together several subjects which are normally discussed separately in their own right.

The cathedral and monastic churches were not parochial churches in the ordinary sense: they were churches for communities of canons and monks and nuns; and those communities employed the labour and paid for the buildings.[1] They did so either out of their general fund of accumulated capital or by persuading others to subscribe to the work in hand. In some few cases, a single benefactor, prelate or prince, bore the whole cost. Why this generosity? Why did the canons of a cathedral or the monks of a monastery choose to spend their money in this way, and why did their benefactors provide them with the means, directly or indirectly? The short answer is that the Catholic faith held such an empire in the minds of men that they were persuaded to build churches to the greater glory of God, and to think no building too magnificent for His service. But we can and ought to be more precise. Certain specific articles of the Catholic faith and certain features of the popular cult were of overwhelming importance in determining both the direction and the volume of this activity.[2]

Foremost among these are the belief in miracles and the belief in the intercession of saints. These hallow certain spots because of events which happened there, or because of the holy relics which they contain, or because of both. The

[1] On the organizers and architects of church-building see A. Hamilton Thompson, 'Cathedral builders of the Middle Ages', *History*, n.s. x (1925), 139–50 and 'Master Elias of Dereham and the King's Works', *Archaeological Journal*, xcvii (1941), 1–35, and John Harvey, *The Gothic World* (1950), especially pp. 1–52.

[2] Professor C. N. L. Brooke has approached the subject from a different point of view in a Rylands Lecture on 'Religious sentiment and church design in the later Middle Ages', *BJRL*, l (1967–8), 13–33, reprinted in his collected essays, *Medieval Church and Society* (1971), pp. 162–82.

Palestinian churches connected with the life of Jesus Christ are of the first sort; of the second one may instance three celebrated centres in Western Europe: the tombs of St. Peter at Rome, of St. Denis near Paris, of St. Edmund at Bury. At each place, a church has incorporated the shrine. What was at first an oratory connected with a sacred incident or a saint became a place for congregational and liturgical worship.

The implications of this development have been the subject of a remarkable study by André Grabar.[1] M. Grabar traces the evolution of oratories known as *martyria* in the first Christian centuries, both in East and West. The cult of martyrs, 'witnesses' *par excellence* of the faith, found monumental expression in buildings of a sepulchral character, and their forms show a distinct and conscious dependence on the *heroa* which celebrated heroes in the pagan world.[2] Even when the shrine did not contain the entire body of a martyr (and already by the fourth century it was not unusual to dismember bodies of the saints) the building normally retained the form of a sepulchre. Many traces, though few complete examples, survive in Western Europe from the period between Constantine and Charlemagne. Some were circular, some were polygonal or trefoil in plan, some were made cruciform (like the palace-chapel of Galla Placidia at Ravenna, because it contained a relic of the true Cross 'a quo habet et nomen et formam').[3] In the fifth century and after, many sanctuaries were built in East and West in honour of the Blessed Virgin Mary, her cult possibly stimulated by the definition of the Council of Ephesus (431). Their architects often adopted the central plan common for *martyria*, and it is interesting to learn from a twelfth-century

[1] *Martyrium. Recherches sur le culte des reliques et l'art chrétien antique*, 3 vols. (Collège de France, Fondation Schlumberger pour les études bizantines, 1946). The related subject of pilgrimage in the early Church is dealt with comprehensively in the important work of Bernhard Kötting, *Peregrinatio religiosa: Wallfahrt in der Antike und das Pilgerwesen in der alten Kirche* (Münster, 1950).

[2] Here M. Grabar's archæological evidence seems to be of weight in a controversy in which the late Père H. Delehaye expressed a contrary opinion (*Les origines du culte des martyrs*, 1912).

[3] Grabar, op. cit. i. 407. Cf. G. Sieffert, 'Ecclesia ad instar dominici sepulchri', *Rev. du moyen âge latin*, v (1949), 197–202. See also Ejnar Dyggve, *History of Salonitan Christianity* (Instituttet for Sammenlignende Kulturforskning, Oslo, 1951).

writer that St. Wilfrid's buildings at Hexham included a church
'in modum turris erecta, et fere rotunda, a quatuor partibus
totidem porticus habens, in honorem sanctae Mariae semper
virginis dedicata'.[1]

M. Grabar's analysis of these forms is fascinating; for a consideration of later, medieval, churches in the West it is specially
significant because he demonstrates 'how the principal churches,
the schools of architecture which created the new styles of the
Middle Ages, followed the line formerly indicated by the Con-
stantinian architects of Rome and accepted and consecrated by
the Church. Instead of creating an independent building, they
treated the enclosure for the relic as an interior *martyrium* or
shrine in the chevet of the basilica.'[2] The shrine usually occupied
the east end of a church, formed as it were a casual excrescence
upon a basilican plan; but it was an excrescence which altered
the whole balance of the building, introducing different planes,
rounded walls, and vaulted roofs.

The effect upon church architecture was overwhelming because the cult of saints and the veneration of their relics became
one of the most prominent features of medieval worship. In
this cult the miraculous played an all-important part. St.
Benedict appears in the *Dialogues* of Gregory the Great as the
wonder-worker rather than the model monk; so it was throughout the Middle Ages—and beyond. Saints were remembered
less for the holiness of their lives than for their miracles. Their
relics were not mere commemorative objects to be gazed at.
Those of Ste. Foy de Conques, carried in procession, could
quell a riot. The body of St. Lambert of Liège could bring to
a successful end the siege of the castle of Bouillon.[3] Others
cured at touch mental and physical diseases. Small wonder,
then, that the clergy of the Middle Ages frequently display
a pious ferocity and lack of scruple in their hunt for relics.
Duchesne has said that the theft of relics was practised throughout Christendom; nor was there any sin so venial in the eyes of
the sinner and of public opinion.[4] Even such a saintly man as

[1] J. Raine, *The priory of Hexham*, i (Surtees Soc. xliv, 1864), 14. Cf. A. W.
Clapham, *Eng. romanesque architecture before the Conquest* (1930), pp. 143 sqq.
and Grabar, op. cit. i. 325–6, 411–13.   [2] Op. cit. i. 580.
[3] E. de Moreau, *Hist. de l'Église en Belgique*, iii (1945), 572–3.
[4] L. Duchesne, *Les premiers temps de l'état pontifical*, 3rd edn. (1911), p. 40.

Hugh of Avalon was so overcome by his devout greed, when confronted by a bone of St. Mary Magdalen in the abbey of Fécamp, that (as his biographer tells us), unable to break it with his fingers he applied first his incisor teeth and then his molars to the task and quickly broke off two bits, which he handed to his attendant to preserve.[1] If anyone doubts the part played by relics in medieval religion, let him look at the numerous inventories surviving from these times,[2] or study those two remarkable volumes entitled *Exuviae sacrae constantinopolitanae* (Geneva, 1877–8) in which the Comte de Riant collected the records of relics looted from Byzantium after the Fourth Crusade.

It is not necessary to expatiate on this cult, which is a thing of common knowledge, but I would emphasize that both the early romanesque crypts, with central chamber and surrounding ambulatory, and the fully developed gothic retrochoir were alike designed to serve it. Abbot Suger explicitly tells us that he replanned St. Denis to admit of easier access for the concourse of pilgrims who thronged to the shrine at festivals.[3] Most of our medieval churches have been denuded of the shrines which were once their chief glory; but despite the English Reformation we still possess the shrine of St. Edward the Confessor *in situ*, much mutilated, behind the high altar of Westminster Abbey. And in the church of St. Sernin of Toulouse one may still see the elaborate arrangement of shrines constructed in the eleventh century round an eastern ambulatory to house those bodies of apostles which Charlemagne is said to have deposited on his return from Spain, and a crypt-full of other relics besides, beneath the high altar.[4]

I will only venture one more illustration. If we examine the

[1] *Magna vita Hugonis*, ed. J. Dimock (RS), p. 317. His excuse and another episode of the same sort are recorded on the next page.

[2] e.g. *Inventories of Christ Church, Canterbury*, ed. J. W. Legg and W. H. St. John Hope (1902), pp. 29–40; *Gesta abbatum S. Albani* (RS), iii. 539–44; J. B. Hurry, *Reading Abbey* (1901), 127–31; *Durham account rolls*, ed. J. T. Fowler (Surtees Soc.), ii. 425–40.

[3] Suger, 'De rebus in administratione sua gestis', xxv in E. Panofsky, *Abbot Suger on the abbey church of St. Denis* (Princeton, 1946), p. 42.

[4] These are not negligible. They include the head of St. Thomas Aquinas and (with very dubious credentials) the bodies of St. Edmund, king and martyr, and St. Gilbert of Sempringham.

history of some of the principal English churches, we find a rebuilding of the east end in the course of the thirteenth century. It happens a little earlier at Canterbury and then, soon after 1200, at Winchester and Rochester. A little later, we see this happening at Worcester, Ely, Durham, Fountains, Westminster. In the latter part of the century, St. Paul's of London, Lincoln and Hereford cathedrals and two great Benedictine churches, Chester and St. Albans, follow suit. In each place one object was evidently to provide a more worthy, magnificent, and spacious shrine for the principal relics. Access must be made easy for the devout. Space was needed, too, if the desire of the faithful to be buried *ad sanctos* were to be fulfilled. King John, it will be remembered, chose to be laid at rest at Worcester near to St. Wulfstan, while his successors sought for their mortal remains propinquity to the shrines of St. Edward or St. Thomas.[1]

One feature of this cult points directly to the next part of my subject. It was early considered proper for altars (whenever possible) to be sanctified by the presence of relics.[2] Gregory the Great instructed the missionaries in England to de-contaminate pagan temples, erect altars, and place relics there.[3] The altar was an essential part of the church. The great cathedral and monastic communities consisted of clerics, and the liturgy developed in their churches demanded first and foremost ample room in the choir and opportunity for processions. Along with the elaboration of day and night offices went important eucharistic developments. The church building was, in a great measure, intended for the celebration of Mass; Mass was not to be celebrated outside consecrated churches and except at consecrated altars.[4] The insistence that there must be relics about the altar meant that on this point, under the church's roof, were focused the doctrines and the liturgy connected with the saints and the eucharist. This was the first

[1] Cf. Suger's Life of Louis VI, c. xxxii (*Œuvres complètes*, ed. A. Lecoy de la Marche (1867), pp. 148–9).

[2] Grabar, op. cit. i. 38 and R. W. Muncey, *A hist. of the consecration of churches and churchyards* (1930), pp. 40–6. *Decretum*, de cons., dist. 1 c. 26 was interpreted in this sense.

[3] *Councils*, ed. Haddan and Stubbs, iii. 37.

[4] *Decretum*, de cons., dist. 1 c. 33.

stage: a concentration of interest on the high altar, with the shrine on the altar, or within it, or beneath it, or projecting eastward from the back of it.

The second stage is a diffusion of interest. The main shrine often becomes self-standing, in a special crypt or in a retrochoir or transept. That was the purpose of those extensions of English churches in the thirteenth century to which I have referred. But here we must also take into account the multiplication of Masses and its consequences. This dates from the earliest period of the Middle Ages. The cult of the Blessed Virgin Mary led to the celebrating of Masses additional to the Masses of the day. Other votive Masses were added, commemorative and expiatory; above all, Masses for the dead, intended to redeem their souls from purgatory. This had the first consequence of causing more monks and clergy to become priests. St. Benedict was never ordained priest. Two centuries after his day the abbey of St. Gall apparently had only two or three priests in a community about fifty strong.[1] Finally, in 1311, the decree *Ne in agro* ensured that practically all monks would proceed to priesthood.[2] By that time monasteries had become, to use Coulton's words, 'great Mass-machines'.[3] And the change was reflected in the design of their churches. From the sixth century onward more than one altar might sometimes be found in a church. The first church of Cluny cannot have had more than two or three altars; the second church, built late in the tenth century had thirteen;[4] the third church, begun a century later, eventually provided at least twice as many.[5] When Suger's church of St. Denis was consecrated in 1144 Mass was celebrated simultaneously at twenty altars. For the same reason, many churches of the Cistercian Order soon developed beyond their primitive simplicity. The first church of Pontigny, built soon after 1114, had one or two altars. Reconstruction completed by 1170 provided for chapels on all sides of the transept. The third and final stage was reached before 1210 when, with

[1] J. M. Clarke, *Abbey of St. Gall* (1926), p. 285.
[2] *Clementin.* 3, 10, 1, para. 8.
[3] G. G. Coulton, *Five centuries of religion*, i. 126.
[4] *Med. studies pres. to Rose Graham* (1950), p. 46.
[5] Rose Graham and A. W. Clapham, 'The monastery of Cluny 910–1155', *Archaeologia*, lxxx (1930), 143–78.

thirteen chapels opening on to the eastern ambulatory, there were twenty-five chapels in the church.[1] This explains a feature of those great reconstructions of the east ends of English churches. The east end was not merely lengthened; it was expanded with a cluster of chapels growing out of the ambulatory round the shrine, and sometimes a second, eastern, transept was added, to contain more altars. This development was not, of course, confined to monasteries. Secular clergy likewise took on Mass-obligations. In all the greater churches of the Middle Ages, as well as many parish churches, votive Masses were daily said or sung. Chantries were founded to ensure perpetual commemoration of individuals; and where the chapels provided by the architects did not allow enough altars for the celebrant chantry-priests, narrow chapels were inserted into the choir or nave-arcade, and altars set against the pillars of the nave.

Thus specific doctrines connected with the saints and the Mass did much to determine the functions of the churches and their shape. Builders not unnaturally worked as a rule from east to west in the construction and reconstruction of churches; the nave mattered least and was often left unfinished. The main lines of the plan were fixed to a certain extent irrespective of architectural style.

The same theme might be developed regarding decoration; for in church the decorative arts, when they become representational, are devoted mainly to the iconography of saints. Quite apart from the influence worked by the cult of any one saint, the very development of main lines of pilgrim-traffic and the exchange of ideas along those routes had profound influence on the evolution of artistic styles. Leaving on one side this vast and fascinating topic,[2] I turn to consider the economic consequences of these doctrines, as they relate to church-building.

'The cultus of relics', wrote Baldwin Brown, 'gave medieval architects much to do and at the same time provided means for

[1] See M. Anselme Dimier, *Recueil de plans d'églises cisterciennes* (2 vols., Paris and N. D. d'Aiguebelle, 1949), i. 36–8.

[2] Cf. A. Kingsley Porter, *Romanesque sculpture on the pilgrimage roads* (10 vols., Boston, 1923); E. Mâle, *L'art religieux au XIIe siècle* (1922), ch. vii; J. Bédier, *Les légendes épiques*, ii (2nd edn., 1917).

achieving the desired ends.'[1] The relics of an important saint were of financial value to their owner. The saint was forever living, exercising a decisive effect on the lives of these who sought his intercession by prayer, and visiting with affliction those who infringed his rights. The church which held his relics was his home. We find this notion expressed in the phraseology of deeds of gift. When a church was endowed in the early Middle Ages a saint was commonly named as the beneficiary or among the beneficiaries. To take two charters at random: between 1060 and 1087 Eude, lord of Blaison, gave an arpent of land to 'God and St. Aubin and his monks' at Angers;[2] about the years 1136–8 Adeliz, wife of Gilbert Fitz Richard, and her children gave land 'to St. Mary and St. Botulf of Thorney'.[3]

Miracles of healing and other wonders proclaimed the saint's sanctity; they were most often performed where his relics rested. Moreover, these sanctuaries had such virtue that the prayers poured forth there, and the Masses sung there, had particular efficacy. So they attracted pilgrims. Besides those pilgrims who went to shrines out of gratuitous piety, were many on whom the pilgrimage was enjoined as penance. I will cite one example only: in 1325, at Rochester,[4] Simon Heyroun confessed to adultery, and his bishop ordered him for penance to go annually for seven years to St. Thomas of Canterbury (note the personification), and within the same period thrice to St. Thomas of Hereford, thrice to St. Edmund of Bury, thrice to St. Mary of Walsingham. He was also to feed one poor person every Friday. His partner in sin was sent on pilgrimage to Santiago de Compostela.

[1] *Anglo-Saxon architecture*, 2nd edn. (1925), p. 183.
[2] *Cartulaire de l'abbaye de S. Aubin d'Angers*, ed. A. Bertrand de Broussillon (1903), i. 153.
[3] *Facs. of Northants. Charters*, ed. F. M. Stenton (Northants. Rec. Soc., 1930), p. 52.
[4] *Reg. Hamonis de Hethe ep. Roffensis*, ed. C. Johnson (CYS), i. 200, cf. 201, 217, 224, 233. In 1275 the archbishop of York ordered a pilgrimage to the Holy Land as penance for adultery. *Reg. Walter Giffard, archbishop of York*, ed. W. Brown (Surtees Soc.), p. 282. See also E. van Cauwenbergh *Les pèlerinages expiatoires et judiciaires dans le droit communal de la Belgique au moyen âge* (Louvain, 1922), and L. Tanon, *Hist. des justices des anciennes églises et communautés monastiques de Paris* (1883), pp. 45–6.

Not only is the economic aspect of this system obvious to us. Medieval churchmen were well aware of the financial implications.[1] Abbot Samson of Bury challenged the barons of the Exchequer to despoil St. Edmund's tomb for King Richard's ransom, and none dared. Thereafter, the abbot invested spare capital in a very precious crest for the shrine of the glorious martyr, for 'no man would dare to lay hands upon it'.[2] A little earlier than this the Winchester annalist reports that 'St. Barnabas first became notable at Hyde Abbey by the miracles wrought by God through his merits, and then that church began to be renovated and improved'.[3] A century earlier a monk of Battle, who had been put in charge of a cell at Exeter, set himself to improve its position. He was at pains to extend as much as possible the fame of the relics by which the place was distinguished and thus acquired lands and churches and tithes in and around the city of Exeter.[4] Bromholm Priory rose suddenly to prosperity after its reception of a piece of the true Cross, stolen from Constantinople in 1205; but that story is too well known to be repeated now.[5] Relics were bought, borrowed, stolen, and manufactured. If they were not well enough known, their owners gave publicity to them and their miracles. The history of relics is full of faked relics and feigned miracles, for the opportunities for fraud were many and the inducement was immense. I shall not discuss this subject beyond observing that the getting of relics and the propaganda for them are often associated significantly with building operations.

When work on the west front of St. Albans was interrupted for lack of funds at the beginning of the thirteenth century, the abbot organized a preaching tour through many dioceses. 'He sent relics, and also a clerk named Amphibalus whom the Lord had raised from the dead after four days, by the merits of St. Alban and St. Amphibalus, so that he might bear visible witness to the miracles of these saints', and in this way he

---

[1] Cf. three valuable chapters (vi–viii) in G. G. Coulton's *Five centuries of religion*, iii (1936).

[2] *Chronicle of Jocelin of Brakelond*, ed. H. E. Butler (1949), p. 97.

[3] *Annales monastici* (RS), ii. 62.

[4] *Chron. mon. de Bello* (Anglia Christiana Soc., 1846), p. 32.

[5] Modern accounts are by G. G. Coulton, op. cit. iii. 90–2 and F. Wormald, 'The Rood of Bromholm', *Journal of the Warburg Institute*, i (1937), 31–45.

accumulated a good deal of money (*non minimam pecuniam coacervavit*).[1] In 1174, after a fire at the abbey of St. Evurtius of Orléans, its abbot, Stephen of Tournai, wrote to the dean of St. Martin's at Tours recommending to him the canons of St. Evurtius who were being sent out with relics to preach and collect gifts.[2] Preaching tours of this sort sometimes went far afield: we have the account of the canons of Laon who, in 1112–13, took their relics overseas to get funds for rebuilding their cathedral, and who went as far as Exeter.[3] In January 1201 King John gave letters of protection and recommendation to brothers John and Elias, monks of St. Eparchus of Angoulême; the church had been burnt to the ground and their abbot was sending them to preach and raise funds in England.[4] Professor Wormald remarked on the synchronizing of the forgeries by the monks of St. Martial of Limoges, designed to prove that St. Martial was an apostle, and the rebuilding of their church between 1017 and 1028. He observed: 'the promulgation of the cult of St. Martial as an apostle would be likely to prove not only glorious but profitable, since pilgrims and subscriptions would be likely to come from it.'[5] Wormald pointed out in passing how the discovery of the bones of King Arthur at Glastonbury in 1191 had coincided with the great rebuilding of that abbey. To take an example from the Lower Rhine: in 1264 seventeen bodies of holy martyrs were providentially dug up in the collegiate church of Xanten when a new eastern choir was under construction.[6]

I do not think that any medieval records which survive enable one to calculate just how much money accrued to any one church through the alms of pilgrims or other gifts and

[1] *Gesta abbatum*, i. 219. The 'invention' of St. Amphibalus was fairly recent (1178, ibid. i. 192–3), but the saint is a wholly fictitious figure.

[2] Migne, ccxi. 318.

[3] V. Mortet, *Recueil des textes relatifs à l'histoire de l'architecture*, i (1911) 319–21. An extremely comprehensive survey of the French material is provided by P. Héliot and M.-L. Chastang, 'Quêtes et voyages de reliques au profit des églises françaises du moyen âge', *Rev. d'histoire ecclés.*, lix (1964), 789–822, lx (1965), 5–32.

[4] *Rotuli chartarum*, ed. T. D. Hardy (Record Comm., 1837), pp. 101a, 103b.

[5] F. Wormald, 'The English saints in the Litany in Arundel MS. 60', *Analecta bollandiana*, lxiv (1946), 86.

[6] *Rev. d'histoire ecclés.*, lvi (1961), 40.

legacies prompted by devotion to the saints. Nor can we often say what proportion of this income was spent on the enlargement and adornment of the structure. There are, to be sure, many fabric accounts which are of utmost value for studying the organization and technique of building. There are also the charters and chronicles recording endowments and the accounts presented by custodians of shrines. Though these records are insufficient for accurate statistical analysis, they are worth attention. According to a statement of income drawn up at Mont St. Michel in 1338, a sixth of the abbey's income was derived from pilgrims.[1] At St. Trond, in eastern Belgium, during the rule of Abbot Adelard II (1055–82), the fame of miracles worked at the tomb of St. Trond produced floods of pilgrims. They offered in enormous quantity not only money but livestock, linen, wax and cheeses. 'In those days', says a later abbot of the house, 'the income of the altar far exceeded all the revenue then or now collected by the abbey.' The abbot spent a large part of these offerings on rebuilding the church; and the new church had a second transept and a spacious crypt.[2] Again, according to the chronicler of Gloucester Abbey, it was the offerings at the tomb of King Edward II which provided the funds for rebuilding the transept and modifying the choir in the middle of the fourteenth century; and had all the offerings gone to the fabric, they would (it was said) have sufficed to rebuild the whole church.[3] Some years ago, the late Canon C. E. Woodruff devoted a study to 'The financial aspect of the cult of St. Thomas of Canterbury.'[4] Using the lengthy series of Treasurers' accounts, he was able to show that the monks received annual offerings between the years 1198 and 1206 amounting on average to £426. 3s. 7d. The offerings at the two shrines of Becket averaged £349. 2s. 6d. and the rest came from other altars. The Treasurer's receipts from all sources averaged £1,406. 1s. 8d. a year; so that the martyr may be said to have produced almost exactly one quarter of the gross income. By the time of Chaucer offerings

[1] L. Delisle, 'Enquête sur la fortune des établissements de l'Ordre de S. Benoît, en 1338', *Notices et extraits des MSS.*, xxxix (1916), 368, 372.
[2] E. de Moreau, op. cit. ii (1940), 251, 291.
[3] *Hist. monast. S. Petri Gloucestriae* (RS), i. 46–7.
[4] *Archaeologia Cantiana*, xliv (1932), 13–32.

had increased in amount, though not perhaps enough to compensate for change in the value of money. Thereafter there was a steep decline in takings.

From late in the eleventh century, pilgrims had more inducement to visit certain churches because of the indulgences offered to visitors by ecclesiastical authority. The relaxation of thirty or forty days of penance was the usual spiritual reward for those who came and piously contributed to the needs of the church. An indulgence of this sort was granted by a papal legate in 1121 for those who visited Westminster Abbey, and prayed and made offerings, on the feast of the martyrdom of St. Peter and St. Paul.[1] Nor were indulgences always restricted to visitors. In 1125 a papal legate, announcing that Bishop Urban of Llandaff had begun to rebuild his church from the foundations and would be unable to complete it without alms, confirmed an indulgence granted by the archbishop of Canterbury to all contributors and relaxed the penance of fourteen days in addition.[2]

The idea of a church as the home of a saint, who rewards benefactors by intercession, appears from the terms of the charters of endowment which the churches received. Laymen who endowed churches expected a *quid pro quo*. That is elaborately expressed by the clerk who in the year 910 drafted for Duke William of Aquitaine the charter recording his foundation of Cluny. 'The ransom of a man's life are his riches;' he says (quoting Proverbs 8:8), 'I will maintain at my own cost persons living together in the monastic profession, in the faith and hope that, if I cannot myself despise all earthly things, yet by maintaining those who do and whom I believe to be righteous in the eyes of God, I shall receive the recompense of the righteous.' The hope of buying salvation is expressed with more usual brevity in a charter, drawn up about the year 1200, now preserved in the John Rylands Library.[3] It begins:

To all Christ's faithful to whom this present writing shall come, Robert Marmion gives greeting in the Lord. Let it be known to you

---

[1] *PUE*, I, ii (1931), 234–6. The authenticity of the indulgence is not altogether beyond doubt.   [2] *Councils*, ed. A. W. Haddan and W. Stubbs, i. 318.
[3] J. R. L., Beaumont charter 43. Cf. The letter of Innocent III absolving Sir Robert Marmion from his vow, Oct.–Nov. 1201 (Pott. 1532).

all that I, for the salvation of my soul and those of Philippa my wife and of all my ancestors and successors and for the release from my journey to Jerusalem (*pro absolutione itineris mei Ierosolimitani*), have granted to God and St. Mary of Barbéry and the monks there serving God, to build and construct their church, five hundred pounds of money of Angers . . .'[1]

The general feeling that the chance of salvation was improved by such piety as this was not enough. People looked for the measured mitigation of penance expressed in indulgences or for some assurance that prayers and Masses would be said for their especial benefit, either for a period or in perpetuity. Donations were attracted by specific promises.[2] The development of Mass-obligations prepares us for finding innumerable transactions of this sort. The churches offer special prayers and Masses to those who help them with this world's goods. While many donations and legacies are simply for the general expenses of the churches or for the communities' food or clothing, some—like Robert Marmion's—are earmarked for building.

In particular, the general type of *fraternitas* offered from early times by churches to their benefactors took on the special form of a fraternity of the fabric to advance building operations. Rose Graham called attention to the earliest known English example, established by Bishop Gilbert Foliot for the completion of St. Paul's Cathedral, about the years 1174–5.[3] Here the priests of the diocese of London each undertook to 'sing thirty Masses for members of the confraternity, fifteen for the living and fifteen for the dead. The cathedral chapter undertook every week to have two Masses in St. Paul's, one for the living and one for the dead. Even if a member died in mortal sin, he should be buried in consecrated ground.' A dozen years later, Archbishop Baldwin proposed to build a church in honour

---

[1] For Robert Marmion see *D.N.B.* s.v. He died in 1218; Philippa was his second wife. The Cistercian abbey of Barbéry was in the diocese of Bayeux. The present charter also included lands in England, which seem to be exchanged for an earlier donation.

[2] Georg Schreiber assembled a wealth of material about this under the heading 'Schenkungsmotive' in his work, *Gemeinschaften des Mittelalters* (Münster, 1948), pp. 99–125.

[3] 'An appeal about 1175 for the building fund of St. Paul's Cathedral Church', *Journal of the Brit. Archaeological Assoc.*, 3rd series, x (1945–7), 73–6.

of St. Thomas and ordained[1] 'a fraternity throughout the province of Canterbury to last for seven years from this year of grace 1186. To all who enter this fraternity and send some donation annually for the said fabric or bequeath it at their death, we remit a third of their penance for those sins truly confessed for which they are doing seven years or more of penance; if their penance be less, we remit sixty days; let slight sins and those forgotten, and offences against parents short of violence, be included in the penance imposed for other sins. To those also who for penance have been excluded from church for a whole year, except for Lent, we grant free access to church. We add, moreover, that all members of the fraternity shall have Christian burial unless they committed suicide or died excommunicate by name. And if a church lies under interdict when a parishioner who is a brother or sister of the fraternity dies, let the interdict be lifted until the brother or sister be buried, and let the bells be rung and the service said for the dead. And if a sister die in childbirth, let her be brought to church and solemnly given Christian burial. Moreover we grant that all who shall have joined this fraternity shall participate in all the Masses, prayers, and observances for the departed[2] which occur in all the churches of the province of Canterbury; and we grant the benefit of this fraternity to their children under the age of fifteen years.' Early in the thirteenth century confraternities were established for limited periods in other cathedral churches of England. In 1202 Bishop Godfrey de Lucy founded one for the repair of the church of Winchester, to last for five years, and at Worcester a confraternity was established on St. Wulfstan's day, 1226, to run for seven years.[3] Bishop Richard Poore of Salisbury, when planning his new cathedral in 1219, directed canons to various English dioceses 'as preachers, or rather as seekers of alms'; Canon Robert Scottus even went as far as Scotland on this business. In 1220 foundation stones were laid at New Sarum and noblemen and

---

[1] *Epistolae Cantuarienses* (RS), pp. 8–9.

[2] 'Observances for the departed': *beneficia*. For this meaning of the word, cf. 'De beneficiis fratrum quae fiunt post obitum alicuius fratris'. *Customary of St. Aug. Canterbury*, ed. E. M. Thompson (H. Bradshaw Soc. 1902), i. 351 and Schreiber, op. cit., pp. 173–4.

[3] *Ann. mon.* (RS), ii. 78, i. 68.

ladies were induced to lay a stone apiece and enter into a seven-year covenant for subscriptions to the fabric fund.[1] These activities were doubtless connected with the confraternity recorded in Poore's synodal statutes,[2] which provided services for deceased brethren and sisters of the fabric. A little later, in 1230, we hear of a *confraria novi operis* at Osney Abbey.[3]

What money these fraternities yielded we do not know; but when St. Hugh, bishop of Lincoln, established a 'new general fraternity of the church of Lincoln' he collected (it was said) a thousand marks a year by this means for the building of the new cathedral.[4] Like Archbishop Baldwin's fraternity, this one mitigated the severity of interdicts, and ensured Christian burial for those whose names were inscribed in the *liber fraternitatis*.[5] The forms of admission of layfolk to benefits of this sort are recorded at Salisbury and at Exeter.[6] Not all the endowments which were applied to the building of churches were of this kind: free-will offerings granted in expectation of reward in Heaven; but in general it was so. I have been concerned with the forms of this inducement, and I shall not dwell on the various forms of gift.

The facts which I have laid before you justify us in treating the medieval cathedrals and monastic churches both as illustrations and products of the Catholic faith of the Middle Ages. (It is not, therefore, surprising that those which have come into the hands of Protestant communions in modern times should prove to be ill-adapted to their present uses.)[7] These churches were deliberately shaped to modes of worship which demanded

[1] *Register of S. Osmund* (RS), ii. 11–13.

[2] *C. & S.* ii. 91. Archbishop Stephen Langton granted an indulgence to those who should join the *confraternitas ecclesie Sar'*. *Acta of Stephen Langton*, ed. K. Major (CYS), p. 66.

[3] *Cartulary of Oseney Abbey*, ed. H. E. Salter (Oxford Hist. Soc.), i. 136. A later example is found at Lichfield in 1361. *Reg. of Wm. Stretton* (Wm. Salt Archaeol. Soc.), pp. 94–6.

[4] Rad. de Coggeshall, *Chron. anglic.* (RS), p. 111, and next note.

[5] *Registrum antiquissimum of ... Lincoln*, ed. C. W. Foster and K. Major (Lincoln Record Soc.), ii. 86, where a letter of St. Hugh is wrongly attributed to Hugh de Wells.

[6] *Salisbury charters and documents* (RS), pp. 212–14; *The Liber pontificalis of Bishop Edmund Lacy*, ed. R. Barnes (Exeter, 1847), pp. 288–90.

[7] Cf. G. W. O. Addleshaw and Frederick Etchells, *The architectural setting of Anglican worship* (1948).

space and magnificence and mystery. The nearness of the saints and the recurrent miracle of the Mass were ideas adapted to various stages of comprehension, by minds crude or refined. The Catholic Church of the Middle Ages never declined to reduce theological doctrines of the most spiritual sort to material expression. The shrine, the altar, the chantry-chapel, not only emphasized beliefs concerning the Communion of Saints and Purgatory and vicarious salvation in their most popular forms; they positively encouraged them. Although the underlying doctrine was that of the Universal Church, devotion was concentrated on local and tangible objects. The calendar of saints and the liturgical year varied from place to place. The pious layman could turn to a saint whose human remains were present in his own church, whose spiritual presence was testified by local miracles, whose favour was bestowed specially on this locality or that class of people or gild-fraternity.[1] There was local pride in the prodigies connected with a shrine, and competition between rival establishments possessed of different relics (or occasionally claiming the possession of the same). Devotion was stimulated by the offer of specific recompense, a recompense all the more urgently desired because of current teaching about hell-fire and the high proportion of the damned. One cannot but recognize that all these doctrines added together, and expressed with the force and even brutality which we find in the sermons and hagiography of the age, gave the clergy of a great church a powerful claim upon the people's alms. Along with the purely religious motive, the existence of which no one would deny, the lowest motive of worldly prudence encouraged the clergy to advertise the miracles performed at their shrines, to

[1] It is not generally realized how common in the later Middle Ages was the veneration accorded to relics of uncanonized persons. For a discussion of what may be called 'popular canonization' see E. W. Kemp, *Canonization and authority in the Western Church* (1948), pp. 116–28. Cf. J. C. Russell, 'The canonization of opposition to the King in Angevin England', in *Anniversary essays in med. hist. by students of C. H. Haskins* (1929). Cf. cases recorded in *Hist. mon. Gloucestriae* (RS), i. 32; *Ann. mon.*, ii. 266; Coulton, *Five centuries*, i. 545–6; *Reg. of John de Grandisson, bishop of Exeter*, ed. F. C. Hingeston-Randolph, iii (1899), 1231–4. For the votive wax figures and pilgrim's badge in honour of Edmund Lacy, bishop of Exeter, which have been discovered in the cathedral, see *The Antiquaries Journal*, xxix (1949), 164–8.

multiply the indulgences granted at their altars. The spirit of emulation made builders anxious to surpass neighbouring churches.[1]

In other words, the clergy of the greater churches were impelled for reasons both good and bad to build magnificently, and generally they built beyond their means. That explains why it so often happened that the choir-altars were consecrated, long before the final dedication of a church, as soon as the choir was complete; and the dedication of the whole church was apparently permitted as soon as its walls were raised.[2] In the fine fifteenth-century Flemish service-book which is now Rylands Latin MS. 39, the feast *in dedicatione ecclesie* is illustrated by a delightful picture of a bishop proceeding round a church to anoint the consecration-crosses with chrism; either the nave or the choir (it is not clearly indicated) has only the beginnings of a roof, dominated by 'a huge pair of wheels for raising stones'.[3] Maybe those who planned these buildings sometimes feared that the inflow of alms would diminish or dry up once the work was finished: the crane which stood for centuries on the unfinished south tower of Cologne Cathedral was a visible appeal for funds. Be that as it may, it was exceptional for a great church to be constructed by a single generation of men. More often it was the work of centuries. Some cathedrals (Cologne, Florence, Toulouse for example) were never completed in the Middle Ages. They may be taken to symbolize the unattained ideal of the medieval Church, seeking always to explain the immaterial by the material.

---

[1] Harvey, *The Gothic World*, p. 8.

[2] Cf. the first canon of the legatine Council of London, 1237: 'que perfectis parietibus sunt constructe' (*C. & S.* ii. 246).

[3] M. R. James, *Catalogue of the Latin MSS. in the John Rylands Library at Manchester* (1921), i. 100, and ii., pl. 92.

Index

Only a selection of proper names is given, but all medieval place-names not identified in the texts above are, where possible, cross-referred to the modern equivalents. Texts printed above are listed under the heading: Manuscripts